CHILDREN'S RIGHTS AND COMMERCIAL COMMUNICATION IN THE DIGITAL ERA

CHILDREN'S RIGHTS AND COMMERCIAL COMMUNICATION IN THE DIGITAL ERA

Towards an empowering regulatory framework for commercial communication

Valerie Verdoodt

INTERSENTIA
Cambridge – Antwerp – Chicago

Intersentia Ltd
8 Wellington Street
Cambridge | CB1 1HW | United Kingdom
Tel.: +44 1223 736 170 | Fax: +44 1223 736 169
Email: mail@intersentia.co.uk
www.intersentia.com | www.intersentia.co.uk

Distribution for the UK and Ireland:
NBN International
Airport Business Centre, 10 Thornbury Road
Plymouth, PL6 7 PP
United Kingdom
Tel.: +44 1752 202 301 | Fax: +44 1752 202 331
Email: orders@nbninternational.com

Distribution for Europe and all other countries:
Intersentia Publishing nv
Groenstraat 31
2640 Mortsel
Belgium
Tel.: +32 3 680 15 50 | Fax: +32 3 658 71 21
Email: mail@intersentia.be

Distribution for the USA and Canada:
Independent Publishers Group
Order Department
814 North Franklin Street
Chicago, IL60610
USA
Tel.: +1 800 888 4741 (toll free) | Fax: +1312 337 5985
Email: orders@ipgbook.com

Children's Rights and Commercial Communication in the Digital Era. Towards an empowering regulatory framework for commercial communication

Cover image: by Annelien Hofmans

ISBN 978-1-78068-868-8 (hardcover)
ISBN 978-1-78068-941-8 (PDF)
D/2020/7849/15
NUR 822

GPRC
Guaranteed
Peer Reviewed
Content

British Library Cataloguing in Publication Data. A catalogue record for this book is available from the British Library.

PREFACE

On 20 November 2019 the United Nations Convention on the Rights of the Child celebrates its 30th anniversary. In 1989, when the Convention was adopted, children came across advertising on television, on billboards in the street, in shops and through leaflets in their mailbox. Over the past 30 years, the way in which children are targeted by advertisers and the formats that are used have changed significantly. Think of advergames, influencer marketing, and behavioural targeted advertising. The specific features of these formats, such as their immersive, interactive and personalised nature, make it difficult for children to understand the commercial and persuasive intent of the commercial messages directed at them.

Valerie Verdoodt's doctoral research presents an original and timely fundamental rethinking of the regulatory framework of commercial communication from a children's rights perspective. Offering a carefully considered, well-documented overview and in-depth evaluation of several legislative frameworks, policy documents, self- and co-regulatory initiatives and literature from a variety of disciplines, she has worked towards the development of children's rights-inspired recommendations for an empowering regulatory framework for online commercial communication aimed at children. It is a subject with great societal relevance which contributes to the further realisation of children's rights in the digital environment.

Dr. Verdoodt convincingly concludes that the children's rights framework requires a balance between *empowering* children to cope with advertising (i.e. by educating them and providing them with the necessary opportunities to practice their commercial decision-making skills) and *protecting* them against harmful or misleading advertising and advertising that processes their personal data in an opaque manner (i.e. by recognizing the limitations to advertising literacy and providing additional protections). She found that, at present, the regulatory framework puts too much emphasis on empowerment with much of the responsibility resting on the shoulders of children and their parents, thereby tipping the empowerment-protection scales out of balance. She helpfully suggests that combining all the elements of the regulatory toolbox is the only way to restore that balance. This toolbox includes *inter alia* the enhanced enforcement of the regulatory framework, stimulating the collaboration between regulatory bodies, improving the structure and enforcement of advertising Alternative Regulatory Instruments and carrying out children's rights impact assessments that respect the multi-dimensionality of rights, when developing advertising and marketing campaigns.

The author's research did not only result in this book but was also published in reputable journals and edited volumes and presented at an impressive number of conferences and expert fora around the world, contributing to the international and national visibility of her work on children's rights in the digital environment. At a time when Member States of the Council of Europe are in the process of implementing the 2018 Recommendation on Guidelines to respect, protect and fulfil the rights of the child in the digital environment and the United Nations Committee on the Rights of the Child is drafting a new General comment on this issue, Valerie Verdoodt's research in this field will undoubtedly inspire many actors, including fellow scholars, policymakers, regulators, advertisers ànd the public.

Prof. dr. Eva LIEVENS
Professor in Law & Technology
Ghent University
14 November 2019, Ghent

CONTENTS

ABBREVIATIONS

AC Authority	Advertising Code Authority
AC Committee	Advertising Code Committee
ACC	Audiovisual commercial communication
ARI's	Alternative regulatory instruments
ASA	Advertising Standards Authority
AVMS Directive/ AVMSD	Audiovisual Media Services Directive
BCAP	Broadcast Committee of Advertising Practice
BCAP Code	Code of Broadcast Advertising
BPRs	Best Practice Recommendations
CAHENF	Ad hoc Committee for the Rights of the Child
CAP	Committee of Advertising Practice
CAP Code	Code of Non-broadcast Advertising, Sales Promotion and Direct Marketing
CFREU	Charter of Fundamental Rights of the European Union
CJEU	Court of Justice of the European Union
Code on E-Commerce	Code of Conduct on e-Commerce and Interactive Marketing
COE	Council of Europe
CRBP	Children's rights and business principles
EASA	European Advertising Standards Alliance
EC	European Commission
ECHR	European Convention on Human Rights
ECtHR	European Court of Human Rights
EDPS	European Data Protection Supervisor
EESC	European Economic and Social Committee
EP	European Parliament
FEDMA	Federation of European Direct Marketing
GDPR	General Data Protection Regulation
IAB Europe	Interactive Advertising Bureau Europe
ICC	International Chamber of Commerce
ICC Code	Consolidated ICC Code on Advertising and Marketing Communication Practice
JEP	Jury for Ethical Practices
OBA	Online behavioural advertising

OECD	Organisation for Economic Cooperation and Development
Ofcom	Office of Communications
OP	Optional Protocol on a Communications Procedure
Social Code: YouTube	Social Code: Guidelines for advertising in online video
SRC	Stichting Reclame Code
SRO	Self-regulatory organisation
TFEU	Treaty on the Functioning of the European Union
TWFD	Television Without Frontiers Directive
UCP Directive/ UCPD	Unfair Commercial Practices Directive
UNCRC	United Nations Convention of the Rights of the Child
UNCRC Committee	United Nations Committee on the Rights of the Child
VSPs	Video-sharing platform services
WHO	World Health Organisation

INTRODUCTION

1. BACKGROUND

Children's advertising literacy in the digital era. Nowadays, children grow up in a commercialised environment, where they are confronted with advertising and marketing on a daily basis. From a very young age, they already display a level of brand consciousness, even starting from the age of 2 years old.[1] Children are an attractive target group for advertisers, as they not only represent the primary market (i.e. they can purchase products or services with their weekly allowance), but also the secondary market (i.e. influence on their parents' purchasing behaviour) and even the so-called future market (i.e. themselves as adults with full commercial decision-making capacities).[2] The digital advertising industry plays an important role in the creation and maintenance of good-quality content and digital platforms for children and, as such, offers opportunities for children's participation and empowerment. At the moment, the dominant business model for online services is still advertising-based. Rather than paying for services online, users' personal data are collected in exchange and commercial communications form part of the digital environments in which children play, communicate and search for information.[3] For instance, children play entertaining advergames online, they transform the pictures and videos they send as snaps to their friends with sponsored filters, they participate in challenges launched by brands (e.g. the 'Oreo challenge')[4] and upload TikTok (formerly known as musical.ly)[5] clips of brand songs or containing a certain product. The persuasive tactics employed by the advertising industry

---

1 J. Bakan, *Childhood Under Siege: How Big Business Ruthlessly Targets Children* (Random House 2012); Liselot Hudders and others, 'Shedding New Light on How Advertising Literacy Can Affect Children's Processing of Embedded Advertising Formats: A Future Research Agenda' (2017) 46 Journal of Advertising 333.

2 A. Garde, 'Advertising Regulation and the Protection of Children-Consumers in the European Union: In the Best Interests of … Commercial Operators?' [2011] International journal of children's rights 523, 152.

3 V. Verdoodt and E. Lievens, 'Targeting Children with Personalised Advertising: How to Reconcile the Best Interests of Children and Advertisers' in Gert Vermeulen and Eva Lievens (eds), *Privacy and Data Protection under Pressure: Transatlantic tensions, EU surveillance, and big data* (Maklu 2017).

4 See for numerous examples: https://www.youtube.com/results?search_query=oreo+challenge.

5 K. Flynn, 'Musical.Ly Is Quietly Starting Another Big Advertising Push' <https://digiday.com/marketing/musical-ly-quietly-starting-another-big-advertising-push/> accessed 22 August 2018.

become ever more sophisticated with the lines between commercial messages and non-commercial content being increasingly blurred.[6] Furthermore, due to technological developments and advanced computational capacities, children are being tracked online and their personal data are used for advertising purposes. Indeed, in addition to the apparent privacy and data protection concerns associated with such behaviour monitoring, there are also clear issues with the insights such monitoring gives commercial operators regarding the increased capacity to tailor commercial offerings to individual children's interests. More specifically, commercial communications are more and more targeted at specific individuals, including children, who have been profiled as potentially interested in or receptive to the products or services that are promoted.[7] In other words, the advertising techniques used in the digital environment raise significant issues vis-à-vis children's advertising literacy. In the scope of this book, children's advertising literacy should be understood as comprising different elements (1) the personal knowledge they have about advertising, the persuasive intent, and the advertising techniques that are used to target them (i.e. the cognitive dimension); (2) their ability to develop thoughts about the moral appropriateness of a specific advertising format and their general moral evaluations (i.e. the moral dimension); and (3) their ability to regulate their emotions when exposed to advertising.[8] Children find it difficult to recognise and critically process advertising messages in the digital environment, which ultimately affects their commercial decision-making, autonomy and empowerment (*infra*).

The reconfiguration of children's rights. The commercialisation of children's digital environments has significant implications for children's rights and their implementation. Children are granted a variety of rights under the United Nations Convention on the Rights of the Child ("UNCRC"), which are relevant in the context of advertising and marketing. The digitisation and commercialisation significantly influences not only how children can exercise their rights, but also how these rights may be supported or neglected. This reconfiguration necessitates a translation of the relevant children's rights and

---

6 I. Vanwesenbeeck and others, 'Minors' Advertising Literacy in Relation to New Advertising Formats – Identification and Assessment of the Risks' (2016) <www.adlit.be> accessed 16 November 2017.

7 V. Verdoodt, D. Clifford and E. Lievens, 'Toying with Children's Emotions, the New Game in Town? The Legality of Advergames in the EU' (2016) 32 Computer Law & Security Review 599.

8 L. Hudders and others, 'Children's Advertising Literacy in a New Media Environment: An Introduction to the AdLit Research Project', *Etmaal van de Communicatiewetenschap, Proceedings* (2015) <http://hdl.handle.net/1854/LU-5811593> accessed 5 February 2018. For further reading on the different dimensions of advertising literacy, the reader can be referred to P. De Pauw, 'Children's Advertising Literacy: Empowering Children to Cope with Advertising – A Multi-Perspective Inquiry in Children's Abilities to Critically Process Contemporary Advertising' (Ghent University 2018) <https://biblio.ugent.be/publication/8561253/file/8561256.pdf> accessed 31 August 2018.

principles into standards and guidelines, not only for policy and regulation on digital advertising, but also for businesses that address their digital advertising campaigns to children and even for parents and children themselves.

A FRAGMENTED REGULATORY FRAMEWORK. The children's rights and principles of the UNCRC form an important frame in light of which existing advertising regulation should be evaluated. The regulatory framework should enable the reconciliation of the rights and interests of children and advertisers in relation to new forms of commercial communication. The protection of children against certain forms of commercial communication has long been considered an objective of general interest. In consumer policy and regulation, the universal trend is to limit the commercial pressure on children, caused by advertising and marketing and more broadly commercial practices targeted to children. At the EU level, the legal protections are spread across various instruments, regulating both the delivery and the content of the commercial message. In addition, the advertising industry has been very active in developing self-regulation, especially regarding the protection of children. Accordingly, the current regulatory framework is fragmented into both legislative and alternative regulatory instruments (i.e. self- and co-regulation), containing a myriad of legal requirements for advertisers. To address the fragmentation, a holistic approach is followed by building on literature in children's rights law, advertising and marketing law, data protection law and advertising self-regulation.

RESEARCH PURPOSE. The above forms the context of this research, the overall objective of which was to develop substantive and procedural and/or organisational elements for the regulatory framework on commercial communication aimed at children in the digital environment, ensuring that children can grow up to be critical and advertising literate human beings and in this sense become empowered adults. This overall objective is further divided into five purposes. First, the emerging trends in the area of commercial communication and the impact on children's advertising literacy are described and analysed. Second, the children's rights and principles of the United Nations Convention on the Rights of the Child are translated into the specific context of advertising and marketing aimed at children. Third, the existing regulatory framework (including both legislation and alternative regulatory instruments) on commercial communication is mapped and critically evaluated in light of the translated children's rights and principles, to identify any gaps or overlaps regarding emerging trends in advertising and marketing. Fourth, the procedural and organisational elements of a selection of alternative regulatory instruments at the national level are examined and compared. Fifth, recommendations for the regulatory framework are made to overcome the identified substantive gaps or overlaps, as well as for the structuring and organisation of self- and co-regulatory systems in this area.

Research question and hypothesis. The research starts from the hypothesis that due to the fragmentation of the current framework of legislation and self- and co-regulation for commercial communication aimed at children, potential gaps and/or overlaps in relation to new forms of commercial communication may exist, calling children's ability to make informed commercial decisions (and the long-lasting effects on their development) into question. Therefore, the main research question this book answers is formulated as follows: What are the substantive and procedural and/or organisational elements a regulatory framework on new forms of commercial communication aimed at children needs from a children's rights perspective, in order to ensure that children can grow up to be critical and advertising literate human beings?

2. DELINEATION

Research scope. This book examines and evaluates the legislative and self- and co-regulatory framework for commercial communication, focusing on new advertising formats. Whereas the aim of the research is to be as comprehensive as possible, it has been necessary to carefully delineate its exact scope, due to the vastness of the subject matter. In this respect, the focus lies on commercial communications that are specifically aimed at children, rather than those to which children are exposed to but are in fact aimed at adults. It concentrates on those rules that contribute to the means of delivery of the advertisements (i.e. the specific form or persuasive technique used) rather than the actual content of the commercial message. This implies that – although highly important for the protection of minors, offline as well as online – rules which target specific products (e.g. advertising for tobacco, alcohol, or unhealthy foods) will not be covered as such.[9]

Territorial scope. Aside from the United Nations children's rights framework, what is mainly covered is legislation and alternative regulatory instruments (ARIs) at the European Union level. However, a limited functional comparative analysis of national (i.e. Belgium, United Kingdom and the Netherlands) self- and co-regulatory systems in this context is performed, not only to gain insights in the interplay between legislation and alternative regulatory instruments,

9 However, these rules did form part of the extensive mapping exercise conducted within the frame of the AdLit Project, and interested readers are referred to Valerie Verdoodt, Eva Lievens and Liesbeth Hellemans, 'Mapping and Analysis of the Current Legal Framework on Commercial Communication Aimed at Minors. A Report in the Framework of the AdLit Research Project.' (2015) <www.adlit.be> accessed 20 November 2017; Valerie Verdoodt, Ingrid Lambrecht and Eva Lievens, 'Mapping and Analysis of the Current Self- and Co-Regulatory Framework on Commercial Communication Aimed at Minors. A Report in the Framework of the AdLit SBO Project.' <www.adlit.be> accessed 20 November 2017.

but also to develop recommendations for best practices. The Member States that form part of the comparative study have been selected based on a number of considerations: (1) the importance, application and acceptance of ARIs in the particular Member State, (2) the level of development of the ARIs, (3) the differences in organisation or structure (i.e. co-regulatory system vs. self-regulatory system) and (4) language constraints[10] (for more information on the selection of the national ARIs see part III).

Insights from social science research. Finally, the protection and empowerment of children in the context of new forms of advertising is closely related to social science research. The persuasive tactics employed by these new forms and the actual impact on children's advertising literacy – and ultimately their commercial decision-making – are crucial elements to be taken into account when evaluating the current regulatory framework. To reach a thorough understanding of these elements, the research builds on the insights on new forms of commercial communication and their specific features gained by social scientists (i.e. the AdLit Project, *infra*).

3. STRUCTURE AND METHODOLOGY OF THE RESEARCH

The book is composed of three parts, all of which contain two chapters, followed by a conclusion.

Descriptive analysis of the research setting. The first chapter of the first part essentially introduces the concept of commercial communications aimed at children in the digital age to contextualise the research. It considers how children process commercial communications and what impact the specific features of new forms of commercial communications have on their advertising literacy. The chapter consists of a descriptive analysis of the relevant academic and advertising industry writings. More specifically, it is supported by state of the art social science disciplines within the framework of the AdLit project ("Advertising literacy in a new media environment", SBO-IWT).[11] This interdisciplinary project actively involved and received feedback from various

10 For instance, no systems of the Nordic EU Member States were selected, although they are also considered to be relatively experienced in the use of alternative forms of regulation, especially in the areas of consumer protection, media management and regulating good market behaviour. L. Senden and others, 'Mapping Self- and Co-Regulation Approaches in the EU Context' (Utrecht Centre for Shared Regulation and Enforcement in Europe 2015) 21 <https://ec.europa.eu/digital-single-market/en/content/mapping-self-and-co-regulation-approaches-eu-context> accessed 7 August 2018.

11 Www.adlit.be

stakeholders, including *inter alia* societal and educational organisations, policy makers and the advertising industry. Within AdLit, empirical research was performed on individual (i.e. age) and social contextual variables (i.e. parenting, peer influence and socio-economic household situation) and their impact on children's advertising literacy. These research findings support the legal-theoretical approach of the book and underpin the evidence-based character of the final recommendations. Furthermore, the chapter provides some insights into the need for a strong and empowering regulatory framework for commercial communication aimed at children, by analysing the policy history and the evolving regulatory context.

Descriptive-interpretative analysis of the children's rights framework. The second chapter of the first part consists of a descriptive-interpretative analysis and examines in detail the children's rights and principles at stake and how they have been balanced not only against each other, but also against the fundamental rights of others (e.g. advertisers). The main questions it aims to answer are: which children's rights and principles are at stake and what is their role in regulating new advertising formats aimed at children? The research addresses the societal debate of paternalism versus empowerment, which goes to the heart of the protection of children's rights. It aims to clarify the factors that are important to consider when striking this balance in the context of children's ability to cope with new forms of commercial communication. The analysis starts with an in-depth investigation of the United Nations Convention on the Rights of the Child and the relevant articles of the Charter of the Fundamental Rights of the European Union and the European Convention on Human Rights. Furthermore, the interpretation and recommendations by relevant bodies and organisations such as *inter alia* the UN Committee on the Rights of the Child, the Council of Europe, the EU institutions, the OECD, as well as by academic scholarship are examined. The children's rights and principles are interpreted in the specific context of commercial communication and form the analytical framework in light of which the existing regulatory framework on commercial communication is evaluated.

Descriptive mapping and analysis of the regulatory framework at EU level. In chapter one of part two of this book, the current legislative and self- and co-regulatory framework for commercial communication aimed at children is mapped and analysed. This includes several different areas of law, including media law, consumer protection law and data protection law. The main question it aims to answer is: What legal protections for children against certain forms of commercial communication can be found in both legislative (i.e. media law, consumer protection law and data protection and privacy law) and alternative regulatory instruments (i.e. self- and co-regulation)? The mapping exercise is structured according to different contexts or instruments at the EU level: (1) the consumer protection context, (2) the Audiovisual Media Services Directive, (3) the e-Commerce Directive, (4) the General Data Protection Regulation and the framework for ePrivacy. In addition, it discusses self- and co-regulatory instruments at the EU level that cover these contexts (to gather insights on the relation between advertising self- and co-regulation and legislation). This overview forms a necessary preparatory step to the actual evaluation of the current regulatory framework.

Critical-evaluative analysis of the regulatory framework at EU level. Chapter two of part two builds on the mapping exercise and critically evaluates how new advertising formats fit within the regulatory framework. The goal of this chapter is to examine whether these new forms of advertising are also covered by existing rules and protections and to identify any gaps or overlaps that would hinder the effective realisation of children's rights and principles. The research consists of three case studies that have been selected on the basis of their popularity and effectiveness when targeted towards children (i.e. as established in social science research). The case studies include: (1) advergames, (2) targeting children with personalised advertising and (3) digital influencers and vlogging advertising. On the basis of the evaluation, a number of substantive gaps are identified in the regulatory framework.

Functional comparative analysis of national alternative regulatory instruments. After having studied in detail the substantive elements of the regulatory framework in the previous parts of the research, the third part of the book explores procedural and organisational elements. Considering the important role of self-regulation in the advertising sector and the encouragement for the development of alternative regulatory instruments at the EU level, the research focuses on a selection of national ARIs. The aim is to gather insights into best practices for the structuring and development of such instruments in the area of commercial communication.

Conclusion and recommendations. On the basis of the research conducted, the book concludes with a number of recommendations for a future-proof regulatory framework on commercial communication aimed at children in the digital environment, in order to ensure that children can grow up to be critical and advertising literate human beings. Recommendations are targeted towards EU and/or national legislators and/or policy makers.

PART I

CHILDREN'S RIGHTS AND ADVERTISING LITERACY IN THE DIGITAL ERA

CHAPTER I
SETTING THE SCENE

STRUCTURE OF THE CHAPTER. As a necessary prelude to the legal analysis, this chapter starts by exploring the essential components of the research topic, being children, new forms of commercial communication and advertising literacy. Second, it continues by discussing the need for a regulatory framework that empowers children to cope with advertising and marketing in the digital environment. Finally, as the research topic is studied from a children's rights perspective, the chapter explains the reasons for and implications of such an approach.

SECTION I. CLARIFICATION OF THE CONSTITUTIVE ELEMENTS

INTRODUCTION. To illustrate the issue of new forms of commercial communication aimed at children, this section first clarifies the constitutive elements of this book and then provides an overview of the emerging trends in the area of commercial communication.

1. CHILDREN, COMMERCIAL COMMUNICATION AND ADVERTISING LITERACY

1.1. Definition of a child

NO UNIFORM LEGAL DEFINITION. When studying topics related to children, one comes across a variety of notions to indicate the targeted persons, with 'minors', 'adolescents', 'youth', 'youngsters' and 'young persons' as some of the terms that are most frequently used.[12] These terms can be found across different legislative and policy documents. First of all, the United Nations Convention on the Rights of the Child has opted for the notion 'child', which it defines as "*every human being below the age of eighteen years of age unless under the law applicable to the*

[12] E. Lievens, *Protecting Children in the Digital Era: The Use of Alternative Regulatory Instruments*, vol 105 (Martinus Nijhoff Publishers 2010) 27.

child, majority is attained earlier".[13] While the drafters of the Convention were eager to ensure a broad application, this provision also safeguards a certain amount of flexibility for those countries in which the legal age of majority is set below or above eighteen years.[14] The legal age of majority determines when children are considered to be adults before the law and when they are allowed to access certain rights or lose certain protections (e.g. the minimum age for consent to engage in sexual activity, or to the processing of their personal data).[15] The age threshold will depend on the purpose of the law or policy in question.[16] In the Council of Europe's Cybercrime Convention, the term 'minors' is chosen, which entails "*all persons under 18 years of age*" (unless a Party requires a lower age limit not less than 16 years of age).[17] Furthermore, LIEVENS highlights that policy documents at the EU level[18] use the words child[19] and minor[20] alternately, without providing any clarification or definition.[21] Aside from this, certain scholars have interpreted the different concepts as well. ETZIONI, for instance, clarifies the distinction between children, teenagers and minors as follows:

> *"Children refers to those twelve and under, and teenagers refers to those between the ages of thirteen and eighteen. Minors is used to refer to both groups together"*.[22]

It has also been argued that the term 'child' is more general and used in different contexts compared to the term 'minor', which is mostly linked to the legal discourse and the age of majority.[23] Regardless of the different notions used,

---

13 Article 1 United Nations Convention of the Rights of the Child, 20.11.1989, <www.ohchr.org/en/professionalinterest/pages/crc.aspx> accessed 11.05.2018.

14 S. Detrick, *A Commentary on the United Nations Convention on the Rights of the Child* (Martinus Nijhoff Publishers 1999).

15 European Union Agency for Fundamental Rights, 'Mapping Minimum Age Requirements Concerning the Rights of the Child in the EU' (2017) <http://fra.europa.eu/en/publication/2017/mapping-minimum-age-requirements-concerning-rights-child-eu> accessed 4 January 2018.

16 E. Lievens and others, 'Children's Rights and Digital Technologies' in Ursula Kilkelly and Ton Liefaard (eds), *International human rights of children* (Springer 2018).

17 Article 9, para. 3 Council of Europe, Convention on Cybercrime, ETS No. 185, 23.11.2001, Budapest, <http://conventions.coe.int/Treaty/EN/Treaties/Html/185.htm> accessed 11.05.2018; Lievens, *Protecting Children in the Digital Era: The Use of Alternative Regulatory Instruments* (n 12).

18 European Parliament and Council, 'Recommendation 2006/952/EC of 20 December 2006 on the Protection of Minors and Human Dignity and on the Right of Reply in Relation to the Competitiveness of the European Audiovisual and on-Line Information Services Industry'.

19 Defined as "*a young person especially between infancy and youth*" in Merriam Webster's Online Dictionary, Child, <www.m-w.com/dictionary/child> accessed 11.07.2018.

20 Defined as "*a person who has not attained majority*" in Merriam Webster's Online Dictionary, Minor, < www.m-w.com/dictionary/minor> accessed 11.07.2018.

21 Lievens, *Protecting Children in the Digital Era: The Use of Alternative Regulatory Instruments* (n 12) 27–28.

22 A. Etzioni, 'On Protecting Children from Speech' (2004) 79 Chicago-Kent Law Review 43.

23 Lievens, *Protecting Children in the Digital Era: The Use of Alternative Regulatory Instruments* (n 12).

the distinction is made on the basis of a person's age or on the basis of maturity and the age of discernment. Setting an age threshold for the acquisition of rights or the loss of certain protections is difficult as a balance is needed between the protection and empowerment of the child.[24] In this regard, the evolving capacities of the child need to be taken into account.[25] Finally, certain policy documents in the area of media law make a further distinction between 'child' and 'youth', according to various age limits.[26]

SOCIAL SCIENCE RESEARCH. In the context of children and new forms of commercial communication it is also important to look at social science research, where the notion of a child may be defined differently. Of course, the interpretation of the notion of a child and childhood is, however, not straightforward and may be culturally dependant.[27] Nevertheless, social scientists do agree on the fact that age is an important factor for the evaluation of the effect of advertising on children. In particular, research has shown that children's advertising literacy develops over the years together with their cognitive capacities.[28] In general, younger children *"attend to and interpret information in different ways than do their older counterparts"*.[29] Social science research uses specific categories linked to stages of advertising literacy, such as 0–5 years, 8–12 years 12–15 years and 16–18 years of age.[30] However, it is significant to note that capacities and skills of children of the same age can vary widely, for instance due to personality differences or gender characteristics.[31]

---

24 R. Hodgkin and P. Newell, 'Implementation Handbook for the Convention on the Rights of the Child: Fully Revised Third Edition' (UNICEF 2007) <https://www.unicef.org/publications/index_43110.html> accessed 10 November 2017.

25 See also UN Committee on the Rights of the Child, 'General Comment No. 20 (2016) on the Implementation of the Rights of the Child during Adolescence'.

26 For instance, The Flemish Community Media Decree Media Decree defines a 'child' as a person under the age of 12 years and makes a distinction with 'youth' being a person aged between 12 and 16 years (Article 2, 15° and 18° of the Belgian Decree of 27 March 2009 of the Flemish Community on radio and television, *BS.*, 30 April 2009 (hereafter 'the Flemish Community Media Decree'). The Ofcom Broadcasting Code on the other hand speaks of children when under 15 years (Section 1: Protecting the Under-Eighteens, Ofcom Broadcasting Code, < https://www.ofcom.org.uk/__data/assets/pdf_file/0005/100103/broadcast-code-april-2017.pdf> accessed 11.07.2018).

27 Lievens, *Protecting Children in the Digital Era: The Use of Alternative Regulatory Instruments* (n 12).; Ian Hutchby and J Moran-Ellis, *Children, Technology, and Culture: The Impacts of Technologies in Children's Everyday Lives* (Routledge 2001) 1.

28 V. Cauberghe and others, 'Reclamewijsheid Bij Kinderen En Jongeren: Onderzoeksrapport in Opdracht van Vlaams Ministerie van Cultuur, Jeugd, Sport En Media' (2012) <https://biblio.ugent.be/publication/4130480/file/4130494> accessed 25 October 2017.

29 V. C. Strasburger and B. J. Wilson, *Children, Adolescents, and the Media* (SAGE Publications 2002) 12.

30 Cauberghe and others (n 28).

31 Strasburger and Wilson (n 29) 13.

Use of notions. For the purpose of this book, the notions 'child', 'minor', 'adolescent' and 'youngster' are used interchangeably. Where the age is of particular importance to the topic that is discussed this will be emphasised and explained. In this regard, the analysis integrates insights of other disciplines such as communication science and pedagogy, gained within the context of the AdLit project (*supra*).

1.2. Commercial communication

Commercial communication: an overarching concept. A second constitutive element of this book is commercial communication. From a legal perspective, one can refer to the definition that was inserted by the European Commission in its 1996 Green Paper on Commercial Communications in the Internal Market, stating that it entails "*all forms of communication seeking to promote either products, services or the image of a company or organisation to final consumers and/or distributors*".[32] Thus, it is an overarching concept which covers a broad variety of promotional messages. When analysing the regulatory framework for commercial communications, the terminology used may vary per instrument (e.g. advertising[33], audiovisual commercial communication[34] or commercial communication[35]) and it may change over time.[36] From an industry perspective, one can refer to the definition of the International Chamber of Commerce ("ICC"), which states that it covers "*any publicity activity intended as part of a marketing process for goods or services*".[37]

32 European Commission, 'Green Paper on Commercial Communications in the Internal Market' <http://europa.eu/documents/comm/green_papers/pdf/com96_192_1_en.pdf> accessed 15 March 2018.

33 Directive 2005/29/EC of the European Parliament and the Council of 11 May 2005 concerning unfair business-to-consumer commercial practices in the internal market and amending Council Directive 84/450/EEC, Directives 97/7/EC, 98/27/EC and 2002/65 /EC of the European Parliament and of the Council and Regulation (EC) No 2006/2004 of the European Parliament and of the Council ('Unfair Commercial Practices Directive') 2005.

34 Directive 2010/13/EU of the European Parliament and of the Council of 10 March 2010 on the coordination of certain provisions laid down by law, regulation or administrative action in Member States concerning the provision of audiovisual media services (Audiovisual Media Services Directive) 2010.

35 Directive 2000/31/EC of the European Parliament and of the Council of 8 June 2000 on certain legal aspects of information society services, in particular electronic commerce, in the Internal Market (Directive on electronic commerce) 2000.

36 For instance, with regard to regulation of audiovisual media, Castendyk clarifies that the introduction of the general concept of "audiovisual commercial communication" was necessary in order to cover advertising in a larger context of audiovisual media services. More specifically, this new concept was to cover audiovisual commercial communications of all kinds, including advertising, sponsorship, teleshopping, split screens, interactive advertising and product placement. R. Chavannes and O. Castendyk, 'Directive 2007/65/EC "Audiovisual Media Services Directive"' in O. Castendyk, E. Dommering and A. Scheuer (eds), *European Media Law* (Kluwer Law International 2008).

37 International Chamber of Commerce, 'Policy Statement on Freedom of Commercial Communication, 240/474 Rev'.

Similar to the European Commission's definition, it may cover various activities, such as advertising but also public relations, sales promotion, direct marketing, etc. Furthermore, the ICC also provides a specific definition of advertising – as a form of commercial communication – entailing commercial messages carried by a variety of media (e.g. television, press, telephone, radio).[38] Finally, certain communication science scholars have also referred to commercial communication as an overarching concept.[39] However, communication scientists also use other terms such as 'marketing communications'[40], 'advertising', 'persuasive communication', etc.

USE OF NOTIONS. For the purpose of this book, the notions 'commercial communication', 'commercial message', 'promotional message', 'advertising' and 'marketing' may be used interchangeably. However, if a regulatory instrument uses a specific notion, this notion will be used in conformity (e.g. the notion 'audiovisual commercial communication' will be used when discussing the AVMS Directive). Furthermore, the word 'new' is used to indicate that the forms of commercial communication rely on one or more of the emerging trends that are further discussed *infra* (e.g. *new* forms of commercial communication, *new* advertising formats, *new* advertising techniques).

1.3. *Advertising literacy*

CHILDREN'S ADVERTISING LITERACY. Children grow up in a commercialised environment in which they, from an early age, come across advertising for a multitude of products and services.[41] Throughout their childhood, they learn how to cope with the overload of such commercial information and develop critical decision-making skills.[42] Scholars refer in this regard to children's 'advertising literacy', which includes their advertising-related knowledge, attitudes, and skills, such as the ability to recognise commercial messages, to understand the persuasive intent of such messages, and to critically evaluate them.[43] Children already display some level of brand consciousness at a very

---

38 Conversely, the mere appearance of a brand or product does not necessarily mean that there is a marketing communication.

39 G. Siegert, B. von Rimscha and S. Grubenmann (eds), *Commercial Communication in the Digital Age: Information or Disinformation?* (1 Edition, Walter de Gruyter 2017).

40 P. De Pelsmacker, M. Geuens and J. Van Den Bergh, *Marketing Communications: A European Perspective, 6/E* (Pearson 2017) <http://catalogue.pearsoned.co.uk/educator/product/Marketing-Communications-A-European-Perspective/9781292135762.page> accessed 15 March 2018.

41 B. Gunter, *Kids and Branding in a Digital World* (Manchester University Press 2016).

42 Cauberghe and others (n 28); Esther Rozendaal and others, 'Reconsidering Advertising Literacy as a Defense Against Advertising Effects' (2011) 14 Media Psychology 333. ibid.

43 Cauberghe and others (n 27); Rozendaal and others (n 41); S. Livingstone and E. J. Helsper, 'Does Advertising Literacy Mediate the Effects of Advertising on Children? A Critical Examination of Two Linked Research Literatures in Relation to Obesity and Food Choice' (2006) 56 Journal of Communication 560; D. M. Boush, M. Friestad and G. M. Rose,

young age (even starting from the age of 2 years old).[44] This is part of the reason why advertisers and marketers target children from the earliest stages of their lives, essentially transforming them into young consumers.

Digital natives in a changing media landscape. The current media landscape is undergoing significant changes due to technological advancements and is characterised by an increased convergence between traditional and digital media. Research has shown that children's use of traditional media (i.e. radio and print) is steadily declining, with the exception of television.[45, 46] Yet, even with television, important evolutions can be noted, as children nowadays use different screens to watch television content (i.e. computer, tablet, smartphone)[47] and increasingly consume video-on-demand services.[48] Children all across the world are engaging in digital environments in which they play, communicate and search for information. As per Livingstone et al., "*an estimated one in three of all Internet users in the world today is below the age of 18*".[49] Children are early adopters of information and telecommunications technologies, which have a crucial role in empowering them by enabling communication and education. They access the web at a very young age[50], via their own devices[51] or ask their parents to borrow theirs to go online. The duration of internet usage

---

'Adolescent Skepticism toward TV Advertising and Knowledge of Advertiser Tactics' (1994) 21 Journal of Consumer Research 165.

44 Gunter (n 40); Hudders and others, 'Shedding New Light on How Advertising Literacy Can Affect Children's Processing of Embedded Advertising Formats' (n 1).

45 Research conducted in 2017 by OfCom, the UK Media Regulator, shows that the television set remains the most widely used device for watching TV content. However, YouTube is becoming increasingly popular and there have been big increases in the number of younger children watching YouTube. Ofcom, 'Children and Parents: Media Use and Attitudes Report 2017' (2017) <https://www.ofcom.org.uk/__data/assets/pdf_file/0020/108182/children-parents-media-use-attitudes-2017.pdf> accessed 11 July 2018.

46 B. Zarouali and others, 'Mediabezit En -Gebruik Bij Minderjarigen. Een Rapport in Het Kader van Het AdLit Onderzoeksproject' (2015) <www.adlit.be/output> accessed 11 July 2018.

47 Zarouali and others, 'Mediabezit En -Gebruik Bij Minderjarigen. Een Rapport in Het Kader van Het AdLit Onderzoeksproject' (n 45).

48 According to Brasel, "*Consumers no longer sit down to simply watch television or read a newspaper; instead, they watch television while surfing the Internet on a laptop, cellphone by their side, splitting their attention between multiple screens and media sources*". S. A. Brasel, 'How Focused Identities Can Help Brands Navigate a Changing Media Landscape' (2012) 55 Business Horizons 283.

49 S. Livingstone, J. Carr and J. Byrne, 'One in Three: Internet Governance and Children's Rights' (Centre for International Governance Innovation and the Royal Institute of International Affairs 2015) 22 <https://www.cigionline.org/publications/one-three-internet-governance-and-childrens-rights> accessed 11 July 2018.

50 Up to 70% of 3–4 year olds are active online. Zarouali and others, 'Mediabezit En -Gebruik Bij Minderjarigen. Een Rapport in Het Kader van Het AdLit Onderzoeksproject' (n 46).

51 From the age of 12, the smartphone becomes a major part of the media consumption of children. Zarouali and others, 'Mediabezit En -Gebruik Bij Minderjarigen. Een Rapport in Het Kader van Het AdLit Onderzoeksproject' (n 45).

and the preferred online activities may vary according to age. For example, certain studies in Flanders have shown that younger children primarily enjoy playing videogames[52] and watching videos online via websites or apps, whereas teenagers are more present on social media.[53]

Impact on commercial communication. The changes in the modern media environment also have an impact on advertising and marketing practices. As traditional and new media are consumed interchangeably and consumers' attention is split between multiple screens and media sources, the competition for 'eyeballs' has become even more difficult for advertisers. Brasel clarifies that "*brands must be hyper-focused, displaying a single consistent message that resonates on simple personality and affective dimensions across all consumer touchpoints, from media channels to in-store and environmental brand exposures*".[54] Against this backdrop, several emerging trends in the area of commercial communication aimed at children can be identified, which will be the subject of discussion of the next section.

2. EMERGING TRENDS IN THE AREA OF COMMERCIAL COMMUNICATION AND CHILDREN[55]

2.1. *Advertising in the digital era*

Introduction. The digital environment in which children spend a lot of their time[56], is increasingly permeated with sophisticated, interactive and personalised forms of advertising.[57] Children have difficulties understanding the persuasive tactics employed by these new forms of advertising, which raises important questions from both a societal and legal perspective.

Persuasive tactics. The most significant difference between traditional and new forms of commercial communication lies in the persuasive tactics that are

52 Zarouali and others, 'Mediabezit En -Gebruik Bij Minderjarigen. Een Rapport in Het Kader van Het AdLit Onderzoeksproject' (n 45).

53 Furthermore, the study showed that the number of children that uses social media gradually grows with their age. D. Bastien and others, 'Apestaartjaren: De Digitale Leefwereld van Kinderen En Jongeren' (Mediawijs 2018) <https://drive.google.com/file/d/1ArMVpbG55QmNWcOTz6ScjFWBBnrDClxm/view?usp=embed_facebook> accessed 24 August 2018.

54 Brasel (n 48).

55 In the context of this book, the concepts 'new advertising formats' or 'new forms of commercial communication' refer to these emerging trends: integration, interaction, personalisation and emotional appeal.

56 S. Chaudron and others, *Young Children (0–8) and Digital Technology: A Qualitative Exploratory Study across Seven Countries.* (Publications Office 2015) <http://dx.publications.europa.eu/10.2788/00749> accessed 6 November 2017.; Livingstone, Carr and Byrne (n 49).

57 Verdoodt, Clifford and Lievens (n 7).

employed. Traditional formats (e.g. TV commercials) primarily spread factual or propositional messages, for instance by focusing on the product quality and characteristics.[58] In addition, certain persuasive tactics are used, including *inter alia* repetition and linking them to positive stimuli such as humour.[59] Conversely, new formats (e.g. advergames, sponsored content on social media) employ more subtle tactics. According to De Pauw et al., these tactics function at a preconscious level, and rather than aiming to inform consumers about products and services they attempt to effectuate a better brand recall and attitude.[60] This is achieved through constant exposure to brands or products[61], as well as through implicit persuasion by what Nairn and Fine define as a 'positive affect transfer' of amusing and captivating media content to the brand or product it integrates.[62]

Children's advertising literacy. The specific tactics of new forms of commercial communication, including their (1) integrated, (2) interactive, (3) personalised nature as well as (4) their emotive appeal, are particularly appealing to children.[63] As such, they allow for a more effective persuasive commercial message, as they positively influence children's attitudes towards products or brands and have a real impact on their purchasing decisions. Indeed, many children have great difficulty applying their advertising literacy skills when it comes to these new tactics or advertising trends.[64] Accordingly, it remains crucial for children to be able to recognise and understand the persuasive tactics of these new forms of commercial communication.

---

58 E. S. Moore and V. J. Rideout, 'The Online Marketing of Food to Children: Is It Just Fun and Games?' (2007) 26 Journal of Public Policy & Marketing 202.

59 E. Rozendaal, M. Buijzen and P. Valkenburg, 'Children's Understanding of Advertisers' Persuasive Tactics' 329.

60 P. De Pauw and others, 'From Persuasive Messages to Tactics: Exploring Children's Knowledge and Judgement of New Advertising Formats' [2017] New Media and Society 1.

61 S. Auty and C. Lewis, 'Exploring Children's Choice: The Reminder Effect of Product Placement' (2004) 21 Psychology and Marketing 697; Haiming Hang, 'Online Game Advertising and Children: A Literature Review', *Advances in Advertising Research* (University of Bath 2015) <http://opus.bath.ac.uk/45052/> accessed 7 November 2017.

62 A. Nairn and C. Fine, 'Who's Messing with My Mind?: The Implications of Dual-Process Models for the Ethics of Advertising to Children' (2008) 27 International Journal of Advertising 447.

63 B. Zarouali and others, 'Online Reclamewijsheid Bij Kinderen: Herkennen En Begrijpen van Reclamebanners En de Rol van Need for Cognition En Reclamewijsheidslessen' (2016) 44 Tijdschrift voor communicatiewetenschap.-Houten 24; M. Buijzen, E. A. Van Reijmersdal and L. H. Owen, 'Introducing the PCMC Model: An Investigative Framework for Young People's Processing of Commercialized Media Content' (2010) 20 Communication Theory 427; Nairn and Fine (n 61); K. Daems and P. De Pelsmacker, 'Marketing Communication Techniques Aimed at Children and Teenagers. A Research Report within the Frame of the AdLit Project.' (2015) <www.AdLit.be/output> accessed 11 July 2018.

64 Hudders and others, 'Children's Advertising Literacy in a New Media Environment' (n 8); S. An, H. S. Jin and E. H. Park, 'Children's Advertising Literacy for Advergames: Perception of the Game as Advertising' (2014) 43 Journal of Advertising 63.

2.2. *Integration*

Types of integration. A first widespread persuasive tactic in this area is the fluid integration of commercial messages into non-commercial content (e.g. a programme).[65] Although this convergence has started quite some time ago, it reached new heights within the digital environment.[66] The idea behind integration is that commercial communication is most effective when the consumer does not recognise it as such.[67] According to Buijzen et al., there are three types of integration: (1) format, (2) thematic and (3) narrative integration.[68] Format integration relates to the embedding of a commercial message into a specific editorial context (e.g. an advertisement in the same style as a news article, a sponsored story in a person's social media newsfeed). Thematic integration entails that commercial messages are integrated into thematically congruent content, for instance sports brand logos at football games.[69] Finally, narrative integration entails that the commercial message is integrated in the narrative of certain media content (e.g. product placement in a television program or vlog). Aside from these types of integration, commercial communication may also be integrated in different media at the same time. Advertisers nowadays tend to make use of a holistic marketing or advertising strategy, targeting children with the same commercial message through different media.[70] By combining the effects of the different media platforms, the campaign may achieve a viral effect.[71]

Persuasive tactic. When children are exposed to branded environments for an extended period of time, the lines between advertising and programme content are blurred.[72] By seamlessly integrating the commercial message in the storyline and the images of the media content, potential irritation or resistance on the child's behalf may be bypassed. Particularly for younger children, their ability to engage with integrated forms of commercial communication in a critical manner is less developed.[73] According to the Organisation for Economic Cooperation and Development ("OECD"), "*Children have insufficient*

---

65 Various other terms are used when talking about this trend in commercial communication, such as "sponsored", "promoted", "native", etc.

66 S. M. Grimes, 'Kids' Ad Play: Regulating Children's Advergames in the Converging Media Context' (2008) 8 International Journal of Communications Law and Policy 162.

67 S. L. Calvert, 'Children as Consumers: Advertising and Marketing' [2008] Journal of Consumer Research 205.

68 Buijzen, Van Reijmersdal and Owen (n 63).

69 Buijzen, Van Reijmersdal and Owen (n 63).

70 Daems and De Pelsmacker (n 63).

71 K. Tutaj and E. A. van Reijmersdal, 'Effects of Online Advertising Format and Persuasion Knowledge on Audience Reactions' (2012) 18 Journal of Marketing Communications 5.

72 Daems and De Pelsmacker (n 63).

73 M. C. Martin, 'Children's Understanding of the Intent of Advertising: A Meta-Analysis' [1997] Journal of Public Policy & Marketing 205.

understanding of how Internet content is produced and financed, which is also a reason why they have difficulty critically assessing advertising messages."[74] The societal impact of the blurred lines between commercial and non-commercial content is significant. Indeed, integrated advertising techniques avail themselves of the fact that consumers are unable to entirely ignore the commercial message, as it is inherently linked with the informational element.[75] Consumers may experience greater difficulties when it comes to recognising persuasive commercial messages, which undermines their ability to process the message critically.[76] This trend in commercial communication has become even more popular due to consumer fatigue and an apparent increasing immunity to traditional digital advertising (such as display ads)[77] and the increased use of ad blocking technologies.[78]

Children's advertising literacy. Research has shown that children can better recognise traditional television commercials as a form of commercial communication as compared to the following new formats relying on integration: advergames, sponsored content and brand placement.[79] Although children can easily recognise and understand the concept of advertising banners, they have less understanding of the persuasive intent of commercial communication when exposed to advergames and sponsored content. They also find it more difficult to recognise these new forms of commercial communication as advertising, compared to television and online banners. According to De Pauw et al., children in general do not actively look out for commercial communication that is embedded into entertaining or interactive media content. This also entails that children do not reflect on the tactics such new forms of commercial communication employ (e.g. positive affect transfer, the collection of personal data).[80] According to Nairn and Fine, these techniques are particularly likely to persuade young consumers implicitly.[81] Similar to children, teenagers find it more difficult to recognise integrated social

74 OECD, 'The Protection of Children Online – Recommendation of the OECD Council' (2012) <https://www.oecd.org/sti/ieconomy/childrenonline_with_cover.pdf> accessed 12 July 2018.

75 L. Hellemans, E. Lievens and P. Valcke, 'Playing Hide-and-Seek? A Legal Perspective on the Complex Distinction between Commercial and Editorial Content in Hybrid Advertising Formats' (2015) 17 info 19.

76 Cauberghe and others (n 28); Rozendaal and others (n 42).

77 Wharton University, 'A New Marketing Royalty: Why Digital Influencers Are on the Rise' (*Knowledge@Wharton*) <http://knowledge.wharton.upenn.edu/article/new-marketing-royalty-rise-digital-influencers/> accessed 20 November 2017.

78 D. Clifford and V. Verdoodt, 'Ad-Blocking-the Dark Side of Consumer Empowerment: A New Hope or Will the Empire Strike Back?' (2016), BILETA Conference, University of Hertfordshire.

79 Vanwesenbeeck and others (n 6). This is also in line with earlier research An, Seung Jin and Hae Park (n 64).

80 De Pauw and others (n 60).

81 Nairn and Fine (n 62).

media advertisements (i.e. news feed) when compared to traditional television commercials.[82]

2.3. *Interaction*

Interactivity. Another important trend in the area of commercial communication is the use of interaction or in other words the involvement of the consumer in the advertising campaign. McMillan and Hwang identified three dimensions of interactivity, namely user control, direction of communication, and time.[83] User control relates to the ability of the user to search for and control the amount of information online. The direction of communication in a digital context will often be two-way, as internet users are able to communicate and interact with others online. The third dimension, time, refers to synchronisation, as interaction may take place simultaneously or delayed.[84] Aside from these three dimensions, scholars have argued that interactivity in the context of commercial communication can be characterised by different features.[85] For instance, modern commercial communication campaigns or strategies make use of the constant connectivity of young people and their extensive use of digital media. Furthermore, interactivity is often connected to other trends, such as personalisation and integration (e.g. social games where the advertising message is placed in a context in which peers play a central role[86], targeted advertisements on social media).

Persuasive tactic. Interactive advertising formats such as advergames or branded mobile applications have proven to be an extremely useful tool for advertisers and in particular when targeted towards children. Such techniques allow for the development of a positive product or brand association through the delivery of fun interactive content.[87] As a result, children are no longer merely passive receivers of commercial communications. Instead, they become

82 B. Zarouali and others, 'The Impact of Online Peer Communication on Adolescents' Persuasion Knowledge and Attitudes toward Social Advertising', *Paper presented at Etmaal van de Communicatiewetenschap 2017* (2017).

83 S. J. McMillan and J. Hwang, 'Measures of Perceived Interactivity: An Exploration of the Role of Direction of Communication, User Control, and Time in Shaping Perceptions of Interactivity' (2002) 31 Journal of Advertising 29.

84 V. Cauberghe and P. De Pelsmacker, 'Advergames: The Impact of Brand Prominence and Game Repetition on Brand Responses' (2010) 39 Journal of Advertising 5; Daems and De Pelsmacker (n 62).

85 Daems and De Pelsmacker (n 63).

86 E. Rozendaal and others, 'Children's Responses to Advertising in Social Games' (2013) 42 Journal of Advertising 142.

87 A. D. Cheyne and others, 'Marketing Sugary Cereals to Children in the Digital Age: A Content Analysis of 17 Child-Targeted Websites' (2013) 18 Journal of Health Communication 563; A. Nairn and H. Hang, 'Advergames: It's Not Child's Play: A Review of Research' (Commissioned by the Family and Parenting Institute 2012) <www.agnesnairn.co.uk/policy_reports/advergames-its-not-childs-play.pdf> accessed 8 November 2017.

actively involved in the advertising process for instance by creating or sharing content themselves or by networking with peers.[88] Advertisers stimulate young consumers to share and create content in order to promote their own brands, products and services within children's personal networks (e.g. through likes and comments, by using sponsored filters in photo's, by sharing videos containing brand songs or featuring products).[89]

CHILDREN'S ADVERTISING LITERACY. Children experience a lot of difficulties when applying their advertising literacy skills to interactive and social advertising. It is generally recognised that peers such as friends or classmates play an important socialisation role in shaping children's commercial decision-making.[90] BANERJEE and DITTMAR clarify that when children grow up, they start believing that the possession of certain products and brands determines the quality of their friendships.[91] In this sense, the peer group sets the standard for the brands and products that are cool and desirable. According to ROZENDAAL et al., peer influence also plays an important role in the context of social games, making children more susceptible to the persuasive effects of advertising integrated within these games.[92] In line with these findings, ZAROUALI et al. discovered that online peer communication on social media generally leads to lower advertising literacy amongst teenagers towards commercial communications that appear on their newsfeeds.[93]

2.4. Personalisation

PERSONALISATION. A third trend that has emerged in recent years is the personalisation of commercial communications. The significant technological progress, globalisation and the emergence of new business models have contributed to the collection and processing of personal data on an ever-increasing scale. Children's personal data is being collected in unprecedented quantities, by businesses, governments, schools, and other organisations, leading to children's lives being increasingly 'datafied'.[94] Children's online

---

88 Daems and De Pelsmacker (n 62); K. C. Montgomery and J. Chester, 'Interactive Food and Beverage Marketing: Targeting Adolescents in the Digital Age' (2009) 45 Journal of Adolescent Health S18.

89 Daems and De Pelsmacker (n 63).

90 G. P. Moschis and G. A. Churchill, 'Consumer Socialization: A Theoretical and Empirical Analysis' (1978) 15 Journal of Marketing Research 599; Rozendaal and others (n 85).

91 R. Banerjee and H. Dittmar, 'Individual Differences in Children's Materialism: The Role of Peer Relations' (2008) 34 Personality & Social Psychology Bulletin 17.

92 Rozendaal and others (n 86).

93 Zarouali and others, 'The Impact of Online Peer Communication on Adolescents' Persuasion Knowledge and Attitudes toward Social Advertising' (n 82).

94 D. Lupton and B. Williamson, 'The Datafied Child: The Dataveillance of Children and Implications for Their Rights' (2017) 19 New Media & Society 780; S. van der Hof, 'I Agree, or

behaviour is being tracked by means of cookies[95] and plug-ins[96]; joining a social media platform or downloading an app usually involves a transfer of personal information; advergames offer content tailored to the age or sex of the child; and interconnected toys interact with children and even record conversations.[97] The harvested data is converted into profiles[98], on the basis of which advertisers are able to target children with personalised advertisements and tailor their marketing campaigns.[99]

PERSUASIVE TACTIC. It has been argued that personalised advertising techniques allow for a more effective transmission of the commercial message, as advertisers can respond explicitly to a specific user's developmental level and knowledge base.[100] This is a distinct advantage when it comes to building a strong and lasting personal interaction and connection with the child consumer. Indeed, studies have shown that commercial messages that correspond with the interests and behaviour of consumers will lead to a more positive brand attitude, as the message is perceived as less intrusive, more relevant and useful, ultimately increasing consumers' purchase intentions.[101] In addition, YAN et al. found

Do I: A Rights-Based Analysis of the Law on Children's Consent in the Digital World' (2016) 34 Wis. Int'l LJ 409.

95 F. J. Zuiderveen Borgesius, 'Personal Data Processing for Behavioural Targeting: Which Legal Basis?' (2015) 5 International Data Privacy Law 163; E. Kosta, 'Peeking into the Cookie Jar: The European Approach towards the Regulation of Cookies' (2013) 21 International Journal of Law and Information Technology 380.

96 In 2015, an international network of data protection authorities conducted a privacy sweep of 1494 children's websites and apps, which showed that 67% of the websites and apps was collecting children's personal data and 50% shared this personal data with third parties. Global Privacy Enforcement Network (2015) Results of the 2015 Global Privacy Enforcement Network Sweep. Global Privacy Enforcement Network, 'Children's Privacy Sweep' (2015) <http://194.242.234.211/documents/10160/0/GPEN+Privacy+Sweep+2015.pdf>; Nairn and Fine (n 62).

97 S. Chaudron and others, 'Kaleidoscope on the Internet of Toys – Safety, Security, Privacy and Societal Insights' (European Commission) JRC Technical Report <http://publications.jrc.ec.europa.eu/repository/bitstream/JRC105061/jrc105061_final_online.pdf> accessed 6 February 2018.

98 F. Bosco and others, 'Profiling Technologies and Fundamental Rights and Values: Regulatory Challenges and Perspectives from European Data Protection Authorities', *Reforming European Data Protection Law* (Springer 2015) <http://link.springer.com/chapter/10.1007/978-94-017-9385-8_1> accessed 11 August 2017., 4.

99 For a more detailed analysis of profiling and personalised advertising, see part II, chapter II, section II of this book.

100 Calvert (n 67).; Cauberghe and others (n 28).

101 L. F. Bright and T. Daugherty, 'Does Customization Impact Advertising Effectiveness? An Exploratory Study of Consumer Perceptions of Advertising in Customized Online Environments' (2012) 18 Journal of Marketing Communications 19. A. Ghose and S. Yang, 'An Empirical Analysis of Search Engine Advertising: Sponsored Search in Electronic Markets' (2009) 55 Management Science 1605; R. S. Moore, C. A. Stammerjohan and R. A. Coulter, 'Banner Advertises-Website Context Congruity and Color Effects on Attention and Attitudes' (2005) 34 Journal of Advertising 71.

that the click-through rates of advertisements employing behavioural targeting techniques increased enormously.[102]

Children's advertising literacy. With regard to children's advertising literacy in the context of personalised advertising, several important considerations can be made. First, the tracking of consumers' online information and activities often happens covertly. Boerman et al. argue that this covertness may be harmful as well as unethical, since consumers are not aware of the persuasive techniques used.[103] Furthermore, although the advertising sector has rapidly adopted personalisation techniques, research on the effects thereof on children's advertising literacy remains scarce.[104] De Pauw et al. found that while children between 9 and 11 recognised a personalised advertisement (not integrated in the media content), few of them immediately understood that the advertisement was based on previous browsing behaviour.[105] In general, children's commercial literacy increases gradually as they get older. For instance, research has shown that children between 12 and 16 years old have less knowledge of social media advertising and are less critical than youngsters above 16 years.[106] However, studies on personalised advertising and adolescents, a group of avid social media users who are frequently exposed to such advertising, paint an interesting picture. The level of personalisation of advertising may be different depending on the types and amount of personal data used.[107] If the level of personalisation of a commercial message is too high, consumers may view this as a breach of their privacy.[108] Zarouali et al. confirmed this in a study on the impact of retargeting on adolescents.[109] First, the direct effect of retargeted advertising on adolescents' purchase intention was indeed higher than for non-retargeted advertising, meaning that, in general, adolescents responded quite favourably to this advertising technique. However, the study also found that a retargeted advertisement indirectly leads to a negative effect

---

102 J. Yan and others, 'How Much Can Behavioral Targeting Help Online Advertising?', *Proceedings of the 18th international conference on World wide web* (ACM 2009) <http://dl.acm.org/citation.cfm?id=1526745> accessed 25 October 2017; De Pauw and others (n 60).

103 S. C. Boerman, S. Kruikemeier and Frederik J Zuiderveen Borgesius, 'Online Behavioral Advertising: A Literature Review and Research Agenda' (2017) 46 Journal of Advertising 363.

104 B. Zarouali and others, '"Do You like Cookies?" Adolescents' Skeptical Processing of Retargeted Facebook-Ads and the Moderating Role of Privacy Concern and a Textual Debriefing' (2017) 69 Computers in Human Behavior 157.

105 De Pauw and others (n 60).

106 De Pauw and others (n 60).

107 Boerman, Kruikemeier and Zuiderveen Borgesius (n 103).

108 M. L. Anteunis and G. van Noort, 'Interactivity Effects in Social Media Marketing on Brand Engagement: An Investigation of Underlying Mechanisms, The 10th ICORIA Conference Berlin' (2011). In relation to this, research has shown that there could even be 'reactance', where consumers mentally resist persuasive attempts and even do the opposite of the advertiser's wishes. J. van Doorn and J.C. Hoekstra, 'Customization of Online Advertising: The Role of Intrusiveness' (2013) 24 Marketing Letters 339.

109 Zarouali and others, '"Do You like Cookies?' (n 104).

on the purchase intention when adolescents are made aware that their personal information was being used to target the commercial message at them. In other words, personalisation techniques may also trigger scepticism and privacy concerns. In addition, another study by Zarouali et al. uncovered rather worrying findings about adolescents' understanding of personalised advertising techniques employed in social media.[110] The study shows that although the level of advertising literacy of children for these techniques gradually increases when they get older, almost half of 17 year-olds have a really low understanding of persuasion tactics and most of them did not understand the data processing practices behind the advertisements. Considering these results, it can also be questioned whether adults would be better equipped to recognise and critically reflect on personalised advertising and make well-balanced decisions regarding their privacy.

2.5. *Emotional appeal*

Consumers are emotional creatures. To a certain extent, it can be argued that all commercial communications aim at triggering an emotional response of consumers. More specifically, marketers aim to evoke emotional responses in order to create awareness, positive brand association, and an emotional desire for a product or service.[111] Already in 1957, Martineau argued that

> *"Psychologists unhesitatingly state that the main appeal which advertising uses and the one which we can place our main reliance is the emotional, in the sense that we are trying to create suggested association with strong motive power."*[112] (Emphasis added)

In this regard, both positive and negative appeals may be used to elicit an emotional response.[113] Whereas positive appeals promise positive emotions as a result of the use or purchase of the advertised product or service[114], negative appeals associate negative consequences for those who fail to comply with the marketing message.[115] In 1977, Reed and coalson tracked the historical increase of emotional appeals in advertising and attributed technological development as

110 B. Zarouali and others, 'Adolescents' Advertising Competences and Institutional Privacy Protection Strategies on Social Networking Sites: Implications for Regulation'.

111 Verdoodt, Clifford and Lievens (n 7).

112 P. Martineau, 'Motivation in advertising' (1957) 15 as cited by O Lee Jr Reed and John L Jr Coalson, 'Eighteenth-Century Legal Doctrine Meets Twentieth-Century Marketing Techniques: F.T.C. Regulation of Emotionally Conditioning Advertising' (1976) 11 Georgia Law Review 733.

113 N. Henley, R. J. Donovan and H. Moorhead, 'Appealing to Positive Motivations and Emotions in Social Marketing: Example of a Positive Parenting Campaign' (1998) 4 Social Marketing Quarterly 48.

114 Reed and Coalson (n 112).

115 Verdoodt, Clifford and Lievens (n 7).

a key-determining factor in its rise.[116] More recently, due to major technological advancements and increased computational capabilities, emotions have now become detectable in the online world and have raised the interest of a broad variety of commercial entities.[117] For instance, a leaked internal Facebook document revealed that the platform allows advertisers to target users during moments when they feel insecure and worthless.[118] This reflects an emerging trend relating to the use of neuroscience techniques to shape advertising and marketing strategies, which allows advertisers to connect on an even deeper level with consumers.[119] Such techniques or applications are designed to bypass rational consumer behaviour, making use of the fact that emotions play a key role in decision-making and that consumers are mostly unaware of them.[120] In other words, neuromarketing aims at influencing consumers' decision-making at an unconscious level (i.e. by stimulating subconscious mechanisms within the brain).[121] By studying the impact of advertising and marketing stimuli on the brain, advertisers adapt campaigns to generate more powerful and longer-lasting positive responses from consumers.[122]

Persuasive tactics. In the words of Lerner et al., "*emotions constitute potent, pervasive, predictable, sometimes harmful and sometimes beneficial drivers of decision making*".[123] Emotions can shape decision-making in two important ways: (1) certain emotions are associated with different patterns of cognitive assessments that allow to predict the outcome of the decision-making process (e.g. anger or joy) and (2) emotions influence how individuals process

116 Reed and Coalson (n 112).

117 D. Clifford, 'Citizen-Consumers in a Personalised Galaxy: Emotion Influenced Decision-Making, a True Path to the Dark Side?' (2017).

118 W. Christl, K. Kopp and P. Urs Riechert, 'How Companies Use Personal Data against People' (Cracked Lab – Institute for Critical Digital Culture 2017) <http://crackedlabs.org/dl/CrackedLabs_Christl_DataAgainstPeople.pdf> accessed 13 October 2017.

119 D. Ariely and G. S. Berns, 'Neuromarketing: The Hope and Hype of Neuroimaging in Business' (2010) 11 Nature Reviews Neuroscience 284; Amani Al Abbas, Weifeng Chen and Maria Saberi, 'The Impact of Neuromarketing Advertising on Children'.

120 E. Laureckis and À. M. Miralpeix, 'Ethical and Legal Considerations in Research Subject and Data Protection' in A. R. Thomas and others (eds), *Ethics and Neuromarketing: Implications for Market Research and Business Practice* (Springer International Publishing 2017) <https://doi.org/10.1007/978-3-319-45609-6_5> accessed 27 August 2018; Ariely and Berns (n 118).

121 Morin explains that consumers are unable to describe their own cognitive processes, which has many subconscious components. Thus traditional methods of marketing research, such as interviews and focus groups have significant limitations. C. Morin, 'Neuromarketing: The New Science of Consumer Behavior' (2011) 48 Society 131.

122 T. Voorhees, D. L. Spiegel and D. Cooper, 'Neuromarketing: Legal and Policy Issues' <https://www.cov.com/files/upload/White_Paper_Neuromarketing_Legal_and_Policy_Issues.pdf> accessed 28 August 2018.

123 J. S. Lerner and others, 'Emotion and Decision Making' (2015) 66 Annual Review of Psychology 799.

information and whether they do so superficially or in detail.[124] According to CLIFFORD, the use of these techniques for advertising and marketing purposes potentially undermines a person's rationality as understood as a legal paradigm and, as such, individual autonomy given that the law has traditionally separated 'rationality' from emotions.[125] Advertisers aim at inducing emotional responses with consumers to create awareness and positive brand associations. In turn, this will evoke an emotional desire for the advertised product or service. Emotional appeals can be used both for the content and the delivery of the commercial message. With regard to the latter, gamification elements are often used to exploit cognitive biases, including when a marketing campaign is targeted at children.[126] For instance, by using elements such as countdowns (e.g. counting down the time left until a certain offer is no longer valid), marketers make use of people's loss aversion and their tendency to evaluate potential losses as larger and more significant than equivalent gains. Considering the new trends in emotion detection and targeting (i.e. personalisation and neuromarketing), the potential capacity to personalise the link between positive moods and the effect of an advertising campaign raise clear legal–ethical issues (e.g. protection against misleading or aggressive advertising practices, privacy infringements).[127]

CHILDREN'S ADVERTISING LITERACY. Specifically with regard to children, it has been recognised that highly affective media content does not motivate children to process the content critically. Indeed, as children need all their cognitive capacities to process and understand the media content, they do not have the capacity to critically evaluate the commercial message.[128] Furthermore, the affect-based nature of new advertising formats not only limits children's motivation and ability to process an advertising message elaborately, but also to apply their advertising literacy skills as a defence against the persuasive message.[129]

---

124 C. R. Hullett, 'The Impact of Mood on Persuasion: A Meta-Analysis' (2005) 32 Communication Research 423; Clifford (n 116).

125 Clifford (n 117).

126 R. Terlutter and M. L. Capella, 'The Gamification of Advertising: Analysis and Research Directions of In-Game Advertising, Advergames, and Advertising in Social Network Games' (2013) 42 Journal of Advertising 95.

127 A. Kramera, J. E. Guillory and J. T. Hancock, 'Experimental Evidence of Massive-Scale Emotional Contagion through Social Networks' (2014) 111 PNAS 8788.

128 S. An and S. Stern, 'Mitigating the Effects of Advergames on Children: Do Advertising Breaks Work?' (2011) 40 Journal of Advertising 43; Rozendaal and others (n 42); M. K. J. Waiguny, M. R. Nelson and R. Terlutter, 'The Relationship of Persuasion Knowledge, Identification of Commercial Intent and Persuasion Outcomes in Advergames – the Role of Media Context and Presence' (2014) 37 Journal of Consumer Policy 257.

129 E. Rozendaal, *Advertising Literacy and Children's Susceptibility to Advertising* (9789491211065 2011) <https://dare.uva.nl/search?identifier=59a96c2a-1dd8–4fbc-8ac1–1c0cf4836420> accessed 8 February 2018.

3. CONCLUDING REMARKS

This section first clarified the constitutive elements of the book (children, commercial communication and advertising literacy) and then explored the emerging trends in the area of commercial communication. Four major trends were identified: integration, interaction, personalisation and the use of emotional appeal. These trends and the persuasive tactics behind them present significant obstacles for children to activate their advertising literacy skills (i.e. their ability to recognise and critically assess the commercial message). The societal impact of these new forms of commercial communication raises questions regarding the regulation thereof. Therefore, the next section explores the regulatory context and the policy agenda, and it addresses the need for future-proof regulation and a children's rights-based approach.

SECTION II. THE NEED FOR A FUTURE-PROOF REGULATORY FRAMEWORK IN LIGHT OF CHILDREN'S RIGHTS

Introduction. The protection of children against certain forms of commercial communication has long been considered an objective of general interest. In this regard, a broad variety of provisions regulating different aspects or forms of commercial communication can be found across various legislative instruments at the international, EU and national level. In addition, the advertising industry has understood for a long time the importance of consumer trust in advertising and has been very active in the development of self-regulatory initiatives. This section begins by briefly discussing this evolving regulatory context and addresses the fragmentation of existing legislation and the rise of alternative regulatory instruments in the area of commercial communication. Furthermore, this section provides an overview of the policy discourse on new forms of commercial communication (i.e. the emerging trends analysed in the previous section)[130] and their impact on children's advertising literacy. Finally, this section elaborates on the need for a future-proof and empowering regulatory framework and outlines several elements that are important in this regard.

---

130 I.e. advertising formats that make use of techniques such as integration, interaction, personalisation, and emotional appeal.

1. EVOLVING REGULATORY CONTEXT IN THE DIGITAL ENVIRONMENT

1.1. A fragmented legal framework for commercial communication in the EU

A COMPLEX LEGAL FRAMEWORK UNDER REVIEW. At the EU level, there is a myriad of laws regulating commercial communication aimed at children. Indeed, rather than having a single piece of legislation devoted exclusively to new forms of commercial communication, existing instruments and provisions have been retrospectively adapted to new technologies and services.[131] As mentioned, new advertising formats have specific features that make them particularly appealing to children. They are often digital (e.g. advergames) or hybrid (e.g. advertisements on smart/connected tv's) and as such, the exact application or interplay of the different regulatory frameworks is complex. The EU legislators have, for instance, restricted the marketing of certain products (e.g. alcohol) and services[132], provided rules specifically applicable to audiovisual commercial communications (i.e. the Audiovisual Media Services Directive, "AVMS Directive") and adopted general rules on misleading and aggressive advertising (i.e. the Unfair Commercial Practices Directive, "UCP Directive").[133] Aside from this, advertisers and advertising networks increasingly process children's personal data, which allows them to tailor and personalise commercial communication based on children's online behaviour. Such data processing activities are only allowed if the rules of the EU data protection framework (i.e. the General Data Protection Regulation, "GDPR" and ePrivacy framework) are respected. The existing legislative framework has been undergoing significant reforms, as part of the European Commission's Digital Market Strategy for Europe (*infra*). First, in its 2015 Communication the Commission stated that it would review the AVMS Directive, with a particular focus on *inter alia* the rules on the protection of minors as well as the advertising rules.[134] Second, the Commission also added the review of the ePrivacy Directive to its Strategy, once the EU rules on data protection were adopted (i.e. the GDPR).[135] In addition, the European Commission launched a Fitness Check of consumer and marketing law in 2016. Its aim was to test whether the existing directives remain fit for purpose on the basis of a set of criteria.[136]

---

131 'New Forms of Commercial Communications in a Converged Audiovisual Sector' (European Audiovisual Observatory 2012).

132 As mentioned, this falls outside the scope of the book.

133 Vanwesenbeeck and others (n 6) 104.

134 European Commission, 'Communication from the Commission to the European Parliament, the Council, the European Economic and Social Committee and the Committee of the Regions on a Digital Single Market Strategy for Europe. [COM(2015)192 Final] 11' 10.

135 European Commission, 'Communication from the Commission to the European Parliament, the Council, the European Economic and Social Committee and the Committee of the Regions on a Digital Single Market Strategy for Europe. [COM(2015)192 Final] 11' (n 134) 13.

136 These criteria include effectiveness, efficiency, coherence, relevance and EU added value.

Based on the results, the Commission then determined whether there was a need for further action at the EU level, to improve the implementation or application of the directives. The legislative framework and its ongoing reforms is further mapped, analysed and evaluated in part II of this book.

SELF- AND CO-REGULATION. Aside from legislative instruments, the regulatory framework on commercial communication also consists of a broad variety of alternative regulatory instruments which also form an important part of the book.

1.2. The rise of alternative regulatory instruments

THE RATIONALE BEHIND ADVERTISING SELF-REGULATION. The advertising industry has traditionally actively participated in the regulatory process at national, European and international level, leading to a variety of self- and co-regulatory initiatives, some more general[137], some specifically across different sectors (e.g. food[138], alcohol[139], cosmetics, toys)[140], and formats. According to BURLETON, The Times already emphasised the role of advertising agencies in regulating commercial communication in 1909 by suggesting that

> *"The best modern advertising has the publication of facts for its basis. The day of successful claptrap and vulgarity, still more the day of exaggerated and deceptive misrepresentation, is quickly passing away. So far from these being fostered by advertising agents, the whole tendency of the best and most successful agents is to repress them."*[141]

According to DUROVIC et al. alternative regulatory instruments ("ARIs") are more prevalent in the area of advertising than in other areas of consumer law.[142] The significant role of the advertising sector in regulating commercial

---

137 Such as the ICC Code. International Chamber of Commerce, 'Consolidated Code of Advertising and Marketing Practice' <https://cdn.iccwbo.org/content/uploads/sites/3/2011/08/ICC-Consolidated-Code-of-Advertising-and-Marketing-2011-English.pdf> accessed 14 November 2017.

138 Such as the EU Pledge, for more information see www.eu-pledge.eu/.

139 Such as the Covenant on advertising and marketing of alcohol drinks issued by the Belgian Brewers, Signed on 25 January 2013, <www.belgianbrewers.be/nl/verantwoordelijkheid/arnoldus-groep-convenant/> accessed 17 October 2016.

140 L. Wilks and others, 'Mapping Exercise Report on Self-Regulation. Prepared for the European Commission DG SANCO Institute for Social Marketing. The Open University & University of Stirling.' <https://ec.europa.eu/health/archive/ph_determinants/life_style/alcohol/forum/docs/regulation_en.pdf> accessed 12 July 2018.

141 E. Burleton, 'The Self-Regulation of Advertising in Europe' (1982) 1 International Journal of Advertising 333.

142 M. Durovic and H. W. Micklitz, *Internationalization of Consumer Law: A Game Changer* (Springer 2017) 26 <https://kclpure.kcl.ac.uk/portal/en/publications/internationalization-of-consumer-law(6cab25a6-6b64-4837-ab12-523c9a8dfe53)/export.html> accessed 12 July 2018.

communication results from different factors, the first of which is the importance of consumer trust and a company's reputation.[143] More specifically, the profit of traders is heavily dependent on the consumer trust in the products and services they promote.[144] Additionally, as traditional advertising formats (e.g. television commercials) are highly visible and identifiable, often using the company or brand names, any shortcomings are more readily detectable and traceable.[145] Therefore, the sector has a strong interest in safeguarding fair advertising and sanctioning misleading or aggressive forms of commercial communication, as such practices would be detrimental to advertising's overall acceptance and effectiveness.[146] In addition, the advertising sector is characterised by a strong degree of organisation by its main actors, who have set up many associations and meta-associations at various levels (e.g. international, European and national). Through these associations all kinds of codes of conduct for different forms of commercial communication have been developed. A final incentive lies in the desire to avoid government regulation. In this regard, VERBRUGGEN mentions that "*pressures by the government to undertake legislative or executive action have been crucial for the adoption and further development of these codes*".[147] In this regard, the United Nations Committee on the Rights of the Child has highlighted the important role of the State in providing adequate incentives for the private sector to adopt such fair advertising practices. More specifically, the Committee recommends the following:

> "*States should ensure that marketing and advertising do not have adverse impacts on children's rights by adopting appropriate regulation and encouraging business enterprises to adhere to codes of conduct and use clear and accurate product labelling and information that allow parents and children to make informed consumer decisions*".[148]

The development of ARIs regulating commercial communication aimed at children in the digital environment forms part of the current international and

143 P. Verbruggen, 'Case Study Report – Transnational Private Regulation in the Advertising Industry. Conducted within the Framework of the Research Project Constitutional Foundations of Transnational Private Regulation' (2011) <www.hiil.org/data/sitemanagement/media/HiiL%20Case%20Study%20Advertising%20Executive%20Summary.pdf> accessed 12 July 2018.

144 F. Weber, 'The Law and Economics of Self-Regulation in Advertising' (2014) 3 Journal of European Consumer and Market Law 5.

145 J. J. Boddewyn, 'Advertising Self-Regulation: True Purpose and Limits' (1989) 18 Journal of Advertising 19, 20.

146 Boddewyn (n 145) 20.

147 Verbruggen, 'Case Study Report – Transnational Private Regulation in the Advertising Industry. Conducted within the Framework of the Research Project Constitutional Foundations of Transnational Private Regulation' (n 143).

148 UN Committee on the Rights of the Child, 'General Comment No. 16 (2013) on State Obligations Regarding the Impact of the Business Sector' (2013) 16.

EU policy agenda (*infra*). In its 2012 Recommendation on the Protection of Children Online, the OECD recognised that children face significant consumer risks when surfing online (related to *inter alia* embedded advertisements, privacy-invasive practices, age-inappropriate content).[149] To protect children against such risks, most countries have implemented multi-layered policies, which entail (1) legal measures, (2) self- and co-regulation, (3) technical measures and (4) awareness-raising and education. In this regard, the OECD stresses that those who are best placed to protect children in a concentrated market with substantial network effects (such as social networks or search engines) are the largest providers themselves.[150] Any ARIs in this context would be most effective if they are consolidated (i.e. have overarching principles that are applicable across sectors, for instance for the definition of a child) and independently evaluated.[151] In EU policy documents, self-regulation is often mentioned as a more flexible system of regulation than legislation, and as such particularly well suited for achieving tangible results in the specific context of children's protection and empowerment in the digital environment.[152]

Broad variety of initiatives. As mentioned, ARIs regulating commercial communication can be found at different levels (i.e. international, regional, national) and the scope of the rules contained in them may vary (e.g. applicable to all advertising formats, applicable to specific formats or to certain products). As early as 1937, the most important international self-regulatory organisation ("SRO"), the International Chamber of Commerce, adopted the first International Code of Advertising and Marketing Communication Practice[153], which served as a basis for most self-regulatory codes worldwide and even for national legislation in more than 35 countries. However, as Verbruggen points out, different legal traditions and market structures have led to major differences in the adoption of the provisions in the national context.[154] Indeed, ARIs regulating commercial

149 OECD (n 74).

150 OECD (n 74) 42–43.

151 OECD (n 74) 42–43.

152 Lievens, *Protecting Children in the Digital Era: The Use of Alternative Regulatory Instruments* (n 12); European Parliament, 'Resolution of 15 December 2010 on the Impact of Advertising on Consumer Behaviour' 5; European Commission, 'Communication from the Commission to the European Parliament, the Council, the European Economic and Social Committee and the Committee of the Regions on a European Strategy for a Better Internet for Children' 6 <https://eur-lex.europa.eu/legal-content/EN/TXT/PDF/?uri=CELEX:52012DC0196&from=EN> accessed 16 March 2018.

153 ICC (2006). Advertising and Marketing Communication Practice. Accessed at www.iccwbo.org/Advocacy-Codes-and-Rules/Document-centre/2011/Advertising-and-Marketing-Communication-Practice-(Consolidated-ICC-Code)/ on 17.10.2016.

154 Verbruggen, 'Case Study Report – Transnational Private Regulation in the Advertising Industry. Conducted within the Framework of the Research Project Constitutional Foundations of Transnational Private Regulation' (n 143).

communication do have a strong regional character.[155] In Europe, the European Advertising Industry began coordinating the efforts of national SRO's in the early nineties, by setting up the European Advertising Standards Alliance ("EASA") in 1992. Furthermore, certain sectors have been particularly active in adopting ARIs regulating commercial communication aimed at children. For instance, driven by the global problem of child obesity, several pledges by the food sector to change food and beverages marketing to children have emerged over the years.

Drawbacks to ARIs on commercial communication. Nevertheless, scholars agree that there are a number of drawbacks to self-regulation, such as a lack of effective enforcement, a low level of transparency and it has been questioned whether it should be a tool to safeguard human rights.[156] Furthermore, even though co-regulation partly addresses these drawbacks, confusion or uncertainty may occur for instance when the structure and procedures are not carefully laid out from the start or when the role of all actors is not clearly described.[157] In order to overcome these drawbacks and set a benchmark for effective ARIs, the European Commission designed "Principles for better self- and co-regulation" covering the phases of conception and implementation (discussed *infra* part III, chapter I).

ARIs and regulatory tools. ARIs often fall back on or make use of so-called regulatory tools. Examples of regulatory tools in the context of commercial communication are technology (e.g. advertising cues, labels, parental control mechanisms, identification mechanisms) or supporting mechanisms such as education and advertising literacy. These tools embody the concept of empowerment and may help children to cope with commercial communication. Important to note is that their use also needs to respect the broader legal framework, including children's rights (e.g. their right to privacy, freedom of expression).[158]

Concluding remark. It can be concluded that an extensive regulatory framework for commercial communication is in place at the international, EU and national level, and it is fragmented into legislative and alternative regulatory instruments. The next section focuses more specifically on how "new" advertising and marketing practices (cfr. the emerging trends as discussed *supra*) have been introduced into the policy discourse at international and EU level.

---

155 Durovic and Micklitz (n 142) 36.

156 B. E. Baarsma, 'Afwegingskader Bij Het Gebruik van Zelfreguleringsinstrumenten' (2010) 1 Tijdschrift voor Toezicht <https://dare.uva.nl/search?identifier=4dfccb8b-1f3e-41d3–898a-fcab1453b4f0> accessed 22 March 2018; Lievens, *Protecting Children in the Digital Era: The Use of Alternative Regulatory Instruments* (n 11).

157 Lievens, *Protecting Children in the Digital Era: The Use of Alternative Regulatory Instruments* (n 12).

158 Lievens, *Protecting Children in the Digital Era: The Use of Alternative Regulatory Instruments* (n 12) 230.

2. CHILDREN AND NEW FORMS OF COMMERCIAL COMMUNICATION IN POLICY DOCUMENTS

Three main objectives on the policy agenda. When analysing policy documents dealing with children and new forms of commercial communication, three major policy objectives can be identified: (1) the protection of children against commercial pressure online and certain forms of advertising; (2) children's privacy and data protection online and (3) the need for children's education and advertising literacy. What follows is a selection of relevant policy documents at both the international and European Union level that refer to one (or more) of these objectives.

2.1. *International policy documents*

2.1.1. OECD Recommendation on the protection of children online

Recognition of children's consumer risks online. In 2012, the Organisation for Economic Co-operation and Development issued its Recommendation on the protection of children online, which "*includes principles for all stakeholders involved in making the Internet a safer environment for children and educating them towards becoming responsible digital citizens*".[159] The Recommendation was drafted after the OECD conducted a report in 2011 on the risks that children are exposed to online and the policies that protect them.[160] An important issue that is raised by the report is the protection of children against commercial pressure online. The OECD recognises that children are targeted as consumers on the internet and deserve specific protection in this regard.[161] More specifically, the report underlines several consumer risks that children are faced with online, such as receiving inappropriate or hidden commercial messages, as well as risks related to their privacy and personal data. Interesting to note is that the OECD is currently reviewing and scoping the developments in the area of child protection online, in order to keep the 2012 Recommendation relevant and up to date.[162]

Principles for digital policymaking. The Recommendation also mentions three principles that governments need to take into account when developing policies for the protection of children online, which are also relevant in the context of online advertising and marketing. First, policymakers should foster the empowerment of children and parents, by providing safe digital environments for children to participate in and by supporting parents in their

159 OECD (n 74) 6.
160 OECD (n 74) 6.
161 OECD (n 74) 25.
162 OECD (n 74).

primary role of evaluating and minimising risks online (as well as offline), including advertising-related risks (e.g. misleading or harmful advertisements, privacy infringements). Second, there should be a balance between the protection and participation of the child online, and as such, policymakers should pay due account of the principle of proportionality. Digital policy should also be consistent with the fundamental values of democratic societies (e.g. the freedom of expression, privacy protection and the free flow of information), as they are also applicable to children. Third, the rapid evolution of new technologies (including innovative marketing practices) and the development process of children necessitates a certain degree of flexibility. In this regard, the OECD recommends that policies are age-appropriate and technology neutral to ensure their sustainability.[163]

2.1.2. Council of Europe

A. Declaration of the Committee of Ministers on protecting the dignity, security and privacy of children on the Internet

Concerns for the profiling of children for commercial purposes. The protection of children in the online environment against commercial and privacy risks forms an important priority of the Council of Europe ("CoE"). Already in 2008, the Committee of Ministers – the CoE's statutory decision-making body – expressed its concerns regarding "*the profiling of information and the retention of personal data regarding children's activities for commercial purposes*".[164] Even though the Committee recognises the internet as an important means for children's communication, information and education, it also expresses concerns about the long term storage of and access to children's data that may be damaging to their dignity, privacy and security when they grow up. In other words, the Committee recognises the potential negative impact of the commercial profiling of children on their development. To address these issues, the Declaration requires that there should be no lasting and permanently accessible record of the content created by children which challenges their dignity and privacy, or otherwise renders them vulnerable now or in the future, unless in the context of law enforcement. Therefore, the Member States were invited to explore the feasibility of removing or deleting such content within a reasonably short time span.[165]

---

163 OECD (n 74) 8.

164 Council of Europe, Committee of Ministers, 'Declaration of the Committee of Ministers on Protecting the Dignity, Security and Privacy of Children on the Internet'.

165 Council of Europe, Committee of Ministers, 'Declaration of the Committee of Ministers on Protecting the Dignity, Security and Privacy of Children on the Internet' (n 164).

B. Strategy on the Rights of the Child

Children's digital rights as a priority area. The Council of Europe has also expressed that the realisation of children's rights such as the right to privacy in the digital environment is one of its most important priorities for the period 2016 to 2021. In its Strategy on the Rights of the Child, the CoE recognises on the one hand that new technologies provide children with important opportunities for exercising their participation rights (e.g. the right to education, right to freedom of expression). On the other hand, the CoE underlines the risks that children face online, for instance exposure to harmful content, but also privacy and data protection issues. In this regard, the Strategy also mentions the increasing generational divide, with parents and teachers struggling to catch up with technological developments.[166] The CoE will address these issues by offering guidance and support to Member States in "*ensuring children's participation, protection and provision rights in the digital environment*".[167] The aim of this guidance and support is threefold: (1) to effectively change legislation and digital policy to protect children in the online environment; (2) to empower children to fully enjoy the potential of ICT; and (3) to offer education concerning digital citizenship and to tackle radicalisation and online hate speech.[168] The implementation of the Strategy is monitored by the Ad hoc Committee for the Rights of the Child ("CAHENF"), composed of representatives of all 47 Member States.[169]

C. Recommendation CM/Rec(2018)7 of the Committee of Ministers to member States on Guidelines to respect, protect and fulfil the rights of the child in the digital environment

Business responsibilities for children's digital rights. In July 2018, the Council of Europe released a Recommendation on the rights of the child in the digital environment.[170] Although it is the primary responsibility of the State to protect children's rights, the Council highlights in its Recommendation that businesses have a responsibility to respect human rights (*infra* part

166 Council of Europe, 'Strategy on the Rights of the Child 2016–2021' (2016) 9 <https://rm.coe.int/168066cff8> accessed 2 August 2017.

167 Council of Europe, 'Strategy on the Rights of the Child 2016–2021' (n 166) 20.

168 Council of Europe, 'Strategy on the Rights of the Child 2016–2021' (n 166) 21.

169 To support the Ad hoc Committee with the development of comprehensive Guidelines, a Drafting Group of Specialists on Children and the Digital Environment has been established. Council of Europe, 'Children's Rights Committee' (*Council of Europe Portal: Children's Rights*) <https://www.coe.int/en/web/children/cahenf> accessed 19 March 2018.

170 Council of Europe, Committee of Ministers, 'Recommendation CM/Rec(2018)7 of the Committee of Ministers to Member States on Guidelines to Respect, Protect and Fulfil the Rights of the Child in the Digital Environment' <https://search.coe.int/cm/Pages/result_details.aspx?ObjectId=09000016808b79f7>.

III).[171] More specifically, the Council states that all relevant public and private stakeholders share responsibility for ensuring the rights of children in the digital environment. It is up to the State to have the measures or mechanisms in place that are necessary to require businesses to meet their responsibilities in respecting the rights of children.[172]

Digital advertising as an area of concern. The Council also explicitly mentions the risk of harm from advertising as one of the areas of concern for children's healthy development and well-being in the digital environment.[173] In its Recommendation, the Council underlines that children have a right to be protected from all forms of exploitation in the digital environment. More specifically, it is up to the States to "*take measures to ensure that children are protected from commercial exploitation in the digital environment, including exposure to age-inappropriate forms of advertising and marketing.*"[174] Furthermore, States are recommended to ensure that the industry does not engage in unfair commercial practices towards children. This entails that digital advertising and marketing towards children must be clearly distinguishable to them as such. Moreover, all relevant stakeholders are recommended to limit the processing of children's personal data for commercial purposes.

2.2. *EU policy documents*

Advertising and the information paradigm in the EU. In the European Union, the internal market in which goods, persons and services can move freely among the Member States, is one of the fundamental aspects of the European integration. However, real market integration calls for consumers who are sufficiently informed and aware of the types of goods and services that are available to them.[175] This is where advertising plays an important role, and where the freedom of commercial expression allows commercial operators to encourage consumers to engage in (cross-border) transactions.[176] Moreover,

---

171 UN Committee on the Rights of the Child, 'General Comment No. 16 (2013) on State Obligations Regarding the Impact of the Business Sector' (n 148).

172 Council of Europe, Committee of Ministers, 'Recommendation CM/Rec(2018)7 of the Committee of Ministers to Member States on Guidelines to Respect, Protect and Fulfil the Rights of the Child in the Digital Environment' (n 170).

173 Council of Europe, Committee of Ministers, 'Recommendation CM/Rec(2018)7 of the Committee of Ministers to Member States on Guidelines to Respect, Protect and Fulfil the Rights of the Child in the Digital Environment' (n 170).

174 Council of Europe, Committee of Ministers, 'Recommendation CM/Rec(2018)7 of the Committee of Ministers to Member States on Guidelines to Respect, Protect and Fulfil the Rights of the Child in the Digital Environment' (n 169), para 57.

175 Garde (n 2).

176 The European Court of Human Rights has introduced commercial communication into the domain of freedom of expression decades ago, with the case concerning an advertisement for the Scientology Church. *X and Church of Scientology v Sweden, 5 May 1979, Appn 7805/77.*

Garde explains that it also fits in with the model of consumer protection of the EU, relying on the belief that for consumers to take full advantage of the opportunities offered by a wider internal market and move beyond their national borders, they must be informed.[177] In this regard, the European Commission underlines that "*empowered and informed consumers can more easily make changes in lifestyle and consumption patterns contributing to the improvement of their health, more sustainable lifestyles and a low carbon economy*".[178] However, for the information paradigm to be successful, the information provided to consumers must be of sufficient quality and adequate to guide consumers in their commercial decision-making and to effectively enable them to protect themselves.[179]

The protection of the child as a legitimate interest. Furthermore, free movement of course has its limits and there are important non-commercial interests that require adequate protection and legislation, such as consumer protection or health related concerns. For instance, Garde mentions existing restrictions on the marketing of certain goods and services like tobacco, alcoholic beverages, unhealthy foods, gambling).[180] These concerns are even more serious when children are involved, as their commercial decision-making skills are less developed than adults and they generally have a lower level of advertising literacy. Furthermore, the Court of Justice of the European Union ("CJEU") supports the rights of the child as a "*legitimate interest which, in principle, justifies a restriction on a fundamental freedom guaranteed by the EC Treaty, such as the free movement of goods*".[181] Keeping children safe in the

---

177 Garde (n 2).

178 European Commission, 'Communication from the Commission to the Council, the European Parliament and the European Economic and Social Committee – EU Consumer Policy Strategy 2007–2013 – Empowering Consumers, Enhancing Their Welfare, Effectively Protecting Them' 11 <https://eur-lex.europa.eu/legal-content/EN/TXT/PDF/?uri=CELEX:52007DC0099&from=EN> accessed 20 March 2018.

179 S. Wheaterill, *EU Consumer Law And Policy* (2nd ed. edition, Edward Elgar Pub 2005); Garde (n 2) 2.

180 A. Garde, 'Advertising Regulation and the Protection of Children-Consumers in the European Union: In the Best Interests of … Commercial Operators?' [2011] International journal of children's rights 523.

181 *C 244/06 Dynamic Medien Vertriebs GmbH v Avides Media AG* (CJEU); Lievens, *Protecting Children in the Digital Era: The Use of Alternative Regulatory Instruments* (n 12). Although this case did not relate to the protection of children against advertising or marketing practices (it related to the importation by a company of Japanese cartoons called 'Animes' in DVD or video cassette format from the United Kingdom to Germany and the lack of an age-limit label), the reasoning of the Court is also relevant by analogy in this specific context. See also article 24 of the Charter of Fundamental Rights of the European Union, which explicitly protects childrens rights, *infra* chapter II, section I.

digital environment has been the subject of intense policy debate in the EU since the rise of the internet as a public means of communication.[182]

2.2.1. European Parliament Resolution of 15 December 2010 on the impact of advertising on consumer behaviour

Risks of new forms of advertising. Back in 2010, the European Parliament ("EP") already explicitly recognised that new advertising practices online and via mobile devices may cause several issues that need to be solved, in order to maintain a high level of protection of internet users.[183] According to the EP, advertising may be harmful on the basis of the nature of the advertised product, such as tobacco or alcohol, or because of the use of gender-stereotypes. Furthermore, a form of advertising that the EP denounces in particular in its Resolution is hidden internet advertising, such as comments posted on social networks, forums and blogs.[184] The direct or indirect financing of such actions by businesses is also condemned. The problem with such hidden advertising practices is that it is very difficult for consumers to distinguish the commercial message from mere opinions. As a result, they might make the wrong decisions, believing that the information originates from an objective source. In relation to these practices, the EP calls on the European Commission and the Member States to ensure a proper application of the Unfair Commercial Practices Directive (*infra*) and to develop information and awareness campaigns for consumers. Tackling hidden advertising at an EU level would allow to clean up the market and boost consumer confidence.[185] Another element of new forms of commercial communication that the EP voices its concerns about is personalisation and the use of intrusive advertising practices (e.g. geolocation, using social media, retargeting). In this regard, companies that are both content providers and advertising sales houses (e.g. social media platforms, video-sharing platforms) present important risks for cross-referencing data collected in the course of each of these activities.[186]

Children are a particularly vulnerable group of consumers. The EP considers children and adolescents to be particularly vulnerable to aggressive

---

182 B. O'Neill, E. Staksrud and S. McLaughlin (eds), *Towards a Better Internet for Children? Policy Pillars, Players and Paradoxes* (Nordicom 2013).

183 European Parliament, 'Resolution of 15 December 2010 on the Impact of Advertising on Consumer Behaviour' (n 152).

184 European Parliament, 'Resolution of 15 December 2010 on the Impact of Advertising on Consumer Behaviour' (n 152) 6.

185 European Parliament, 'Resolution of 15 December 2010 on the Impact of Advertising on Consumer Behaviour' (n 152) 6.

186 European Parliament, 'Resolution of 15 December 2010 on the Impact of Advertising on Consumer Behaviour' (n 152) 6.

marketing and advertising and as such in need of specific protection.[187] More specifically, the EP argues that children and adolescents are greatly receptive and curious beings that lack a certain level of maturity, making them easily influenced by new information and communication technologies. In this regard, the EP advocates an evidence-based approach and calls on the European Commission to conduct a detailed analysis of the impact of aggressive and misleading advertising on vulnerable consumers, and in particular on children and adolescents (*infra*). The Resolution also mentions certain protections for children that could be implemented or further developed by the Member States, including *inter alia* restrictions on TV advertising addressed to children during programmes mainly watched by children, restrictions on targeted advertising to children and on advertisements that display harmful behaviour or attitudes (e.g. drugs, eating disorders).

Self-regulation and corporate social responsibility. In addition, the EP addresses the responsibility of the advertising industry that comes with "*the impact of widespread and pervasive advertising*".[188] In this regard, self-regulation could support the existing legislative framework and the Member States are encouraged to establish formally recognised self-regulatory authorities.[189] In addition, the advertising industry can also play an important role by cultivating a culture of corporate awareness and responsibility.

Positive aspects of advertising. In relation to the latter, the EP also highlights the positive aspects of advertising in its Resolution. In particular, the EP specifies that advertising fosters competition and competitiveness; is likely to limit abuses of dominant positions; and encourages innovation on the market. As a result, advertising increases consumer choice and lowers the prices of products and services on the market. Furthermore, consumers will also receive information on new products. Advertising revenues are also crucial for financing content creation and safeguarding a dynamic and competitive media landscape, as well as contributing to a diverse and independent press in Europe.[190] In this sense, advertising revenue also allows for the development of media content and digital platforms specifically for children. Finally, the EP underlines that

187 European Parliament, 'Resolution of 15 December 2010 on the Impact of Advertising on Consumer Behaviour' (n 152) 8.

188 European Parliament, 'Resolution of 15 December 2010 on the Impact of Advertising on Consumer Behaviour' (n 152) 5.

189 However, the EP recognises that there are certain drawbacks to self-regulation and that it can never entirely replace legislation, especially with regard to the protection of consumers' personal data.

190 European Parliament, 'Resolution of 15 December 2010 on the Impact of Advertising on Consumer Behaviour' (n 152) 3.

advertising can play an important role in fighting stereotypes and prejudices based on racism, sexism and xenophobia.[191]

2.2.2. European Parliament Resolution of 22 May 2012 on a Strategy for Strengthening the Rights of Vulnerable Consumers

Children are vulnerable consumers that need protection. The European Parliament repeated the need for an in-depth study of the existing regulatory framework on advertising in its 2012 Resolution in order to evaluate whether stricter rules are needed when it comes to children and young people. The Resolution illustrates a particular concern for children's health, as they increasingly suffer from problems like obesity and sedentariness. In this regard, the EP points to the fact that children are more sensitive to advertising for food that is high in fat, salt or sugar.[192] Therefore, the EP urges the European Commission to include the protection of children in this context (and especially against aggressive or misleading TV and online advertising) as a priority on the Consumer Agenda. The EP also repeats its concerns about the impact of the routine use of online behavioural advertising and intrusive advertising practices, in particular through the use of social media.[193]

Consumer empowerment. Furthermore, the EP advocates that vulnerable consumers should be empowered, entailing that their capacity to take optimal decisions is strengthened. This could be achieved by the provision of clear and understandable information and consumer education. Nevertheless, the EP expresses its concerns that empowerment alone would not be sufficient as "*their vulnerability may originate from their difficulty in accessing or assessing the information given to them*".[194] As such, it is crucial that vulnerable consumers, like children, are not misled.

---

191 European Parliament, 'Resolution of 15 December 2010 on the Impact of Advertising on Consumer Behaviour' (n 152) 4.

192 European Parliament, 'European Parliament Resolution of 22 May 2012 on a Strategy for Strengthening the Rights of Vulnerable Consumers (2011/2272(INI))' 7.

193 European Parliament, 'European Parliament Resolution of 22 May 2012 on a Strategy for Strengthening the Rights of Vulnerable Consumers (2011/2272(INI))' (n 192) 9.

194 European Parliament, 'European Parliament Resolution of 22 May 2012 on a Strategy for Strengthening the Rights of Vulnerable Consumers (2011/2272(INI))' (n 192) 5.

2.2.3. Opinion of the European Economic and Social Committee on a framework for advertising aimed at young people and children (September 2012)

Protections for children against certain forms of advertising. The European Economic and Social Committee ("EESC")[195] also participated in the debate on the protection of children against certain forms of advertising. More specifically, in its 2012 Opinion the EESC discusses the development of legislative or other measures for the protection of children and young people against those forms of commercial communication that would "*use children improperly or target them in a harmful way, or expose them by any means to messages that could harm their sound physical, mental or moral development*".[196] The EESC explicitly recognises that advertising aimed at children may present additional risks depending on the age-group involved, which could harm their physical, mental or moral health. Accordingly, the Opinion highlights a number of advertising practices (content-related) that should not be used when advertising to children, including incitements to over-consumption and the use of violent, racist, xenophobic, erotic or pornographic content. Furthermore, several elements that require further scrutiny are mentioned in the Opinion, including children's behaviour on social media according to their age and social background; the phenomenon of children choosing 'idols' or 'lifestyles' as definers of their personality, which are in turn exploited by advertising; the use of children's images in advertising; children being specifically targeted by advertising. The EESC also recommends to set a universal minimum age for advertising specifically aimed at children at the EU level, to ensure the smooth operation of the internal market.[197] Additionally, more restrictive, cross-cutting measures are needed for protecting children's rights in the context of advertising, and especially audiovisual and digital commercial communication.

Increased exposure to online advertising. With regard to online advertising, the EESC points to the fact that children increasingly have access to a television and the internet in their bedroom. As such, this presents difficulties for the mediating role of parents in mitigating the effects of advertising. Moreover, as the internet plays an important role in the daily lives of children, they are increasingly exposed to new advertising and marketing techniques.

---

195 The EESC is an EU advisory body composed of representatives of workers' and employers' organisations and other interest groups, which issues opinions on EU matters to the European Commission, the Council of the EU and the European Parliament. For more information see https://europa.eu/european-union/about-eu/institutions-bodies/european-economic-social-committee_en.

196 European Economic and Social Committee, 'Opinion of the European Economic and Social Committee on a Framework for Advertising Aimed at Young People and Children' 1.

197 European Economic and Social Committee (n 196) 2–3.

Therefore, the EESC highlights that special emphasis on children's education and information concerning digital technologies and on how to interpret advertising messages is needed, both in school and at home.[198]

Shortcomings of the current regulatory framework. Finally, the EESC stresses that the existing regulatory framework is failing in adequately protecting children's rights in the context of advertising. More specifically, the legal framework is complex and confusing, partly because of the different transposition and implementation of the legislative instruments in the Member States. The fact that advertising self-regulation has been developed at the international and Member State level does not remove the need to "*guarantee a high level of respect for children and their protection in order to ensure their physical, mental and moral development, with concern for their own interests, their wellbeing and the preservation of the family environment and ties*".[199]

2.2.4. European Parliament Resolution of 20 November 2012 on protecting children in the digital world

Children and the risks of digital advertising. In line with its earlier resolutions that addressed the protection of children against certain forms of commercial communication, the European Parliament expressed its main concerns again in 2012, this time specifically focusing on the digital environment. As a general principle, the EP underlines that advertising targeted at children should be responsible and moderate. However, in the digital environment children are exposed to age-inappropriate, aggressive or misleading advertising[200], as well as to risks to their privacy and dignity. For instance, minors should be made aware[201] of and protected from online exposure to advertising that encourages overspending and the purchase of virtual goods or credits with their mobile phones. Thus, the EP urges the Commission again to include the protection of children against both aggressive or misleading TV and online advertising in its main priorities.

2.2.5. European Commission Communication on a European Strategy for a Better Internet for Children (2012)

Children's specific needs and vulnerabilities. Inspired by the United Nations Convention on the Rights of the Child (*infra*, chapter II), the European

198 European Economic and Social Committee (n 196) 4–5.
199 European Economic and Social Committee (n 196) 9.
200 European Parliament, 'European Parliament Resolution of 20 November 2012 on Protecting Children in the Digital World' 6.
201 In this regard, the Member States are encouraged to promote systematic education and training for children.

Commission launched its EU Strategy for a Better Internet for Children in 2012, which tries to find the balance between empowering and educating children on the one hand and offering protection where needed on the other hand. According to the EC, children have specific needs and vulnerabilities and although they are generally perceived as 'digital natives', research has shown that there is a serious digital skills deficit amongst Europe's children.[202] For this and other reasons (such as market fragmentation and the failure of the market to deliver protection measures and quality content for children across Europe), the EC was of the opinion that a strategy for Europe was needed to *"create a safer, enriching environment for all EU children"*.[203]

Protecting children against certain forms of advertising, promoting self-regulation. In its Communication, the European Commission included several action points concerning the protection of children against certain forms of online advertising and overspending. As children have not fully developed the ability to engage critically with advertising messages[204], the Commission stresses that there should be standards for commercial messages on children's websites that allow a level of protection comparable to that of audiovisual commercial communication (*infra*, part II chapter I). Moreover, the Commission addresses the issue of behavioural advertising and underlines that no such segments should be created to target children. The advertising industry is encouraged to comply with the existing requirements or restrictions for digital advertising and to further develop self-regulatory standards to ensure that children are not exposed to inappropriate advertising in any form of online media. Indeed, in its Strategy, the Commission underlines its preference for more flexible and more adaptable self-regulatory tools and education, over regulation.[205] Furthermore, the Commission itself promises to step up enforcement of existing EU rules, encourage the industry to further develop self-regulatory standards and look into further legislation if self-regulatory measures fail to deliver.[206]

---

202 The EC mentions that although 38% of 9–12 year-olds in Europe who use the internet reportedly have a social media profile, only 56% of the 11–12 year-olds says they know how to tweak their privacy settings. K. Ólafsson, S. Livingstone and L. Haddon, 'Children's Use of Online Technologies in Europe' 40.

203 European Commission, 'Communication from the Commission to the European Parliament, the Council, the European Economic and Social Committee and the Committee of the Regions on a European Strategy for a Better Internet for Children' (n 152) 6.

204 European Commission, 'Communication from the Commission to the European Parliament, the Council, the European Economic and Social Committee and the Committee of the Regions on a European Strategy for a Better Internet for Children' (n 152) 5.

205 European Commission, 'Communication from the Commission to the European Parliament, the Council, the European Economic and Social Committee and the Committee of the Regions on a European Strategy for a Better Internet for Children' (n 152) 2.

206 European Commission, 'Communication from the Commission to the European Parliament, the Council, the European Economic and Social Committee and the Committee of the Regions on a European Strategy for a Better Internet for Children' 13 <https://eur-lex.europa.

2.2.6. European Commission Green Paper: Preparing for a Fully Converged Audiovisual World: Growth, Creation and Values (2013)

A CONVERGING MEDIA LANDSCAPE. Considering the ongoing transformation of the audiovisual media services landscape, the European Commission published a Green Paper to open the discussions on the implications of the increased convergence of media services. In its Green Paper, the EC highlights that traditional broadcasting services and the internet are increasingly merging, resulting in the expansion of viewing possibilities (e.g. connected TV sets, PCs, tablets and other mobile advices) and opportunities to interact with friends or with the TV programme itself. However, this transformation also raises important questions for the protection of consumers, including specific groups such as minors.[207] The Commission foresees that this convergence will also have an impact in the future on a number of legal instruments, including *inter alia* the Audiovisual Media Services Directive and the e-Commerce Directive, but also the frameworks on consumer protection, data protection and electronic communications.

NEW FORMS OF COMMERCIAL COMMUNICATION. The relationship between these instruments will also become more visible in the context of convergence and innovative advertising techniques. The Commission expresses concerns about several new advertising techniques, such as commercial overlays that are shown without the consent of users and broadcasters, disguised commercial communications and personalisation tools. Accordingly, the Commission poses several questions for public consultation on this specific topic:

- *"Will the current rules of the AVMSD regarding commercial communications still be appropriate when a converged experience progressively becomes reality? Could you provide some concrete example?*
- *What regulatory instruments would be most appropriate to address the rapidly changing advertising techniques? Is there more scope for self/co-regulation?*
- *Who should have the final say whether or not to accept commercial overlays or other novel techniques on screen?"*[208]

Furthermore, the Commission underlines the importance of the EU data protection framework for increasing consumer trust in the innovative business

eu/legal-content/EN/TXT/PDF/?uri=CELEX:52012DC0196&from=EN> accessed 28 March 2018.

207 European Commission, 'Green Paper: Preparing for a Fully Converged Audiovisual World: Growth, Creation and Values, COM(2013) 231 Final.' 4.

208 European Commission, 'Green Paper: Preparing for a Fully Converged Audiovisual World: Growth, Creation and Values, COM(2013) 231 Final.' 15.

models that are emerging in the digital environment, and refers to the recent reforms in this regard (i.e. the General Data Protection Regulation, *infra*).

Self-regulation as an appropriate complement to legislation. The Green Paper also mentions the use of self-regulation as an appropriate complement to the regulatory approach, considering the global and complex nature of the internet.[209] Related to this, the Commission already launched an initiative in 2012 with businesses to develop a code of good practice for self- and co-regulation exercises, resulting in a number of principles for better self- and co-regulation.[210]

Executive summary of responses to the public consultation. The gathered responses to the consultation show that several public bodies and consumer groups are concerned about the impact of convergence on the relationship between the AVMS and e-Commerce Directives.[211] First, it is difficult to determine the exact scope of the AVMS Directive and it may be interpreted differently across Member States. Second, certain respondents were also concerned about new advertising techniques such as when third party online advertising is overlaid onto broadcasting content, which would be covered by two separate Directives.

2.2.7. European Commission Communication on A Digital Single Market Strategy for Europe (2015)

Digital Single Market Strategy. The European Commission followed up on the repeated calls by the European Parliament to prioritise the protection of children against certain forms of advertising and on the concerns expressed by various stakeholders during the public consultation. The objective of protecting children against new forms of commercial communication forms part of the European Commission Strategy on a Digital Single Market for Europe. The main goal of the Strategy is to have

> *"a market in which the free movement of goods, persons, services and capital is ensured and where individuals and businesses can seamlessly access and exercise online activities under conditions of fair competition, and a high level of consumer*

209 European Commission, 'Green Paper: Preparing for a Fully Converged Audiovisual World: Growth, Creation and Values, COM(2013) 231 Final.' 12.

210 European Commission, 'Principles for Better Self- and Co-Regulation' <https://ec.europa.eu/digital-single-market/sites/digital-agenda/files/CoP%20-%20Principles%20for%20better%20self-%20and%20co-regulation.pdf> accessed 12 July 2018.

211 European Commission, 'Executive Summary of Contributions to the Public Consultation – Green Paper Preparing for a Fully Converged Audiovisual World' 6.

and personal data protection, irrespective of their nationality or place of residence" (emphasis added).[212]

By achieving this goal, the Commission is convinced that Europe will be able to maintain its position as a world leader in the digital economy. To realise such a digital single market, the Strategy contains several actions, including a number that relate to commercial communications and the protection of children.

ACTIONS FOR COMMERCIAL COMMUNICATION AND CHILD PROTECTION: REVIEW OF EXISTING LEGAL INSTRUMENTS. First, the Commission addresses the changing media landscape and the changing viewing habits of users (i.e. consumption of audiovisual media content increasingly via the internet and portable devices). Second, the Commission recognises that the framework regulating audiovisual media services[213] – at the time – already contained a set of minimum rules for traditional broadcasts and on-demand audiovisual media services, including rules on commercial communications and the protection of minors. However, as part of the Strategy, the functioning of these rules in light of the converging media landscape were to be analysed. Third, in relation to privacy and data protection, the Commission aims at achieving the highest standards and, therefore, decided to assess the functioning of the rules applicable to electronic communications services.[214]

3. NEW FORMS OF COMMERCIAL COMMUNICATION CALL FOR FUTURE-PROOF REGULATION

WHY REGULATE. When developing recommendations for future-proof regulation, it is important to take into account the underlying goal of such regulation. In the context of commercial communication aimed at children, regulation entails restrictions on the use of certain types of persuasive tactics, and thus the behaviour of certain actors (i.e. advertisers). Therefore, there should be a compelling reason to regulate.[215] A first reason refers to the effectiveness of new forms of commercial communications and the impact of the persuasive tactics used on children's advertising literacy (as analysed above). Secondly, the increased exposure of children to commercial messages, especially in the digital environment, also has certain unintended effects on children's development. Finally, aside from the

212 European Commission, 'Communication from the Commission to the European Parliament, the Council, the European Economic and Social Committee and the Committee of the Regions on a Digital Single Market Strategy for Europe. [COM(2015)192 Final] 11' (n 134) 3.

213 I.e. the 2010 Audiovisual Media Services Directive (*infra*, part II chapter I).

214 I.e. the ePrivacy Directive (*infra*, part II chapter I).

215 By analogy see Lievens, *Protecting Children in the Digital Era: The Use of Alternative Regulatory Instruments* (n 12) 38.

impact on children's advertising literacy and development, the precautionary principle should always be considered in the context of child protection.

3.1. *Effects of commercial communication on children's development and advertising literacy*

Impact on children's advertising literacy. A first reason why these new advertising formats necessitate an empowering regulatory framework is children's development and their cognitive capacities. As mentioned, the specific features of new forms of commercial communication make them particularly appealing to children, which renders them vulnerable to persuasion.[216] Children find it difficult to use their advertising literacy skills when it comes to new forms of commercial communication as they do not recognise them as such and therefore cannot critically reflect upon their messages. From an ethical point of view, it has been questioned whether it is acceptable or responsible to target young consumers with commercial messages, if they do not recognise them as such.[217] Children may face the risk of being manipulated if it is unclear to them that certain information, content or entertainment is in fact a persuasive commercial message. They are generally more trusting than adults and, as such, more prone to commercial pitches.

Unintended effects of advertising and marketing on children. In addition, there are certain unintended effects of commercial communication which need to be kept in mind. First of all, social scientists have witnessed an increase in parent-child conflicts as a consequence of nag behaviour or so-called 'pester power'.[218] The ubiquity of commercial messages in children's lives may lead them to become more materialistic and attach more value to money.[219] An extreme opinion in this regard originates from Bakan, who claims in his book that "*big businesses are transforming our children into obsessive and narcissistic*

---

216 Vanwesenbeeck and others (n 6); Hudders and others, 'Shedding New Light on How Advertising Literacy Can Affect Children's Processing of Embedded Advertising Formats' (n 1); Rozendaal (n 129).

217 M. J. Austin and M. L. Reed, 'Targeting Children Online: Internet Advertising Ethics Issues' (1999) 16 Journal of Consumer Marketing 590.

218 L. McDermott and others, 'International Food Advertising, Pester Power and Its Effects' (2006) 25 International Journal of Advertising 513; L. Hudders and others, 'Children's Advertising Literacy for New Advertising Formats: The Mediating Impact of Advertising Literacy on the (Un)Intended Effects of Advergames and Advertising Funded Programs.' in P. Verlegh, H. Voorveld and M. Eisend (eds), *Advances in Advertising Research (Vol. VI)* (Springer Fachmedien Wiesbaden 2016) <http://link.springer.com/10.1007/978-3-658-10558-7_19> accessed 29 March 2018.

219 M. Buijzen and P. M. Valkenburg, 'The Effects of Television Advertising on Materialism, Parent-Child Conflict, and Unhappiness: A Review of Research' (2003) 24 Journal of Applied Developmental Psychology 437; S. J. Opree, *Consumed by Consumer Culture? Advertising's Impact on Children's Materialism and Life Satisfaction* (9789462590335 2014) <http://dare.uva.nl/search?arno.record.id=467433> accessed 30 March 2018.

mini-consumers, media addicts and pharmaceutical industry guinea pigs".[220] An illustration can be found in children's changing food choices, as research has revealed that children who played advergames promoting less healthy foods were more likely to select less healthy food options than those who played advergames promoting healthier food options, which may lead to long term health concerns such as obesity.[221] Thus, new advertising formats call into question children's ability to make informed commercial decisions, which may have long-lasting effects on their development.

3.2. *Precautionary principle*

THE PRECAUTIONARY PRINCIPLE: CONCEPT AND ORIGIN. Aside from the impact on children's advertising literacy and development, it has been argued that in relation to delicate issues such as the context of child protection, one should always defer to the 'precautionary principle'.[222] According to the Merriam Webster dictionary, precaution can be defined as "*care taken in advance and a measure taken beforehand to prevent harm or secure good*".[223] In line with this definition, the precautionary principle embraces a 'better safe than sorry' approach, requiring action before there is strong proof of harm.[224, 225] Similarly, NARYANAN *et al.* clarify that the principle deals with decision-making and risk regulation in situations where there is scientific uncertainty, but that its exact formulation is highly debated.[226] The principle originates from the field

220 Bakan (n 1).

221 J. L. Harris, J. A. Bargh and K. D. Brownell, 'Priming Effects of Television Food Advertising on Eating Behavior' (2009) 28 Health Psychology: Official Journal of the Division of Health Psychology, American Psychological Association 404; Montgomery and Chester (n 87); European Parliament, 'European Parliament Resolution of 22 May 2012 on a Strategy for Strengthening the Rights of Vulnerable Consumers (2011/2272(INI))' (n 191). Accordingly, these studies highlight the important informative role of commercial communication and its potential positive impact on society. For instance, the commercial message could promote healthy products to children or motivate them to behave in a good way (e.g. eat healthy).

222 Lievens, *Protecting Children in the Digital Era: The Use of Alternative Regulatory Instruments* (n 12) 38.

223 X., 'Precaution', Merriam-Webster Dictionary, retrieved from https://www.merriam-webster.com/dictionary/precaution on 6 April 2018.

224 It should also be noted that the notion of harm in itself is a complex one. According to the Merriem Webster Dictionary, harm is defined as physical or mental damage. However, what is harmful can be culture-dependent and it may evolve over time. Lievens, *Protecting Children in the Digital Era: The Use of Alternative Regulatory Instruments* (n 12) 61. Furthermore, in the context of advertising, it is difficult to keep up with emerging trends and to measure the actual or future impact on children.

225 P. Harremoes and others, *The Precautionary Principle in the 20th Century: Late Lessons from Early Warnings* (Routledge 2013) 4–5; Lievens, *Protecting Children in the Digital Era: The Use of Alternative Regulatory Instruments* (n 11) 38.

226 According to the authors: "*it has many, much-debated formulations, ranging from very weak (for example, that regulation should be permitted when risks are uncertain) to very strong (for example, that any action with an uncertain risk should be barred completely until the actor can*

of environmental policy, where it was used as a means to bridge uncertain scientific information and a political responsibility to act in order to prevent damage to the public health and to ecosystems.[227] More specifically, several scholars have traced its origins to the 'Vorsorgeprinzip' in 1970's West German environmental policy, which commands that "*the damages done to the natural world (which surrounds us all) should be avoided in advance and in accordance with opportunity and possibility*".[228] Over the years, is has been cited in various legal instruments, policy documents and case law at the international, EU and national level.[229]

The precautionary principle in EU policy and legislation. At the EU level, the principle has also emerged as an autonomous principle inspired by the constitutional traditions in the EU Member States. It was officially introduced into EU law by the Treaty of Maastricht[230] and is referred to in article 191 of the Treaty on the Functioning of the European Union in the context of environmental policy.[231] However, the European Commission has clarified that the principle has a much broader scope of application:

> *"Although the precautionary principle is not explicitly mentioned in the Treaty except in the environmental field, its scope is far wider and covers those specific circumstances where scientific evidence is insufficient, inconclusive or uncertain and there are indications through preliminary objective scientific evaluation that there are reasonable grounds for concern that the potentially dangerous effects on the*

---

prove that the risks are acceptable". A. Narayanan, J. Huey and E. W Felten, 'A Precautionary Approach to Big Data Privacy' in S.Gutwirth, R. Leenes and P. De Hert (eds), *Data Protection on the Move*, vol 24 (Springer Netherlands 2016) 12 <http://link.springer.com/10.1007/978-94-017-7376-8_13> accessed 6 April 2018.

227 M. Martuzzi and J. Tickner, *The Precautionary Principle: Protecting Public Health, the Environment and the Future of Our Children* (WHO Regional Office for Europe 2004) 7–8 <www.euro.who.int/__data/assets/pdf_file/0003/91173/E83079.pdf> accessed 9 April 2018.

228 J. E. Fenstad and K. Matsuura, 'The Precautionary Principle, World Commission on the Ethics of Scientific Knowledge and Technology (Published by UNESCO)' 52, 9–10; Lievens, *Protecting Children in the Digital Era: The Use of Alternative Regulatory Instruments* (n 11) 39; Martuzzi and Tickner (n 226) 10; A. Szajkowska, 'The Impact of the Definition of the Precautionary Principle in EU Food Law' 24, 175.

229 For an overview see Lievens, *Protecting Children in the Digital Era: The Use of Alternative Regulatory Instruments* (n 11); K. Garnett and D. J. Parsons, 'Multi-Case Review of the Application of the Precautionary Principle in European Union Law and Case Law' (2017) 37 Risk Analysis 502; L. Costa, 'Privacy and the Precautionary Principle' (2012) Vol. 28 Computer Law & Security Review, 14.,

230 Treaty on European Union, *Official Journal C 191, 29/07/1992*, <https://eur-lex.europa.eu/legal-content/EN/TXT/?uri=celex:11992M/TXT> *accessed 12 July 2918.*

231 Article 191 TFEU states that: "2. *Union policy on the environment shall aim at a high level of protection taking into account the diversity of situations in the various regions of theCommunity. It shall be based on the precautionary principle and on the principles that preventive action should be taken, that environmental damage should as a priority be rectified at source and that the polluter should pay*" (Emphasis added).

environment, human, animal or plant health may be inconsistent with the chosen level of protection."[232]

This was also confirmed by the Court of Justice of the European Union in *Artegodan*, in which it recognises the precautionary principle as a general principle of EU law.[233] Accordingly, the EU institutions must consider the precautionary principle in their policy-making in order to ensure a high level of environmental, health and consumer protection.[234] In this regard, the European Commission has established common guidelines on the application of the precautionary principle. First, there are three specific conditions that need to be adhered to: (1) the fullest possible scientific evaluation should be conducted to determine as far as possible the degree of scientific uncertainty; (2) there should be a risk assessment of the potential consequences of inaction; and (3) all interested parties should participate in the examination of precautionary measures once the results of the scientific evaluation are available.[235] Second, the Communication mentions the general principles of risk management that apply whenever the precautionary principle is invoked, which entail that the measures taken on the basis of the principle should be proportional, non-discriminatory, consistent, based on an cost-benefit analysis of action or inaction, subject to review in light of new scientific evidence and capable of assigning responsibility for producing the scientific evidence needed.[236]

The precautionary principle and food advertising. The precautionary principle has also been mentioned in the context of (digital) advertising, and more specifically related to unhealthy food. Despite the steady emergence of academic analysis exploring and supporting the correlation between (digital) advertising for unhealthy foods and child obesity, there is still no clear evidence of any direct and causal relation.[237] The World Health Organisation ("WHO") urges State actors and policy makers to keep up with the changes in the digital environment as the current lack of regulation of unhealthy food marketing to children online leaves them without protection. According to the WHO, such a

232 Commission of the European Communities, 'Communication from the Commission on the Precautionary Principle, COM(2000) 1 Final' 9.

233 *T-74/00 Artegodan GmbH and Others v Commission of the European Communities (Joined cases T-74/00, T-76/00, T-83/00, T-84/00, T-85/00, T-132/00, T-137/00 and T-141/00)* (Court of First Instance) §§183–184.

234 Szajkowska (n 228) 175.

235 European Commission, 'The Precautionary Principle – Summaries of EU Legislation' (30 November 2016) <https://eur-lex.europa.eu/legal-content/EN/TXT/?uri=LEGISSUM%3Al32042> accessed 9 April 2018.

236 Commission of the European Communities (n 232) 3.

237 In fact the correlation may be due to other factors such as environmental or social factors encouraging children to become overweight. D. Barnabé and others, 'The Effect of Advertising and Marketing Practices on Child Obesity, A Study Requested by the European Parliament's Committee on the Environment, Public Health and Food Safety.' (2007) 12–13.

"wait-and-see" approach is not in line with the precautionary principle, nor with the United Nations Convention on the Rights of the Child (*infra*).[238]

The precautionary principle and new forms of commercial communication. In line with the above, and considering that (1) new innovative advertising formats are constantly emerging, yet (2) research on the impact of digital advertising on children's development and advertising literacy is struggling to catch up, the precautionary principle could arguably be considered as a justification of the creation of regulatory protections for children against (potentially) harmful digital advertising. Moreover, the precautionary principle has also been mentioned by scholars in the context of privacy and data protection, where it is argued that a broad scope of application of the principle is required in order to counteract real but intangible privacy harms that are difficult to quantify.[239]

4. TAKING A CHILDREN'S RIGHTS APPROACH

A children's rights-based approach. Since the adoption of the United Nations Convention on the Rights of the Child ("UNCRC"), it has been generally recognised that children are entitled to fundamental rights (*infra* part I chapter II). In this regard, van der Hof explains that the UNCRC "*signifies a paradigm shift from a welfare-based approach towards a rights-based approach with respect to children*", which recognises children as active rightsholders.[240] In general, the term 'rights-based' is broadly used to indicate that work is influenced by international human rights standards.[241] However, according to Lundy and McEvoy, these international standards are a legal articulation of a broader philosophical perspective and should be understood within the paradigm in

238 More specifically, the Convention aims at treating children's interests as a primary concern and balancing their protection and participation rights, which requires a more proactive approach rather than a wait-and see approach. World Health Organization (Regional Office for Europe), 'Tackling Food Marketing to Children in a Digital World: Trans-Disciplinary Perspectives – Children's Rights, Evidence of Impact, Methodological Challenges, Regulatory Options and Policy Implications for the WHO European Region' 21 <www.euro.who.int/__data/assets/pdf_file/0017/322226/Tackling-food-marketing-children-digital-world-trans-disciplinary-perspectives-en.pdf> accessed 9 April 2018.

239 Costa (n 229); O. Lynskey, *The Foundations of EU Data Protection Law* (Oxford University Press 2015) 83–84; B. van der Sloot, 'Where Is the Harm in a Privacy Violation? Calculating the Damages Afforded in Privacy Cases by the European Court of Human Rights' (2017) 4 <https://bartvandersloot.com/onewebmedia/Bart%20van%20der%20Sloot%20-%20PLSC.pdf> accessed 29 August 2018.

240 Van der Hof (n 94).

241 L. Lundy and L. McEvoy, 'Childhood, the United Nations Convention on the Rights of the Child and Research: What Constitutes a Rights-Based Approach' in M. Freeman (ed), *Law and Childhood* (Oxford University Press) 77 <https://www.qub.ac.uk/research-centres/CentreforChildrensRights/ChildrensRights-BasedResearch/> accessed 29 August 2018.

which they have been developed.[242] A children's rights approach is underpinned by the general principles of the UNCRC, which guide the interpretation of the rights in practice.[243] Moreover, it embodies the multidimensionality of the children's rights framework and balances the different dimensions of protection, participation and provision.[244] In addition, FREEMAN argues that a human rights-based approach distinguishes itself from other moral discourses by "*drawing our attention to the persons that have rightful entitlements*".[245] More specifically, the codification of these standards places important obligations on the state (i.e. to protect, respect and remedy, *infra*).[246] To achieve an effective implementation of the UNCRC, states should develop a child rights perspective throughout their government, parliament and judiciary.[247] UNICEF clarifies that taking a children's rights-based approach means that human rights and child rights principles should guide policy-making in all sectors. More specifically,

> "*a child rights-based approach integrates the norms, standards and principles of the international human rights system into the plans, policies and processes of programme development for children*".[248]

Therefore, in this book a children's rights approach is followed, where key children's rights principles and standards are used as a critical lens to examine the existing regulatory framework for commercial communication aimed at children. More specifically, children's protection, empowerment and opportunities for autonomy are explored in light of the challenges posed by new forms of commercial communication. Such an approach entails two steps: (1) the children's rights and principles that have been codified in international law are defined as the norms and standards for child well-being in the specific context of commercial communication and (2) the key EU legal commitments to children's rights in this context are identified and evaluated. In relation to the second step, the book examines the legality of new trends in the area of

242 Lundy and McEvoy (n 241).

243 General UN Committee on the Rights of the Child, 'General Comment No. 5 (2003) General Measures of Implementation of the Convention on the Rights of the Child (Arts. 4, 42 and 44, Para. 6)' (2003) 4.

244 In her research, VAN DER HOF has used the three p's as conceptual lenses through which she analyses children's data protection, in order to ensure a balanced approach. van der Hof (n 94).

245 M. Freeman, *Human Rights* (EPZ ed edition, Polity Press 2002). See also Gerison Lansdown, *The Evolving Capacities of the Child* (Florence 2005).

246 Lundy and McEvoy (n 241).

247 UN Committee on the Rights of the Child, 'General Comment No. 5 (2003) General Measures of Implementation of the Convention on the Rights of the Child (Arts. 4, 42 and 44, Para. 6)' (n 243) 4.

248 UNICEF, 'Main Principles – Child Rights Approach' (*UNICEF*) <https://www.unicef.org/tdad/index_55678.html> accessed 4 April 2018.

commercial communication and evaluates whether the current regulatory framework adequately protects and empowers children to deal with new forms of commercial communication, in light of their fundamental rights. The focus also lies on developing the capacities of duty-bearers at all levels (i.e. states, businesses, parents) to meet their obligations to respect, protect and fulfil rights, as well as on developing the capacities of rights-holders (i.e. children) to claim their rights.[249]

SECTION III. INTERIM CONCLUSION

CONSTITUTIVE ELEMENTS. In this chapter, the central elements of the book were delineated and analysed. First, the essential building blocks 'children', 'commercial communication' and 'advertising literacy' were examined. It can be concluded that emerging trends in the area of commercial communication have specific features (i.e. integration, interaction, personalisation and emotional appeal) that make it difficult for children to apply their advertising literacy skills. The persuasive tactics behind these advertising techniques negatively affect their capacity to critically evaluate the commercial message and, ultimately impact children's commercial decision-making in both the online and offline world.

THE NEED FOR A FUTURE-PROOF REGULATORY FRAMEWORK. Second, the central problem of this book was presented: the need for a future-proof regulatory framework for commercial communication in light of children's rights. The evolving regulatory context and the protection of children against new forms of commercial communication as a policy objective were explored. More specifically, three recurring themes were identified in policy documents at the international and EU level: protecting children against commercial pressure in the digital environment, protecting children's privacy and data protection and empowering children through education and fostering their advertising literacy. However, considering the effectiveness of new advertising formats, especially when targeted to children, it is questioned whether the existing regulatory framework for commercial communication – which is fragmented into legislative instruments (of which a number are under review or have been reviewed recently) and alternative regulatory instruments – achieves these policy goals. Even though the impact on children's lives of the increased commercialisation may not (yet) be entirely clear or scientifically proven, it was argued that the precautionary principle justifies a thorough mapping and evaluation of the instruments in light of children's rights and might be considered as a justification for additional regulatory protections for children if needed.

249 UNICEF (n 248).

CHAPTER II

THE ROLE OF CHILDREN'S RIGHTS IN REGULATING NEW FORMS OF COMMERCIAL COMMUNICATION

Introduction. The aim of this chapter is to gain a deeper understanding of the role of children's rights in regulating new forms of commercial communication. The chapter starts by providing a brief introduction to children's fundamental rights at the international and EU level. It then identifies which children's rights are at stake, studies how they have been reconfigured in the context of commercial communication and interprets them in this specific context. This interpretation forms the analytical framework for the evaluation of the legislative and alternative regulatory instruments in the following parts of the book.

SECTION I. INTRODUCING THE CHILDREN'S RIGHTS FRAMEWORK

Introduction. Before studying the relevant children's rights and principles, it is important to take a step back and look at how children's rights have emerged, at both the international and European level. This section also introduces children's rights in a digital environment, considering the increased digitisation of children's worlds.

1. CHILDREN'S RIGHTS AT INTERNATIONAL LEVEL

1.1. From subject of protection to active rightsholders

From subject of protection... The idea that children are active holders of rights and, as such, form a separate social and legal category is only a recent creation.[250] Until the end of the Middle Ages, the dominant attitude towards children in the Western countries was one of indifference. It was only during

250 E. Verhellen, *Convention on the Rights of the Child – Background, Motivation, Strategies, Main Themes* (Garant 2005) 11–16.

the 16th to 18th century that the idea of children as a separate group with specific characteristics and expected behaviour gained prominence. Back then, children were regarded as innocent creatures in need of education, as compared to the "worldly-wise" adults.[251] Alongside this societal attitude towards children, vulnerability and incapacity have also been the bedrock of the Western legal conception of children.[252] At the beginning of the 20th century, the first child protection laws emerged and compulsory education was introduced in most countries.[253] In 1924, the League of Nations adopted the Declaration on the Rights of the Child, which marked the starting point of a journey towards full recognition of children's rights in international law.[254]

...TO ACTIVE RIGHTSHOLDERS. Nowadays, it is generally recognised that the human rights framework is not only applicable to adults but also to children as a specified group. In fact, the United Nations Convention on the Rights of the Child[255] is the most widely accepted instrument of international law, with 193 countries having ratified it (including all EU Member States).[256] For the first time in history, children are considered to be active subjects of rights and granted a number of fundamental human rights (i.e. children's rights).[257] The rights guaranteed can be divided according to the traditional subdivision of human rights into civil/political (i.e. the child as citizen, e.g. freedom of speech), socio-economic (e.g. right to education, leisure and play) and cultural rights (e.g. rights related to arts and culture) or alternatively into the three P's: provision (e.g. education), protection (e.g. against economic exploitation) and participation (e.g. freedom of speech) rights.[258]

---

251 Verhellen (n 250) 11–16.

252 In most situations, children still need an adult representative to initiate legal proceedings on their behalf and their vulnerability has often been invoked to justify this difference in treatment. S. Clark, 'Child Rights and the Movement from Status to Agency: Human Rights and the Removal of the Legal Disabilities of Vulnerability' (2015) 84 Nordic Journal of International Law 183. Another example can be found in common law, where only certain contracts with minors are entirely valid, namely contracts for necessaries and beneficial contracts of service. All other contracts are voidable at the option of the minor reflecting their vulnerable status and restricted capacity to contract. Verdoodt, Clifford and Lievens (n 7) 604.

253 Verhellen (n 250) 11–16.

254 The Declaration, for instance, enshrined children's right to be given the means necessary for them to develop normally both at a material and spiritual level. Declaration on the Rights of the Child, 1924, <www.un-documents.net/gdrc1924.htm> accessed 12 July 2018.

255 United Nations Convention on the Rights of the Child, 20 November 1989, <www.ohchr.org/en/professionalinterest/pages/crc.aspx> accessed 12 July 2018.

256 Interesting to note is that although the US is signatory to the Convention, up until now it has not ratified it. See Status of Ratification Interactive Dashboard, http://indicators.ohchr.org/ (Last Updated: 8 June 2017).

257 Verhellen (n 250) 87; S. Ruxton, 'Children's Rights in the European Union: What about Us? : Next Steps. Brussels: The European Children's Network' (2005) 105 <https://www.crin.org/en/docs/Ruxton%20Report_WhatAboutUs.pdf> accessed 8 November 2017; Clark (n 252).

258 Garde (n 2); A. Osler and H. Starkey, 'Children's Rights and Citizenship: Some Implications for the Management of Schools' (1998) 6 The International Journal of Children's Rights 313; Annemie

Protection, Provision and Participation. Most of the provisions of the UNCRC are protectionist in nature, as children's perceived special vulnerability inspired the drafters to include protections against certain situations that are particularly dangerous for children (e.g. article 11 on illicit transfer abroad, article 33 involvement with illegal drugs).[259] However, the UNCRC also emphasises the capacities and strengths of children as rightsholders.[260] Indeed, one of the essential elements of the UNCRC is the belief that children should not be regarded merely as vulnerable victims, but also as social actors who need support while growing up.[261] As such, the UNCRC also has a provision dimension, as children have the right to be provided with the resources, the skills and services needed for their development (i.e. to safeguard basic care and nurture).[262] In addition, the UNCRC has a participation dimension, requiring that children are enabled to play an active role in society, for instance by allowing them to have a voice in the decision-making process on policy issues which affect them.[263]

1.2. The United Nations Framework

Normative value. The UNCRC was adopted by the UN General Assembly on the 20th of November 1989[264] and entered into force on the 2nd of September 1990. Its provisions are legally binding for the signatory states. The Court of Justice of the European Union has explicitly recognised the legal binding force[265] of the UNCRC for the EU Member States:

> *"The Court has already had occasion to point out that the International Covenant on Civil and Political Rights is one of the international instruments for the protection of*

Dillen, 'Children between Liberation and Care: Ethical Perspectives on the Rights of Children and Parent–Child Relationships' (2006) 11 International Journal of Children's Spirituality 237.

259 J. Willems, *Developmental and Autonomy Rights of Children* (2007) <http://intersentia.be/nl/developmental-and-autonomy-rights-of-children.html> accessed 8 November 2017.

260 Ruxton (n 257) 28.

261 Ruxton (n 257) 17. For instance, the formal phrasing "*the exercise by the child of the rights recognized in the present Convention*" in article 5, expresses the fact that children are active subjects of rights. R. Hodgkin and P. Newell, 'Implementation Handbook for the Convention on the Rights of the Child: Fully Revised Third Edition' (*UNICEF*) 85 <https://www.unicef.org/publications/index_43110.html> accessed 26 February 2018.

262 J. Fortin, *Children's Rights and the Developing Law* (Cambridge University Press 2003) 10–11.

263 Lievens, *Protecting Children in the Digital Era: The Use of Alternative Regulatory Instruments* (n 12). In the digital environment, this could be the right to engage and communicate with their friends and family in a safe manner.

264 Previous international documents on children's rights were: "Declaration on the Rights of Child", adopted by the League of Nations in 1924, and the 1959 "UN Declaration on the Rights of Child", which was adopted unanimously by the General Assembly of the United Nations on 20 November 1959, < www.un-documents.net/a14r1386.htm> accessed 12 July 2018. For a detailed overview see G. Van Bueren, *International Law on the Rights of the Child* (Springer Netherlands 1995) 11–16.

265 This entails that after accession or ratification of the Convention, states can no longer adopt national laws which are in breach of the Convention.

> *human rights of which it takes account in applying the general principles of Community law [...]. That is also true of the Convention on the Rights of the Child referred to above which, like the Covenant, binds each of the Member States".*[266] (Emphasis added)

Aside from its legally binding nature, the UNCRC also enjoys a significant moral force due to its status as the most highly ratified instrument in international law.[267] There is, however, no consensus on the direct effect or self-executive force of the UNCRC.[268] The actual implementation of the provisions is left up to the discretion of the national legislators.[269] Indeed, the UNCRC provisions mostly address States, who are responsible for taking measures implementing the treaty in their national legal systems. This entails *inter alia* reforming national laws, providing resources and services and monitoring the impact of legislation and policies on children's lives and the enjoyment of their rights. Furthermore, children's rights impact assessments need to be built into government at all levels and as early as possible in the development of policies and laws.[270] In this regard, the UNCRC requires States to submit periodic reports to the UNCRC Committee on the measures they have adopted and the progress they have made giving effect to the rights enshrined in the Convention.[271] VERHELLEN argues that the Convention does not exist in a legal vacuum. By translating children's rights into national law they can be refined and enhanced, depending on the willingness in the Member States to make the Convention enforceable.[272] The principles of the UNCRC contain the key guidelines for establishing children's rights policies, as recognised in the EU Strategy on the Rights of the Child.[273] It functions as a comprehensive framework against which legislative or self- and co-regulatory proposals that directly or indirectly affect children should be evaluated.[274] Furthermore,

---

266 *Parliament v Council* [2006] CJEU C-540/03 [37].See also: Verhellen (n 249) 147; S. Meuwese, M. Blaak and M. Kaandorp, *Handboek Internationaal Jeugdrecht* (Ars Aequi Libri 2005) 3.

267 U. Kilkelly, 'The Best of Both Worlds for Children's Rights? Interpreting the European Convention on Human Rights in the Light of the UN Convention on the Rights of the Child' (2001) 23 Human Rights Quarterly 308, 310.

268 Cf. for instance: Verhellen (n 250) 84–86; Meuwese, Blaak and Kaandorp (n 266) 4.

269 The Committee on the Rights of the Child, however, does emphasise that it "*welcomes the inclusion of sections on the rights of the child in national constitutions, reflecting key principles in the Convention, which helps to underline the key message of the Convention – that children alongside adults are holders of human rights*": UN Committee on the Rights of the Child, 'General Comment No. 5 (2003) General Measures of Implementation of the Convention on the Rights of the Child (Arts. 4, 42 and 44, Para. 6)' (n 243).

270 Lundy and others (2012) The UN Convention on the Rights of the Child: a study of legal implementation in 12 countries. Unicef UK.

271 Article 44 UNCRC.

272 Verhellen (n 250) 84–87.

273 European Commission, 'Towards an EU Strategy on the Rights of the Child, COM(2006) 367 Final' 6 <https://eur-lex.europa.eu/legal-content/EN/TXT/PDF/?uri=CELEX:52006DC0367&from=NL> accessed 26 July 2018.

274 Ruxton (n 257) 17.

the CJEU has repeatedly stressed that it takes the UNCRC into account when applying the general principles of EU law.[275]

Definition of a child and its evolving capacities. The central aim of the children's rights framework is to contribute to children's personal or psychological development. According to article 1 UNCRC, a child is considered to be

> *"every human being below the age of eighteen years unless under the law applicable to the child, majority is attained earlier".*[276]

The age of 18 years is a general upper benchmark, meaning that signatory states have to provide special protection to every child below this limit.[277] However, article 1 takes into account the social and cultural differences of the signatory states, by allowing national legislation to deviate from this benchmark.[278] In this regard, the UNCRC Committee has stressed that signatory states should take into account the overarching principles of the UNCRC when setting such age limits through legislation.[279] An important principle in this regard is the evolving capacities of the child principle, which embodies the balance between recognising that children are active agents in their own lives who should be heard, respected and given increased autonomy in exercising their rights, and being entitled to protection in accordance with their relative immaturity and youth.[280] It is a principle of interpretation, which recognises that when children grow older and acquire enhanced capabilities, the need for direction by their parents or others reduces. In turn, children's capacity to take responsibility for decisions affecting their lives grows.[281] Children are a highly differentiated group, with a broad variety of factors impacting their development and their capacities are viewed differently across the world.

---

275 *C 244/06 Dynamic Medien Vertriebs GmbH v Avides Media AG* (n 181) para 93; *Parliament v. Council* (n 266) para 37.

276 Article 1 UNCRC.

277 Interesting to note is that the starting point of childhood and the acquisition of rights is not defined in the Convention. This is because the drafters did not want to take a position on abortion, which would have made the Convention's universal acceptance impossible. Hodgkin and Newell (n 261) 3.

278 Examples of deviations include a lower age at which the child attains majority in civil matters or assumes criminal responsibility. Hodgkin and Newell (n 261) 5.

279 See also the best interests of the child principle (*infra*). Lievens and others (n 16) 5.

280 Lansdown (n 245).

281 According to Lansdown, the principle should be understood as a multidimensional concept: (1) recognising children's development, competence and emerging personal autonomy, which are promoted through the realisation of the UNCRC rights (i.e. the developmental dimension); (2) respecting their capacities and the transfer of rights from adults to children based on their level of competence (i.e. the participatory dimension); and (3) protecting children – as they are still evolving – by both parents and the state from participation in or exposure to harmful behaviour (i.e. the protective dimension). Lansdown (n 245).

The Convention recognises that children in different environments and cultures will acquire competencies at different ages. As a result, Lansdown stresses that "*children require varying degrees of protection, participation and opportunity for autonomy in different contexts and across different areas of decision-making*".[282]

Monitoring and complaint mechanism. Until recently, the UNCRC did not foresee an actual mechanism for complaint-handling. Accordingly, children could not file complaints and there was no option for testing the Convention in specific cases by the courts.[283] This changed with the adoption of the Optional Protocol on a Communications Procedure ("OP") in 2011, which enabled the filing of complaints regarding specific violations of children's rights under the UNCRC.[284] As such, the Protocol provides a means through which children's legal rights and access to remedies can be strengthened.[285] As per Clark,

> "*their legal status as children is not in itself an obstacle to legal capacity to sue for violations of their human rights*".

In other words, the complaint mechanism also echoes the legal transformation from children to active holders of rights. The Protocol entered into force in April 2014 and has up until now been signed by 51 and ratified by 39 states.[286] It establishes a quasi-judicial mechanism that allows children[287] and/or their representatives to file complaints with the United Nations Committee on the Rights of the Child ("UNCRC Committee") in relation to specific infringements of their rights under the UNCRC (*infra*).[288] The UNCRC Committee also monitors the implementation of the Convention in the different States and can issue critical remarks or recommendations.[289] As it is up to the States to take

---

282 Lansdown (n 245) 3.

283 E. Lievens, 'A Children's Rights Perspective on the Responsibility of Social Network Site Providers' (2014) 3 <https://www.econstor.eu/bitstream/10419/101441/1/795276834.pdf> accessed 7 November 2017.

284 United Nations, 'Optional Protocol to the Convention on the Rights of the Child on a Communication Procedure' <https://treaties.un.org/doc/source/signature/2012/ctc_4-11d.pdf> accessed 12 July 2018.

285 Clark (n 252) 216–217.

286 For a real time update see https://treaties.un.org/pages/ViewDetails.aspx?src=TREATY&mtdsg_no=IV-11-d&chapter=4&lang=en accessed 13 July 2018.

287 This is a logical and necessary outcome of with the right of the child to be heard as enshrined in article 12 UNCRC. S. C. Grover, *Children Defending Their Human Rights Under the CRC Communications Procedure* (Springer Berlin Heidelberg 2015) 4.

288 Grover (n 287). The Committee on the Rights of the Child is the body of 18 Independent experts that monitors implementation of the Convention on the Rights of the Child by its State parties (see *infra* enforcement). For more information see www.ohchr.org/EN/HRBodies/CRC/Pages/CRCIndex.aspx.

289 Kilkelly (n 267) 309.

the recommendations into account, the role of the Committee is "*advisory and non-adversial in nature and its success relies on diplomacy rather than legal sanction*".[290] The entering into force of the procedure allows the Committee to take up a more proactive role in enforcing state compliance.[291] Although the decisions of the Committee are non-binding, signatory parties commit themselves to follow the decisions and provide redress to victims.[292] Important to note is that complaints can only be made after exhausting domestic remedies.[293] Accordingly, a complainant needs to provide evidence of engaging with existing domestic complaints mechanisms. Aside from the possibility to file individual complaints, article 9 of the OP foresees the possibility of friendly settlements. However, the effectiveness of the Communications Procedure has also received some criticism by academics. Particularly the exclusion of collective complaints[294] and the fact that signatory states may decide to not recognise certain powers of the UNCRC Committee are conceived as weaknesses of the mechanism.[295] Finally, to foster the implementation of the UNCRC in an adequate manner, the Committee has also issued several implementation guidelines for the States.[296]

---

290 Kilkelly (n 267) 309.

291 Previously, the Committee only had the report of the state party and the information and context therein. G. Waschefort, *International Law and Child Soldiers* (Bloomsbury Publishing 2014) 157. The Committee may also take interim measures to avoid irreparable damage to children.

292 The state party is required to give serious consideration to the decision. A. Parkes, *Children and International Human Rights Law: The Right of the Child to Be Heard* (Routledge 2013) 242.

293 For instance, in Belgium, children and/or their representatives have access to preliminary remedies via alternative dispute resolution mechanisms, temporary relief with the presiding judges of the courts of first instance, they may file complaints seeking a sanction and/or compensation (against businesses and/or the state) with certain administrative authorities (e.g. the children's rights commissioner, the data protection authority), or have access to judicial mechanisms. For a more detailed overview see Faculty of Law Antwerp, 'Access to Remedy in Belgium – The United Nations Guiding Principles on Business and Human Rights (UNGP) in Belgium, State-Based Judicial and Non-Judicial Mechanisms That Provide Access to a Remedy' (Federal Institute for Sustainable Development (FISD 2017) <https://www.sdgs.be/sites/default/files/publication/attachments/brochure_acces_to_remedy_in_belgium_2017.pdf> accessed 16 July 2018; Similarly, in Ireland, several legal and quasi-legal remedies are open to children and families whose rights under the UNCRC have been violated (e.g. courts, the Equality Tribunal, the Ombudsman for Children's office). Children's Rights Alliance, 'Briefing Note on the Optional Protocol to the UN Convention on the Rights of the Child on a Communications Procedure' <www.childrensrights.ie/sites/default/files/information_sheets/files/BriefingNoteUNCRC3rdOptProtocol170914.pdf> accessed 12 July 2018.

294 Grover explains that representatives of child victim complainants, such as NGOs or children's parents or the complainants themselves are blocked from bringing complaints as a group, unless each and every one of the group is accurately identified. Grover (n 287) 23.

295 Grover (n 287) 218; Waschefort (n 291) 156.

296 For more information see UN Committee on the Rights of the Child, 'General Comment No. 5 (2003) General Measures of Implementation of the Convention on the Rights of the Child (Arts. 4, 42 and 44, Para. 6)' (n 243).

2. EUROPEAN CHILDREN'S RIGHTS LAW

INTRODUCTION. European children's rights law has been developed by the Council of Europe and the European Union. Although the CoE and the EU share the same fundamental values such as human rights, democracy and the rule of law, they remain separate entities performing different – but complementary – roles.[297] The development of these two frameworks are significantly informed by the international children's rights framework.[298]

2.1. *Fundamental human rights for all, including children*

INFORMED BY THE INTERNATIONAL FRAMEWORK. Although the European Union itself is not a party to the UNCRC, all the Member States have ratified the Convention.[299] In this regard, the European Commission stated in its 2011 Communication on an EU Agenda for the Rights of the Child that the

> *"standards and principles of the UNCRC must continue to guide EU policies and actions that have an impact on the rights of the child"*.[300]

Likewise, the Council of Europe is not legally bound to the UNCRC as an organisation, but all its Member States are individual parties to the Convention.[301] Over the years, both the Council of Europe and the European Union have increasingly built on the UNCRC when adopting their fundamental human rights instruments. The provisions of these instruments that contain obligations for Member States concerning children's rights must be interpreted in light of the UNCRC.[302] As such, it is the most powerful children's rights instrument in Europe.[303]

---

297 Council of Europe, 'The Council of Europe and the European Union: Different Roles, Shared Values' <https://www.coe.int/en/web/portal/european-union> accessed 30 August 2018.

298 E. Canetta and others, 'EU Framework of Law for Children's Rights' (European Parliament) <www.europarl.europa.eu/RegData/etudes/note/join/2012/462445/IPOL-LIBE_NT(2012)462445_EN.pdf> accessed 12 July 2018.

299 Only States can be signatories to the Convention, but the EU as an institution could bind itself through unilateral declaration or the conlusion of an accession Protocol. Canetta and others (n 298) 9.

300 European Commission, 'Communication from the Commission to the European Parliament, the Council, the European Economic and Social Committee and the Committee of the Regions: An EU Agenda for the Rights of the Child, COM (2011) 60' 3 <https://eur-lex.europa.eu/legal-content/EN/TXT/PDF/?uri=CELEX:52010DC0245R(01)&from=EN> accessed 16 July 2018.

301 European Union Agency for Fundamental Rights, 'Handbook on European Law Relating to the Rights of the Child' (2015) 30 <http://fra.europa.eu/en/publication/2015/handbook-european-law-child-rights> accessed 12 July 2018.

302 European Union Agency for Fundamental Rights (n 301) 30.

303 Verhellen (n 250) 132.

THE COUNCIL OF EUROPE FRAMEWORK. The Council of Europe[304] has had a clear mandate to protect and promote human rights ever since its establishment. In 1950, the Council adopted its main human rights treaty, the European Convention on Human Rights ("ECHR")[305], protecting democracy and human rights. It creates an international obligation to comply for the Member States and has thus been incorporated by all of them in their national laws. Furthermore, the Convention established the European Court of Human Rights ("ECtHR")[306] to ensure compliance of the contracting parties with their obligations under the Convention.

The Convention only explicitly refers to children in two instances[307] and as such, the scope for enforcing and protecting children's rights was not immediately evident.[308] Nevertheless, the general provisions of the ECHR are applicable to everyone – including children – and several of the guaranteed rights are relevant for children.[309] The CoE has also explicitly recognised a fundamental right to education, which is of particular significance to children's lives.[310] In addition, the ECtHR has often referred to the UNCRC throughout its extensive case law on children's rights.[311] Aside from the Convention and related case law, the

304 The Council of Europe is an international organisation in Strasbourg, counts 47 Member States and was formed right after the Second World War to promote democracy and protect human rights in Europe. It should not be confused with the institution of the European Council (which consists of the heads of state or government from the Member States, as well as the President of the European Commission) or with the European Union (which consists – at the time of writing – of 28 Member States that have delegated a certain part of their sovereignty on specific matters of joint interests). Nonetheless, all the members of the European Union are also member of the Council of Europe. For more information see www.coe.int/aboutcoe/index.asp?l=en&page=nepasconfondre.

305 European Convention on Human Rights. CETS No. 005 1950.

306 The European Court of Human Rights is composed by a judge of each of the parties to the Convention and can examine cases brought by nationals of Member States and non-Member States, nationals of non-Member States, Council of Europe Member States against another Member State. See www.coe.int/aboutcoe/index.asp?l=en&page=nepasconfondre.

307 Article 5 on deprivation of liberty and Article 6.1 on the special protection to be awarded to children at public court hearings.

308 Kilkelly (n 267) 308.

309 Of particular relevance to children are the right to respect for private life (Article 8), the prohibition of torture (Article 3), the right to life (Article 2), the prohibition of slavery and forced labour (Article 4) and the right to a fair trial (Article 6).

310 Additional Protocol no.1. Article 2. Retrieved from www.coe.int/en/web/echr-toolkit/protocole-1.

311 Verhellen (n 250) 133; European Union Agency for Fundamental Rights (n 301) 23. For instance in HARROUDJ V. FRANCE the ECtHR decided that "the positive obligations that Article 8 lays on the Contracting States in this matter [a case concerning adoption], they must be interpreted in the light of the Convention on the Rights of the Child of 20 November 1989". See *Harroudj v France* [2013] ECtHR 43631/09. Other examples include *inter alia*: *Maslov v Austria* [2008] ECtHR 1638/0323; *Keegan v Ireland* [1994] ECtHR 16969/90; *KT v Norway* [2008] ECtHR 26664/03; *Sahin v Germany* [2003] ECtHR 30943/96; *S and Marper v the United Kingdom* [2008] ECtHR 30562/04.

CoE has developed other legal standards for the protection of specific children's rights, including *inter alia* their economic and social rights[312], their procedural rights[313] and their right to protection against sexual exploitation.[314] Finally, as mentioned (*supra*, chapter I), the actualisation of children's rights online forms an important part of the CoE's Strategy on the Rights of the Child (2016–2021).[315]

Charter of Fundamental Rights of the EU. In contrast to the Council of Europe framework, the original treaties of the European Communities did not explicitly refer to human rights or their protection.[316] Cases concerning human rights violations in areas within the scope of EU law that came before the European Court of Justice were brought into the so-called general principles of EU law. In order to position fundamental rights more visibly within EU law, the EU proclaimed the European Charter of Fundamental Rights of the European Union (Charter) in 2000, covering a whole range of civil, political, economic and social rights of EU citizens, while also synthesising the constitutional traditions and international obligations common to the different Member States.[317]

The Charter enshrines children's rights and obliges Member States to foresee such protection and care for children, which is necessary for their wellbeing. Article 24 of the Charter recognises that children are independent and autonomous holders of rights.[318] Children are explicitly granted a right to freedom of expression[319] and may benefit from the general rights of the Charter (e.g. right to education, private life). Furthermore, the Charter recognises the best interests of the

312 European Social Charter. European Treaty Series – No. 163 1996. Many of the rights guaranteed by the Charter are relevant to children, including the right of the family to social, legal and economic protection (article 16) and the right to protection of health (article 11). In addition, the Charter contains a number of rights that are specifically applicable to children: the right of children and young persons to protection (article 7), the right of children and young persons to social, legal and economic protection (article 17). For more information see Secretariat of the European Social Charter, 'Children's Rights under the European Social Charter' <https://rm.coe.int/1680474a4b> accessed 14 January 2018.

313 European Social Charter. European Treaty Series – No. 163.

314 Convention on the Protection of Children against Sexual Exploitation and Sexual Abuse (Lanzarote Convention), CETS No. 201. 2012.

315 Council of Europe, 'Strategy on the Rights of the Child 2016–2021' (n 166).

316 A. Williams, 'Human Rights in the EU' in Damian Chalmers and Anthony Arnull (eds), *The Oxford Handbook of European Union Law* (Oxford University Press 2015) 252 <www.oxfordhandbooks.com/view/10.1093/oxfordhb/9780199672646.001.0001/oxfordhb-9780199672646-e-10> accessed 17 July 2018.

317 European Union Agency for Fundamental Rights and Council of Europe (eds), *Handbook on European Data Protection Law* (Re-ed, Publ Office of the Europ Union [u.a] 2014) 20 <https://www.echr.coe.int/Documents/Handbook_data_protection_ENG.pdf> accessed 25 July 2018.

318 European Commission, 'Communication from the Commission to the European Parliament, the Council, the European Economic and Social Committee and the Committee of the Regions: An EU Agenda for the Rights of the Child, COM (2011) 60' (n 300).

319 "Such views shall be taken into consideration on matters which concern them in accordance with their age and maturity."

child principle[320], in light of which any EU policy that directly or indirectly affects children must be designed, implemented and monitored.[321] Although initially the Charter was merely a political instrument, it became legally binding as EU primary law (see Article 6 (1) of the Treaty on the European Union) with the entering into force of the Lisbon Treaty on the 1st of December 2009.[322] As mentioned, the CJEU has also expressly recognised in its case law that children's rights need to be protected and requires EU law to take due account of the UNCRC.[323] Finally, the EU has also developed a conscious EU strategy on the rights of the child.[324]

Definition of a child. In Europe, the same legal parameter of what constitutes a child is used as the UNCRC framework.[325] Indeed, most Council of Europe instruments refer to the UNCRC definition. Furthermore, although there is no single definition of a child under EU law, the UNCRC definition is generally adopted in contexts where EU action complements actions of the Member States.[326]

3. CHILDREN'S RIGHTS AND NEW FORMS OF COMMERCIAL COMMUNICATION

Children's rights protected offline must also be protected online. Since the creation of the UNCRC, there has been general agreement concerning children's entitlement to fundamental rights that are of importance in the (digital) media environment.[327] Across the world, children are engaging in digital environments in which they play, communicate and search for information. As mentioned above, children are early adopters of information and telecommunications technologies, with almost one third of internet users being

320 Para 2 Article 24 Charter of Fundamental Rights of the European Union.

321 Canetta and others (n 298) 19.

322 The competence of the EU regarding children is limited to the elements contained in Articles 81 and 82 TFEU.

323 For example case C-540/03, *European Parliament v Council of the European Union* (2006) ECR 5769, 37; as mentioned by Canetta and others (n 298) 8. This was initially left to national traditions and public international law.

324 European Commission, 'Towards an EU Strategy on the Rights of the Child, COM(2006) 367 Final' (n 273).

325 European Union Agency for Fundamental Rights (n 301) 17–18.

326 The age at which children acquire rights can be different in certain EU law instruments, for example the Young Workers Directive distinguishes between young people (all under 18s) and adolescents (aged 15 to 18). Directive 94/33/EC of 20 August 1994 on the protection of young people at work, OJ 1994 L 216, Art. 3. In other areas of EU law (e.g. education, migration) it is left up to the Member States to decide, and in those contexts the CRC definition is generally adopted. European Union Agency for Fundamental Rights (n 301) 18. See also European Union Agency for Fundamental Rights (n 15).

327 Lievens, 'A Children's Rights Perspective on the Responsibility of Social Network Site Providers' (n 283) 3–4. The rights concerning traditional media mostly fall under article 17 of the UNCRC (i.e. access to information, mass media and protection against harmful content).

younger than 18 years old.[328] In this regard, the Council of Europe highlights in its Strategy on the Rights of the Child (2016–2021) that information and communication technologies affect their enjoyment of fundamental rights.[329] Indeed, the digitisation of children's worlds[330] significantly influences not only how they can exercise their rights, but also how these rights may be supported or neglected.[331] Almost every child's right now has a digital dimension (*infra*) and as such the principles and provisions of the children's rights framework should be looked at through a digital lens.[332]

New forms of advertising and marketing reconfigure children's rights. An important domain in which children's rights are reconfigured by internet use, is advertising and marketing.[333] In their digitised worlds, children and teenagers are increasingly confronted with hybrid, immersive and personalised commercial messages. This commercialisation has significant implications for children's rights and their protection (e.g. concerning responsibilities for the protection and proper implementation of the framework). In this regard, children's rights and principles require a translation into standards and guidelines, not only for policy and regulation that addresses children's rights in relation to new advertising and marketing techniques, but also for businesses that address their commercial communication to children and even for parents and children themselves.

SECTION II. CHILDREN'S RIGHTS AND PRINCIPLES IN THE CONTEXT OF COMMERCIAL COMMUNICATION

Introduction. This section investigates the role of the children's rights framework in regulating new forms of commercial communication aimed at children. More specifically, it identifies the principles that lie at the root of the

328 Livingstone, Carr and Byrne (n 49) 1.

329 Council of Europe, 'Strategy on the Rights of the Child 2016–2021' (n 166).

330 Oneal Irwin clarifies that a lifeworld is "*the place where we work, play, live and breath*". In this lifeworld, a human-technology connection takes place, which causes a transformation through our "*everyday perception and lived experience of it*". S. O'Neal Irwin, *Digital Media: Human-Technology Connection* (Rowman & Littlefield 2016) 12.

331 A. Third and others, *Children's Rights in the Digital Age [Documento Elettronico]: A Download from Children around the World* (Young and Well Cooperative Research Centre 2014).

332 More specifically it was argued that "*a digital-age specific interpretation of every article, adapted to today's realities*" should be applied. UN Committee on the Rights of the Child, 'Report of the 2014 Day of General Discussion "Digital Media and Children's Rights"' (2014) 10 <www.ohchr.org/Documents/HRBodies/CRC/Discussions/2014/DGD_report.pdf> accessed 26 October 2017. See also Lievens and others (n 16).

333 Livingstone, Carr and Byrne (n 49) 12.

United Nations children's rights framework and looks at how they might be understood or enacted in the specific context of new advertising and marketing techniques. Furthermore, the role and responsibilities of the relevant actors for realising children's rights in a commercial communication context are briefly examined.

1. OVERARCHING PRINCIPLES THAT UNDERPIN A CHILD RIGHTS PERSPECTIVE

FOUR BASIC PRINCIPLES. In the context of the UNCRC, the role of States lies in fulfilling clear obligations to each and every child. We have seen that to achieve an effective implementation of the Convention, states should develop a children's rights perspective throughout their government, parliament and judiciary.[334] According to the UN Committee on the Rights of the Child, such a perspective should consider the four key principles of the UNCRC, which form the basis for interpreting the other provisions.[335] The principles highlight the fundamental values underlying the Convention, and aim at ensuring a common philosophical approach. According to RUXTON, *"the principles constitute a vision of the child as an individual, whose integrity must be respected"*.[336]

1.1. Children's development lies at the heart of the framework

NO CONCRETE AND IMPLEMENTABLE DEFINITION. Perhaps the most fundamental human right's principle of the child is enshrined in article 6 UNCRC which stipulates the right to have their lives protected from the moment of birth, as well as their right to be able to survive, grow and develop appropriately.[337] Article 6 is much broader than the mere survival of the child and should be interpreted in a comprehensive manner.[338] Although fostering children's development is one of the central aims of the Convention, the notion is not clearly defined. Both the Convention in Article 27 and the UNCRC Committee in its General Comment no. 5 on general measures for the implementation of the Convention, interpret

---

334 UN Committee on the Rights of the Child, 'General Comment No. 5 (2003) General Measures of Implementation of the Convention on the Rights of the Child (Arts. 4, 42 and 44, Para. 6)' (n 243) 4.

335 UN Committee on the Rights of the Child, 'General Comment No. 5 (2003) General Measures of Implementation of the Convention on the Rights of the Child (Arts. 4, 42 and 44, Para. 6)' (n 243) 4.

336 Ruxton (n 257) 16.

337 The right can be traced back to the 1924 Geneva Declaration, which states that "the child must be given the means requisite for its normal development, both materially and spiritually". Geneva Declaration of the Rights of the Child 1924.

338 M. Nowak, *Article 6: The Right to Life, Survival, and Development* (Martinus Nijhoff Publishers 2005) 2.

development as a holistic concept, encompassing several dimensions (i.e. the physical, mental, spiritual, moral and social dimension).[339] Furthermore, the UNCRC Committee has often referred to development in its jurisprudence as the process of becoming an adult, during which the child develops 'normally' or in a 'healthy' manner.[340]

Optimal development approach. Furthermore, Peleg stresses that during the drafting process of the Convention the discussions also focused on the desired result of the development process, namely the fulfilment of the child's human potential.[341] First, the UNCRC strives for an optimal approach, for instance with article 29 UNCRC, which defines the aims of education, requiring that education enables the child to develop to their fullest potential. In this sense, it has been argued that children have 'the right to become an optimal person'.[342] Article 6 is understood as the platform for other developmental principles enshrined in the Convention, such as the child's best interests and the evolving capacities of the child principles, as well as for other rights that may enable children to reach their fullest potential, including *inter alia* the right to information and freedom of thought, school and educational goals and the right to participation in leisure and play.[343] This perspective also recognises children as individuals and allows taking into account their inner capacities and their opinions on what they consider to be in their best interest.[344] As there is no one right way to develop, the right to optimal development recognises that every child has different experiences and will therefore develop in different ways, as long as it enables the child to fulfil his or her potential.[345]

Minimal development approach. The optimal development theory has been contested by scholars arguing that reality forces us to be more modest in our ambitions. A minimal approach is advocated, which attempts to temper high expectations and to better connect with the relative autonomy of children and their rights, and the responsibility of parents in this regard, while preventing

339 UN Committee on the Rights of the Child, 'General Comment No. 5 (2003) General Measures of Implementation of the Convention on the Rights of the Child (Arts. 4, 42 and 44, Para. 6)' (n 243).

340 N. Peleg, 'The Child's Right to Development' (UCL (University College London) 2012).

341 Peleg (n 340).

342 UN Committee on the Rights of the Child, 'General Comment No. 5 (2003) General Measures of Implementation of the Convention on the Rights of the Child (Arts. 4, 42 and 44, Para. 6)' (n 243); Willems (n 259).

343 Lansdown (n 245); General UN Committee on the Rights of the Child, 'General Comment No. 1 (2001) Article 29 (1): The Aims of Education'.

344 UN Committee on the Rights of the Child, 'General Comment No. 5 (2003) General Measures of Implementation of the Convention on the Rights of the Child (Arts. 4, 42 and 44, Para. 6)' (n 243).

345 Peleg (n 340).

excessive government interference.[346] WEIJERS argues that if the optimal development of the child is the desired outcome of the development process, it would lead to paternalistic intervention by the government in the lifestyle and parenting methods of parents, and in his opinion the government should only intervene when needed to prevent damage to the development of the child.[347] It is argued here that such a paternalistic approach would arguably go against children's participatory rights, such as the right to be heard (article 12 UNCRC, *infra*), or the participatory dimension of development (i.e. autonomy). Nevertheless, LIEFAARD's point that the minimal development view is too narrow in light of the UNCRC is convincing. As an alternative, LIEFAARD advocates a children's rights-based approach, which takes into account children's healthy and holistic development (as promoted by the UNCRC), as well as the concerns of paternalism and expectations of governments.[348]

BALANCING PROTECTION AND PARTICIPATION IN THE CONTEXT OF NEW ADVERTISING TECHNIQUES. The right to development under the UNCRC also has different dimensions that need consideration. The UNCRC Committee emphasises that children should be able to develop the necessary life skills to face the challenges they can expect to be confronted with in real life.[349] These life skills include the ability to make balanced decisions, resolve conflicts in a peaceful manner, be a critical thinker etc. Thus, it is contended that in order to be in line with the underlying child's right to develop to their fullest potential, children should be educated and empowered to cope with digital advertising (i.e. ad literate) so that they can grow up to be critical, informed consumers who make their own conscious choices in today's new media environment. However, the sophistication, immersiveness and opaqueness of modern advertising practices provides a significant challenge in this respect. Therefore, it is argued that children need protection against those advertisements that they do not recognise as such and cannot critically process, thereby rendering it impossible for them to make a balanced commercial decision, and ultimately having a negative impact on their right to development. As per the UNCRC Committee,

> *"children, as users of information technologies and recipients of information, may be exposed to actually or potentially harmful advertisements, spam, sponsorship,*

346 I. Weijers, 'Grondslagen van Jeugdstrafrecht', *Jeugdstrafrecht in internationaal perspectief* (3de edn, Boom Lemma uitgevers 2014) <https://www.jongbloed.nl/boek/9789089740212/jeugdstrafrecht-ido-weijers> accessed 16 November 2017.

347 Weijers (n 346).

348 T. Liefaard and others, 'Het belang van het kind en de hooggespannen verwachtingen van het IVRK' (Boom Criminologie 2016) <http://hdl.handle.net/1887/45678> accessed 16 November 2017.

349 UN Committee on the Rights of the Child, 'General Comment No. 1 (2001) Article 29 (1): The Aims of Education' (n 343).

personal information and content which is aggressive, violent, hateful, biased, racist, pornographic, unwelcome and/or misleading".[350]

The Committee further discussed this topic during its Day of General Discussion on digital media and children's rights in 2014. During the discussions, it was suggested to align the Committee's position with the UN Special Rapporteur in the field of cultural rights. The latter had recommended State parties to adopt legislation, which would "*prohibit all forms of advertising to children under 12 years of age, regardless of the medium, support or means used, with the possible extension of such prohibition to 16 years of age and to ban the practice of child brand ambassadors*".[351] However, the child's right to development also has an important participation dimension that should be kept in mind. According to Fortin, children will be unable to make a successful transition to adulthood unless they are given opportunities to practice their decision-making skills and are provided with a dry-run of adulthood.[352] From this perspective, banning all forms of advertising aimed at children would not be compatible with the right to development. The European Parliament advocates a more nuanced approach, by stressing that children need to be protected against harmful practices such as aggressive or misleading advertising (e.g. advertising which encourages overspending and the purchase of virtual goods or credits with their mobile phones).[353]

Responsibilities for States and parents. Article 18 defines that both states and parents have responsibilities regarding the development of children. First, parents have the primary responsibility when it comes to the upbringing and development of their children, in a manner consistent with the evolving capacities of the child. It should be emphasised that the rights parents have, are functional rights rather than autonomous parental rights, meaning that they are conducive to children's rights.[354] The principle of the evolving capacities of the child requires that once children are competent to exercise their rights, they should be able to do so.[355] The balancing act between children's capacity to exercise their rights and their relative lack of experience is also a necessary

---

350 General UN Committee on the Rights of the Child, 'General Comment No. 13 (2011) The Right of the Child to Freedom from All Forms of Violence' (2011).

351 UN Committee on the Rights of the Child, 'Report of the 2014 Day of General Discussion "Digital Media and Children's Rights"' (n 332) 16.

352 Fortin (n 262) 11.

353 European Parliament (Committee on Culture and Education), 'Report on Protecting Children in the Digital World (2012/2068(INI))' (2012) <www.europarl.europa.eu/sides/getDoc.do?pubRef=-//EP//NONSGML+REPORT+A7-2012-0353+0+DOC+PDF+V0//EN> accessed 8 November 2017.

354 D. Reynaert, M. Bouverne-de-Bie and S. Vandevelde, 'A Review of Children's Rights Literature Since the Adoption of the United Nations Convention on the Rights of the Child' (2009) 16 Childhood 518, 525.

355 Thus, when children become more and more competent, parents have to fulfil fewer parental responsibilities. Reynaert, Bouverne-de-Bie and Vandevelde (n 354) 525. States should take

exercise in the context of commercial communication.[356] From a certain age, they will be better equipped to understand the (commercial) impact of marketing and advertising and therefore better equipped to exercise their rights. For instance, a recent study by Ofcom, the British independent Regulator for Media and Communication, indicates that children's commercial media literacy gradually increases between the ages of 12 to 15 years.[357] However, one should also be mindful of the emerging trends in commercial communication where the impact of advertising literacy is restricted (e.g. advertising that appeals to our emotions or personalised advertising, *supra*). Second, States must respect this parental responsibility and aid and support services to parents. Moreover, it is the role of the State to encourage children to develop their personality and identity to grow up to become self-reliant and responsible adults.[358]

Challenges of parenting in a commercialised world. Parents, however, also face significant parenting challenges because of the increased commercialisation. A first one relates to the increased pressure to buy that is fuelled by advertising and marketing. Indeed, social scientists have witnessed an increase in parent-child conflicts as a consequence of nag behaviour or so-called 'pester power'.[359] Second, it is important to keep in mind that adults do not necessarily have a better understanding of new advertising and marketing techniques than their children, especially when it comes to complex targeting techniques and data processing practices. In this sense, Van der Hof underlines that parents are not necessarily more empowered than their children in making decisions regarding the processing of their personal data (depending on the age and maturity of the child).[360] Indeed, parents are often expected to be gatekeepers and supervisors, yet, for numerous reasons they themselves might not be media or advertising literate enough, to understand the complexity of children's digital lives. States have a duty to provide "*parents and legal guardians with appropriate assistance in the performance of their child-rearing responsibilities*".[361] An example of such assistance in relation

this principle into account when establishing minimum ages on particular issues. Lansdown (n 245) 7; Lievens and others (n 16).

356 It implies on the one hand offering the fullest possible protection to all children from harm, for example, misleading or aggressive advertising, while encouraging and nurturing rights relating to children's autonomy, such as freedom of expression, which allow them to grow and participate in society. See also Lansdown (n 245) 15.

357 S. Livingstone and K. Olafsson, 'Children's Commercial Media Literacy: New Evidence Relevant to UK Policy Decisions Regarding the GDPR. LSE Media Policy Project Blog.' <http://blogs.lse.ac.uk/mediapolicyproject/2017/01/26/childrens-commercial-media-literacy-new-evidence-relevant-to-uk-policy-decisions-regarding-the-gdpr/> accessed 17 July 2018.

358 S. van der Hof and M. Groothuis (eds), *Innovating Government, Normative, policy and technological dimensions of modern government*, (The Hague: T M C Asser, Berlin/Heidelberg: Springer, 2011).

359 Rozendaal and others (n 42); McDermott and others (n 218).

360 Van der Hof (n 94).

361 Article 18 para 2 UNCRC.

to new forms of commercial communications could be the provision of adequate information by States to parents about children's use of digital technologies and associated commercial risks and opportunities.[362] In this regard, the UN Committee on the Rights of the Child has confirmed that States have a duty

> *"to provide adequate training and support to parents and other caregivers [...], to enhance their technical skills, inform them about the risks and potential harm, learn about how children use technology and be able to support children in using digital media and ICTs in a responsible and safe manner".*[363]

Responsibilities of the advertising industry. Advertising and marketing may have an important impact on children's development and, as such, several children's rights are at stake in this context (discussed *infra*). Accordingly, the advertising industry has an important role to play in the protection and promotion of children's rights throughout their advertising and marketing activities. The UNCRC Committee stresses that the industry has important responsibilities concerning children's rights, and it is up to the State to ensure that the industry meets their responsibilities.[364] The responsibilities of the advertising industry under the children's rights framework and the role of advertising self- and co-regulation in this context are further discussed in part III of the book.

1.2. Non-discrimination in advertising or marketing

Non-discrimination as an umbrella right. A second guiding principle of the UNCRC (as well as of other human rights instruments[365]) can be found in article 2, which protects children against all forms of discrimination. It relates to the underlying idea that all children are born with fundamental rights and freedoms and should not be discriminated against for being children, or on any other basis (e.g. gender, race, religion).[366] As children have less power

---

362 E. Lievens, 'Is Self-Regulation Failing Children and Young People? Assessing the Use of Alternative Regulatory Instruments in the Area of Social Networks', *European media policy for the twenty-first century : assessing the past, setting agendas for the future* (Routledge 2016).

363 UN Committee on the Rights of the Child, 'Report of the 2014 Day of General Discussion "Digital Media and Children's Rights"' (n 332).

364 UN Committee on the Rights of the Child, 'General Comment No. 16 (2013) on State Obligations Regarding the Impact of the Business Sector' (n 148).

365 For instance, the Universal Declaration of Human Rights (1948), the International Covenant on Civil and Political Rights (1966) and the International Covenant on Economic, Social and Cultural Rights (1966) all attribute important value to the principle of non-discrimination. However, according to Besson, the principle has not sufficiently been developed in these instruments for them to effectively counter child discrimination. S. Besson, 'The Principle of Non-Discrimination in the Convention on the Rights of the Child' (2005) 13 International Journal of Children's Rights 433, 444.

366 More specifically, the UN Human Rights Committee defines discrimination as *"any distinction, exclusion, restriction or preference which is based on any ground such as race, colour, sex, language, religion, political or other opinion, national or social origin, property,*

than adults in nearly all cultures, they are more prone to discrimination.[367] According to Abramson, the right to non-discrimination is an umbrella right and, as such, it attaches to or forms part of other rights of the Convention.[368] All rights apply to all children without exception, and it is up to the State to put into place protection mechanisms and take positive actions to promote children's rights free of discrimination.[369] The UNCRC Committee stresses that, in order to mitigate discrimination, States may have to introduce changes in their national legislation[370], administration and allocation of resources, but also in their educational system to change attitudes.[371] According to McGonagle, children should be educated about their right to non-discrimination as well as their responsibility to not discriminate themselves when interacting with others in the digital environment.[372] Moreover, the UNCRC requires States to "*actively identify individual children and groups of children the recognition and realisation of whose rights may demand special measures*".[373] This implies that the right to non-discrimination does not necessarily mean that all children should be treated the same, or as adults.[374] The UNCRC Committee makes a distinction between discriminatory and differential treatment and sometimes special measures may be necessary to foster the rights of certain groups of children.[375]

---

birth or other status, and which has the purpose or effect of nullifying or impairing the recognition, enjoyment or exercise by all persons, on an equal footing, of all rights and freedom." Human Rights Committee, 'General Comment 18 on Non-Discrimination', 10/11/1989, HRI/GEN/I/Rev. 5.

367 F. Sheahan, 'Translating the Right to Non-Discrimination into Reality. Save the Children' (2005) <https://resourcecentre.savethechildren.net/sites/default/files/documents/2617.pdf> accessed 8 November 2017.

368 B. Abramson, *Article 2: The Right of Non-Discrimination* (BRILL 2008).

369 Such positive action could include review of legislation, strategic planning, monitoring, raising awareness, education etc. Sheahan (n 367).

370 In this regard, Besson mentions that the CRC Committee has repeatedly stressed that the principle of non-discrimination also applies to private institutions and individuals. This should be reflected into national legislation. Besson (n 365) 450.

371 UN Committee on the Rights of the Child, 'General Comment No. 5 (2003) General Measures of Implementation of the Convention on the Rights of the Child (Arts. 4, 42 and 44, Para. 6)' (n 243).

372 T. McGonagle, 'A Survey and Critical Analysis of Council of Europe Strategies for Countering "Hate Speech"', *The Content and Context of Hate Speech: Rethinking Regulation and Responses* (Cambridge University Press 2012) 456–498 <http://dare.uva.nl/search?metis.record.id=385322> accessed 8 November 2017. In this regard, Lievens et al. stress that children should have the necessary tools and skills to act against and deal with the harms that may result from *inter alia* online discrimination. Furthermore, policies should be extended to overcome digital exclusion, and they should be flexible to the extent that they can address the needs of all children. Lievens and others (n 16).

373 General UN Committee on the Rights of the Child, 'General Comment No. 5 (2003) General Measures of Implementation of the Convention on the Rights of the Child (Arts. 4, 42 and 44, Para. 6)' (2003).

374 The principle of non-discrimination prohibits a different treatment of similar situations, without an objective justification. Besson (n 365) 435.

375 For instance with regard to children with disabilities. W. Vandenhole, *Non-Discrimination and Equality in the View of the UN Human Rights Treaty Bodies* (Intersentia nv 2005) 185.

In relation to (new) advertising and marketing techniques and the right to non-discrimination, several considerations are relevant.

Digital exclusion and age discrimination. Non-discrimination requires all children having equal[376] access to the digital environment, as it forms an important gateway for exercising their participation rights (e.g. right to freedom of expression, right to play, right to freedom of association).[377] More specifically, children should be protected from age discrimination in access to *inter alia* facilities, services, information and goods. The media has an important role to play in facilitating access to the digital commodities children need to exercise their participation rights. Children are often represented in the (digital) media as a vulnerable group of internet users, with stories of child abuse and online grooming making the headlines.[378] The storytelling lacks nuance and disregards the distinction between the large group of children who do quite well online and those who are particularly vulnerable considering their cognitive (in)capabilities and socio-emotional problems.[379] Furthermore, the broader issues of children's rights, and in particular their participation rights, are often not considered newsworthy. Mascheroni et al. have argued that this "*media framing of online risks might pose a challenge to awareness-raising and education campaigns: children are more often exposed to stories that might be instilling fear rather than empowering them to take action and to stand up for themselves*".[380]

Personalisation and equality of children as consumers. Digital exclusion is also closely related to the phenomenon of personalisation and the application of consumer profiles. In this regard, Van der Hof warns for the often invisible underlying processes of data processing and knowledge creation, which allows social sorting (i.e. systematically categorising and classifying individuals for purposes of identification or risk assessment). More specifically, Van der Hof stresses that "*Social sorting can create and reinforce social differences, for instance, by excluding the economically deprived from commercial services or by targeting*

---

376 Equality and non-discrimination are two statements of the same principle, i.e. a positive and negative one. Besson (n 365) 434.

377 Lievens and others (n 16).

378 G. Mascheroni, A. Jorge and L. Farrugia, 'Media Representations and Children's Discourses on Online Risks: Findings from Qualitative Research in Nine European Countries' (2014) 8 Cyberpsychology: Journal of Psychosocial Research on Cyberspace <https://cyberpsychology.eu/article/view/4310> accessed 18 July 2018.

379 In this regard, Wolak et al. have pointed to a difficult problem for public policy, namely addressing the risks of this vulnerable minority in a manner that is proportionate and without extending undue surveillance to the majority of children which is only occasionally naïve and risk-taking. J. Wolak and others, 'Online "Predators" and Their Victims: Myths, Realities, and Implications for Prevention and Treatment.' (2008) 63 American Psychologist 111; Sonia Livingstone, Leslie Haddon and London school of economics and political science, *EU Kids Online: Final Report*. (London school of economics and political science 2009).

380 Mascheroni, Jorge and Farrugia (n 378).

certain minority groups in society".[381] Furthermore, personalisation may result in differential treatment of consumers, for instance through price differentiation[382] or by restricting consumer choice and diminishing preferences.[383] This again may raise significant problems regarding the exercise of children's participation rights in the digital environment.

Stereotyping, gender and racial discrimination. Finally, an important consideration is the fact that stereotypes and discriminatory messages (for instance based on gender) frequently recur in marketing and advertising both offline and online. Children are particularly vulnerable to such practices, as they tend to place trust in characters from TV programmes, picture-books, TV games, toy advertising etc.[384] From a very young age, they learn by imitation and mimicking what they experience and, in this sense, discrimination in advertising has a significant impact on children's development and how they view themselves. In addition, stereotyping may constitute a barrier to a balanced and equal access to information communication technologies for children.[385] In order to battle gender discrimination in digital media, the Council of Europe called on the Member States to take action and promote equality.[386] The advertising industry, as well as providers of new media such as social networks or video-sharing platforms may also play an important role here.[387]

---

381 S. Van Der Hof, 'I Agree, or Do I: A Rights-Based Analysis of the Law on Children's Consent in the Digital World' [2016] Wis. Int'l LJ 34, 118; S. van der Hof and C. Prins, 'Personalisation and Its Influence on Identities, Behaviour and Social Values', *Profiling the European Citizen* (Springer, Dordrecht 2008) 122 <https://link.springer.com/chapter/10.1007/978-1-4020-6914-7_6> accessed 8 November 2017.

382 M. S. Kirsch, 'Do-Not-Track: Revising the EU's Data Protection Framework to Require Meaningful Consent for Behavioral Advertising' (2011) 18 Rich. JL & Tech. 1, 17. For example through dynamic pricing, which entails that service providers ask different consumers to pay different prices. van der Hof and Prins (n 381) 122.

383 Van der Hof and Prins (n 381) 122.

384 European Parliament (Committee on Women's Rights and Gender Equality), 'Report on How Marketing and Advertising Affect Equality between Women and Men (2008/2038(INI))' (2008) <www.europarl.europa.eu/sides/getDoc.do?pubRef=-//EP//NONSGML+REPORT+A6-2008-0199+0+DOC+PDF+V0//EN> accessed 8 November 2017.

385 Citation Ms. Sandberg in UN Committee on the Rights of the Child, 'Report of the 2014 Day of General Discussion "Digital Media and Children's Rights"' (n 332) 10. In this regard, the EU Kids Online project concluded that "*the historic tendency for boys, especially when younger, to have more places to use the internet, to get online earlier, and for more of them to use the internet than girls, appears to be disappearing.*" Livingstone, Haddon and London school of economics and political science (n 379) 6.

386 In this regard, the Council of Europe adopted a new recommendation on gender equality which also covers the Internet, social media and the role of advertising. Council of Europe, 'Recommendation CM/Rec(2019), Preventing and Combating Sexism, 27 March 2019 <https://rm.coe.int/prems-055519-gbr-2573-cmrec-2019-1-web-a5/168093e08c> accessed 17 September 2019.

387 Council of Europe (Parliamentary Assembly, 'Recommendation 2092 (2016) – Fighting the over-Sexualisation of Children' (2016) <https://assembly.coe.int/nw/xml/XRef/Xref-XML2HTML-EN.asp?fileid=22938&lang=en> accessed 8 November 2017.

1.3. *The best interests of the child as a primary consideration for regulators, policymakers, advertisers and parents*

THE STANDARD FOR ALL UNCRC PROVISIONS. Article 3 UNCRC requires that the best interests of the child shall be a primary consideration in all actions concerning children. As such, the principle requires governments, public and private bodies to conduct child impact assessments and evaluate the impact of any proposed law, policy or decision on children's rights[388], including rules on digital advertising. The Convention does not provide a definition of the concept, allowing a diversified and tailor-made implementation.[389] According to the UNCRC Committee, the concept is threefold: (1) a substantive right for the child to have his or her interests assessed and taken as a primary consideration when different interests are being considered[390]; (2) a fundamental, interpretative legal principle requiring that if a legal provision is open to more than one interpretation, the interpretation which most effectively serves the child's best interests should be selected; and (3) a procedural guarantee that whenever a decision has to be made affecting a specific child or a group of children, the decision-making process must include an assessment of the impact of the decision on the child or children concerned.[391] Furthermore, the meaning of the best interests should be determined on a case-by-case basis, according to "*the specific situation of the child or children concerned, taking into consideration their personal context, situation and needs*".[392] The concept has also been discussed in academic literature. EEKELAAR, for instance, is of the opinion that the 'best interests' should be understood as:

> "*Basic interests, for example to physical, emotional and intellectual care developmental interests, to enter adulthood as far as possible without disadvantage; autonomy interests, especially the freedom to choose a lifestyle of their own*".[393]

---

388 UN Committee on the Rights of the Child, 'General Comment No. 5 (2003) General Measures of Implementation of the Convention on the Rights of the Child (Arts. 4, 42 and 44, Para. 6)' (n 243).

389 Van Der Hof (n 381) 120.

390 The Committee clarifies that: *Article 3, paragraph 1, creates an intrinsic obligation for States, is directly applicable (self-executing) and can be invoked before a court.* UN Committee on the Rights of the Child, 'General Comment No. 14 (2013) on the Right of the Child to Have His or Her Best Interests Taken as a Primary Consideration (Art. 3, Para.1)' (2013) 2.

391 In this regard, there is an obligation on the States to show in their justificiation of a decision how the right has been respected, what has been considered in the child's best interests and on the basis of what criteria, and how the balance had been made. UN Committee on the Rights of the Child, 'General Comment No. 14 (2013) on the Right of the Child to Have His or Her Best Interests Taken as a Primary Consideration (Art. 3, Para.1)' (n 390) 2.

392 UN Committee on the Rights of the Child, 'General Comment No. 14 (2013) on the Right of the Child to Have His or Her Best Interests Taken as a Primary Consideration (Art. 3, Para.1)' (n 390) 32.

393 John Eekelaar, 'The Interests of the Child and the Child's Wishes: The Role of Dynamic Self-Determinism' (1994) 8 International Journal of Law, Policy and the Family 42.

The principle sets the standard that underpins all the other provisions of the Convention.[394] According to Tobin, the principle is informed as well as constrained by the other UNCRC principles and rights. In this sense, a proposed outcome for a child cannot be said to be in the child's best interests when it conflicts with the provisions of the Convention.[395] The UNCRC Committee confirms that it is an indeterminate, dynamic and subjective[396] concept, which requires an assessment appropriate to the specific context.[397]

Responsibilities and best interests assessments. The UNCRC Committee clarifies that a best interests assessment consists of "evaluating and balancing all elements necessary to make a decision in a specific situation for a specific individual child or a group of children".[398] The principle also requires that States must ensure that the best interests of the child are taken as a primary consideration in decisions and actions undertaken by the private sector. In the context of digital advertising, this could be interpreted as requiring that the parties involved in the advertising chain must consider the best interests of children when developing advertising and marketing campaigns targeting this particular group of consumers.[399] Furthermore, it implies the creation of mechanisms to assess the impact of government actions or the activities of the business sector on children, and to effectively take these results into account when shaping policy and regulation.[400] Finally, the principle requires States to ensure the necessary protection and care for the child (para. 2) when individual parents are unable or unwilling to protect the child, and thus to function as a safety net.[401]

---

394 In fact, the CRC refers to the child's best interests in several provisions, including *inter alia* article 9 on the separation from parents, article 10 on family reunification and article 18 on parental responsibilities.

395 John Tobin, 'Beyond the Supermarket Shelf: Using a Rights Based Approach to Address Children's Health Needs' (2006) 14 The International Journal of Children's Rights 275, 287.

396 Different societies may attribute different meaning to it. Michael Freeman, *Article 3: The Best Interests of the Child* (2007) 27–28. Examples of practices that are incompatible with the child's best interests principle can be extracted from the UNCRC reports, such as *inter alia* corporal punishment, female genital mutilation, a low minimum age for marriage,

397 UN Committee on the Rights of the Child, 'General Comment No. 14 (2013) on the Right of the Child to Have His or Her Best Interests Taken as a Primary Consideration (Art. 3, Para.1)' (n 390) 2.

398 The Committee also provides some examples of elements that should be taken into account, such as the characteristics of the child (e.g. age, sex, level of maturity, experience, etc), the child's views, the child's right to education, etc. UN Committee on the Rights of the Child, 'General Comment No. 14 (2013) on the Right of the Child to Have His or Her Best Interests Taken as a Primary Consideration (Art. 3, Para.1)' (n 390) 7.

399 Verdoodt and Lievens (n 3).

400 UN Committee on the Rights of the Child, 'General Comment No. 14 (2013) on the Right of the Child to Have His or Her Best Interests Taken as a Primary Consideration (Art. 3, Para.1)' (n 390) 11; Hodgkin and Newell (n 261) 43.

401 Hodgkin and Newell (n 261).

1.4. *Offering children a voice in the decision-making process*

Children's right to be heard. The fourth guiding principle of the children's rights framework can be found in article 12 UNCRC, the right to be heard. The principle entails that children should be able to actively participate in the promotion, protection and monitoring of their rights.[402] The UNCRC Committee explains that this means that children should have a voice in the decision-making, policymaking and the preparation and evaluation of laws and measures concerning them.[403] The notion of participation highlights the need for dialogue and information-sharing between children, adults and other stakeholders, so that children can learn how their views can shape the outcome of such processes.[404]

Children's participation and development. The second paragraph of article 12 requires that children's views need to be given due weight in accordance with their age and level of maturity. In other words, if the child matures, his or her views shall have increasing weight, for instance in the assessment of a child's best interests.[405] Eekelaar argues that the underlying goal of the principle is "*to bring a child to the threshold of adulthood with the maximum opportunities to form and pursue life-goals which reflect as closely as possible an autonomous choice*".[406] This does not entail a full delegation of decision-making to the child, but rather allowing children to make decisions in controlled conditions, in order to enhance their capacities for mature well-founded choices (*supra*).[407]

Children's right to be heard by the advertising industry. To achieve children's participation online, they should not only be consulted when developing legislation or policies (e.g. initiatives fostering safe use of digital media), but also when setting up services and other measures relating to digital media and ICT, and hence by the industry.[408] This also applies to advertisers, who need to consult children when developing digital marketing campaigns for children (e.g. in the context of personalised advertising this means consulting

---

402 This principle applies to all measures adopted by Governments to implement the Convention. Ruxton (n 257) 129.

403 UN Committee on the Rights of the Child, 'General Comment No. 12 (2009) The Right of the Child to Be Heard'.

404 To achieve such an exchange of information, states are encouraged to create platforms with all stakeholders, especially children, at the national, regional and international level. UN Committee on the Rights of the Child, 'Report of the 2014 Day of General Discussion "Digital Media and Children's Rights"' (n 332).

405 UN Committee on the Rights of the Child, 'General Comment No. 14 (2013) on the Right of the Child to Have His or Her Best Interests Taken as a Primary Consideration (Art. 3, Para.1)' (n 390).

406 Eekelaar (n 393) 53.

407 V. Morrow (2004) 15 Kings College Law Journal. as cited by Freeman (n 396) 7.

408 UN Committee on the Rights of the Child, 'Report of the 2014 Day of General Discussion "Digital Media and Children's Rights"' (n 332) 22.

children when carrying out a data protection impact assessment).[409] The age and level of maturity of the child will also play an important role in such an assessment. Furthermore, RUXTON calls for the development of child friendly and accessible spaces, in which children can express themselves, for example using technology such as (mobile) phones or the internet in general.[410] New media environments such as social network platforms (e.g. Facebook, Snapchat, Instagram) and blogs have lowered the threshold for sharing and self-expression significantly.[411] The companies providing these online services to children should also consult children and take into account their interests when developing a corporate social responsibility strategy (*infra*).[412]

2. CHILDREN'S RIGHTS RECONFIGURED BY NEW FORMS OF COMMERCIAL COMMUNICATION

MULTI-DIMENSIONALITY OF THE RIGHTS AT STAKE. Aside from the general principles of the UNCRC, several children's rights are at stake in the context of commercial communication aimed at children, implying responsibilities for different actors (i.e. the State, parents and the business sector).[413] As mentioned, the framework comprises three different perspectives[414]: participation, protection and provision. However, many rights in the digital age are actually multi-dimensional and should be considered and acknowledged in such a manner at different levels.[415] Therefore, this section analyses how the relevant

409 Verdoodt and Lievens (n 3).

410 Ruxton (n 257) 33.

411 Lievens, *Protecting Children in the Digital Era: The Use of Alternative Regulatory Instruments* (n 12) 271.

412 E. Lievens, 'Children's Rights and Media : Imperfect but Inspirational', *Children's rights law in the global human rights landscape isolation, inspiration, integration?* (Routledge 2017) <http://hdl.handle.net/1854/LU-8532067> accessed 10 November 2017; UNICEF, UN Global Compact and Save the Children, 'Children's Rights and Business Principles' (2012) <https://www.unglobalcompact.org/docs/issues_doc/human_rights/CRBP/Childrens_Rights_and_Business_Principles.pdf> accessed 14 November 2017. See also the 2014 ITU Guidelines for Industry on Child Online Protection, recommending industry to draw "*upon internal and external expertise and consult with key stakeholders, including children, on child online safety mechanisms to obtain ongoing feedback and guidance on company approaches*". International Telecommunications Union, 'Guidelines for Industry on Child Online Protection.' <https://www.itu.int/en/cop/Documents/bD_Broch_INDUSTRY0809.pdf> accessed 19 July 2018. As cited by Lievens and others (n 16).

413 The UNCRC is a comprehensive instrument and groups rights specifically created for children, as well as child-specific versions of general fundamental rights. Kilkelly (n 267) 311.

414 VAN DER HOF talks in this regard of the conceptual frameworks of protection, emancipation and participation, and development. These conceptual frameworks should be used as lenses for the analysis of legal provisions, to ensure a balanced approach towards legal issues involving children. Van Der Hof (n 381) 120.

415 For instance, LIEVENS et al. argue that although the right to privacy in the digital environment is often reduced in legal and policy documents to data protection, it also has

rights and responsibilities can be understood in the specific context of commercial communication. The research considers the multi-dimensionality of the children's rights identified as relevant and takes into account the four fundamental principles of the UNCRC (*supra*). It aims to provide a balanced lens for the further analysis of the legal and self-regulatory framework on commercial communication aimed at children.

2.1. *Freedom of expression and access to information (article 13 UNCRC, article 10 ECHR, article 11 CFEU)*

A PREREQUISITE FOR CHILDREN'S DEVELOPMENT. A first right that is relevant in an advertising context is the freedom of expression, a fundamental right in any democratic society and deemed "*one of the basic conditions for its progress and for the development of every man*".[416] This fundamental right has been included into a wide variety of international[417], European[418, 419] and national[420] legislative texts. Article 13 UNCRC stipulates that this right includes

> "*the freedom to seek, receive and impart information and ideas of all kinds, regardless of frontiers, either orally, in writing or in print, in the form of art, or through any other media of the child's choice*".[421]

---

an important participatory dimension "*insofar as it as it is part and parcel of individual autonomy, a necessary precondition of participation*". As such, children should be consulted during the policymaking process and their perceptions of privacy should be duly taken into account. Lievens and others (n 16).

416 *Perna v Italy* [2003] ECtHR 48898/99 [39].

417 At the international level the most important ones are Article 19 of the 1948 Universal Declaration on Human Rights, 10 December 1948 and Article 19 of the 1966 UN International Covenant on Civil and Political Rights United Nations, 16 December 1966.

418 At the European level, the core provision guaranteeing this right is article 10 of the ECHR, which enshrines the freedom to hold opinions and to receive and impart information and ideas without interference by any public authority, and regardless of frontiers. Article 10 encompasses both the passive obligation for States to refrain from interfering with the freedom of expression of their citizens as well as the positive duty to ensure that this freedom is not too restricted by private persons or organisations. According to the European Court of Human Rights, States may be required to actively take measures to protect their citizens, "*even in the sphere of relations between individuals*". D. Voorhoof, 'Vrijheid van meningsuiting' in Y. Haeck and J. Vande Lanotte (eds), *Handboek EVRM : deel 2 : artikelsgewijze commentaar*, vol 1 (Intersentia 2004) 925. See for instance: *Özgür Gündem v Turkey* [2000] ECtHR 23144/93 [42–43].

419 At the European Union level, article 11 of the Charter corresponds to article 10 ECHR and guarantees that everyone has the right to freedom of expression, to hold opinions and to receive and impart information and ideas without interference by public authority. Furthermore, this Article requires respect for the freedom and pluralism of the media. Article 11 Charter of the Fundamental Rights of the European Union, para 2.

420 In Belgium, the relevant provisions are articles 19, 25 and 150 of the Belgian Constitution.

421 LIEVENS highlights that according to the UNCRC Committee it is not sufficient to merely include the 'general' right to freedom of expression applicable to everyone in a country's constitution. It is necessary, to also expressly incorporate the child's right to freedom of

The article has a broad scope of application and extends to all means of information sharing. As such, it will also be applicable to information shared via the internet or any other (future) communication technology.[422] According to Smith, the right is important for the development of the child, and it should not be affected by the fact that children may not have the same capacities as adults.[423] The UNCRC Committee mentions children's right to freedom of expression and access to information in the context of online advertisements promoting certain types of products and messages that potentially have an adverse impact on children's development. More specifically, in this regard, the Committee urges Member States to adopt measures to protect children in digital media, without violating their right to information and freedom of expression.[424]

Balancing protection and participation of the child... The right to freedom of expression is not an absolute right, but restrictions must be provided by law and necessary "*for respect of the rights or reputations of others, or for the protection of national security or of public order, or of public health or morals*" (para. 2).[425] Furthermore, whenever restrictions are imposed, regard must be had for the child's best interests, and whether such limitations unduly restrict children's use of or access to certain types of expression.[426] However, finding the right balance between the freedom of expression and information, and the protection of minors can be difficult. Tackling certain content which is deemed harmful to minors could lead to unwanted side-effects to the freedom of expression of adults, as they should be able to access the content freely.[427]

...while considering the protection of commercial speech. When conducting the balancing exercise, it is important to keep in mind that the

expression in legislation. Lievens, 'Children's Rights and Media' (n 412). See for instance: United Nations Committee on the Rights of the Child (1996). General Guidelines for Periodic Reports, CRC/C/58: "*States parties are requested to provide information on the measures adopted to ensure that the civil rights and freedoms of children set forth in the Convention, in particular those covered by articles 7, 8, 13 to 17 and 37 (a), are recognized by law specifically in relation to children and implemented in practice, including by administrative and judicial bodies, at the national, regional and local levels, and where appropriate at the federal and provincial levels*".

422 Lievens, *Protecting Children in the Digital Era: The Use of Alternative Regulatory Instruments* (n 12) 272.

423 L. Smith, 'Convention on the Rights of the Child: Freedom of Expression for Children' in T. McGonagle and Y. Donders (eds), *The United Nations and Freedom of Expression and Information: Critical Perspectives* (Cambridge University Press 2015) 146.

424 UN Committee on the Rights of the Child, 'General Comment No. 16 (2013) on State Obligations Regarding the Impact of the Business Sector' (n 148).

425 The grounds for restrictions are identical to the grounds listed in article 19 para. 3 of the International Covenant of Civil and Political Rights.

426 Smith (n 423) 146.

427 Lievens, *Protecting Children in the Digital Era: The Use of Alternative Regulatory Instruments* (n 12) 312–313.

European Court of Human Rights has introduced commercial communication into the domain of freedom of expression decades ago.[428] Indeed, the Court recognises the protection of article 10 of the European Convention on Human Rights for "*information of a commercial nature*". Accordingly, the balancing test of paragraph 2 of article 10 will be applicable to any restriction of or interference with the freedom of commercial speech. For instance, the Court has applied the balancing test for its decisions on the admissibility of national advertising bans[429], violations of public morals[430] and humorous advertising.[431] In principle, the Court deems national authorities to be in a better position to give their opinion on the necessity of content restrictions than the international judge. Thus, the Court recognises broad discretion for national policy on restrictions on the content of advertising.[432] However, the margin of appreciation in such cases is not unlimited.

---

[428] In 1973 with the case concerning an advertising for the Scientology Church. *X and Church of Scientology v Sweden* [1979] ECtHR 7805/77.

[429] For instance in *Markt Intern Verlag GmbH and Beermann v Germany* [1989] ECtHR 10572/83.

[430] For instance, in *Sekmadienis Ltd. V Lithuania*, the ECtHR held that fining a clothing company for its "Jesus" and "Mary" advertising campaign breached its freedom of expression. More specifically, the Court decided that not every use of religious symbols in advertising campaigns would violate public morals. According to the Court, "*the domestic authorities failed to strike a fair balance between, on the one hand, the protection of public morals and the rights of religious people, and, on the other hand, the applicant company's right to freedom of expression*". In this regard, MILKAITE clarifies that the judgment of the Court does not mean the religious symbols can always be used for advertising purposes. Public authorities that evaluate the 'morality' of such commercial messages should, however, provide proper and sufficient reasons explaining whether and how the religious symbols used offend religious people and "*especially the public morals which rarely derive from just one (religious) tradition*". I. Milkaite, 'Sekmadienis Ltd. v. Lithuania: Can Religious Figures Be Featured in Commercial Advertising?' <https://strasbourgobservers.com/2018/03/13/sekmadienis-ltd-v-lithuania-can-religious-figures-be-featured-in-commercial-advertising/> accessed 30 August 2018.

[431] According to the Court, the advertisements were able to contribute to a debate of general interest to some degree, as they dealt in a satirical manner with events that had been the subject of public debate. *Bohlen and Ernst August von Hannover v Germany* [2015] ECtHR 53495/09. See Dirk Voorhoof, 'European Court of Human Rights: Bohlen and Ernst August von Hannover v. Germany' (*IRIS Merlin – The Audiovisual Law Information Wizard*) <http://merlin.obs.coe.int/iris/2015/5/article1.en.html> accessed 30 August 2018.

[432] "*Otherwise the Court would have to re-examine the facts and all circumstances of each case. The Court must confine its review to the question whether the measures taken on the national level are justifiable in principle and proportionate*". *Markt Intern Verlag GmbH and Beermann v Germany* (n 429). See also J. Kabel, 'Swings on the Horizontal – The Search for Consistency in European Advertising Law. Legal Observations of the European Audiovisual Observatory' (Council of Europe, European Audiovisual Observatory 1994) 4. Cases that reflect this approach include inter alia: *Casado Coca v Spain* [1994] ECtHR Series A., No. 285., where the Court held that even "*objective, truthful advertisements might be restricted in order to ensure respect for the rights of others or owing to the special circumstances of particular business activities and professions.*"; *Markt Intern Verlag GmbH and Beermann v Germany* (n 429); *X and Church of Scientology v. Sweden* (n 428).

2.2. *Freedom of thought (article 14 UNCRC)*

An absolute right to freedom of thought. Children also have a right to freedom of thought, conscience and religion under article 14 UNCRC.[433] As part of their development process, children need access to information to form and formulate their opinions. The practical implementation of the freedom of thought is, therefore, intertwined with other children's rights, such as *inter alia* the right to access to mass media sources and right to freedom of expression. Article 14 is aimed at state parties, who must ensure the specific right for children, by adopting legislation and taking measures.[434] However, the exercise of the right remains within the minds of children, because as soon as they express their thoughts, it will fall within the sphere of the right to freedom of expression or the right to privacy.[435] Significant to note, is that restrictions on the freedom of thought are not allowed, contrary to for instance the freedom of expression.[436]

The impact of new advertising and marketing techniques. New advertising and marketing techniques have an increasing impact on society's cultural values as well as individuals' beliefs and aspirations (e.g. food consumption, tastes, beauty canons). In this regard, the UN General Assembly Special Rapporteur in the field of cultural rights reports that

> *"the dominance of specific narratives and world views promoted through commercial advertising and marketing in public spaces, family and private spheres, combined with an increased deployment of techniques that may influence people at a subconscious level, raises particular concerns in terms of freedom of thought, opinion and, more widely, cultural freedom."*[437]

---

433 This right can also be found in the following articles: article 18 of the Universal Declaration on Human Rights, article 18 of the International Covenant on Civil and Political Rights, and article 9 of the European Convention on Human Rights and Fundamental Freedoms, article 10 CFEU.

434 E. Brems, *A Commentary on the United Nations Convention on the Rights of the Child – Article 14: The Right to Freedom of Thought, Conscience and Religion* (Martinus Nijhoff Publishers 2006) 10–11.

435 In this sense, Brems argues that the right to freedom of thought never played an important role as an independent right. Brems (n 434) 11.

436 Hodgkin and Newell (n 261) 195. However, there is no consensus on this issue. For example, Meuwese, Blaak and Kaandorp argue that restrictions are allowed. According to these authors, the third paragraph – which contains possible grounds for exception – applies to the freedom of thought as well (although it is formulated as follows: "*Freedom to manifest one's religion or beliefs may be subject only to such limitations as are prescribed by law and are necessary to protect public safety, order, health or morals, or the fundamental rights and freedoms of others*"): Meuwese, Blaak and Kaandorp (n 266) 131.

437 F. Shaheed, 'Report of the Special Rapporteur in the Field of Cultural Rights' (2014) A/69/286 3 <https://digitallibrary.un.org/record/755488> accessed 19 July 2018.

Children may face the risk of being manipulated if it is unclear to them that certain information, content or entertainment is in fact a persuasive commercial message.[438] Furthermore, as mentioned above, it has been argued that the ubiquity of commercial messages in children's lives and the promotion of lifestyles based on consumption may lead them to become more materialistic and attach more value to money.[439] According to Arnold and Thompson, individual consumers (including children) operate within a sociocultural, economic and political framework, that shapes their thinking patterns and feelings in the marketplace.[440] New advertising and marketing techniques arguably help shape this framework for children from a very young age. In this regard, the Special Rapporteur also underlines the potential risk of normalising commercialisation when embedding marketing and advertising programmes in the school environment.[441] The influence that commercial communication may assert over children's decision-making, necessitates an assessment of the means used by the advertising industry, considering children's rights, including their right to freedom of thought.[442]

Parental guidance. Parents and legal guardians have a right and a duty to provide guidance to the child in the exercise of his or her right to freedom of thought, in a manner consistent with the evolving capacities of the child.[443] According to Brems, this right is an accessory to the child's right, rather than an autonomous parental right.[444] States are not only obliged to respect this parental duty, but in certain cases they may also have to intervene to encourage or oblige parents to fulfil their duty.[445]

2.3. *Freedom of association (article 15 UNCRC)*

Children's right to freedom of association. Another right for children which could be relevant in a commercial and digital context is the right to freedom of association and peaceful assembly, as enshrined in article 15 of the

438 An illustration can be found in children's changing food choices, as research has revealed that children who played advergames promoting less healthy foods were more likely to select less healthy food options than those who played advergames promoting healthier food options, which may lead to long term health concerns such as obesity. Montgomery and Chester (n 88) 65.

439 S. J. Opree and others, 'Children's Advertising Exposure, Advertised Product Desire, and Materialism: A Longitudinal Study' (2014) 41 Communication Research 717.

440 Shaheed (n 437) 3.

441 In certain UN Member States advertising and marketing is already present in schools (e.g. in Brasil). Shaheed (n 437) 15.

442 Shaheed (n 437) 12.

443 Article 14 paragraph 2 UNCRC. Meaning that for children with normal mental capacities, the role of their parents diminishes when they grow older.

444 Brems (n 434) 25.

445 Brems (n 434) 28.

Convention.[446] It is up to States to recognise that children have such a right. Similar to the freedom of expression, the right to freedom of association is not absolute but restrictions should be conform to the law and need to be necessary in a democratic society.[447] According to Daly, the scope of article 15 could be understood as remarkably broad, encompassing children's family relationships, school attendance, rights in public places, etc.[448] Moreover, it is argued that children need their right to associate with friends in public to be promoted by the Convention because they often have nowhere to go[449], both in an offline and online context.[450] In relation to the latter, the Council of Europe has clarified how the right applies in an online context (to all users, not just to children). More specifically, it entails the "*freedom to choose any website, application or service in order to form, join, mobilise and participate in social groups*"; "*the right to protest peacefully online*"; and the "*the freedom to use available online tools to participate in local, national and global public policy debates, legislative initiatives and public petitions and to participate in policy-making relating to how the Internet is governed.*"[451]

The role of social media in exercising this right. Social media platforms can play an important role in the realisation of this participation right, as it offers clear opportunities for forming or joining groups. However, as the business models of these online platforms are usually based on the collection of user data and the provision of behavioural advertising, they may also raise issues from a children's rights perspective (e.g. right to privacy, right to protection against economic exploitation). The fact that certain service providers[452] do not offer their services to young children may also negatively impact children's rights to participate in online public spaces.[453]

---

446 Equivalents in other human rights treaties are article 20 of the Universal Declaration on Human Rights, article 22 of the International Covenant on Civil and Political Rights, and article 11 of the European Convention on Human Rights and Fundamental Freedoms. The Belgian government made the same reservation as for article 13, cf. *supra*.

447 And in the interests of national security or public safety, public order, the protection of public health or morals, or the protection of the rights and freedoms of others (para. 2 Article 15 UNCRC).

448 A. Daly, *A Commentary on the United Nations Convention on the Rights of the Child, Article 15: The Right to Freedom of Association and to Freedom of Peaceful Assembly* (Brill 2016) <http://booksandjournals.brillonline.com/content/books/9789004258839> accessed 14 November 2017; Lievens and others (n 15).

449 Daly (n 448); Lievens and others (n 16).

450 Lievens and others (n 16).

451 Council of Europe, 'Recommendation CM/Rec(2014)6 of the Committee of Ministers to Member States on a Guide to Human Rights for Internet Users' (2014) <https://search.coe.int/cm/Pages/result_details.aspx?ObjectID=09000016804d5b31> accessed 19 July 2018.

452 E.g. Facebook and Snapchat restricts their services to under 13s due to US Children's Online Privacy Protection Act (COPPA).

453 Lievens and others (n 16).

2.4. *Right to privacy (article 16 UNCRC, article 8 ECHR, articles 7 and 8 CFEU[454])*

THE RIGHT TO PRIVACY IS ENSHRINED IN SEVERAL LEGAL INSTRUMENTS. Children's right to privacy has gained increasing attention in recent years. The right to privacy is crucial in a digital media environment, where advertisers target children with commercial messages in their personal sphere, through their mobile phones, tablets, or even their connected toys (*infra*). Article 16 of the UNCRC protects children from arbitrary or unlawful interferences with their privacy, family, home or correspondence, nor should there be unlawful attacks on their honour and reputation, which is considered inherent in any truly democratic society.[455] This entails interferences by state authorities and private organisations.[456] Moreover, paragraph 2 stipulates that there should be legislation in place which protects children against such interferences. Similarly, the right to privacy is also enshrined in article 8 of the European Convention on Human Rights[457], which not only protects an individual from interference by public authorities, but also entails several positive obligations for the State.[458] Such positive obligations may "*involve the adoption of measures designed to secure respect for private life even in the sphere of the relations of individuals between themselves*".[459] Any restriction on the right to privacy must be (1) in accordance with the law, (2) necessary in a democratic society and (3) have a legitimate interest. States are also granted a certain margin of appreciation when establishing restrictions.[460] As per KILKELLY, in areas such as the protection of children, the margin of appreciation has been considered to be especially wide.[461] Finally, the Charter of Fundamental Rights of the EU not only embraces the right to private and family life (article 7[462]), but also explicitly establishes the right to data protection and thus raises the level of

---

454 Charter of Fundamental Rights of the European Union (2000/C 364/01). Retrieved from www.europarl.europa.eu/charter/pdf/text_en.pdf.

455 The right to privacy is also included in articles 7 and 8 of the Charter of Fundamental Rights of the European Union. International equivalents are article 12 of the Universal Declaration of Human Rights and article 17 International Covenant on Civil and Political Rights.

456 Hodgkin and Newell (n 261) 216.

457 According to article 8 ECHR, "*everyone has the right to respect for his private and family life, his home and his correspondence*".

458 U. Kilkelly, 'The Right to Respect for Private and Family Life: A Guide to the Implementation of Article 8 of the European Convention on Human Rights, Human Rights Handbooks, No 1' (Council of Europe 2003) Human rights handbooks, No 1 <www.refworld.org/docid/49f17e212.html> accessed 13 November 2017.

459 *X and Y v The Netherlands* [23].

460 Kilkelly (n 458) 6.

461 Kilkelly (n 458) 7.

462 Article 7 of the Charter determines that "*everyone has the right to respect for his or her private and family life, home and communications*".

protection to that of a fundamental right.[463] More specifically, article 8 of the Charter determines that

> *"Everyone has the right to the protection of personal data concerning him or her. In addition, such data must be processed fairly for specified purposes and on the basis of the consent of the person concerned or some other legitimate basis laid down by law. Everyone has the right of access to data which has been collected concerning him or her, and the right to have it rectified".*

Article 8 also establishes that an independent authority shall control compliance with these obligations.

A POSITIVE OBLIGATION FOR STATES. The European Court of Human Rights has recognised the importance of children's right to privacy and the protection of their personal data in a digital environment throughout its case law. According to GROOTHUIS, the Court has imposed a positive obligation upon States – inherent to article 8 ECHR[464] – to adopt a legislative framework protecting children from any grave types of interferences with their private lives, such as sexual exploitation online.[465] Although no case dealt specifically with the use of children's personal data for advertising purposes up until now, it can be argued that Member States also have a positive obligation to adopt a legislative framework to protect children from unfair advertising practices (i.e. economic exploitation, *infra*). Indeed, GROOTHUIS argues that – following the case law of the ECtHR – Member States have an obligation to keep their national legislation up to date, to protect children against forms of exploitation by new technologies or social developments in the digital environment. This positive obligation is

---

463 Although the UNCRC does not explicitly include a right to data protection, The EU's Fundamental Rights Agency's observes that Under international law, the right to data protection is part of the child's right to privacy contained in Article 16 of the UNCRC.

464 The ECtHR rarely refers to the UNCRC in its case law on article 8 ECHR. In this regard, GROOTHUIS believes that the Court could strenghten its case law by referring to articles 16 (2) and (3) UNCRC on the prohibition of arbitrary or unlawful interferences with children's privacy and article 3 (2) UNCRC on State responsibility. See M. M. Groothuis, 'The Right to Privacy for Children on the Internet: New Developments in the Case Law of the European Court of Human Rights', *Minding Minors Wandering the Web: Regulating Online Child Safety* (TMC Asser Press, The Hague 2014) 151–152 <https://link.springer.com/chapter/10.1007/978-94-6265-005-3_8> accessed 13 November 2017.

465 Groothuis (n 464) 154–155. See also the case of *K.U. v Finland*, concerning a 12-year-old child who had become the target of an advertisement of a sexual nature on an internet dating site without his knowledge, which included his age, name, a photo, etc. The ECtHR had to decide whether or not internet service providers had to disclose the identity of the private user who had uploaded the information on a website that made the child a target for paedophiles. The Court held that "*both the public interest and the protection of the interests of victims of crimes committed against their physical or psychological well-being require the availability of a remedy enabling the actual offender to be identified and brought to justice.*" *KU v Finland* [2008] ECtHR 2872/02.

not fulfilled by merely abstaining from interfering with children's rights and freedoms. In fact, it has two dimensions. First, the State will have to 'secure' that these rights and freedoms may effectively be enjoyed by individuals in their jurisdiction (i.e. the obligation to provide for adequate legal protection). This may require actively taking steps to protect individuals against violation of their rights by others, be it individuals or companies, by adopting legal frameworks or encouraging self- or co-regulation.[466] Second, the positive obligation also entails that States may have to take the steps necessary to make the legal protection of the right effective (i.e. practical enforcement).[467]

Different dimensions of privacy. The advancements in internet technologies have led to the further (commercial) encroachment on the private sphere.[468] Increased computing capabilities allow commercial entities to profile children's online behaviour and preferences, based on which children are targeted with tailored marketing campaigns.[469] In this context, it has been argued that the right to privacy has different dimensions in the digital environment which need to be considered, i.e. a protection and participation dimension.[470] On the one hand, children's private lives should remain free from unreasonable constraints from the State or from other actors such as commercial entities online. In relation to the latter, children often do not grasp the scope of the underlying data processing activities and business models of online actors. According to the OECD for example, children lack the awareness and capacity to foresee the potential long-term privacy consequences of the disclosure of their personal data online.[471] Moreover, research has shown that children generally consider themselves having a right to privacy online from their parents or peers (i.e. social privacy), rather than from the State or commercial intrusion (e.g. tracking for behavioural advertising purposes).[472] As a result, they form a particularly vulnerable group of online users that require protection.

466 I. M. Sunde, 'Enforcing Legal Protection against Online Violation of Privacy' in D.J.B. Svantesson and S Greenstein (eds), *Nordic Yearbook of Law and Informatics 2010–2012, Internationalisation of Law in the Digital Information Society* (Ex Tuto Publishing 2013) <https://brage.bibsys.no/xmlui/handle/11250/174974> accessed 13 November 2017.

467 *Osman v the United Kingdom* [1998] ECtHR 23452/94. as mentioned by Sunde (n 466) 47.

468 Verdoodt, Clifford and Lievens (n 7).

469 A 2015 privacy sweep of children's websites and apps by an international coalition of data protection authorities, found that a majority of these websites and apps collects personal data of the young visitors without providing adequate information (see also *infra*). Global Privacy Enforcement Network (n 96). Furthermore, in 2017, the coalition found that website privacy notices are too vague and generally inadequate.

470 Lievens and others (n 16).

471 OECD (n 74) 32.

472 Ofcom, 'Social Networking – A Quantitative and Qualitative Research Report into Attitudes, Behaviours and Use' (Ofcom 2008) <http://news.bbc.co.uk/2/shared/bsp/hi/pdfs/02_04_08_ofcom.pdf> accessed 19 July 2018; Lievens and others (n 16).

THE RIGHTS TO PRIVACY AND DEVELOPMENT IN THE CONTEXT OF PROFILING AND ONLINE BEHAVIOURAL ADVERTISING. On the other hand, the right to privacy has an important participatory dimension, as it is essential for individual autonomy and self-determination, and a precondition of participation. This relates to having control over the aspects of the identity one wants to project to the outside world, or according to ROUVROY and POULLET more fundamentally

> *"the capacity of the human subject to keep and develop his personality in a manner that allows him to fully participate in society without however, being induced to conform his thoughts, beliefs, behaviours and preferences to those thoughts, beliefs, behaviours and preferences held by the majority".*[473]

In other words, the rights to privacy and data protection aim at safeguarding the human capacity for reflexive self-determination[474] and, as such, also link to the child's rights to development, freedom of expression and freedom of thought. In this regard, SAVIRIMUTHU warns that the increased role of algorithms in defining children's consumer experience should not disregard the value of a child's emotional space, which should not be subject to the inside the box-thinking that constitutes profiling-based decisions.[475] Profiling and behavioural targeting have the capacity not only to compartmentalise children, but also to shape their preferences and interests accordingly, ultimately affecting their autonomy and development.[476] We have seen that the right to development in a digital and commercialised setting entails that children's basic needs are fulfilled, so that they can optimally develop into independent adults. This right guides the interpretation of the other provisions of the UNCRC, including the right to privacy. Related to this, ARIELY and BERNS argue that the creation of profiles has a potential negative impact on the development of children. The authors stress that the collection and use of personal data for the purpose of profiling may undermine children's rights to experiment freely with and critically reflect upon their interactions, as the digital environment they are exploring and are communicating in is no longer free of supervision and tracking.[477] In other words, this form of supervision could have

---

473 A. Rouvroy and Y. Poullet, 'The Right to Informational Self-Determination and the Value of Self-Development: Reassessing the Importance of Privacy for Democracy', *Reinventing Data Protection?* (Springer, Dordrecht 2009) 59 <https://link.springer.com/chapter/10.1007/978-1-4020-9498-9_2> accessed 13 November 2017.

474 This is also what RICHARDS denotes as "intellectual privacy", i.e. having our processes of generating ideas protected of the surveillance or interference by others before we make them public. N. Richards, *Intellectual Privacy: Rethinking Civil Liberties in the Digital Age*, vol 6 (Oxford University Press 2016).

475 J. Savirimuthu, 'Unfair Commercial Practies, the Consumer Child and New Technologies: What Should We Regulate? Some Policy Provocations' (2014) <https://www.liverpool.ac.uk/media/livacuk/law/european-childrens-rights-unit/BriefingNote.pdf> accessed 13 November 2017.

476 Verdoodt and Lievens (n 3).

477 Ariely and Berns (n 119). as cited by Savirimuthu (n 475).

important chilling effects on children, for instance in the form of an unwillingness to search for certain information. Furthermore, the lack of children's control over the management of their personal data also affects their ability to develop, learn and experiment with their own identity.[478] In this context, there is again an important tension between participation and protection which States should keep in mind when developing guidance documents and policies for the processing of children's personal data. States have a responsibility to develop guidelines for increased transparency and raise awareness of profiling activities and behavioural advertising, both amongst children and parents. However, it is also important to recognise the limitations of transparency and empowerment of children (and their parents for that matter) when it comes to data processing practices.[479] In this regard, KEYMOLEN mentions the concept of 'invisible invisibility', which entails that *"the invisibility of these actions makes it rather difficult to escape the state of confidence and actively engage with the question if curators are trustworthy and if the actions they undertake are in line with the interests of the users."*[480] Children's right to privacy, therefore, requires specific protections for children when it comes to the processing of their personal data for advertising purposes.[481] Here too, the age and level of maturity of the child will play an important role.[482] Companies collecting children's personal data for advertising purposes must also take their responsibility[483] and carry out a thorough data protection impact assessment with attention to the interests and rights of children (*infra*). Finally, it should be kept in mind that parents keeping track of a child's use of the internet and other new media or their digital correspondence, for instance through software, could constitute a violation of the child's right to privacy.[484] When deciding on the use of such paternalistic measures, parents should take the child's best interests into consideration, and consult the child about the information that is disclosed to their parents, in accordance with their age and maturity.

DIGITAL DURABILITY. Finally, as mentioned, children have a right to explore and experiment with their own identity, both in the offline and online environment. Digital durability and outdated information may present significant challenges in

---

478 Ariely and Berns (n 119). as cited by Savirimuthu (n 475).

479 Personal data collected through profiling may not only be used for improving or adapting the device or service, but also for other purposes such as targeted advertising on other websites or apps. E. Keymolen, *Trust on the Line: A Philosophical Exploration of Trust in the Networked Era* (Wolf Legal Publishers 2016) 154.

480 Keymolen (n 479) 154.

481 For example, default limitations on the processing of children's personal data for profiling purposes could be considered (*infra*).

482 V. Verdoodt and E. Lievens, 'De AVG Bekeken Vanuit Een Kinderrechtenperspectief Pluspunten, Knelpunten & Vraagstukken' (2017) Computerrecht 155.

483 K.C. Montgomery and J. Chester, 'Data Protection for Youth in the Digital Age: Developing a Rights-Based Global Framework' (2015) 1 European Data Protection Law Review 277, 291.

484 Lievens, *Protecting Children in the Digital Era: The Use of Alternative Regulatory Instruments* (n 12) 271.

this respect. Children and youngsters are often not (yet) capable of understanding the potential long-term consequences of sharing their or other people's personal data online – in fact this may be true for most people given that the privacy implications can be incremental and obscure.[485] Accordingly, they should be provided with the possibility to have certain information deleted when they grow up, so that they are not bound by visions, statements or preferences in which they can no longer find themselves. In practice, however, exercising this right may not always be easy. First, VAN DER HOF makes an important distinction between (1) 'data given' – which is information given or published by the individuals themselves and of which they can ask to be deleted; (2) 'data given off' or observed data[486] – of which most people are unaware that they are being collected and, hence, most likely unable to delete; and (3) 'inferred data'[487] – such as profiles, which are equally difficult to be aware of and to delete.[488] Furthermore, BLUME points to the fact that all relevant interests (e.g. the public interest) should be taken into consideration.[489]

2.5. *Right to have a diversity of mass media sources to choose from (article 17 UNCRC)*

THE DIGITAL ENVIRONMENT IS CHILDREN'S GATEWAY TO INFORMATION. Another right which is important in the context of new forms of commercial communication aimed at children, is enshrined in article 17, the right to access to a diversity of media and information. More specifically, this article requires states to provide children with access to

> *"information and material from a diversity of national and international sources, especially those aimed at the promotion of his or her social, spiritual and moral well-being and physical and mental health".*

---

485 OECD (n 74). In this regard, BOYD mentions four characteristics of data that are important: persistence, replicability, scalability and searchability. For more information see D. boyd, 'Social Network Sites as Networked Publics: Affordances, Dynamics, and Implications' in Z Papacharissi (ed), Networked self: Identity, community, and culture on social network sites (Routledge) <https://www.danah.org/papers/2010/SNSasNetworkedPublics.pdf> accessed 9 November 2018.

486 This category of data does not merely consist of content (i.e. communications, social media posts, pictures and video's etc.) but also of metadata (e.g. MAC-address, usage, social connections, how often you call whom, when and where, and other location data). van der Hof (n 94) 104–105.

487 According to VAN DER HOF, *"the data given and given off – and other data – are captured, processed, and then analyzed with algorithms, which results in new knowledge consisting of patterns and correlations. Therefore, knowledge about someone can be inferred that was perhaps not disclosed by individuals because they perceived it as too personal to share online."* van der Hof (n 94) 105–106.

488 Van der Hof (n 94) 104–106.

489 For example, some children will later become public figures (e.g. politicians) and will soon be of interest to a wider audience. P. Blume, 'The Data Subject' (2015) 1 European Data Protection Law Review 258. For this reason, the exercise of the right to data erasure and the retention of data should be viewed from a dynamic and fundamental rights perspective. See also Verdoodt and Lievens (n 482).

The reasoning behind this provision is that for the exercise of other fundamental rights (e.g. the right to freedom of expression, the right to be heard), children need to have access to media and information.[490] According to Wheatly Sacino, the essence of article 17 is the diversity in mass media sources[491] and State's duty to ensure that children and adolescents have access to "*a variety of producers and disseminators of movies, television and radio programs, books, magazines, the Internet and other mass media communications*".[492, 493] In addition, States have a series of obligations for encouraging other actors to produce and distribute material that promotes children's and adolescents' well-being[494], which arguably could include the advertising industry. Following this interpretation, the right to access to media has an important provision dimension, but it undoubtedly also has a participation dimension (i.e. access), as well as a protective dimension (i.e. encourage the development of guidelines for the protection of the child against harmful material, a basis for taking actions against certain harmful content). The digital environment is an important gateway to information and according to the Council of Europe it is a primary source for information and communication for children.[495] However, no similar right can be found in other major human rights instruments. In this regard, the UN Special Rapporteur on the promotion and protection of the right to freedom of opinion and expression believes that States have "*a positive obligation to promote or facilitate the right to freedom of expression and the means necessary to exercise this right, which includes the internet*".[496] Furthermore, the European Court of Human Rights has recognised that "*the Internet plays an important role in enhancing public's access to news and facilitating the dissemination of information in general*".[497] Finally, research has shown that children themselves in fact consider access to digital media to be a fundamental right.[498]

490 Meuwese, Blaak and Kaandorp (n 266) 144–145.

491 Without such a diverity of sources, there will be a lack of diversity in the content availble to children, limiting their choice as media consumers. S. Wheatley Sacino, *A Commentary on the United Nations Convention on the Rights of the Child, Article 17: Access to a Diversity of Mass Media Sources* (Brill 2011) 7.

492 Sacino (n 491) 5.

493 Article 17 also refers to the "*important function performed by the mass media*", but does not provide any further clarifications on the concept. The Council of Europe, however, interprets this notion broadly, encompassing both traditional and online media. Council of Europe, 'Internet Governance – Council of Europe Strategy 2016–2019: Democracy, Human Rights and the Rule of Law in the Digital World' <https://rm.coe.int/16806aafa9> accessed 10 November 2017.

494 Sacino (n 491) 11.

495 Council of Europe, 'Internet Governance – Council of Europe Strategy 2016–2019: Democracy, Human Rights and the Rule of Law in the Digital World' (n 493).

496 F. La Rue, 'Report of the Special Rapporteur on the Promotion and Protection of the Right to Freedom of Opinion and Expression' (2011) <www2.ohchr.org/english/bodies/hrcouncil/docs/17session/A.HRC.17.27_en.pdf> accessed 10 November 2017.

497 Lievens, 'Children's Rights and Media' (n 412). See *MTE v Hungary* [2016] ECtHR 22947/13. See also Lievens and others (n 16).

498 Third and others (n 331).

Implications of the commercialisation of children's digital media. The increased commercialisation of children's digital media poses certain challenges for the implementation of article 17 in practice. First, digital media may transmit commercial messages which are harmful to children (i.e. protection). For instance, when harmful products or services are promoted, such as gambling, alcohol or unhealthy foods, or when portraying unrealistic body images.[499] Second, the increased personalisation of digital services and targeting of advertising and marketing of media content or other services may in practice result in a restricted consumer choice (i.e. participation). Finally, article 17 also requires States to provide children with age-appropriate information on their rights (i.e. provision), which may be difficult to achieve in practice. To overcome such challenges, States are encouraged to pursue a proactive policy that stimulates the cultural, educational and informational potential of media when it comes to children[500], not only in relation to media content, but also regarding commercial communication aimed at them. Such a policy should focus *inter alia* on protecting the child against harmful commercial influences through the media and on safeguarding children's access to a diversity of information and media sources. As mentioned, parents also have an important responsibility under article 18 UNCRC to offer appropriate direction and guidance to children (in a manner consistent with the evolving capacities of the child) when exercising their rights.[501] This provision could be interpreted as implying that parents have a responsibility to (do their best to) support their children in their approach to new media and commercial communication.[502] Furthermore, States must "*render appropriate assistance to parents and legal guardians in the performance of their child-rearing responsibilities*" (*infra*).[503] This 'assistance' could, for example, consist of States providing adequate information to parents, regarding the risks of certain media or advertising to which their children can be exposed.[504]

---

499 UN Committee on the Rights of the Child, 'General Comment No. 16 (2013) on State Obligations Regarding the Impact of the Business Sector' (n 148) 8–9; OECD (n 74) 32.

500 D. Voorhoof, *Media(Recht) En Kinder(Recht)En* (Mys & Breesch 1994) 30.

501 For more details on parental responsibility, see M. Couzens, 'Autonomy Rights versus Parental Autonomy' in A. Alen (ed), *The UN Children's rights Convention: theory meets practice* (Intersentia 2006).

502 The United Nations General Assembly has also touched upon the responsibilities of parents et al. in this respect: "*19. Encourage measures to protect children from violent or harmful web sites, computer programmes and games that negatively influence the psychological development of children, taking into account the responsibilities of the family, parents, legal guardians and caregivers*": United Nations General Assembly, 'Resolution – A World Fit for Children, A/RES/S-27/2' (2004) 23 Refugee Survey Quarterly 225. as cited by Lievens, *Protecting Children in the Digital Era: The Use of Alternative Regulatory Instruments* (n 12) 277.

503 Article 18 para. 2 UNCRC.

504 Hodgkin and Newell (n 261) 236.

2.6. *Right to education and (advertising) literacy (articles 28 and 29 UNCRC)*

Education and literacy as a means for children's development. As mentioned, to be in line with children's right to development, they should not only be protected from harmful or misleading advertising but also be educated and empowered to cope with commercial communication (i.e. advertising literate). It is therefore important to analyse children's education rights under the Convention in this context, which are enshrined in articles 28 and 29. These rights have a dual dimension, on the one hand requiring States to provide access to educational information to all children and on the other hand to enable children to develop the life skills to optimally use such educational and informational sources and strengthen their capacity to enjoy the full range of human rights.[505] Considering this second dimension, children's education rights should be viewed in conjunction with the general principles and rights of the Convention, in particular the right to development, as well as children's participation rights such as *inter alia* the child's right to freedom of expression and the right to freedom of association.[506] According to the Council of Europe, the process of developing skills to use new media and technologies should go hand-in-hand with learning about the enjoyment of children's rights and freedoms online.[507]

Advertising literacy skills. Whereas article 28 contains the right to education[508], article 29 adds a qualitative meaning to it by establishing the aims of education, i.e. the holistic development of the full potential of the child (and as such linking back to the child's right to development).[509] As children are in the process of becoming adults, their situation can always be perceived as one of

505 Lievens and others (n 16); UN Committee on the Rights of the Child, 'General Comment No. 1 (2001) Article 29 (1): The Aims of Education' (n 343) 2. This dual perspective can also be seen in several international policy documents, such as OECD (n 74); Council of Europe, 'Recommendation CM/Rec(2014)6 of the Committee of Ministers to Member States on a Guide to Human Rights for Internet Users' (n 451).

506 M. Verheyde, *Article 28: The Right to Education* (Martinus Nijhoff Publishers 2006) 2.

507 Council of Europe, 'Recommendation Rec(2006)12 of the Committee of Ministers to Member States on Empowering Children in the New Information and Communications Environment' (2006) 2 <https://www.coe.int/en/web/freedom-expression/committee-of-ministers-adopted-texts/-/asset_publisher/aDXmrol0vvsU/content/recommendation-rec-2006-12-of-the-committee-of-ministers-to-member-states-on-empowering-children-in-the-new-information-and-communications-environment> accessed 10 November 2017.

508 According to Verheyde, the UNCRC's education rights can be categories as (1) the right to education (i.e. the provisions regarding the practical organisation and content of education), (2) the right in education (i.e. the protection and participation rights of children in school settings and (3) the right through education (i.e. the indirect implementation of the Convention's standards by means of human rights education. Verheyde (n 506) 2.

509 UN Committee on the Rights of the Child, 'General Comment No. 1 (2001) Article 29 (1): The Aims of Education' (n 343) 2.

education. Education in this sense goes far beyond formal schooling and entails according to the UN Committee on the Rights of the Child:

> *"the broad range of life experiences and learning processes which enable children, individually and collectively, to develop their personalities, talents and abilities and to live a full and satisfying life within society".*[510]

According to Verheyde, the life skills children are entitled to develop include *inter alia* the ability to make well-balanced decisions, to develop a healthy lifestyle and critical thinking[511], which are all crucial when it comes to coping with new advertising and marketing techniques. Therefore, it is argued that children should also be enabled to become advertising literate adults, which means that they should be able to develop and use their advertising-related knowledge, attitudes, and skills, such as the ability to recognise commercial messages, to understand the persuasive intent of such messages, and to critically evaluate them, both offline and online.[512] Nevertheless, it is important to keep in mind the limitations of advertising literacy and the problems associated with certain advertising techniques (e.g. personalisation and emotional targeting). This links back to the requirement imposed by the children's rights framework of finding a balance between empowering the child (i.e. by encouraging their advertising literacy) and protecting the child (i.e. from harmful or misleading advertising).

Advertising literacy policies and initiatives. There is broad consensus that the digital environment offers many benefits for children's education and development, but also that education and literacy initiatives are crucial means to empower children in this environment.[513] In this regard, States should promote advertising literacy initiatives and develop policies considering the children's rights framework.[514] In addition, it is argued that there should be specific protection measures for children against those advertising techniques where advertising literacy is not effective.

2.7. *Right to engage in play and recreational activities (article 31 UNCRC)*

Play and recreation contribute to children's development. Article 31 explicitly recognises the importance of play and recreation in children's lives,

---

510 UN Committee on the Rights of the Child, 'General Comment No. 1 (2001) Article 29 (1): The Aims of Education' (n 343) 2.

511 Verheyde (n 506).

512 Rozendaal and others (n 42); Livingstone and Helsper (n 43).

513 Lievens and others (n 16).

514 Such programmes or initiatives should be reviewed and evaluated on a continuous basis, considering the constant evolution of digital advertising and marketing techniques. Lievens and others (n 16). In this regard, the Council of Europe recommends that familiarisation with new technologies and services should begin from an early stage of school education.

due to its positive impact on the social, cognitive and personal development of the child. More specifically, article 31 requires States to

> *"recognize the right of the child to rest and leisure, to engage in play and recreational activities appropriate to the age of the child and to participate freely in cultural life and the arts".*

According to David, the distinction between the terms 'play' and 'recreational activities' lies in the degree of formality and organisation of the activities. More specifically, 'play' can be understood as unstructured informal activities of children uncontrolled by adults, whereas 'recreation' refers to more organised and formal activities such as sports or creative arts.[515] New media technologies like social networking, mobile apps and online games can play an important role by facilitating access to a variety of playful, social, cultural and artistic activities.[516] The UN Committee on the Rights of the Child has underlined that:

> *"Children in all regions of the world are spending increasing periods of time engaged in play, recreational, cultural and artistic activities, both as consumers and creators, via various digital platforms and media, including watching television, messaging, social networking, gaming, texting, listening to and creating music, watching and making videos and films, creating new art forms, posting images."*[517]

In this regard, States are encouraged to develop policies and adopt measures that are needed to enable all children to take full advantage of the opportunities of the digital environment.[518] This entails that children should have (equal) access to the internet and new media technologies (*supra*), and are educated and provided with the necessary skills to use and reap the benefits of such technologies.

An increased commercialisation of play. Furthermore, an important consideration in relation to article 31 is that, nowadays, children and their families are exposed to increased marketing and a commercialisation of play. It was one of the major concerns brought forward by the Committee on the Rights of the Child, during its Day of General Discussion in 2014. In

---

515 P. David, *A Commentary on the United Nations Convention on the Rights of the Child, Article 31: The Right to Leisure, Play and Culture* (Brill 2006).

516 Hodgkin and Newell (n 261) 470; Meuwese, Blaak and Kaandorp (n 266) 260. as cited by Lievens, *Protecting Children in the Digital Era: The Use of Alternative Regulatory Instruments* (n 12) 278.

517 UN Committee on the Rights of the Child, 'General Comment No. 17 (2013) on the Right of the Child to Rest, Leisure, Play, Recreational Activities, Cultural Life and the Arts (Art. 31)' (2013).

518 UN Committee on the Rights of the Child, 'General Comment No. 17 (2013) on the Right of the Child to Rest, Leisure, Play, Recreational Activities, Cultural Life and the Arts (Art. 31)' (n 517).

this regard, the Committee argues that parents experience more and more pressure to purchase certain toys and games which may be harmful to their children's development.[519] In addition, children themselves are being targeted by game and toy manufacturers, who embed commercial messages directly into children's gaming experiences both online and offline. Examples of such a marketing strategy include the delivery of commercial messages through in-game advertising, advergames, or even interactive, connected toys.[520] As mentioned, the data processing activities underlying these advertising techniques go beyond children's understanding and therefore often happen without their or their parents' meaningful consent.[521] The Committee also fears that global marketing in this context can serve to weaken children's active participation in the traditional cultural and artistic life of their community.[522] To overcome this, the UN Committee on the Rights of the Child underlines that article 31 requires specific actions of States in the context of marketing and media. More specifically, States "*must review their policies concerning the commercialisation of toys and games to children, including through children's television programmes and directly related advertisements, with particular regard to those promoting violence, girls or boys in a sexual way and reinforcing gender and disability stereotypes*". Finally, States are also recommended to limit exposure to advertising during peak viewing hours for children.[523]

---

519 The Committee mentions the following examples: "*products that promote television programmes with established characters and storylines which impede imaginative exploration; toys with microchips which render the child as a passive observer; kits with a pre-determined pattern of activity; toys that promote traditional gender stereotypes or early sexualization of girls; toys containing dangerous parts or chemicals; realistic war toys and games.*" UN Committee on the Rights of the Child, 'General Comment No. 17 (2013) on the Right of the Child to Rest, Leisure, Play, Recreational Activities, Cultural Life and the Arts (Art. 31)' (n 517) 15.; see also UN Committee on the Rights of the Child, 'Report of the 2014 Day of General Discussion "Digital Media and Children's Rights"' (n 332).

520 For instance, a recent review report of the terms of use of connected toys by the Norwegian Consumer Council, found that the myfriendCayla doll was "*embedded with pre-programmed phrases, through which they endorse different commercial products. For example, the doll Cayla will happily talk about how much she loves different Disney movies.*" Finn Myrstad, 'Connected toys violate European consumer law : Forbrukerrådet' (6 December 2016) <https://www.forbrukerradet.no/siste-nytt/connected-toys-violate-consumer-laws/> accessed 23 July 2018.

521 F. Lupiáñez-Villanueva and others, 'Study on the Impact of Marketing through Social Media, Online Games and Mobile Applications on Children's Behaviour' (European Commission 2016) <http://ec.europa.eu/consumers/consumer_evidence/behavioural_research/docs/final_report_impact_marketing_children_final_version_approved_en.pdf> accessed 10 November 2017.

522 General UN Committee on the Rights of the Child, 'General Comment No. 17 (2013) on the Right of the Child to Rest, Leisure, Play, Recreational Activities, Cultural Life and the Arts (Art. 31)' (2013) 15.

523 General UN Committee on the Rights of the Child, 'General Comment No. 17 (2013) on the Right of the Child to Rest, Leisure, Play, Recreational Activities, Cultural Life and the Arts (Art. 31)' (2013) 15.

2.8. *Protection against economic exploitation (article 32 UNCRC)*

Broadening the notion of "economic exploitation". A right which has not been mentioned frequently in the context of advertising is enshrined in article 32 of the Convention, i.e. the right to protection against economic exploitation. Although the Convention does not offer a definition of the notion 'economic exploitation', article 32 is generally interpreted as the child's right to protection against child labour.[524] Nevertheless, it can be argued that this notion is perhaps much broader, especially in the digital era. The notion combines two distinct elements: (1) economic and (2) exploitation. First, 'economic' implies that there is a material interest, i.e. a certain gain or profit through the production, distribution or consumption of goods and services.[525] The UN Committee on the Rights of the Child recognises that this material interest may have an impact on the economy of either the State, the community or the family. In the context of commercial communication, the economic element could be the fact that certain goods and services are advertised towards children, potentially leading to an increased consumption of the advertised goods or services and, hence an increased gain or profit for the brand or company. This material interest of the company in turn has a direct impact on the targeted child and its family (i.e. on their consumption pattern).

Exploitative advertising and marketing. Secondly, according to the Committee's interpretation, 'exploitation' means '*taking unjust advantage of another for one's own advantage or benefit*'.[526] More specifically, this includes manipulation, misuse, abuse, victimisation, oppression or ill-treatment. In this regard, the OECD has stressed that children are exposed to significant consumer risks in the digital environment. Indeed, they may face *inter alia "embedded ads, privacy-invasive practices, age-inappropriate content, as well as the exploitation of their incredulity and inexperience resulting in economic risks such as overspending or online fraudulent transactions"*.[527] Furthermore, van der Hof argues that treating children as the product rather than customers when offering them online services, for instance by collecting their personal data and using it or reselling it for advertising purposes can also be perceived as a form of economic exploitation.[528] The Committee underlines that States have an important role in

---

524 L. Swepston, *A Commentary on the United Nations Convention on the Rights of the Child, Article 32: Protection from Economic Exploitation* (Brill 2012) <http://booksandjournals.brillonline.com/content/books/9789004231467> accessed 13 November 2017.

525 General UN Committee on the Rights of the Child, 'UNCRC Discussion Day 1993, Economic Exploitation of Children, CRC/C/20' (1993) 3 <www.ohchr.org/EN/HRBodies/CRC/Documents/Recommandations/exploit.pdf>.

526 UN Committee on the Rights of the Child, 'UNCRC Discussion Day 1993, Economic Exploitation of Children, CRC/C/20' (n 525) 3.

527 OECD (n 74).

528 S. van der Hof, 'I Agree, or Do I: A Rights-Based Analysis of the Law on Children's Consent in the Digital World' (2016) 34 Wis. Int'l LJ 409, 123.

adequately incentivising the advertising industry to adopt fair advertising and marketing practices.[529]

2.9. *Procedural rights (articles 6 and 13 ECHR, article 47 CFEU)*

Finally, children also have rights that grant them a number of procedural guarantees, which are particularly relevant for the research on the structure of alternative regulatory instruments for advertising and marketing (see *infra* part III).

RIGHT TO A FAIR TRIAL. First, children have a right to a fair trial, as enshrined in article 6 of the ECHR, which provides that

> *"1. In the determination of his civil rights and obligations or of any criminal charge against him, everyone is entitled to a fair and public hearing within a reasonable time by an independent and impartial tribunal established by law."*[530]

Thus, article 6 ECHR is applicable in either criminal cases or non-criminal cases where civil rights and obligations are at stake. The ECtHR has developed an autonomous interpretation of the concept of "civil rights and obligations", entailing *inter alia* that the right to a fair trial only comes into play if there is a dispute concerning civil rights which is genuine and of a serious nature[531] and relates to an actual right.[532] This dispute can either be between individuals or between an individual and the state.[533] The ECtHR has clarified that an inherent aspect of the procedural safeguards enshrined in article 6 is the right to access to a court.[534] Furthermore, several procedural requirements are put forward by article 6: (1) a fair and public hearing and a publicly pronounced judgement, (2) a hearing must occur within a reasonable time frame, (3) cases need to be dealt with by an independent and impartial tribunal established by law.[535]

---

529 UN Committee on the Rights of the Child, 'General Comment No. 16 (2013) on State Obligations Regarding the Impact of the Business Sector' (n 148).

530 The second and third paragraph of Article 6 ECHR continue with a presumption of innocence and a non-exhaustive list of rights which are linked to the notion of fair trial in criminal cases. As criminal cases will be rare in the context of commercial communication aimed at children, the analysis focuses on the first paragraph dealing with non-criminal cases where civil rights are at stake.

531 *Sporrong and Lönnroth v Sweden* [1982] ECtHR Application no. 7151/75; 7152/75.

532 The ECtHR has clarified that the substantive right relied on by the applicant in the national courts must have a legal basis in the State concerned. Directorate of the Jurisconsult of the European Court of Human Rights, 'Guide on Article 6 of the European Convention on Human Rights – Right to a Fair Trial' 7–8 <https://www.echr.coe.int/Documents/Guide_Art_6_ENG.pdf> accessed 17 May 2018.

533 Lievens, *Protecting Children in the Digital Era: The Use of Alternative Regulatory Instruments* (n 12) 324.

534 *Golder v The United Kingdom* [1975] ECtHR Application no. 4451/70.

535 For a more detailed discussion see Lievens, *Protecting Children in the Digital Era: The Use of Alternative Regulatory Instruments* (n 12) 323–327.

RIGHT TO AN EFFECTIVE REMEDY. Another right which could be relevant to the research is the children's right to an effective remedy under article 13 ECHR, which provides that

> *"Everyone whose rights and freedoms as set forth in this Convention are violated shall have an effective remedy before a national authority notwithstanding that the violation has been committed by persons acting in an official capacity."*

Although it is an independent right[536], the right to an effective remedy will normally be invoked in conjunction with another fundamental right. The ECtHR has clarified the essence of article 13:

> *"The object of Article 13, as emerges from the Travaux préparatoires is to provide a means whereby individuals can obtain relief at national level for violations of their Convention rights before having to set in motion the international machinery of complaint before the Court".*[537]

Each of the Contracting Parties to the ECHR are left with a degree of national procedural autonomy. More specifically, they are allowed to choose the form of remedies offered to meet their obligations under the ECHR. RAINEY et al. highlight that such remedies do not necessarily have to be judicial, but may include non-judicial mechanisms such as Ombudsman procedures.[538] There are two questions that need to be asked in the context of article 13 ECHR, (1) does the applicant have an arguable complaint? And (2) is the national remedy effective? First, with regard to the arguability test, the ECtHR decides on the issue on a case-by-case basis.[539] Second, the remedies provided must be effective in practice as well as in law. The ECtHR has clarified throughout its case law that the remedy must be one which enables the applicants to raise their rights in a timely manner, and to have them considered in national proceedings.[540]The violation should not only be terminated but any consequence thereof should also be neutralised.[541]

CONCLUDING REMARK. Within the scope of this study, the issue that is most interesting is which procedural guarantees or organisational elements can be recommended for alternative regulatory instruments, in light of children's procedural rights. This question will be further analysed in part III of the book.

---

536 This entails that a violation of a substantive right of the ECHR (e.g. the right to privacy) does not have to be established first.

537 *Kudla v Poland* [2000] ECtHR 30210/96 [152].

538 B. Rainey, E. Wicks and C. Ovey, *Jacobs, White and Ovey: The European Convention on Human Rights* (Oxford University Press 2017) 139.

539 Rainey, Wicks and Ovey (n 538) 138.

540 Rainey, Wicks and Ovey (n 538) 141.

541 Lievens, *Protecting Children in the Digital Era: The Use of Alternative Regulatory Instruments* (n 12) 329.

CONCLUSION

AN ANALYTICAL FRAMEWORK FOR THE REGULATORY FRAMEWORK FOR COMMERCIAL COMMUNICATION

Children's rights and new forms of commercial communication. The first section of this chapter introduced the children's rights framework and explored children's rights in the digital era. From this analysis, it can be concluded that both the digitisation and the commercialisation of children's worlds impacts not only how children can exercise their rights but also how these rights may be protected, promoted or neglected. In order to address this reconfiguration of children's rights and adapt to the new reality – children as early adopters of new technologies accessing commercialised digital environments for play, communication and information from a very young age – a specific interpretation of the relevant provisions of the UNCRC framework was needed.

Children's rights as an analytical framework for regulation. Therefore, the second section of the chapter focused on the interpretation of the rights and principles in the specific context of commercial communication. Regarding the role of children's rights in regulating advertising, it was argued that the interpretation of the rights and principles should function as a comprehensive analytical framework in light of which the legislative or self- and co-regulatory framework for commercial communication aimed at children should be evaluated. From this interpretative exercise, a number of important outcomes can be highlighted.

A multi-dimensional approach: balancing empowerment and protection. The overarching conclusion of the above analysis is that the tension between the objectives of protection, participation and provision of the child is clearly present in the digital environment. On the one hand, misleading or harmful advertisements online and the collection of children's personal data for advertising purposes raises significant issues in relation to *inter alia* children's rights to development, privacy and protection against economic exploitation. On the other hand, children's right to development and self-determination requires that children are educated and empowered to cope with commercial communication, in accordance with the child's evolving capacities as a 'consumer'. Furthermore, the digital environment offers great opportunities for children's rights to participation, education, and play, and the advertising industry has an important role in the creation and maintenance of good-quality content and online services for children. Accordingly, rather than a purely protectionist approach to regulating new forms of commercial communication, it is contended that a balance is needed between protecting children against those forms of commercial communication that are misleading or harmful or where advertising literacy and education would not be a solution, and between empowering and educating children and allowing them to practice their commercial decision-making skills. Keeping in mind the need for a balance between protection and empowerment, a number of more specific conclusions can be drawn.

Children's autonomy and commercial decision-making. Advertising and marketing infiltrates nearly all aspects of children's online lives, their social media pages, the environments in which they play games, where they search for information, etc. In this regard, it is argued that the increased commercialisation may shape children's thinking patterns and feelings in the market place, which affects a number of rights including their right to development and autonomy, the right to freedom of thought and the right to play. Furthermore, the collection of children's personal data for advertising purposes and the profiling and personalisation impacts their rights to development, privacy and protection against economic exploitation. In relation to this, it is necessary to emphasise that children should be able to maintain their self-determination as well as their autonomy in commercial decision-making and be protected from compartmentalisation. Furthermore, their ability to experiment online without supervision should also be safeguarded.

Education, access to information and advertising literacy. Linking back to the need for a balance between protection and empowerment, the analysis highlighted that children are also entitled to develop the ability to make well-balanced decisions, to develop a healthy lifestyle and their critical thinking, which are all crucial when it comes to coping with advertising and marketing practices. In relation to this, it is contended that children's rights to education and access to information requires that children are provided with the necessary opportunities to mature and practice their advertising-related knowledge, attitudes, and skills, such as the ability to recognise commercial messages, to understand the persuasive intent of such messages, and to critically evaluate them, both offline and online.

Broadening the notion of economic exploitation. However, the analysis of the emerging trends in advertising in the first chapter showed that certain advertising techniques (e.g. targeted advertising, emotional targeting) are extremely effective when used on children. For such advertising practices, the limits of advertising literacy and education and the need for additional protection for children are recognised. More specifically, it is argued that the notion of economic exploitation should be broadened to include exploitative advertising. Targeting children with hidden or misleading commercial messages or collecting children's personal data and using or reselling them for advertising and marketing purposes are practices that would fall under the notion of exploitative advertising.

Procedural safeguards. It was also discussed how children have rights that grant them a number of procedural guarantees, which could be relevant for the structuring and development of advertising self- and co-regulatory instruments. More specifically, their rights to a fair trial and effective remedy demand that whenever civil rights or obligations are at stake (e.g. advertising-related disputes): there should be a fair and public hearing; within a reasonable time; independence and impartiality are to be expected from the decision-making body; and any violation should be terminated and any consequence thereof should be neutralised. These procedural elements will be further discussed in the third part of the book.

Distribution of responsibilities. Finally, the analysis of the children's rights framework identified several actors as having responsibilities for realising these rights in a commercial communication context. Whereas parents have the primary responsibility for the development and upbringing of their children, it is up to the State to implement the rights and principles in their national legal systems, to provide parents with the necessary support and to ensure that businesses meet their responsibilities regarding children's rights. Furthermore, the advertising industry was briefly mentioned as having important responsibilities in respecting and promoting children's rights, which will also be further explored in the third part of the book.

PART II

ASSESSMENT OF THE REGULATORY FRAMEWORK FOR COMMERCIAL COMMUNICATION IN LIGHT OF CHILDREN'S RIGHTS

CHAPTER I
PIECING TOGETHER THE REGULATORY PUZZLE

SITUATION. The first part of the book has provided an introduction to the research topic and addressed the reconfiguration of children's rights and principles in the context of commercial communication. The opening chapter discussed the constitutive elements of the research (i.e. children, commercial communication and advertising literacy) and explored the difficulties that have arisen with these elements in the digital era. It was found that new trends in the area of commercial communication present significant challenges for children's advertising literacy and their commercial decision-making abilities. The examination of the policy agenda at EU and international level (starting from 2008) demonstrated that increasing attention was drawn to the protection of children against the commercial pressure online, children's privacy and data protection and the need for children's advertising literacy education. However, the existing instruments to reach these policy goals are numerous and fragmented into legislation and self- and co-regulation, hence highlighting the need for a detailed mapping and evaluation. The second chapter of the first part then analysed in detail the key children's rights principles and standards and translated them in the specific context of commercial communication. The rights and principles will now be used in the second and third part of the book as a critical lens to evaluate the existing regulatory framework for commercial communication aimed at children.

THE REGULATORY FRAMEWORK. The regulatory framework for commercial communication is fragmented into both legislative and alternative regulatory instruments. This first chapter of the second part of the book aims at piecing together this regulatory puzzle by conducting a mapping exercise of existing advertising regulation at the EU level. It focuses mostly on EU legislation, as these supranational rules were either translated into the national legal order or are directly applicable in all the Member States. Of course, there might be some additional national rules that need to be respected, however, this would entail a far too extended scope of analysis within the framework of this study. At the EU level, there are four important frameworks (or contexts) that need to be taken into account: (1) the consumer protection framework (including the Unfair

Commercial Practices Directive), (2) the audiovisual media services context (including the Audiovisual Media Services Directive), (3) the e-commerce context (including the e-Commerce Directive), (4) the data protection framework (including the General Data Protection Regulation and the ePrivacy Directive). The chapter provides an overview of the relevant provisions of each of these instruments, including the provisions related to their scope of application, the general requirements for commercial communication and the specific protections for children. In addition, within each of these different contexts, an overview of relevant self-regulatory instruments is given.[542]

SECTION I. THE CONSUMER PROTECTION CONTEXT

THE CONSUMER PROTECTION FRAMEWORK. As a first important context, the consumer protection framework is analysed in this section, which consists of those instruments that are applicable to all forms of advertising and marketing, regardless of the format or medium. First, it discusses the provisions of the Unfair Commercial Practices Directive that are relevant in the context of commercial communication. Second, it covers the self-regulatory Code on Advertising Practice of the International Chamber of Commerce, which contains provisions that are applicable to all advertising formats as well as specific protections for children and adolescents. These two instruments form an important layer of protection for children against harmful or misleading commercial communication.

1. UNFAIR COMMERCIAL PRACTICES DIRECTIVE

BACKGROUND: THE PROTECTION OF CHILDREN AS VULNERABLE CONSUMERS. According to article 38 of the EU Charter of Fundamental Rights, consumers are entitled to a high level of consumer protection. In this regard, HELBERGER *et al.* describe that there are two distinct rationales that underlie European consumer law, being (1) empowering consumers as sovereign market actors and providing them with the necessary rights and information to act in that role and (2) protecting consumers in situations where they are the

[542] The selection of the instruments that were included in this chapter was done on a thematic basis, after a preliminary mapping of advertising self-regulatory instruments conducted within the frame of the AdLit Project. For the complete overview see V. Verdoodt, I. Lambrecht and E. Lievens, 'Mapping and Analysis of the Current Self- and Co-Regulatory Framework on Commercial Communication Aimed at Minors. A Report in the Framework of the AdLit SBO Project.' <www.adlit.be> accessed 20 November 2017. The chapter includes instruments at both the international and EU level.

weaker party in commercial dealings and unable to protect their rights, interests and safety themselves.[543] One of the measures adopted by the EU to protect consumers in the internal market is the Unfair Commercial Practices Directive ("UCP Directive"), which prohibits unfair commercial practices.[544] The UCP Directive is not restricted to specific products, media or types of market behaviour and is thus quite broad. It has principle-based provisions, allowing it to catch fast-evolving products, services and sales methods.[545] On the other hand, it is also narrower than most directives as it only applies to business-to-consumer practices and not to all market participants alike.[546] It is based on the principle of full harmonisation and aims to remove internal market barriers and increase legal certainty for both consumers and businesses.[547] The UCP Directive is of particular interest in relation to advertising directed at children as it is one of the cornerstones of EU consumer policy, explicitly recognising that children constitute a group of particularly vulnerable consumers in need of specific protection. The Directive has been receiving increasing attention in the context of for instance in-app purchases.[548]

Interplay with other legal instruments. Due to its broad scope of application, the UCP Directive applies to many commercial practices that are also regulated by other general or sector-specific EU legislation (*infra*). In this regard, the European Commission has clarified that:

> *"The Directive works as a "safety net" ensuring that a high common level of consumer protection against unfair commercial practices can be maintained in all sectors, including by complementing and filling gaps in other EU law".*[549]

543 N. Helberger, F. J. Zuiderveen Borgesius and A. Reyna, 'The Perfect Match? A Closer Look at the Relationship between EU Consumer Law and Data Protection Law' (2017) 5 28, 7.

544 Directive 2005/29/EC of the European Parliament and the Council of 11 May 2005 concerning unfair business-to-consumer commercial practices in the internal market and amending Council Directive 84/450/EEC, Directives 97/7/EC, 98/27/EC and 2002/65 /EC of the European Parliament and of the Council and Regulation (EC) No 2006/2004 of the European Parliament and of the Council ('Unfair Commercial Practices Directive').

545 European Commission, 'Commission Staff Working Document – Guidance on the Implementation/Application of Directive 2005/29/EC on Unfair Commercial Practices, SWD(2016) 163 Final.' (2016) <http://ec.europa.eu/justice/consumer-marketing/files/ucp_guidance_en.pdf> accessed 9 October 2017.

546 F. Henning-Bodewig, 'Directive 2005/29/EC & Directive 2006/114/EC.' in O. Castendyk, E. Dommering and A. Scheuer (eds), *European Media Law* (Kluwer Law International 2008).

547 Recital 5, 12 and 13 UCP Directive.

548 D. Mac Sithigh, 'Multiplayer Games: Tax, Copyright, Consumers and the Video Game Industries' (2014) 5 European Journal of Law and Technology <http://ejlt.org/article/view/324> accessed 28 November 2017.

549 European Commission, 'Commission Staff Working Document – Guidance on the Implementation/Application of Directive 2005/29/EC on Unfair Commercial Practices, SWD(2016) 163 Final.' (n 545).

If provisions of applicable sector-specific legislation overlap with provisions of the UCP Directive, the *lex specialis* rules will prevail.[550] Nevertheless, it has been argued that the Directive applies to providers of audiovisual media service providers and advertisers alongside the AVMS Directive (*infra*), even if recital 82 negates the parallel application of these instruments. More specifically, Cole argues that given their application overlap in the context of new converged media services, the relevance of this exception is debatable.[551]

Full harmonisation. The UCP Directive provides full harmonisation within its broad scope of application. However, a number of important issues still require clarification and it would take many years for the CJEU to resolve all these questions. The Directive also contains a rudimentary regulation of sanctions and leaves it up to the Member State to decide what constitutes adequate and effective means to combat unfair commercial practices.[552]

1.1. Scope and definitions

Scope and definitions. The UCP Directive is applicable to commercial practices, which includes commercial communication such as advertising and marketing by a trader. Such commercial communication has to be "*directly connected with the promotion, sale or supply of a product to consumers*".[553] The Directive aims at protecting consumers from unfair business-to-consumer commercial practices. Relatedly, consumers are to be regarded as "*any natural person who is acting for purposes outside of his trade, business or profession*", which may include children.[554] Important to note is that the Directive only

550 According to article 3(4) UCP Directive: "*in case of conflict between the provisions of this Directive and other Community rules regulating specific aspects of unfair commercial practices, the latter shall prevail and apply to those specific aspects*". Furthermore, Recital 10 clarifies that a provision of EU law will prevail over the UCP Directive if three conditions are fulfilled: (1) it has EU law status, (2) it regulates a specific aspect of commercial practices and (3) there is a conflict or overlap between the two provisions. European Commission, 'Commission Staff Working Document – Guidance on the Implementation/Application of Directive 2005/29/EC on Unfair Commercial Practices, SWD(2016) 163 Final.' (n 545). For a recent example see *Dyson* [2018] CJEU C-632/16.

551 M. Cole, 'New Forms of Commercial Communications in a Converged Audiovisual Sector' [2014] Observatory/Observatoire/Informationsstellen-Shop 41–53 <http://shop.obs.coe.int/en/iris-legal-publications/23-iris-special-new-forms-of-commercial-communications-in-a-converged-audiovisual-sector.html> accessed 16 April 2018; Blázquez and others (n 629) 25.

552 Article 11 (1) UCP Directive. However, a mere self-control system (e.g. code of conduct) would not be sufficient. Consumers need to be able to take legal action or bring the matter before an administrative body. Henning-Bodewig (n 546) 1075. Furthermore, article 13 UCP Directive requires Member States to lay down penalties for infringements of the national provisions that implement the Directive, including an action for injunction and interlocutory protection based thereon.

553 Article 2 (d) UCP Directive.

554 Article 2 (a) UCP Directive.

protects the economic interests of consumers and no other interests like health and safety aspects of products. The Directive stipulates protections against unfair commercial practices on the three distinct levels namely (1) the general clause; (2) two small general clauses specifying protections against misleading and aggressive commercial practices respectively and; (3) a blacklist contained in Annex I that specifies certain practices which are deemed *de facto* unfair as referred to in article 5(5) of the UCP Directive. Although the Directive is constructed in line with the sequence presented in the previous sentence, in effect it operates in reverse with the general clause acting as a safety net.

1.2. Substantive requirements for commercial practices, including advertising

1.2.1. Unfair commercial practice

General rule. The core provision of the Directive is article 5 (1), which contains the general prohibition of unfair commercial practices. According to this article, a commercial practice shall be unfair if

(a) it is contrary to the requirements of professional diligence, and
(b) it materially distorts or is likely to materially distort the economic behaviour with regard to the product of the average consumer whom it reaches or to whom it is addressed, or of the average member of the group when a commercial practice is directed to a particular group of consumers.

Thus, there is a two-step criterion for determining unfairness.[555] First, the lack of professional diligence of the trader and second, the influence on the economic behaviour of the consumer. Although the idea of the Directive is to protect all consumers from unfair commercial practices, the Directive takes as a benchmark the average consumer, who is "*reasonably well-informed and reasonably observant and circumspect*"[556], taking into account social, cultural and linguistic factors.[557] Especially in relation to vulnerable consumers[558], recital 19 stresses that

> *Where certain characteristics such as age, physical or mental infirmity or credulity make consumers particularly susceptible to a commercial practice or to the underlying*

555 Henning-Bodewig (n 546).
556 Article 2 (b) UCP Directive.
557 M. L. Chiarella, 'The Regulation of Child Consumption in European Law: Rights, Market and New Perspectives' (Social Science Research Network 2009) SSRN Scholarly Paper ID 1440251 5 <https://papers.ssrn.com/abstract=1440251> accessed 28 November 2017. European Commission, 'Commission Staff Working Document – Guidance on the Implementation/Application of Directive 2005/29/EC on Unfair Commercial Practices, SWD(2016) 163 Final.' (n 545) 37.
558 Chiarella (n 557).

> *product and the economic behaviour only of such consumers is likely to be distorted by the practice in a way that the trader can reasonably foresee, it is appropriate to ensure that they are adequately protected by assessing the practice from the perspective of the average member of that group. (emphasis added)*

For instance, children might be particularly vulnerable to advertisements about videogames, whereas teenagers are often targeted by rogue traders that promote appealing products by exploiting teenagers' immaturity and their lack of attention or reflection (e.g. mobile phone services ad saying that by subscribing to the service, they will make friends more easily).[559] However, the average consumer test is not a statistical test.[560] National courts and authorities will have to exercise their own faculty of judgment, having regard to the case-law of the Court of Justice of the European Union, to determine the typical reaction of the average consumer in a given case. This is also why the European Commission thought it was appropriate to include in the list of practices which are in all circumstances unfair a provision which, without imposing an outright ban on advertising directed at children, protects them from direct exhortations to purchase (*infra*).[561]

1.2.2. Misleading commercial practice

Misleading commercial practices. Deception is one of the examples the UCP Directive mentions, where unfairness should be assumed in particular.[562] There are two types of deception, (1) misleading commercial practices and (2) misleading omissions. A commercial practice will be misleading if an average consumer takes a transactional decision which he would normally not have taken, because he is deceived.[563] The assessment should take into account the facts and circumstances of the specific case. Moreover, particular points of reference include the nature of the product, its main characteristics, the price, etc.[564] A misleading omission on the other hand concerns material information needed by the average consumer, to make an informed transactional decision, thereby causing him or her to take a decision which he or she would not have taken otherwise.[565] As mentioned, the benchmark is the average consumer (this can be a child when the commercial communication is aimed at children). Finally, the Directive has added a practice which is relevant for new advertising

559 European Commission, 'Commission Staff Working Document – Guidance on the Implementation/Application of Directive 2005/29/EC on Unfair Commercial Practices, SWD(2016) 163 Final.' (n 545) 45.
560 Recital 18 UCP Directive.
561 Recital 18 as well as article 5.3. and Annex I, point 28 UCP Directive.
562 Henning-Bodewig (n 546) 1073.
563 Article 6 UCP Directive.
564 See article 6 (1) subparagraphs a-g UCP Directive.
565 Article 7 UCP Directive.

formats to its blacklist of practices which are under all circumstances prohibited. More specifically, Annex I prohibits:

> *practices using editorial content in the media to promote a product where a trader has paid for the promotion without making that clear in the content or by images or sounds clearly identifiable by the consumer (misleading commercial practices)*[566] *(Emphasis added)*

This could be of particular relevance for advertisements posted by bloggers or Twitter account holders who are being paid to do so by the brand.[567]

1.2.3. Aggressive commercial practice

Aggressive commercial practices. The UCP Directive protects consumers against so-called 'aggressive' commercial practices. According to the UCP Directive, marketing techniques are aggressive, if they "*by harassment, coercion or undue influence significantly impair the freedom of choice or conduct of the average consumer*".[568] Although actual harassment or coercion (including the use of physical force) are not realistic in the context of advertising, the milder form of influence – undue influence – could be applicable.[569] The qualification of undue influence will depend on the specificities of the particular case. Therefore, when it comes to children, the assessment should take into account children's innocence resulting in a much lower threshold than for adults. Of particular relevance is the provision which protects children from direct exhortations to purchase. Indeed, Annex I lists the following practices as being aggressive:

> *"practices which include in an advertisement a direct exhortation to children to buy advertised products or persuade their parents or other adults to buy advertised products for (aggressive commercial practices)."*

Thus, the key element here is the direct exhortation to children. Accordingly, it is an unfair practice for sellers to exhort children to pester an adult to buy advertised products. This ban is valid for all media, including television as well as internet advertising.[570] For instance, the TV advertisement "Your favourite

566 Annex I, point 28 and 11 UCP Directive.

567 L. Scaife, *Handbook of Social Media and the Law* (Informa Law from Routledge 2015) 346.

568 Article 8 UCP Directive.

569 By undue influence is meant that the company holds a position of power in relation to the consumer and exploits this to exert pressure, in order to significantly restrict the consumer's ability to make an informed decision. Article 2 (j) UCP Directive.

570 European Commission, 'Communication To The European Parliament, The Council And The European Economic And Social Committee On the Application of the Unfair Commercial Practices Directive – Achieving a High Level of Consumer Protection Building Trust in the Internal Market' (2013) <https://eur-lex.europa.eu/legal-content/EN/TXT/?uri=celex%3A52013DC0138> accessed 31 July 2018.

book is now out on DVD – tell your dad to buy it for you!" would constitute an aggressive commercial practice, prohibited under the Unfair Commercial Practices Directive.[571] Conversely, mere indirect exhortations do not automatically constitute unfair commercial practices. An indirect exhortation requires an intermediate step between the advertisement and the decision to buy, and only generally presents the options to do this. For instance in a case before the Austrian Supreme Court, a website operator had advertised a video game for schoolchildren (up to 14 years) both on the website and on Austrian television.[572] The advertisement contained general wording such as 'now available' and 'available in retail'. In addition, it included info on how to order the product (e.g. reference to the website link). Both the court at first instance and the court of appeal ruled that these advertisements were direct exhortations aimed at children. However, the Austrian Supreme Court overruled these decisions as these were only indirect exhortations.

1.3. Refit exercise

Outcome of the Refit exercise. In 2017, the European Commission conducted a comprehensive evaluation of the six directives that have built up the core horizontal EU consumer and marketing law, including the UCP Directive.[573] In its Fitness Check report, the Commission concluded that

> *"the substantive rules of the evaluated directives are capable of addressing the existing consumer problems, including new infringements in the online environment even if they were adopted before the age of e-commerce kicked in".*[574]

Therefore, rather than reviewing the legislative instruments, the Commission stressed that the key solution to achieving a higher level of consumer protection lies in a combination of a better enforcement of the existing rules and increased awareness among consumers, traders and enforcement bodies.[575] In this regard,

---

571 European Commission, 'Communication To The European Parliament, The Council And The European Economic And Social Committee On the Application of the Unfair Commercial Practices Directive – Achieving a High Level of Consumer Protection Building Trust in the Internal Market' (n 570).

572 Austrian Supreme Court, *Videospiel D-Universe,* 9 July 2013, https://webgate.ec.europa.eu/ucp/public/index.cfm?event=public.cases.showCase&caseID=570&articleID accessed 31 July 2018.

573 The other Directives that formed part of the Refit Exercise are the Unfair Contract Terms Directive 93/13/EEC, the Price Indication Directive 98/6/EC, the Consumer Sales and Guarantees Directive 1999/114/EC, the Injunctions Directive 2009/22/EC and the Misleading and Compartive Advertising Directive 2006/114/EC.

574 European Commission, 'Commission Staff Working Document: Executive Summary of the Fitness Check Report, SWD(2017) 208 Final' 2.

575 European Commission, 'Commission Staff Working Document: Executive Summary of the Fitness Check Report, SWD(2017) 208 Final' (n 574) 2.

the recent revision of the Consumer Protection Cooperation and the new Regulation (EU) 2017/2394 can be mentioned.[576] This Regulation, which will be applicable as of 17 January 2020, lays down a framework for cooperation for national authorities from all countries in the European Economic Area to jointly address breaches of consumer rules when the trader and consumer are established in different countries.[577]

2. SELF-REGULATION: ICC-CODE

International Chamber of Commerce ("ICC"). Aside from legislative instruments, the industry itself has also played a significant role in the protection of consumers against harmful commercial practices. At the international level, the business organisation bringing together numerous enterprises of different sectors all over the world is the ICC. The main activities of the organisation are setting rules, resolving disputes and policy advocacy. The ICC collaborates with the United Nations, the World Trade Organisation and several other bodies. It has been offering guidance on marketing and advertising ever since 1937 and its Code on Advertising Practice ("ICC Code") has been the foundation of many self-regulatory initiatives of the advertising sector.[578] Moreover, its provisions have also served as a basis for the development of the Directive on misleading and unfair advertising in 1987 as well as the predecessor of the AVMS Directive, the Television without Frontiers Directive (*infra*), with respect to television advertising in 1984.[579] More specifically, it is based on the general principles of honesty, legal compliance, truthfulness and decency of advertisements by providing ethical guidelines that create a level playing field for advertisers across different sectors and using different advertising formats. As such, the ICC believes that there is less of a need for legislative action.[580] The Code aims at enhancing harmonisation and coherence of the rules, however, the ICC itself does not have any powers to require national SRO's to adopt or implement the Code in a uniform way.[581] Each national ICC Committee or

---

576 Regulation (EU) 2017/2394 of the European Parliament and of the Council of 12 december 2017 on cooperation between national authorities responsible for the enforcement of consumer protection laws and repealing Regulation (EC) No 2006/2004.

577 For instance, the Network regularly carries out EU-wide screenings of websites ('sweeps') to check whether a given sector is complying with consumer rules. For more information see https://ec.europa.eu/info/sites/info/files/factsheet_ensuring_consumer_rights_en.pdf.

578 Durovic and Micklitz (n 142) 36.

579 European Audiovisual Observatory, 'Co-Regulation of the Media in Europe' (2003) <https://www.ivir.nl/publicaties/download/IRIS-Special-Co-regulation-of-the-Media-in-Europe.pdf> accessed 31 July 2018.

580 ICC, 'ICC and the Code' <www.codescentre.com/about-us.aspx> accessed 31 July 2018.

581 P. Verbruggen, 'Enforcement of Transnational Private Regulation of Advertising Practices: Decentralization, Mechanisms and Procedural Fairness' in Fabrizio Cafaggi (ed),

group may appoint delegates to take part in meetings of the ICC Commission on Marketing and Advertising, which convenes twice a year to examine marketing- and advertising- related policy issues of interest to world business. More in particular, the Commission revises drafts of codes, rules and opinions and outlines strategies for the future.

2.1. Scope and definitions

SCOPE. The ICC Code applies to:

> *"All advertising and other marketing communications for the promotion of any kind of goods and services, corporate and institutional promotion included".*

More specifically, it applies to commercial communications in their entirety, including all words, music, images, etc. The revised Code covers both traditional and new forms of commercial communication, following the ICC policy decision of 2006. It also includes a chapter on digital interactive media techniques (Chapter D) on all kinds of platforms or devices. Moreover, the Code contains specific provisions regulating the use of online behavioural advertising.

DEFINITION OF A CHILD. As there are significant differences in defining the term "child" across different countries, the provisions of the ICC Code that apply when advertising is aimed at children should be interpreted according to local rules. Important to note is that in the context of the data protection rules (e.g. rules on behavioural advertising), there are specific provisions of the Code that are applicable to children 12 years and under (e.g. the parental consent requirement). In this regard, the ICC has clarified in its Statement on Code Interpretation (2016) that the Code distinguishes between children (under 13s) and youngsters (under 18s). The ICC opted for this distinction because of the following reasons:

> *"the very real differences in teens' interests as compared to children, the practical impediments to obtaining parental consent where data collection from teens is concerned, sensitivities about teen privacy rights, and respect for freedom of commercial communications where the principal audience is adults".*[582]

Moreover, the ICC recognises the different cognitive abilities and stresses that rules that try to treat teenagers like children are simply unworkable.[583]

Enforcement of Transnational Regulation: Ensuring Compliance in a Global World (Edward Elgar Publishing 2012) 304.

582 ICC, 'ICC Releases Statement on Age Considerations for Marketing and Advertising to Children and Teens – ICC – International Chamber of Commerce' (2016) <https://iccwbo.org/media-wall/news-speeches/icc-releases-statement-age-considerations-marketing-advertising-children-teens/> accessed 31 July 2018.

583 The reality of the matter is that teenagers often have money, whereas children usually do not.

Reasonable consumer. The provisions of the ICC Code should be interpreted in light of the advertising format used and its potential impact on the 'reasonable consumer'. Accordingly, regard must be had for the characteristics of the targeted consumer group, including their knowledge, experience, but also cultural, social and linguistic factors. This is of particular importance when the targeted consumer group consists of children, as their natural credulity and inexperience should be kept in mind.[584]

The following subsections provide an overview of the provisions that are applicable to all advertising formats (including *inter alia* television advertisements, digital advertisements such as advergames and personalised advertising). It includes both general principles as well as principles that are only applicable if the commercial communication is aimed at children.

2.2. *Substantive requirements for all advertising formats*

Basic Principles. Article 1 of the ICC Code lists the basic principles upon which all the other provisions are built. First of all, commercial communication needs to be honest and it should not abuse the trust of consumers. More specifically, it must not exploit consumers' lack of experience or knowledge, which in relation to children could be of particular importance. Furthermore, commercial communication should be decent (article 3 ICC Code) and truthful (article 5 ICC Code).

Identification. A crucial requirement for both traditional and new forms of commercial communication is the identification requirement of article 9 of the ICC Code. This provision requires that:

> *"Marketing communications should be clearly distinguishable as such, whatever their form and whatever the medium used."*

In particular, the Code stresses that in cases where the advertisement appears on a medium which contains news or other editorial content, the advertisements should be portrayed in such a way that it is readily recognisable as such and that the identity of the advertiser is also apparent. Similarly, commercial messages should not be disguised as for example private blogs, user-generated content or independent reviews.

2.3. *Specific protections for children*

Special care for children. Of particular relevance to the protection of children and young people against certain forms of advertising is article 18 of the ICC Code. This article requires special care from advertisers and marketers that

[584] Article 18 ICC Code; ICC, 'Interpretation of the Consolidated ICC Code' (2014) <www.codescentre.com/icc-code/general-provisions.aspx#gen1> accessed 31 July 2018.

develop advertising campaigns for children and young people. More specifically, (1) such advertisements should not undermine positive social behaviour, lifestyles and attitudes; and (2) products that are unsuitable for children should not be advertised in media targeted to them, or advertisements targeted towards children should not appear on media where the editorial content is not suitable for children (e.g. an online wineshop). In addition, the ICC Code highlights three important aspects which advertisers and marketers need to take in to account:

Table 4: ICC Code Provisions on children and young people (Source: article 18 ICC Code)

Focus	Article 18 ICC Code – Children and young people
Children's inexperience and credulity	When demonstrating a product's performance and use: – Do not understate the skill needed to produce the result shown; – Do not exaggerate the true characteristics of the product (e.g. size, value, durability); – Provide sufficient info if additional products are needed. Enable children to be able to distinguish between reality and fantasy. Ensure that commercial communications directed to children should be clearly distinguishable to them as such.
Avoidance of harm	– Do not use any statement or visual treatment that could harm children mentally, morally or physically; – Do not portray children in unsafe situations or encourage them to engage in harmful actions.
Social values	– Do not suggest that possession or use of the product will give physical, psychological or social advantages over other children (or that not possessing the product would result in a disadvantage); – Have regard for parents' authority and respect social and cultural values; – Do not include a direct appeal to children to persuade their parents to buy the specific product; – Present the price in such a way that children have a realistic perception of the value of the product (e.g. do not imply that the product is within reach of the family budget); – When inviting children to contact the marketer, encourage them to obtain parental consent.

SECTION II. THE AUDIOVISUAL MEDIA SERVICES CONTEXT

Background. Since the development of audiovisual media, companies have naturally used this means of communication to inform viewers on their products and services. The first steps towards an EU audiovisual policy date back to the early 1980s, triggered by the developments of satellite broadcasting.[585] As broadcast signals did not stop at the national border, the EU adopted certain minimum

585 'EU Audiovisual and Media Policies – Historical Framework| Europa' <http://ec.europa.eu/archives/information_society/avpolicy/reg/history/index_en.htm> accessed 23 July 2018.

standards on audiovisual media in 1989 for all Member States in the Television without Frontiers Directive ("TWFD").[586] In relation to advertising, the TWFD regulated certain aspects which are largely typical for television advertising such as hidden advertisements, sponsorship, the separation of programmes and commercials and maximum hourly amounts. For other aspects of advertising, the TWFD took a more horizontal approach by laying down specific rules for instance in relation to the protection of minors and restrictions for the protection of health.[587] Due to the technological and market developments this framework was revised and amended in 1997 and 2007 and finally renamed Audiovisual Media Services Directive ("AVMS Directive") and codified in 2010.[588] Since its revision in 2007, new types of services and user experiences have emerged, which significantly changed people's viewing habits and particularly among the younger viewers. Although the television remains an important screen for consuming audiovisual media content, more and more viewers have moved to tablets and smartphones to watch content on demand. In this regard, the European Commission announced in its Digital Single Market Strategy that it would review the functioning of the rules of the AVMS Directive in 2016, under the Regulatory Fitness and Performance Programme (REFIT) of the Better Regulation Framework.[589] The goal of the review was to ensure that Europe's audiovisual media landscape is made fit for purpose in the digital age. In preparation of this review, the Commission launched a public consultation in July 2015, to gather inputs on the functioning and impact of the Directive and on policy options for the future of the Directive.[590] The synopsis report showed a lack of consensus amongst the various stakeholders concerning commercial communications.[591] The revision of the AVMS Directive followed the Ordinary Legislative Procedure whereby the European Commission, the European Parliament and the Council act jointly and

---

586 E.J. Dommering, 'General Introduction Towards a European Media Law' in O. Castendyk, E.J. Dommering and Alexander Scheuer (eds), *European Media Law* (Kluwer Law International 2008) 14.

587 'EU Audiovisual and Media Policies – History of TVwF| Europa' <http://ec.europa.eu/archives/information_society/avpolicy/reg/history/historytvwf/index_en.htm> accessed 23 July 2018.

588 O. Castendyk and L. Woods, 'Part 2 – European Media Law' in O. Castendyk, E. Dommering and A. Scheuer (eds), *European Media Law* (Kluwer Law International 2008) 273.

589 European Commission, 'REFIT Evaluation and Impact Assessment of the EU Audiovisual Media Services Directive 2010/13/EU (AVMSD)' <http://ec.europa.eu/smart-regulation/roadmaps/docs/2015_cnect_006_cwp_review_avmsd_iia_en.pdf> accessed 2 April 2018.

590 European Commission, 'Contributions and Preliminary Trends of the Public Consultation on Audiovisual Media Services (AVMSD)' (*Digital Single Market*) <https://ec.europa.eu/digital-single-market/en/news/contributions-and-preliminary-trends-public-consultation-audiovisual-media-services-avmsd> accessed 10 April 2018.

591 European Commission, 'Synopsis Report of the Public Consultation on Directive 2010/13/EU on Audiovisual Media Services (AVMSD) – A Media Framework for the 21st Century' 5 <https://ec.europa.eu/digital-single-market/en/news/report-public-consultation-review-audiovisual-media-services-directive-avmsd> accessed 10 April 2018.

on equal footing.[592] The EU legislators explicitly recognised the evolutions in the market of audiovisual media services due to the ongoing convergence of television and internet services in their final text.[593] These evolutions, necessitated the creation of a level-playing field for audiovisual media services. This section focuses on the 2018 version of the AVMS Directive (Directive (EU) 2018/1808).[594]

MINIMUM HARMONISATION. Ever since the TWF Directive the objective of European broadcasting legislation has been minimum harmonisation.[595] The aim of the AVMS Directive is to promote the free movement of audiovisual media services within the EU and at its core is the country of origin principle.[596] To ensure that free movement is acceptable in the different Member States, the AVMS Directive defines certain minimum requirements that audiovisual media service providers must respect.[597] Accordingly, it is left up to the Member States to decide whether or not to enact stricter regulations.[598] The AVMS Directive also contains several concepts that need to be interpreted by the Member States in their national laws. For instance, the concept 'audiovisual media service' is defined by referring to several unclear sub-concepts, all which lack clarity in scope and substance.[599]

---

592 Blázquez and others (n 551) 62. The revised Directive will enter into force after its publication in the EU Official Journal (on the twentieth day). The EP and the Council agreed on the transposition period, which is to last for 21 months. Council of the European Union, 'Proposal for a Directive of the European Parliament and of the Council Amending Directive 2010/13/EU on the Coordination of Certain Provisions Laid down by Law, Regulation or Administrative Action in Member States Concerning the Provision of Audiovisual Media Services (Audiovisual Media Services Directive) in View of Changing Market Realities – Analysis of the Final Compromise Text with a View to Agreement' (2018) 2 <http://data.consilium.europa.eu/doc/document/ST-9817-2018-INIT/en/pdf> accessed 25 July 2018.

593 Recital 1 of the AVMS Directive.

594 To avoid confusion, any references to the former AVMS Directive will be indicated by the term '2010 AVMS Directive'. The version discussed in this section of the book is: Directive (EU) 2018/1808 of the European Parliament and of the Council of 14 November 2018 amending Directive 2010/13/EU on the coordination of certain provisions laid down by law, regulation or administrative action in Member States concerning the provision of audiovisual media services (Audiovisual Media Services Directive) in view of changing market realities. Hereafter AVMS Directive.

595 V. Little, 'Audiovisual Media Services Directive: Europe's Modernization of Broadcast Services Regulations' [2008] Journal of Law, Technology & Policy 14, 223.

596 This entails that providers of audiovisual media services only have to abide by the rules of the Member State with jurisdiction over them, but can operate in all Member States. F. J. Cabrera Blázquez and others, 'On-Demand Services and the Material Scope of the AVMSD' [2016] IRIS Plus, European Audiovisual Observatory 74, 21.

597 Blázquez et al. clarify that a "*receiving member state with stricter rules than those laid down by the AVMSD cannot restrict the reception of services from another member state on the basis of those stricter rules. Exceptions apply in specific circumstances, set out in the AVMSD.*" Blázquez and others (n 596) 21.

598 Article 4 of the AVMS Directive: "*Member States shall remain free to require media service providers under their jurisdiction to comply with more detailed or stricter rules in the fields coordinated by this Directive, provided that such rules are in compliance with Union law.*"

599 R. Mansell and M. Raboy, *The Handbook of Global Media and Communication Policy* (John Wiley & Sons 2011).

Scope. The territorial scope of the AVMS Directive is limited to service providers under EU jurisdiction[600], which requires that they are either (1) established in a Member State[601], (2) use a satellite up-link situated in that Member State[602] or (3) use satellite capacity appertaining to that Member State.[603] As regards its material scope of application, the Directive first of all covers both linear and on-demand audiovisual media services (e.g. scheduled programming delivered via internet or mobile networks).[604] In relation to these services, it adopts a two-tier approach, which entails that certain basic rules apply to all audiovisual media services whereas the rules specific to broadcasters will only apply to linear audiovisual media services. Second, after its latest revision, the scope of the Directive has broadened to include video-sharing platforms[605], for which a number of specific provisions are applicable. Third, social media could also fall within the scope of the Directive, if the provision of programmes and user-generated videos constitutes an essential functionality of that service. The audiovisual content may not be merely ancillary or form only a minor part of the activities of that service.[606]

---

600 Article 2 (1) of the AVMS Directive.

601 According to article 2 para 3 of the AVMS Directive, a media service provider is established in a Member State if *(a) its head office is in that Member State and the editorial decisions about the audiovisual media service are taken in that Member State, or (b) its head office head office in one Member State but editorial decisions on the audiovisual media service are taken in another Member State, it shall be deemed to be established in the Member State where a significant part of the workforce involved in the pursuit of the programme-related audiovisual media service activity operates. If a significant part of the workforce involved in the pursuit of the programme-related audiovisual media service activity operates in each of those Member States, the media service provider shall be deemed to be established in the Member State where it has its head office. If a significant part of the workforce involved in the pursuit of the programme-related audiovisual media service activity operates in neither of those Member States, the media service provider shall be deemed to be established in the Member State where it first began its activity in accordance with the law of that Member State, provided that it maintains a stable and effective link with the economy of that Member State; (c) if a media service provider has its head office in a Member State but decisions on the audiovisual media service are taken in a third country, or vice versa, it shall be deemed to be established in the Member State concerned provided that a significant part of the workforce involved in the pursuit of the audiovisual media service activity operates in that Member State.*

602 Article 2, para 4 a) of the AVMS Directive.

603 Article 2, para 4 b) of the AVMS Directive.

604 The scope of the AVMSD was considerably extended in 2010 in comparison to its predecessor the TWFD, which only covered traditional broadcasting. The intention of the European Commission at the time was that the application of the rules would not be dependent upon the delivery platform used. Chavannes and Castendyk (n 36) 806.

605 Article 1 (aa) of the AVMS Directive defines a video-sharing service as: "*a service as defined by Articles 56 and 57 of the Treaty on the Functioning of the European Union where the principal purpose of the service or of a dissociable section thereof or an essential functionality of the service is devoted to providing programmes, user-generated videos, or both, to the general public, for which the video-sharing platform provider does not have editorial responsibility, in order to inform, entertain or educate, by means of an electronic communications network within the meaning of point (a) of Article 2 of Directive 2002/21/EC and the organisation of which is determined by the video-sharing platform provider, including by automatic means or algorithms in particular by displaying, tagging and sequencing.*"

606 In this regard, it will be up to the European Commission to issue guidelines on the practical application of the criterion of essential functionality.

1. DEFINITIONS

DEFINITIONS. The scope of the Directive can be further delineated by examining the definitions of the main concepts, such as audiovisual media service, audiovisual commercial communication and audiovisual media service provider. The definition of a video-sharing service is discussed in the next chapter, section three, in relation to vlogging advertising.

1.1. Audiovisual media service

DEFINITION. The notion of audiovisual media service is a central definition to which the other definitions of the AVMS Directive relate.[607] An audiovisual media service covers both television broadcasts (linear) and on-demand (non-linear) audiovisual media services (e.g., Netflix) irrespective of the delivery platform used.[608] To qualify as an audiovisual media service, seven (cumulative) constitutive elements need to be fulfilled[609]:

Table 1: Criteria for audiovisual media services[610]

Criterion	Covered	Excluded
Economic activity	A service normally provided for remuneration by a public or private service enterprise.	Primarily non-economic activities not in competition with television broadcasting (e.g. personal websites or weblogs, private communications, or user-generated content, videoblogs without advertising or banners).
Editorial responsibility	Only audiovisual media services in which a professional media service provider is responsible for the editorial design and final compilation of a programme for broadcasting in accordance with a fixed programme schedule or for viewing on-demand from catalogue.	A-posteriori control (e.g. YouTube).

607 Chavannes and Castendyk (n 36) 812.

608 Defined as follows under article 1 (a) (i) of the AVMS Directive "*a service as defined by Articles 56 and 57 of the Treaty on the Functioning of the European Union which is under the editorial responsibility of a media service provider and the principal purpose of which is the provision of programmes, in order to inform, entertain or educate, to the general public by electronic communications networks within the meaning of point (a) of Article 2 of Directive' 2002/21/EC.*"

609 Article 1 (a) (i) AVMS Directive.

610 Valerie Verdoodt, E Lievens and L Hellemans, 'Mapping and Analysis of the Current Legal Framework of Advertising Aimed at Minors.' (2015) <www.adlit.be/output>.

Criterion	Covered	Excluded
Programmes[611]	Moving images with or without sound constituting an individual item in a schedule or catalogue. Including on-demand AVMS.	Audio-only services (e.g. radio, electronic versions of newspapers and magazines, blogs).
Principal purpose or principle purpose of a dissociable section thereof	Focus on audiovisual aspect.	Service with ancillary audiovisual aspect (e.g. websites that contain audiovisual elements only in an ancillary manner like a travel agent, car manufacturer).
Inform, entertain, educate	Impact on the way people form their opinions.	Audiovisual content with no editorial aspects (e.g. webcams of ski resorts), the purpose of the audiovisual content is to promote for purely commercial purpose the product or service advertised (e.g. a video channel on YouTube of a car company with solely promotional videos about cars)[612]
General public	'Mass media', 'that is, which are intended for reception by, and which could have a clear impact on, a significant proportion of the general public'.	Private correspondence (such as e-mail and faxes) or distribution of programmes to a restricted group, 'narrowcasting' (i.e. promotion spots on internal video circuit of supermarket).
Electronic communications network	In line with the e-commerce Directive. Examples are the provision of service via telephone lines (such as xDSL), cable, satellite and wireless communication systems such as GSM, UMTS and Wi-Fi.	Sending films by post.

1.2. Audiovisual commercial communication

RELATIONSHIP AUDIOVISUAL MEDIA SERVICE AND –COMMERCIAL COMMUNICATION. A second important concept of the AVMS Directive is 'audiovisual commercial communication' ("ACC"). Interestingly, the concept has also been included in the definition of an audiovisual media service. As such, depending how article 1(a) is read, it could be argued that audiovisual commercial communication is either a separate category of audiovisual media services in addition to television broadcasts and on-demand services, or something that is not a service in its own right but which forms an integral

611 This category is further discussed below under the heading audiovisual commercial communication.

612 *Peugeot Deutschland GmbH v Deutsche Umwelthilfe eV* [2018] CJEU C-132/17.

part of a television broadcast or on-demand service.[613] This distinction is important as the AVMS Directive provides a set of general requirements for audiovisual media services and a set of specific requirements for audiovisual commercial communications. In other words, it can be questioned whether the general requirements (e.g. the prohibition of hate speech) are also applicable to audiovisual commercial communication. Chavannes and Castendyk explain that the original proposal of the European Commission (2005) did not categorise audiovisual commercial communication as a service, but rather as a separate entity that accompanies audiovisual media services.[614] This is also reflected in the text of article 1 (h) AVMS Directive[615], which defines an audiovisual commercial communication as:

> *"images with or without sound which are designed to promote, directly or indirectly, the goods, services or image of a natural or legal entity pursuing an economic activity; such images accompany or are included in a programme or in a user-generated video in return for payment or for similar consideration or self-promotional purposes. Forms of audiovisual commercial communication include, inter alia, television advertising, sponsorship, teleshopping and product placement." (emphasis added by author)*

The legislator's idea at the time (2010) was to establish a common set of rules applicable to all different forms of promotional activities.[616] This set of rules included for instance rules on the protection of minors, public health provisions, etc. Moreover, the structural function of this article was to cover potential legal gaps and loopholes.[617] From this definition, two key concepts can be extracted, namely (1) images with the purpose to promote and (2) programme.

Purpose to promote. First, the images (with or without sound) as well as the person or entity making them or on whose behalf the communication is made, must have a promotional purpose. To the extent this intent is invisible, circumstantial evidence may help to identify this intent.[618] An indicator can, for example, be found in the fact that an announcement is made against financial compensation or that there are financial interests between the programme

613 For instance, the previous recital 22 of the 2010 AVMS Directive stated that: "*For the purposes of this Directive, the definition of an audiovisual media service should cover mass media in their function to inform, entertain and educate the general public, and should include audiovisual commercial communication* [...]".

614 Chavannes and Castendyk (n 36) 819.

615 P. Valcke and E. Lievens, 'Rethinking European Broadcasting Regulation: Unraveling Europe's Policy for the Digital Media Landscape: Critical Analysis of the Audiovisual Media Services Directive' (VUB Press 2009) 127–164.

616 Chavannes and Castendyk (n 36) 821–822.

617 Chavannes and Castendyk (n 36) 821–822.

618 Similar to the interpretation in the concept of television advertising (see *infra*).

maker and the owner of the product, even when no financial compensation was foreseen.[619]

PROGRAMME. Second, the images should accompany or form part of a programme[620], a set of moving images with or without sound[621] constituting an individual item within a schedule or a catalogue established by a media service provider and the form and content of which are comparable to the form and content of television broadcasting. In short, the images need to be part of a television broadcast (which is scheduled) or an on-demand service (which has a catalogue) in which it seems sufficient for the service provider to have a schedule or catalogue.[622] Under the former AVMS Directive, on-demand services had to be "television-like", meaning that for viewers they had to be comparable with a television broadcast[623] and the nature and the means of access to the service would lead the user to reasonably expect a regulatory protection within the scope of the AVMS Directive. In other words, a service's form and content needed to be sufficiently comparable to the form and content of television broadcasting.[624] This requirement was deleted in the revised AVMS Directive, and as such, programmes of any length, including short video clips, now fall within the scope of the AVMS Directive.[625]

CJEU CASE LAW ON THE SCOPE OF THE AVMS DIRECTIVE. Furthermore, the CJEU has provided clarifications regarding the scope of application of the AVMS Directive in its case law. For instance, in 2015 the CJEU assessed whether newspaper and magazine websites hosting a video section would fall under the definition of a programme and as such, would have to comply with the substantive requirements of the AVMS Directive. Recital 28 of the 2010 AVMS

---

619 *Degheldere vs VRT* [2000] VRM 2000/42; Dirk Voorhoof and Peggy Valcke, *Handboek mediarecht* (Larcier 2014) 561 <http://hdl.handle.net/1854/LU-5766382> accessed 25 July 2018.

620 Article 1 (b) AVMS Directive.

621 Silent movies are included but electronic magazines and newspapers, audio transmissions and radio broadcastes are not.

622 A user cannot select an on-demand service without being able to access the catalogue in some form but that does not mean the catalogue needs to be available in the form of a complete list of programmes: a search engine might equally provide access to the available content and content made available in such a fashion would presumably qualify as constituting an item within a catalogue. A broadcast service: the schedule will generally be publicised in advance, but the service is a broadcasting service even if the schedule becomes apparent by watching the various programmes as they are broadcast; Valcke and Lievens (n 615) 127–164. Chavannes and Castendyk (n 36) 821–822.

623 Chavannes and Castendyk (n 36) 821.

624 However, the notion of programme had – in any case – to be interpreted in a dynamic way, taking into account developments in television broadcasting. Examples of programmes include feature-length films, sports events, situation comedies, documentaries, children's programmes and original drama. Valcke and Lievens (n 615) 127–164.

625 Article 1 (b) of the AVMS Directive.

Directive explicitly excluded electronic versions of newspapers and magazines from its scope and recital 22 stated that the Directive is not applicable to '*all services the principal purpose of which is not the provision of programmes, i.e. where any audiovisual content is merely incidental to the service and not its principal purpose*'.[626] In light of this, the CJEU clarified that recital 28

> *"cannot be understood as meaning that an audiovisual service must systematically be excluded from the scope of [AVMSD] solely on the ground that the operator of the website of which that service is a part is a publishing company of an online newspaper"*.[627]

As such, the CJEU recognised the possibility of abuse and the need for consumer (or viewer) protection.[628] The CJEU continued by stating that a distinction should be made between the video section[629] and other sections of the magazine or newspaper websites to which the AVMS Directive would not apply. In practice[630], this means that websites incorporating both textual and video content, will have to comply with different requirements for the same advertising techniques depending on the medium in which the message is delivered.[631] In light of this, the revised Directive explicitly mentions that a dissociable section of a service that is not an audiovisual media service may also fall within the scope of the Directive, if this specific section complies with the definition.[632]

In February 2018, the CJEU also discussed the meaning of 'accompanying or being included in a programme' and the concepts audiovisual media service and audiovisual commercial communication in the *Peugeot Deutschland* case. Peugeot Deutschland had a video channel on YouTube containing short promotional videos for new passenger car models. In short, the CJEU first decided that such a promotional video channel does not have as its principal purpose the provision of programmes in order to inform, entertain or educate the general public.[633] The purely promotional purpose of the channel suffices to

---

626 According to WOODS: "recital 28 in identifying newspaper and magazines is a form of subspecies of this general rule" in recital 22 AVMS Directive. L. Woods, 'Audiovisual Media Services Regulation and The "Newspaper Exception"'' <http://eulawanalysis.blogspot.com/2015/10/audiovisual-media-services-regulation.html> accessed 24 November 2017.

627 Woods (n 626).

628 Woods (n 626).

629 In this regard, the CJEU confirmed that the length of videos is not the determining factor in such an assessment, and that there needs to be a link between the content of the newspaper website and the videos. Case C-347/14 New Media Online GmbH v. Bundeskommunikationssenat, 21 October 2015.

630 WOODS warns that the difficulty here lies in drawing the boundary between editorial and audiovisual content, especially if there are no structures separating them. Woods (n 626).

631 For instance, the promotion of a good or service integrated within a news article (native advertisement) requires compliance with the requirements for commercial communication in the lex generalis (see *infra* e-Commerce Directive), whereas the promotion in a video format requires compliance with the requirements of the AVMS Directive.

632 Recital 3 of the AVMS Directive.

633 *Peugeot Deutschland GmbH v. Deutsche Umwelthilfe eV* (n 611) paras 21–24.

exclude it from the scope of the definition of an audiovisual media service under article 1(1)(a)(i) of the AVMS Directive. Second, the CJEU analysed whether one single video on the channel could fall under the definition of an audiovisual commercial communication under article 1(1)(a)(ii) of the AVMS Directive. According to the Court, the videos could not be regarded as accompanying or being included in a programme, as they are individual elements independent of one another.[634] Furthermore, the CJEU dismissed Peugeot Deutschland's argument that the promotional images were situated at the beginning and the end of the video concerned, and therefore accompany or are included in that video, which in itself constitutes a programme. According to the Court, such a video is promotional in its entirety and as such, "*it would be artificial to assert that only the images at the beginning and the end of the video pursue advertising purposes*".[635]

1.3. Media service provider

DEFINITION. Another key notion in the AVMS Directive, and more specifically in relation to determining the actor responsible for complying with the requirements for audiovisual commercial communication, is the media service provider. Under the Directive, a media service provider is the natural or legal person with editorial responsibility for the choice of the audiovisual content of the audiovisual media service and determines the manner in which it is organised.[636] This editorial responsibility also constitutes one of the cumulative requirements for the definition of an audiovisual media service.[637] It entails the exercise of effective control both over the selection of the programmes and over their organisation either in a chronological schedule (television broadcasts) or in a catalogue (on-demand audiovisual media services). Even though the concept of 'effective control' is vague and not conclusive, CHAVANNES and CASTENDYK seem to interpret the exercise of effective control in terms of the ability to

> "*authorise the broadcasting or making available of the programme. In other words, the possession of the broadcasting rights determine an entity's possession of effective control, even if the actual technical transmission is performed by another entity.*"[638]

Effective control may be exercised in different ways, for instance, by selecting the programmes that should be acquired for transmission, or determining which

634 *Peugeot Deutschland GmbH v. Deutsche Umwelthilfe eV* (n 611) para 28.
635 *Peugeot Deutschland GmbH v. Deutsche Umwelthilfe eV* (n 611) paras 29–30.
636 Article 1(d) AVMS Directive.
637 Chavannes and Castendyk (n 36) 822–827.
638 Chavannes and Castendyk (n 36) 823. This is also confirmed by Recital 19, which excludes natural or legal persons who merely transmit programmes (for which the editorial responsibility lies with another party) from the definition of a media service provider.

programme should be broadcast during which particular timeslot. Moreover, it needs to be looked at in terms of final or end responsibility for the selection or programming.[639] Important to note is that it does not relate to control over the content of a certain programme.[640] In line with this, editorial responsibility for the programming of a service does not necessarily imply any legal liability under national law for the programme content or the services provided.[641]

2. SUBSTANTIVE REQUIREMENTS FOR AUDIOVISUAL COMMERCIAL COMMUNICATIONS

Restrictions for reasons of public interest. The AVMS Directive contains certain limitations on duration, frequency and harmful content of commercial communications, but also restrictions that enable viewers not to confuse commercial messages with other parts of the programme. According to Oster, these limitations to the freedom of commercial speech may be justified by overriding reasons related to the public interest, as audiovisual media in particular have a great impact on viewers and may shape or even mislead the public opinion.[642] These reasons may be *inter alia* consumer protection, editorial independence of the programme provider and maintaining a certain level of programme quality.

Two-tier approach to linear and on-demand services. The AVMS Directive acknowledges that a number of core societal values should be applicable to all audiovisual media services, including requirements for audiovisual commercial communications. However, it also sets out lighter regulatory requirements for on-demand services as compared to linear services.[643] The reasoning behind this two-tier or graduated approach[644] is that users have a higher degree of control and choice when it comes to on-demand services, as they can decide on the content and the time of viewing.[645] The following subsections first discuss the general principles and provisions for

639 Chavannes and Castendyk (n 36) 824.
640 Chavannes and Castendyk (n 36) 824.
641 Article 1 (c) AVMS Directive.
642 J. Oster, *European and International Media Law* (Cambridge University Press 2016) 168.
643 J. Metzdorf, 'The Implementation of the Audiovisual Media Services Directive by National Regulatory Authorities National Responses to Regulatory Challenges' (2014) 5 JIPITEC <www.jipitec.eu/issues/jipitec-5-2-2014/3998>.
644 This graduated approach entails *inter alia* that aside from the general principle (i.e. the identification principle) applicable to all forms of audiovisual commercial communications, there is an additional principle that applies solely to television advertising (i.e. the separation principle). In addition, the 2010 AVMS Directive contained a number of other restrictions for television advertising, but they were adapted in the latest revision in order to level the playing field between traditional and new media service providers.
645 Recital 55 AVMS Directive; Blázquez and others (n 596) 21.

audiovisual commercial communication which are not specifically aimed at the protection of children but of media viewers in general and are applicable to either all audiovisual media services or exclusively to linear services. It then continues with the specific protections for minors.

2.1. *General principles and provisions*

GENERAL PRINCIPLES. The two most important principles of the AVMS Directive in relation to commercial communication are (1) the principle of identification and (2) the principle of separation.[646] As per SCHAAR, "*these principles codify the fundamental concept of fairness in advertising*".[647] Both principles are aimed at reconciling the principle of freedom to produce (television) advertising with adequate protection for both audiovisual works and the general public, seen as both viewers and consumers.[648] In concreto, compliance with three key principles was envisaged[649]: (1) protecting the consumer, (2) guaranteeing the neutrality of media in view of the economic competition of third parties and (3) ensuring the editorial integrity of television programmes.[650] Protecting the consumer against disguised messages[651] seems the most obvious. If it is not clear what constitutes advertising or when the line between editorial and commercial content is blurred, viewers can be misled as to the nature of what they see. The same is valid in relation to competing market players, who want to be judged fairly and on editorial grounds by the media, not because a competitor has paid more to the media enterprise.[652] Further, the mandatory separation and identification of television advertising guarantees the editorial integrity of television programmes.[653] In an environment in which companies want to be perceived positively, undue influencing of editorial and fictional content

646 M. E. Price and S. Verhulst (eds), *Routledge Handbook of Media Law* (Routledge 2013).

647 O. Schaar, 'Television Advertising, Sponsorship and Teleshopping' in O. Castendyk, E.J. Dommering and A. Scheuer (eds), *European Media Law* (Kluwer Law International 2008) 479.

648 European Commission, 'Interpretative Communication on Certain Aspects of the Provisions on Televised Advertising in the "Television without Frontiers" Directive (2004/C 102/02)' 3.

649 O. Castendyk, 'Directive 89/552/EEC "Television without Frontiers" Directive.' in O. Castendyk, E.J. Dommering and A. Scheuer (eds), *European Media Law* (Kluwer Law International 2008) 312–313; O. Schaar, 'Directive 89/552/EEC "Television without Frontiers" Directive. Article 1 TWFD' in O. Castendyk, E.J. Dommering and A. Scheuer (eds), *European Media Law* (Kluwer Law International 2008) 492–493; O. Castendyk and O. Schaar, 'Directive 2007/65/EC "Audiovisual Media Services" Directive. Article 10 AVMSD' in O. Castendyk, E.J. Dommering and A. Scheuer (eds), *European Media Law* (Kluwer Law International 2008) 945.

650 O. Castendyk, 'Werbeintegration Im TV-Programm – Wann Sind Themen Placements Schleichwerbung Oder Sponsoring?' [2005] ZUM 857.

651 J. Kabel, 'The Search for Consistency in European Advertising Law' [2003] IRIS Plus, Legal Observations of the European Audiovisual Observatory 8, 3; Schaar (n 599) 492–493; Castendyk (n 599) 313.

652 Castendyk (n 649) 313.

653 Schaar (n 649) 492.

is not unlikely. As such activities could undermine the function of television as a "*medium of information, education, social and cultural development and entertainment*"[654], they should be prevented.[655] As phrased by CASTENDYCK

> "*money should not buy love, and it should also not be able to buy 'truth' (i.e. secretly paid expert opinions, disguised as 'independent science') or editorial or fictional content*".[656]

The principles of identification and separation have been implemented in the various Member States by means of national legislative and/or self-regulatory instruments (*infra*).

2.1.1. The principle of identification and other requirements for all forms of audiovisual commercial communication

THE IDENTIFICATION PRINCIPLE. The principle of identification can be found in article 9 (a) of the AVMS Directive (and article 19), which requires that

> "*audiovisual commercial communications shall be readily recognisable as such. Surreptitious audiovisual commercial communication shall be prohibited;*"[657]

Article 9 of the AVMS Directive is applicable to all audiovisual media services. As such, this article links the in 2010 introduced concept of audiovisual commercial communication to the identification principle, while also adding in a second sentence the prohibition of surreptitious audiovisual commercial communication. However, various attempts during the 2010 legislative process to widen the scope of article 9 (i.e. as to integrate the words 'kept quite separable from other parts of the programme service'[658]) as well as further specifying it

[654] Section 228 of the Council of Europe, 'Europe an Treaty Series – No. 132 Explanatory Report to the European Convention on Transfrontier Television' <https://rm.coe.int/16800cb348> accessed 25 July 2018., making reference to the Council of Europe, Committee of Ministers, 'Recommendation No. R (84) 3 of the Committee of Ministers to Member States on Principles on Television Advertising.' <https://rm.coe.int/CoERMPublicCommonSearchServices/DisplayDCTMContent?documentId=09000016804dc8b4> accessed 25 July 2018.

[655] Schaar (n 649) 492.

[656] Castendyk (n 650) 857.

[657] The concept finds its origins in the predecessor of the AVMS Directive, more specifically in article 10 of the Television without Frontiers Directive (TWFD).

[658] The EP was in favour to widen the scope by not only maintaining the principle of identification but also introducing the principle of separation "*audiovisual commercial communication must be clearly identifiable as such and kept quite separable from other parts of the programme service, in terms of both time and space, by optical and acoustic means*". European Parliament, 'Report on the Proposal for a Directive of the European Parliament and of the Council Amending Council Directive 89/552/EEC on the Coordination of Certain Provisions Laid down by Law, Regulation or Administrative Action in Member States

(i.e. adding the words 'distinguishable from editorial content'[659]) were not upheld. The provisions of article 9 apply to all types of audiovisual commercial communication used in linear as well as on-demand media services.[660] As mentioned, the principle of identification is also withheld in article 19 of the AVMS Directive focusing on television advertising and teleshopping.

Additional requirements for all forms of audiovisual commercial communication. Aside from the identification principle and the prohibition on surreptitious advertising, article 9 of the AVMS Directive contains a number of restrictions for audiovisual commercial communications that should be kept in mind, including restrictions on the use of subliminal techniques; discrimination; and encouragements of behaviour prejudicial to health or safety or behaviour grossly prejudicial to the protection of the environment. Finally such communications also must not prejudice respect for human dignity.

2.1.2. The principle of separation and other requirements for television advertising

Principle of separation. As part of the graduated approach, the AVMS Directive contains additional rules that are specifically applicable to television advertising and teleshopping. More specifically article 19 of the AVMS Directive defines that:

> *"Television advertising and teleshopping shall be readily recognisable and distinguishable from editorial content."*

This so-called 'principle of separation' can be traced back to article 10 TWFD, requiring that television advertising and teleshopping shall be kept 'quite separate' from other parts of the programme service. The goal of this principle is to guarantee the editorial integrity of television programmes.[661] Important to note is that it is only applicable to linear audiovisual media services and that

---

Concerning the Pursuit of Television Broadcasting Activities.' (2006). (Amendment 111, Art. 1 point 6, Art. 3 g, point (a)).

659 Also, the proposal to specify the principle of identification further by additionally introducing 'distinguishable from editorial content' was not upheld. European Parliament, 'Report on the Proposal for a Directive of the European Parliament and of the Council Amending Council Directive 89/552/EEC on the Coordination of Certain Provisions Laid down by Law, Regulation or Administrative Action in Member States Concerning the Pursuit of Television Broadcasting Activities.' (n 658). (Amendment 113, Art. 1 point 6, Art. 3 g, point (b)).

660 K. Böttcher and others, 'Directive 2007/65/EC "Audiovisual Media Services" Directive. Article 3 e AVMSD' in O. Castendyk, E. Dommering and A. Scheuer (eds), *European Media Law* (Kluwer Law International 2008) 898.

661 Hellemans, Lievens and Valcke (n 75).

there is no corresponding provision for on-demand services (i.e. the graduated approach).[662] Furthermore, article 19 of the AVMS Directive states that

> *"Without prejudice to the use of new advertising techniques, television advertising and teleshopping shall be kept quite distinct from other parts of the programme by optical and/or acoustic and/or spatial means."*

This specification of the means is broader than the original wording of article 10 TWFD: the option to use 'spatial' means was added during the 2010 revision of the AVMS Directive. Interestingly, recital 81 of the 2010 AVMS Directive emphasises that the principle of separation should not prevent the use of new advertising techniques, which was also confirmed by the European Commission in its 2004 interpretative communication.[663] For example, in relation to split screen advertising (i.e. advertising consisting of the simultaneous or parallel transmission of editorial content and advertising content[664]), the European Commission stressed that the principle of separation between advertising and editorial content should, therefore, not be interpreted as prohibiting it. However, split screen advertising must be in compliance with the principle of separation of the AVMS Directive. Accordingly, split screen advertising must be readily recognisable as such and kept clearly separate from other parts of the programme by acoustic or optical means aimed at preventing the viewer from mistaking advertising for editorial content. According to the EC, "*a spatial separation by optical and/or acoustic means is adequate, provided it identifies advertising clearly and enables the viewer to readily recognise it*".[665]

QUANTITATIVE RULES. Aside from the principle of separation, the Directive also contains certain quantitative rules for television advertising and teleshopping. These rules were adapted during the latest review of the Directive, in order to level the playing field between traditional and new media service providers. First, the revised Directive grants more flexibility to television broadcasters regarding the insertion of advertising and teleshopping commercials. More specifically, the hourly limit of 20% was replaced by a 20% daily limit, which applies between 6am and 6pm. Furthermore, during primetime (i.e. from 6pm

---

662 Castendyk and Schaar (n 649) 947.

663 European Commission, 'Interpretative Communication on Certain Aspects of the Provisions on Televised Advertising in the "Television without Frontiers" Directive (2004/C 102/02)' (n 648).

664 For example, one or more advertising spots appear in a window during the transmission of a programme in such a way that two separate images are visible on the screen. Provided the space set aside for advertising is not excessive, this technique enables the viewer to continue to watch the editorial programme during the transmission of an advertising spot; Commission Interpretative Communication, nr. 41.

665 European Commission, 'Interpretative Communication on Certain Aspects of the Provisions on Televised Advertising in the "Television without Frontiers" Directive (2004/C 102/02)' (n 648) s 47.

to 12 am), broadcast time may not contain more than 20% advertising messages. Additionally, broadcasts of television films, cinematographic productions and news programs may be interrupted by advertising messages or teleshopping commercials once per scheduled period of at least 30 minutes. This is also applicable to children's programmes, provided that the programme lasts at least 30 minutes[666] (i.e. excluding teleshopping commercials as they are forbidden during children's programmes).

2.2. *Protection of minors in relation to audiovisual commercial communication*

PROTECTION OF MINORS. The AVMS Directive contains certain protections for children in relation to audiovisual commercial communications, which apply to both linear and on-demand media services. The basic rule protecting minors in view of audiovisual commercial communication can be found in article 9 (1) g of the Directive.[667] According to this provision:

> *"Audiovisual commercial communications shall not cause physical or moral detriment to minors. Therefore, they shall not*
> - *directly exhort minors to buy or hire a product or service by exploiting their inexperience or credulity,*
> - *directly encourage them to persuade their parents or others to purchase the goods or services being advertised,*
> - *exploit the special trust minors place in parents, teachers or other persons, or*
> - *unreasonably show minors in dangerous situations."*

The phrasing of this provision and in particular the use of the word "directly" limits its scope of application. Indeed, not many advertisements are calling "directly" upon the child to buy a certain product or service or to use their so-called "pester power" to convince their parents into buying it for them. GARDE explains that "*marketing to children tends to be covert*".[668] In this regard, it has been argued that it has become ever more difficult to precisely determine the scope of the EU provisions on the protection of minors.[669] Indeed, the actual level of protection is hard to decipher, especially given the constant evolution of new technologies and economic developments in the field of (on-demand) audiovisual services.

---

666 Children's programmes that are shorter than 30 minutes may not be interrupted by commercials. Article 20 (2) of the AVMS Directive.

667 This provision is applicable to both television advertising and teleshopping as well as to advertising on on-demand services.

668 A. Garde, 'The Best Interests of the Child' in J. Devenny and M. Kenny (eds), *European Consumer Protection: Theory and Practice* (Cambridge University Press 2012) 190.

669 European Audiovisual Observatory, *The Protection of Minors in the Case of New (Non-Linear) Media – European Legal Rules and Their National Transposition and Application* (S. Nikoltchev ed, Council of Europe 2012) 9–10.

Sponsorship and product placement. The Directive also contains restrictions on the amount of marketing to children in programmes, applicable to both linear and on-demand audiovisual media services. First, Member States may further choose to prohibit the showing of a sponsorship logo during children's programmes, documentaries and religious programmes.[670] Second, under the Directive, product placement shall be prohibited in children's programmes.[671] Product placement is any form of audiovisual commercial communication which consists of "*the inclusion of or reference to a product, service or the trade mark thereof so that it is featured within a programme, in return for payment or for similar consideration*".[672] Conversely, the placement of production props or prizes of insignificant value can be included in children's programme.[673]

Limitations to television advertising. Finally, the Directive provides certain protections for children that exclusively apply to television advertising. Aside from the principle of separation, article 20 of the AVMS Directive defines that children's programmes may not be interrupted by television advertising or teleshopping if they are shorter than 30 minutes.[674] Thus, for each scheduled period of at least 30 minutes, a television advertisement may interrupt the programme, but only if the scheduled duration of the programme exceeds 30 minutes. Finally, as mentioned, teleshopping commercials are forbidden during children's programmes.[675]

Product-specific provisions. Furthermore, the Directive provides certain protections for children against all forms of audiovisual commercial communications for harmful products (e.g., food, tobacco, alcohol).[676] However, these provisions are not further discussed in this book as they focus on the

---

670 Article 10 (4) of the AVMS Directive.

671 Article 11 of the AVMS Directive states that "*Product placement shall be allowed in all audiovisual media services, except in news and current affairs programmes, consumer affairs programmes, religious programmes and children's programmes*". (Emphasis added).

672 Article 1(1)(m) AVMS Directive. Angelopoulos clarifies that product placement actually escapes the principle of separation, with transparency as an adequate safeguard for viewer interests (i.e. the identification principle remains applicable). Nevertheless, it is not allowed in children's programmes. C. Angelopoulos, *Product Placement in European Audiovisual Productions* (European Audiovisual Observatory 2010) 10 <http://dare.uva.nl/search?metis.record.id=337442> accessed 25 July 2018.

673 C. Angelopoulos, *Product Placement in European Audiovisual Productions* (European Audiovisual Observatory 2010) 17 <http://dare.uva.nl/search?metis.record.id=337442> accessed 25 July 2018.

674 A programme qualifies as a children's programme if – taking into consideration its content, form and time of transmission – it is targeted at persons below a certain age threshold. This threshold differs in the different EU Member States, for instance in the Netherlands it is set at 12 years whereas in the UK it is set at 16 years. Angelopoulos (n 672) 17. See also Dutch Medialaw 2008, Article 3.19a (2) and Ofcom Broadcasting Code, Section 10.5.

675 Article 20 (2) of the AVMS Directive.

676 Article 9 (1) (d-f) of the AVMS Directive.

content of the commercial message, rather than the advertising format or technique used.

3. SELF-REGULATION

ICC Code. At the international level, the provisions of the ICC Code are also applicable to audiovisual commercial communications (*supra*).

National initiatives. In addition, a broad variety of self-regulatory instruments implementing aspects of the AVMS Directive (i.e. on the protection of minors from harmful audiovisual content in both television broadcasting and in on-demand audiovisual media services and commercial communication) exist at the national level.[677] Considering that the focus of our mapping exercise lies on advertising regulation at the EU level, these instruments are not analysed.

SECTION III. THE E-COMMERCE CONTEXT

1. THE E-COMMERCE DIRECTIVE

Background. The European Union has traditionally invested and encouraged the development of electronic commerce.[678] In 1997, the European Commission launched its European Initiative in the sector of Electronic Commerce, "*to encourage the vigorous growth of electronic commerce in Europe*". To achieve such growth, the Commission recognised the importance of a coherent regulatory framework at the European level, which is based on a number of principles, including the single market freedoms, taking into account business realities and meeting general interest objectives like privacy and consumer protection effectively and efficiently.[679] The main objective of the e-Commerce Directive[680],

---

677 For an overview and assessment of the effectiveness of these national initiatives see European Commission, Directorate-General of Communications Networks, Content & Technology., 'Effectiveness of Self and Co-Regulation Study in the Context of Implementing the AVMS Directive' (2016) <https://ec.europa.eu/digital-single-market/en/news/audiovisual-and-media-services-directive-self-and-co-regulation-study> accessed 30 August 2018.

678 A. R. Lodder and A. D. Murray, *EU Regulation of E-Commerce: A Commentary* (Edward Elgar Pub 2017) 19.

679 European Commission, 'Communication of 18 April 1997: A European Initiative in the Sector of Electronic Commerce' (18 April 1997) <https://eur-lex.europa.eu/legal-content/EN/TXT/?uri=LEGISSUM%3Al32101> accessed 12 April 2018.

680 Directive 2000/31/EC of the European Parliament and of the Council of 8 June 2000 on certain legal aspects of information society services, in particular electronic commerce, in the Internal Market (Directive on electronic commerce). (Hereafter e-Commerce Directive).

adopted in 2000, is to contribute to the proper functioning of the internal market by ensuring the free movement of information society services.[681]

Scope. The territorial scope of the e-Commerce Directive is limited to those service providers that have an establishment[682] in one of the Member States of the EU.[683] The Directive is of a horizontal nature and, as such, applies across all areas of law touching upon the provision of information society services (e.g. private law, criminal law). It provides a light and flexible approach for e-commerce, meaning that the Directive only addresses those elements that are needed to ensure the proper functioning of the internal market.[684] One of these elements requiring regulation is commercial communications in online services.[685]

1.1. Definitions

1.1.1. Information society service

Information society service. According to recital 17, the e-Commerce Directive is applicable to "any service normally provided for remuneration, at a distance by electronic means and at the individual request of a recipient of

681 Article 1 of the e-Commerce Directive.

682 Recital 19 of the e-Commerce Directive clarifies that: *The place at which a service provider is established should be determined in conformity with the case-law of the Court of Justice according to which the concept of establishment involves the actual pursuit of an economic activity through a fixed establishment for an indefinite period; this requirement is also fulfilled where a company is constituted for a given period; the place of establishment of a company providing services via an Internet website is not the place at which the technology supporting its website is located or the place at which its website is accessible but the place where it pursues its economic activity; in cases where a provider has several places of establishment it is important to determine from which place of establishment the service concerned is provided; in cases where it is difficult to determine from which of several places of establishment a given service is provided, this is the place where the provider has the centre of his activities relating to this particular service.*

683 Article 3 (1) and recital 58 clarify that the Directive does not apply to service providers that are established in third countries. More specifically, article 3 (1) states that: 1. *Each Member State shall ensure that the information society services provided by a service provider established on its territory comply with the national provisions applicable in the Member State in question which fall within the coordinated field.* (emphasis added). For more information see J. Riordan, *The Liability of Internet Intermediaries* (Oxford University Press 2016) 380.

684 P. Valcke and E. Dommering, 'Directive 2000/31/EC-'e-Commerce' Directive' in O. Castendyk, E. Dommering and A. Scheuer (eds), *European Media Law* (Kluwer Law International 2008) 1084. Indeed, in its 1997 Communication, the European Commission underlines that regulation is only needed if the free movement of electronic commerce services cannot be effectively achieved by mutual recognition of national rules and of appropriate self-regulatory codes. European Commission, 'Communication of 18 April 1997: A European Initiative in the Sector of Electronic Commerce' (n 679).

685 Aside from this, the Directive also contains other provisions than those related to advertising, but these remain outside the scope of this book.

services". Thus, for a service to fall within the scope of the Directive, it has to be analysed within the context of these four conditions: (1) normally provided for remuneration, (2) at a distance, (3) by electronic means and (4) at the individual request of the recipient. Of these four conditions, the requirement for a service to be provided by electronic means is the most straightforward. It refers to digital, online or mobile services as they are provided and received via electronic equipment. Furthermore, the requirement that the service has to be provided at a distance entails that the parties involved (i.e. the service provider and the consumer) are not simultaneously present. LODDER and MURRAY underline that the crucial aspect in this regard is that parties cannot communicate face-to-face.[686] Third, the requirement that the service is provided at the individual request is fulfilled if, for instance, the user downloads a mobile application or registers on a website in order to receive a certain service. The last condition, however, is less straightforward.

NORMALLY PROVIDED FOR REMUNERATION. The requirement should be interpreted broadly and not merely monetary payment. The e-Commerce Directive clarifies that services financed by advertising are also included under the scope of the Directive (for instance this could include access to website content).[687] More specifically, recital 18 states that

> "*information society services are not solely restricted to services giving rise to on-line contracting but also, in so far as they represent an economic activity, extend to services which are not remunerated by those who receive them, such as those offering on-line information or commercial communications, or those providing tools allowing for search, access and retrieval of data.*"[688]

The Court of Justice of the European Union has supported this by finding that services, as defined by article 57 of the Treaty on the Functioning of the European Union ("TFEU"), do not necessarily require payment by the users themselves.[689] Furthermore, the European Data Protection Supervisor ("EDPS") has stated in its analysis of the overlap between data protection, consumer protection and competition law that it works from the assumption that all three of these areas are applicable to "free" services.[690] Recital 18 of the e-Commerce

686 Lodder and Murray (n 678) 24.

687 Recital 18 e-Commerce Directive.

688 In this regard, LODDER and MURRAY refer to the common phrase 'if something is free, you are the product'. Lodder and Murray (n 678) 22.

689 *Giuseppe Sacchi Reference for a preliminary ruling: Tribunale civile e penale di Biella v Italy* [1974] CJEU C-155/73; *Bond van Adverteerders v the Netherlands* [1988] CJEU C-352/85.

690 European Data Protection Supervisor, 'Preliminary Opinion – Privacy and Competitiveness in the Age of Big Data: The Interplay between Data Protection, Competition Law and Consumer Protection in the Digital Economy' <https://edps.europa.eu/sites/edp/files/publication/14-03-26_competitition_law_big_data_en.pdf> accessed 25 July 2018.

Directive also specifies that whereas television and radio broadcasting would not fall under the definition, services which are transmitted point to point, such as video-on-demand or the provision of commercial communications by electronic mail would be considered information society services. Finally, information society services also include services in hosting information provided by a recipient of the service (e.g. online social networks[691]).

1.1.2. Commercial communication

Commercial communication. Under article 2(f) of the e-Commerce Directive, commercial communication is defined as

> *"any form of communication designed to promote directly or indirectly, the goods, services or image of a company, organisation or person pursuing a commercial, industrial or craft activity or exercising a regulated profession."*".

This definition should be interpreted broadly and entails both direct and indirect promotion, as a way to prevent circumvention of the ban on commercial communications for certain products (e.g., tobacco, alcohol).[692] The commercial character of the communication entails that it promotes goods or services of a certain company or organisation.[693] Excluded from this definition is the mere ownership of a website or e-mail address, linking to a commercial site without getting paid for it, providing information not constituting promotion, consumer-testing services, and price or product comparisons.[694]

1.1.3. Information society service provider

Information society service provider. An information society service provider can be any natural or legal person providing an information society service.[695] This could be *inter alia* social network providers, internet service providers and providers of mobile messenger applications. For a service provider to be established in a Member State of the European Union, it has to effectively pursue an economic activity using a fixed establishment for an indefinite period.[696]

---

691 As confirmed by the CJEU, for instance in *Sabam v Netlog* [2012] CJEU C-360/10.

692 A. Lodder, 'European Union E-Commerce Directive – Article by Article Comments' (Social Science Research Network 2007) SSRN Scholarly Paper ID 1009945 73 <https://papers.ssrn.com/abstract=1009945> accessed 22 November 2017.

693 However, the definition does not extend to promotional messages from organisations such as Greenpeace or Scientology. Valcke and Dommering (n 684) 1097.

694 Valcke and Dommering (n 684) 1097.

695 Article 2 (b) e-Commerce Directive.

696 Article 2 (c) e-Commerce Directive. Furthermore, Article 2 (c) clarifies that "*the presence and use of the technical means and technologies required to provide the service do not, in*

1.2. *Substantive requirements for commercial communications*

Identification and information requirements. The e-Commerce Directive establishes *de facto* obligations for advertisers, by requiring Member States to implement rules regarding the identification of commercial messages and the information to be provided together with commercial communications which are part of or constitute an information society service. In other words, the regulatory regime of the e-Commerce Directive on commercial communications consists of identification and transparency requirements, and in this sense differs from the AVMS Directive (i.e. no specific protection for children).[697] More specifically, article 6 determines the following conditions:

(a) *the commercial communication shall be clearly identifiable as such*[698]*;*
(b) *the natural or legal person on whose behalf the commercial communication is made shall be clearly identifiable;*
(c) *promotional offers, such as discounts, premiums and gifts, where permitted in the Member State where the service provider is established, shall be clearly identifiable as such, and the conditions which are to be met to qualify for them shall be easily accessible and be presented clearly and unambiguously;*
(d) *promotional competitions or games, where permitted in the Member State where the service provider is established, shall be clearly identifiable as such, and the conditions for participation shall be easily accessible and be presented clearly and unambiguously.*

Unsolicited commercial communication. Furthermore, the e-Commerce Directive obliges Member States to implement rules concerning unsolicited commercial communications by electronic mail. In particular, the Member States need to oblige service providers established in their territory who make use of unsolicited commercial communications, to ensure that such communication "*shall be identifiable clearly and unambiguously*".[699] Finally, each Member State must have measures in place to ensure service providers of such communications to consult on a regular basis and respect the opt-out registers, in which natural persons can register if they do not want to receive such commercial communications.[700]

Exemption for hosting providers. Furthermore, the Directive contains a number of liability exemptions for certain service providers.[701] The rationale of

themselves, constitute an establishment of the provider".

697 Oster (n 642) 227.

698 This is the identification principle, which corresponds to article 9 (a) of the AVMS Directive.

699 Article 7 e-Commerce Directive.

700 Article 7 §2 e-Commerce Directive.

701 Nowadays, commercial messages are often spread via social network sites by the users themselves. If such commercial messages are harmful or illegal, the question may rise whether the social network platform could be liable for any damage resulting from this (i.e.

these exemptions is that in the late 1990s several Member State courts had ruled that online intermediaries could be held liable for the content that was uploaded by users. Yet eventually, the idea grew in Europe that intermediaries should be protected against liability for content originating from third parties, but only if they were prepared to cooperate when it comes to content removal or blocking access to illegal or harmful content.[702] These exemptions could be relevant in the situation where third parties upload illegal or harmful advertisements on platforms such as Facebook or YouTube. Article 14 of the e-Commerce Directive contains a liability exemption for providers of hosting services for illegal web content uploaded by the users of the service. In essence, a hosting service is any service which consists of the storage of information at the request of the recipient of the service (e.g. social network providers).[703] Hosting providers can only benefit from the liability exemption if three conditions are fulfilled: (1) absence of knowledge[704] of the illegal web content, (2) absence of control[705] and (3) expeditious action upon obtaining awareness over the illegal activity or web content.[706]

2. SELF-REGULATION: FEDMA CODE OF CONDUCT ON E-COMMERCE & INTERACTIVE MARKETING

Background. In the late nineties consumers had low confidence in e-commerce. At the time, there were a number of legal obstacles to the proper functioning of the internal market, which placed a burden on the development of information society services within the Community.[707] More specifically, divergences

secondary liability). G. Sartor, 'Providers Liability: From the ECommerce Directive to the Future' (European University Institute 2017) 4; P. Van Eecke, 'Online Service Providers and Liability: A Plea for a Balanced Approach' (2011101) 48 Common Market Law Review 1455.

702 Van Eecke (n 701). as cited by B. Van Alsenoy and V. Verdoodt, 'Liability and Accountability of Actors in Social Networking Sites, Spion Project' (2014) 23.

703 Van Alsenoy and Verdoodt (n 702) 23. More specifically: *"A typical example of a hosting service is that of a "webhosting company", which provides web space to its customers who can then upload content to be published on a website. However, the hosting exemption is defined in broad terms and may benefit any online service provider storing information at the request of its users".*

704 Thus, the host may still be held liable once it has obtained knowledge of facts or circumstances from which the illegal activity or web content is apparent. See A. Kuczerawy, 'Intermediary Liability & Freedom of Expression: Recent Developments in the EU Notice & Action Initiative' (2015) 31 Computer Law & Security Review 46.

705 For example, if the illegal content was introduced by an employee of the host, the latter will not be able to benefit from the liability exemption.

706 Van Alsenoy and Verdoodt (n 702) 24.

707 European Economic and Social Committee, 'The Database on Self- and Co-Regulation Initiatives: Federation of European Direct and Interactive Marketing (FEDMA)' (29 January 2007) <https://www.eesc.europa.eu/en/policies/policy-areas/enterprise/database-self-and-co-regulation-initiatives/48> accessed 25 July 2018.

in legislation and legal uncertainty as to which national rules applied to such services negatively affected consumers' confidence. Against this backdrop, the Federation of European Direct Marketing ("FEDMA"), an organisation representing[708] the Direct and Interactive Marketing sector at the European Level[709] issued a Code of Conduct on e-Commerce and Interactive Marketing ("Code on E-Commerce"), following the entering into force of the E-Commerce Directive.[710] With the Code on E-Commerce, FEDMA aims "*to contribute to the growth of an e-commerce environment conducive to online direct marketing and at the same time protective of consumer interests*".[711] In order to remove barriers to the development of cross-border services within the Community which members might offer via the internet, it was considered necessary to establish a set of professional rules on consumer and child protection or public health, and guarantee compliance at the Community level.[712] The Code forms part of FEDMA's trustmark system (i.e. the "Ring of Confidence" for e-commerce). Companies adhering to the Code on E-Commerce can display a Guarantee Seal on their website.[713] In addition, companies accept a consumer complaint resolution mechanism[714] and link to online Alternative Dispute Resolution systems.

---

708 FEDMA's main tasks are the promotion and protection of the Direct and Interactive Marketing sector at pan-European level, as well as providing the sector with information, education and training.

709 Amongst its members are (1) national members, i.e. the national Direct Marketing Associations (hereafter "DMAs") which represent users, service providers and media/carriers of direct marketing and (2) direct company members. FEDMA, 'European Code of Practice for the Use of Personal Data in Direct Marketing' <https://ec.europa.eu/digital-single-market/en/content/european-code-practice-use-personal-data-direct-marketing> accessed 26 July 2018. FEDMA reports to have around 400 direct members in more than 30 countries as well as nearly 10 000 indirect members (through their membership in national Direct Marketing associations). M. Macenaite, 'Protecting Children's Privacy Online: A Critical Look to Four European Self-Regulatory Initiatives' (2016) 7 European Journal of Law and Technology <http://ejlt.org/article/view/473> accessed 21 June 2018.

710 Article 16 of the e-Commerce Directive states that "*Member States and the Commission shall encourage the a) drawing up of codes of conduct at Community level, by trade, professional and consumer associations and organisations, designed to contribute to the proper implementation of articles 5 to 15*".

711 FEDMA, 'Code on E-Commerce & Interactive Marketing' <www.oecd.org/internet/ieconomy/2091875.pdf> accessed 26 July 2018.

712 In this regard, the EU considered that codes of conduct at Community level would be the perfect means to define principles regarding professional ethics in the context of commercial communication. See European Economic and Social Committee (n 707).

713 For serious and/or consistent breaches of the Code, the national DMA may decide to withdraw a FEDMA recognised guarantee seal of a certain marketer. The matter will then be referred to the FEDMA Monitoring Committee for approval before execution. FEDMA, 'Code on E-Commerce & Interactive Marketing' (n 711).

714 As a first step, marketers should have effective in-house complaint mechanisms in place, which should be confidential, free and easy for consumers to access. The marketer should also make every effort to resolve complaints in a satisfactory manner within a specified time period (not exceeding 30 days). If the complaint cannot be dealt with at the in-house level, the consumer should have redress to the National Direct Marketing Associations. Finally,

2.1. *Scope*

SCOPE. With the Code of E-Commerce, FEDMA aims to set a standard of ethical business conduct for online marketers that (1) sell goods or services or (2) provide information as part of, or follow up to a sale (it is applicable to both product or service promotion through the web and/or through email).[715] It is applicable only to online commercial relations between businesses and consumers (including e-commerce and commercial communications). The provisions should be read in conjunction with the other FEDMA Codes (*infra*) and should be interpreted in accordance with the framework of applicable laws.

2.2. *Substantive requirements for commercial communications*

PRINCIPLE OF IDENTIFICATION. The Code on E-Commerce first of all contains a section of provisions that apply to all forms of online commercial communications.[716] These principles reflect the general principles as contained in the e-Commerce Directive.[717] More specifically, article 3.1 of the Code provides that:

- *Consumers can be confident that all online commercial communication shall be clearly identifiable as such.*
- *The originator of the communication (i.e. a natural or legal person) should likewise be clearly identifiable.*
- *All promotional offers and games shall be clearly identifiable as such.*

MISLEADING COMMERCIAL COMMUNICATION. Furthermore, articles 3.3 and 3.4 of the Code protect consumers against misleading commercial communications. More specifically, article 3.3 defines that consumers may not be misled about the nature of the product or service being promoted or offered. Moreover, consumer's freedom to exit sites should not be restricted deceptively. Search terms also have to reflect the content of the site in a fair manner. Article 3.4 on the other hand determines that price comparisons may not be misleading; must contain the start and end date of the offer and; must show any specific conditions that may apply.

---

if a national DMA is unable to solve the problem due to cross-border aspects, FEDMA can investigate the complaint itself. For these situations, the Code foresees that the investigation is conducted by the FEDMA Monitoring Committee. FEDMA, 'Code on E-Commerce & Interactive Marketing' (n 711).

715 Introduction of the FEDMA Code on E-Commerce.

716 Section 6 of the FEDMA Code on E-Commerce.

717 For more information on the e-Commerce Directive see V. Verdoodt, E. Lievens and L. Hellemans, 'Mapping and Analysis of the Current Legal Framework on Commercial Communication Aimed at Minors. A Report in the Framework of the AdLit Research Project.' (2015) <www.adlit.be> accessed 20 November 2017.

Respecting the sensibilities of children. The Code also contains certain rules for marketers that target children or for whom children are likely to constitute a section of their audience. Several factors that define whether or not a commercial communication aimed at children is harmful are highlighted. More specifically, the commercial communication:

- *should not exploit a child's credulity, loyalty, vulnerability or lack of experience;*
- *should take into account the age, knowledge and level of maturity of the intended audience;*
- *should not contain any advertising material suitable only for adults;*
- *should not encourage children to enter adult websites, copy unsafe practices nor communicate with strangers;*
- *should encourage children to obtain parental consent before purchasing goods/services;*
- *should not contain an offer of credit.*

Evidence of advertising claims. Finally, online marketers always need to have evidence for any claims made in their advertisements.[718]

SECTION IV. THE DATA PROTECTION CONTEXT

Background. As mentioned above, the collection of personal data for personalisation and targeted advertising purposes is one of the major trends in the area of commercial communication. Children have become a datafied generation and are increasingly targeted with personalised commercial messages.[719] Under the EU Charter of Fundamental Rights, EU citizens have the right to the protection of their personal data.[720] The EU legislative framework on data protection – which is also applicable to the processing of children's personal data – has been undergoing significant reforms in recent years. First, the Data Protection Directive[721] which was adopted in 1995 (i.e. the old regime),

718 Article 3.5 of the FEDMA Code on E-Commerce.

719 Lupton and Williamson (n 94).

720 The recognition of data protection as a key personal right of EU citizens was also confirmed with the adoption of the Lisbon Treaty, with article 39 TEU and article 16 TFEU providing specific provisions on data protection. Indeed, Article 16 imposes an obligation on the EU legislators to establish a clear and unequivocal legal framework for data protection. D. Clifford, 'EU Data Protection Law and Targeted Advertising: Consent and the Cookie Monster – Tracking the Crumbs of Online User Behaviour' (2014) 5 JIPITEC 195–196 <www.jipitec.eu/issues/jipitec-5-3-2014/4095>.

721 Directive 95/46/EC of the European Parliament and of the Council of 24 October 1995 on the protection of individuals with regard to the processing of personal data and on the free movement of such data 1995.

has been replaced by the EU General Data Protection Regulation ("GDPR")[722], which devotes specific attention to the protection of children's personal data.[723] The GDPR was adopted by the EU Parliament and Council on April 27th, 2016, and became applicable on May 25th, 2018. Although the EU legislators opted for a high level of harmonisation by adopting a regulation, the GDPR still leaves a margin of manoeuvre to the EU Member States regarding the implementation of certain provisions, including a number of provisions that are important for children. Hence, at the moment of writing, the real impact of the changes on the daily lives of children and the exercise of their rights remains unclear. Second, the ePrivacy Directive[724] provides a regulatory regime for the processing of citizen's communications data and operates as a *lex specialis* framework to the requirements provided by the *lex generalis* Regulation (i.e. the GDPR and previously the Data Protection Directive). This legislative instrument is currently also being revised. Aside from these legislative instruments, the advertising industry has developed a number of self-regulatory instruments that play an important role in regulating the delivery of personalised advertising to children.

1. THE GENERAL DATA PROTECTION REGULATION

DATA PROTECTION DIRECTIVE. Up until May 2018, the Data Protection Directive remained the core legal instrument applicable to the processing of personal data in the European Union.[725] The underlying idea of the Directive was that in order to realise a free flow of services, capital, people and goods on the EU's internal market, a free flow of data is necessary. To achieve this, all Member States needed to adhere to a uniform level of data protection.[726] The Data Protection Directive further clarified the privacy principles stemming from fundamental rights documents and defined certain general data protection principles that needed to

722 European Union (Parliament and Council) (2016) Regulation (EU) 2016/679 of 27 April 2016 on the protection of natural persons with regard to the processing of personal data and on the free movement of such data, and repealing Directive 95/46/EC (General Data Protection Regulation), *OJ* 4 May 2016, *L*119/1.

723 In contrast, the recent proposal for an ePrivacy Regulation does not contain specific references to children: Proposal for a Regulation of the European Parliament and of the Council concerning the respect for private life and the protection of personal data in electronic communications and repealing Directive 2002/58/EC (Regulation on Privacy and Electronic Communications) 2017.

724 Directive 2002/58/EC of the European Parliament and of the Council of 12 July 2002 concerning the processing of personal data and the protection of privacy in the electronic communications sector (Directive on privacy and electronic communications) 2002 (OJ L 201) 37.

725 Directive 95/46/EC of the European Parliament and of the Council of 24 October 1995 on the protection of individuals with regard to the processing of personal data and on the free movement of such data (OJ L 281) 31. (hereinafter Data Protection Directive).

726 European Union Agency for Fundamental Rights (FRA) and Council of Europe (2014). *Handbook on European data protection law.* Luxembourg: Publications Office of the European Union, 18.

be taken into account whenever personal data was processed. Due to the nature of this legal instrument, the Member States had to implement the provisions of the Directive in their national legal systems.

General Data Protection Regulation. Although the key principles of data protection remain the same, the GDPR introduces several important changes. The most important changes concerning the processing of children's personal data for advertising purposes and the concerns that may arise regarding the implementation of the provisions in this regard are discussed below.[727]

Territorial scope. With regard to the territorial scope, article 3 of the GDPR provides that the GDPR applies to (1) the processing of personal data in the context of the activities of an establishment of a controller or a processor in the Union, regardless of whether the processing takes place in the Union or not; (2) the processing of personal data of data subjects who are in the Union by a controller or processor not established in the Union, where the processing activities are related to: (a) the offering of goods or services, irrespective of whether a payment of the data subject is required, to such data subjects in the Union; or (b) the monitoring of their behaviour as far as their behaviour takes place within the Union; and (3) the processing of personal data by a controller not established in the Union, but in a place where Member State law applies by virtue of public international law. This expansion of the territorial scope (compared to the Data Protection Directive) entails that foreign businesses processing EU residents' personal data for advertising purposes will have to comply with the rules of the GDPR.

Material scope. The GDPR is underpinned by the premise that natural persons should have control of their own personal data.[728] The material scope of the GDPR is very broad. More specifically, according to article 2, the GDPR applies to

> *"the processing of personal data wholly or partly by automated means and to the processing other than by automated means of personal data which form part of a filing system or are intended to form part of a filing system."*

As such, there are two key concepts that determine the material scope, i.e. (1) processing and (2) personal data. These concepts will be discussed more into detail below.

---

727 This section of the book is a translation and adaptation of the following two articles: Verdoodt and Lievens (n 482); E. Lievens and V. Verdoodt, 'Looking for Needles in a Haystack: Key Issues Affecting Children's Rights in the General Data Protection Regulation' [2017] Computer Law & Security Review <http://linkinghub.elsevier.com/retrieve/pii/S026736491730314X> accessed 3 November 2017.

728 Recital 7 GDPR.

1.1. *Definitions*

A. Personal data and processing

Personal data. According to the article 4 (1) of the GDPR, personal data is

> *"any information relating to an identified or identifiable natural person ('data subject'); an identifiable natural person is one who can be identified, directly or indirectly, in particular by reference to an identifier such as a name, an identification number, location data, an online identifier or to one or more factors specific to the physical, physiological, genetic, mental, economic, cultural or social identity of that natural person".*

An identifiable person is a person who can be identified, directly or indirectly, in particular by reference to an identification number or to one or more factors specific to his physical, physiological, mental, economic, cultural or social identity. In short, a person is identifiable if anyone can ascertain his or her identity, directly or indirectly, through reasonable means.[729] The interpretation of personal data is very broad and includes for instance a person's first name, surname, date of birth, IP address and mobile app data.[730]

Processing. The second key concept that defines the scope of application of the GDPR is "processing". Processing entails according to article 4 (2) of the GDPR:

> *"any operation or set of operations which is performed upon personal data, whether or not by automatic means, such as collection, recording, organization, storage,*

---

729 Recital 26 of the GDPR provides that: "*To determine whether a natural person is identifiable, account should be taken of all the means reasonably likely to be used, such as singling out, either by the controller or by another person to identify the natural person directly or indirectly. To ascertain whether means are reasonably likely to be used to identify the natural person, account should be taken of all objective factors, such as the costs of and the amount of time required for identification, taking into consideration the available technology at the time of the processing and technological developments*".

730 In general, the GDPR applies in any case where the use of apps on smart devices involves the processing of personal data of individuals. Many types of data stored or generated by a mobile device are to be considered personal data. These data usually do not only have a significant impact on the private lives of users but also potentially on other individuals, such as application developers. Often, these data are indeed collected and processed on the device itself and then – in a later stage – transferred to a third party's infrastructure, without the knowledge of the end user. Examples are geo- location data, contacts, unique device and customer identifiers (such as IMEI13, IMSI14, UDID15 and mobile phone number), credit card and payment data, phone call logs, SMS or instant messaging, browsing history, information society service authentication credentials (especially services with social features) pictures and videos and biometrics (such as facial recognition and fingerprint templates). Article 29 Data Protection Working Party, 'Opinion 02/2013 on Apps on Smart Devices, WP202' (2013) 7–8 <http://ec.europa.eu/justice/data-protection/article-29/documentation/opinion-recommendation/files/2013/wp202_en.pdf> accessed 14 November 2017.

adaptation or alteration, retrieval, consultation, use, disclosure by transmission, dissemination or otherwise making available, alignment or combination, blocking, erasure or destruction."

The scope of what constitutes processing is thus extremely broad. Nearly all types of action performed on personal data (such as collection, storage, use, removal etc.) can be qualified as 'processing'.

B. Controller, processor and data subject

Data controller and processor. Article 4 (7) of the GDPR defines a 'controller' as "*the natural or legal person, public authority, agency or other body which, alone or jointly with others, determines the purposes and means of the processing of personal data*". As such, the GDPR allows more than one legally separate entity to act as a controller and decide together to process data for a shared purpose.[731] A 'data processor' on the other hand is "*a natural or legal person, public authority, agency or other body which processes personal data on behalf of the controller*".[732] The Article 29 Working Party[733] has defined two requirements for the qualification as processor, i.e. being a separate legal entity from the controller and processing the personal data on the latter's behalf.[734] In short, a data controller is the entity determining the purpose(s) and means of a personal data processing activity whereas a data processor is the entity who processes the personal data on behalf of the controller. To clarify, a controller can process personal data without contracting the services of a processor. The distinction is fact-based[735] and is complex in an online marketing environment, with its variety of stakeholders involved in the development and distribution of new advertising formats as well as the increasing cross-border and cloud environment setting.

Advertising environment – it's complicated. In an advertising environment, stakeholders may range from app developers to device

731 For a detailed discussion see B. Van Alsenoy, 'Regulating Data Protection: The Allocation of Responsibility and Risk among Actors Involved in Personal Data Processing' (2016).

732 Article 4 (8) GDPR.

733 The Article 29 Data Protection Working Group ("Working Party") is a European advisory body comprising of representatives of the national data protection authorities. Although the opinions of the Working Party are not binding, significant authoritative value is attached to them, as all the Member State are represented in this body. As of 25 May 2018 the Article 29 Working Party ceased to exist and has been replaced by the European Data Protection Board (EDPB). The website of the EDPB can be consulted under the following address: https://edpb.europa.eu/.

734 Article 29 Data Protection Working Party, 'Opinion 1/2010 on the Concepts of "Controller" and "Processor", WP 169' 5 <http://ec.europa.eu/justice/article-29/documentation/opinion-recommendation/files/2010/wp169_en.pdf> accessed 26 July 2018.

735 Article 29 Data Protection Working Party, 'Opinion 1/2010 on the Concepts of "Controller" and "Processor", WP 169' (n 734) 5.

manufacturers, app stores, third parties, and advertisers – all with potential subcontractors and affiliates – and, of course, the data subjects (e.g. children). As such, actors cannot always be clearly defined given the complex factual situation. Multiple entities might determine the purpose and means of processing activities leading to several separate controllers or a joint controllership, which can be the case in a multinational where various subsidiaries participate in the cloud environment.[736] Consider for example an international toy company with subsidiaries (separate legal entities) spread worldwide. The purpose and collection of the personal data could be decided at global and local level in case of a local marketing campaign where, in the end, the collected data will be used at global as well as local level for further marketing purposes. Also, multiple processors could come into play: an infrastructure provider may outsource (part of the) work attributed to him to subcontractors, leading to a cascade of processors. For information purposes, some examples of qualifications as controller or processor in the advertising environment are provided[737], as mentioned by the Article 29 Working Party in their opinion on apps on smart devices.[738]

Table 2: Controller – processor in the advertising chain (Source: Article 29 Data Protection Working Party, 'Opinion 02/2013 on apps on smart devices).

Actor	Potential qualification
App developers	Responsible for the creation of the app and/or making it available to end users, could be qualified as data controllers to the extent they determine purpose and means.
OS and device manufacturers	Can be considered as controllers or even, where relevant joint controllers for any personal data they process for their own purposes, such as the smooth running of the device, security etc. This would include user generated data (such as user details at registration), data automatically generated by the device (for example if the device has a 'phone home' functionality for its whereabouts) or personal data processed by the OS or device manufacturer resulting from the installation or use of apps.
App store	An app store records login credentials as well as the history of previously bought apps. It also asks the user to provide a credit card number that will be stored with the account of the user. The app store is the data controller for these operations. On the contrary, websites that allow the download of an app to be installed on the device without any authentication may find that they are not processing any personal data.

736 For a detailed discussion on the roles and responsibilities of the actors involved in a cloud computing environment, see Van Alsenoy (n 731) 383–425.

737 Article 29 Data Protection Working Party, 'Opinion 02/2013 on Apps on Smart Devices, WP202' (n 730) 9–13.

738 Article 29 Data Protection Working Party, 'Opinion 02/2013 on Apps on Smart Devices, WP202' (n 730).

Actor	Potential qualification
Third parties	Third parties (such as analytics providers and communication service providers) can qualify as data controllers or data processors. When they purely execute operations for the app owner, for example provide analytics within the app, they don't process data for their own purposes nor share these data with developers and as such qualify as data processor. When they, on the other hand, collect information across apps to supply additional services such as analyse figures at a larger scale (app popularity, personalised recommendation), they collect personal data for their own purpose and qualify as data controller.
Metrics provider	A company provides metrics for app owners and advertisers through the use of trackers embedded, by the app developer, within apps. The trackers of the company are therefore able to be installed on many apps and devices. One of its services is to inform app developers what other apps are used by a user, through the collection of a unique identifier. The company defines the means (i.e. trackers) and purposes of its tools before offering them to app developers, advertisers and others and therefore acts as a data controller

CONTROLLER-PROCESSOR RELATIONSHIP. Under the Data Protection Directive, processors were only indirectly accountable in case of non-compliance with the data protection rules. In contrast, the GDPR contains a substantial number of provisions which are directly relevant to processors, imposing on them a range of obligations and rendering them liable towards data subjects.[739] VAN ALSENOY underlines that this also means that processors are accountable to regulators and, as such, can be fined in case of non-compliance with their obligations under the GDPR. Despite the increased obligations imposed upon processors by the GDPR, the nature of the relationship between controllers and processors has remained largely the same. The processor is essentially perceived as an agent of the controller, who may only process personal data in accordance with the instructions of the controller.[740] Furthermore under the GDPR, both the controller[741] and processor[742] may be liable for non-compliance with their obligations.

DATA SUBJECT. As mentioned, the data subject is the individual to whom the personal data relate. The data subject does not have to be identified, but can also just be 'identifiable' (i.e., to be determined, taking into account "*all the means likely reasonably to be used either by the controller or by any other person to*

739 For an overview of all relevant articles see Van Alsenoy (n 731) 269.
740 Van Alsenoy (n 731) 270.
741 Article 82 (2) GDPR states that "*any controller involved in processing shall be liable for the damage caused by processing which infringes this Regulation.*"
742 Article 82 (2) GDPR states that "*a processor shall be liable for the damage caused by processing only where it has not complied with obligations of this Regulation specifically directed to processors or where it has acted outside or contrary to lawful instructions of the controller.*"

identify the said person").[743] Important to note is that the data subject has certain rights which can be enforced against the controller.

1.2. *Principles for the processing of (children's) personal data*

DATA QUALITY PRINCIPLES. The general principles regarding data quality as specified by the GDPR need to be respected when processing children's personal data. More specifically, personal data need to be processed in a fair, lawful and non-excessive manner for a specific purpose and based upon legitimate grounds. The following table provides an overview of the relevant principles of the GDPR and includes some elements that have been interpreted by the Article 29 Working Party.

Table 3: Principles as interpreted by the Article 29 Data Protection Working Party. Source: Article 29 Data Protection Working Party, Opinion 2/2009 on the protection of children's personal data (General guidelines and the special case of schools).

Principle	Article	Comment
Fair, lawful and transparent processing	5 (1)(a) GPDR	The personal data of children need to be processed *lawfully, fairly and in a transparent manner.* Since children's maturity is still developing, this principle needs to be interpreted strictly.[744]
Purpose limitation	5 (1) (b) GDPR	The data can only be collected for *specified, explicit and legitimate purposes* and not further processed in a way incompatible with the initially specified purpose(s).
Data minimisation	5 (1) (c) GDPR	Only *adequate, relevant and non-excessive* data can be collected and/or further processed. The collecting entity needs to carefully consider which data are strictly necessary to meet the goal or, for mobile apps for example, the desired functionality.[745]
Accuracy	5 (1) (d) GDPR	Personal data must be *accurate* and, where necessary, kept *up to date.* Every reasonable step must be taken to ensure that data are inaccurate or incomplete, having regard to the purpose for which they were collected or for which they are further processed, are erased or rectified. In short, only data necessary to reach the purpose can be collected and these data should be kept updated. As children are constantly developing, data controllers must pay particular attention to the duty to keep personal data up-to-date.[746]

743 Recital 26 GDPR.

744 Article 29 Data Protection Working Party, 'Opinion 2/2009 on the Protection of Children's Personal Data (General Guidelines and the Special Case of Schools). WP160.' (2009) 7 <http://ec.europa.eu/justice/policies/privacy/docs/wpdocs/2009/wp160_en.pdf> accessed 27 November 2017.

745 Article 29 Data Protection Working Party, 'Opinion 02/2013 on Apps on Smart Devices, WP202' (n 730) 17.

746 Article 29 Data Protection Working Party, 'Opinion 2/2009 on the Protection of Children's Personal Data (General Guidelines and the Special Case of Schools). WP160.' (n 744) 7.

Principle	Article	Comment
Storage limitation	5 (1) (e) GDPR	When no longer necessary for the purposes of collection, personal data should either be *deleted* or kept in a form which does not allow identification. This principle is particularly important for children. As they are developing a lot, data related to them could very quickly change and become outdated, so that it becomes irrelevant to the original purpose of collection. Such information should be deleted.[747]
Integrity and confidentiality	5 (1) (f) GDPR	Personal data must be processed in a manner that ensures *appropriate security*, including protection against unauthorised or unlawful processing and against accidental loss, destruction or damage, using appropriate technical or organisational measures.
Accountability	5 (2) GDPR	The controller shall be *responsible* for, and be able to demonstrate compliance with, paragraph 1 ('accountability').

1.3. Specific protections for children under the GDPR

COMPARISON WITH THE DATA PROTECTION DIRECTIVE. Under the Data Protection Directive[748] no distinction was made between children and adults. The Directive did not contain any child-specific provisions and, as such, under the terms of the Directive data controllers had to comply with the same set of legal requirements for processing personal data, regardless of the age of the data subjects. However, in turn data subjects could rely on the same rights and principles regardless of their age. In 2006, the European Commission launched its EU Strategy on the Rights of the Child[749], recognising children's rights as a priority across different policy domains. In 2009, the Article 29 Working Party issued an opinion on the protection of children's personal data, referring explicitly to the 2006 Strategy.[750] In this opinion, general principles and guidelines for the processing of children's personal data are discussed (e.g. concerning consent). The Working Party emphasised that the processing of children's personal data requires extra care and should be guided by the best interests of the child principle.[751] This idea has been reiterated in other opinions,

747 Article 29 Data Protection Working Party, 'Opinion 2/2009 on the Protection of Children's Personal Data (General Guidelines and the Special Case of Schools). WP160.' (n 744) 8.

748 For a detailed discussion of the processing of children's personal data under the 'old regime', see Verdoodt, Lievens and Hellemans (n 612).

749 European Commission, 'Towards an EU Strategy on the Rights of the Child, COM(2006) 367 Final' (n 273).

750 Article 29 Data Protection Working Party, 'Opinion 2/2009 on the Protection of Children's Personal Data (General Guidelines and the Special Case of Schools). WP160.' (n 744).

751 According to the Article 29 Working Party, a child's situation needs to be looked at from two points of view, a static and a dynamic one. More specifically, "*from the static point of view, a child is a person who has not yet achieved physical and psychological maturity. From a dynamic perspective, a child is in the process of developing physically and mentally to become an adult.*"

such as the one on smart devices, in which app developers are recommended to interpret the principles of data minimisation and purpose limitation in a more stringent way when children are involved[752], or in its opinion on online behavioural advertising which states that "*ad network providers should not offer interest categories intended to serve behavioural advertising or influence children*".[753]

SPECIFIC PROTECTION UNDER THE GDPR. The fact that children merit 'specific protection' regarding their personal data has now been explicitly acknowledged by the EU legislators in the GDPR. Recital 38 GDPR explains that children are less aware of the risks and the potential consequences of the processing of their personal data on their rights. Moreover, the GDPR recognises that the processing of children's personal data may result in risks to the rights and freedoms of natural persons.[754] Children merit specific protection especially when their personal data is used for marketing purposes, for the creation of profiles and for the collection of their data when using services offered directly to a child.[755] The GDPR refers to this specific protection in several recitals and provisions, sometimes explicitly and at other times more implicitly. The following subsections contain an overview of the new elements of this protection introduced by the GDPR and the potential consequences or issues regarding their implementation in practice.

1.3.1. Definition of a child

LACK OF A DEFINITION. First, it is important to note that the GDPR does not contain a definition of 'a child'. As a result, it is not entirely clear until what age children can benefit from the specific protection that is referred to in recital 38. In its 2009 opinion, the Article 29 Working Party refers in this regard to the relevant international instruments, such as the UNCRC, indicating that a child should be understood as any person under the age of 18 years, unless he or she has acquired legal adulthood before that age.[756] Although this interpretation was integrated in the initial proposal for a GDPR of the European Commission, it disappeared in the later European Parliament and Council iterations.

Article 29 Data Protection Working Party, 'Opinion 2/2009 on the Protection of Children's Personal Data (General Guidelines and the Special Case of Schools). WP160.' (n 744) 4–5.

752 Article 29 Data Protection Working Party, 'Opinion 02/2013 on Apps on Smart Devices, WP202' (n 730) 26.

753 Article 29 Data Protection Working Party, 'Opinion 2/2010 on Online Behavioural Advertising WP 171' (2010) 20 <http://ec.europa.eu/justice_home/fsj/privacy/index_en.htm>.

754 Recital 75 GDPR.

755 Recital 38 GDPR.

756 Article 29 Data Protection Working Party, 'Opinion 2/2009 on the Protection of Children's Personal Data (General Guidelines and the Special Case of Schools). WP160.' (n 744) 3.

EVOLVING CAPACITIES OF THE CHILD. During the legislative process the broad interpretation of children as under-18 gave rise to criticism, including from the US Department of Commerce, which argued that it could have a negative impact on the rights of older children (e.g. 13 or 16 to 18 year olds, *infra*).[757] Yet, from a children's rights perspective, the exercise of the rights under the GDPR should not necessarily be the same for all children. The UNCRC refers to the importance of the evolving capacities of children, and their level of maturity, in exercising their rights.[758] The Article 29 Working Party stressed in this regard that the exercise of children's rights should be adapted to the level of their physical and psychological development.[759]

1.3.2. The age threshold for consent[760]

ARTICLE 8 GDPR. Notwithstanding the possibility for the data controller to rely in certain circumstances on other legitimate grounds for processing (e.g. legitimate interest of the controller, necessary for the performance of a contract)[761], the GDPR is fundamentally built on the notion of the informed data subject, who agrees in a freely given, specific, informed and unambiguous manner[762] to having his or her personal data processed. As such, the GDPR is underpinned by the idea that a transparent and simple explanation of the purpose(s) of the processing of personal data allows a data subject to make an informed decision.[763] It seems obvious that this process is more complex in relation to children. The GDPR does recognise this and has introduced specific 'protection' for children in article 8, which defines the conditions for consent as a legitimate ground for processing children's personal data.[764]

INFORMATION SOCIETY SERVICE. Article 8 is by far the most debated provision of the GDPR in relation to children. The article states that, in relation to the offer of 'information society services' 'directly to a child' and when the data

---

757 Montgomery and Chester (n 483) 289.

758 Article 5 (i.e. evolving capacities of the child) and article 12 (i.e. the right to be heard in accordance with the age and maturity of the child) UNCRC.

759 The Article 29 Working Party explicitly refers to the right to development of the child in this context, laid down in article 6 UNCRC.

760 For an extensive analysis of this issue, cf. M. Macenaite and E. Kosta, 'Consent for Processing Children's Personal Data in the EU: Following in US Footsteps?' (2017) 26 Information & Communications Technology Law 146; van der Hof (n 93).

761 Article 6 GDPR.

762 Cf. the definition of consent in recital 32 GDPR and article 4 (11) GDPR.

763 B.J. Koops, 'The Trouble with European Data Protection Law.' [2014] International Data Privacy Law 3; N. Fisk, 'The Limits of Parental Consent in an Algorithmic World.' <http://blogs.lse.ac.uk/mediapolicyproject/2016/11/28/the-limits-of-parental-consent-in-an-algorithmic-world/>.

764 Note that the third paragraph of article 8 GDPR emphasises that the first paragraph, in relation to these requirements for consent, "*shall not affect the general contract law of Member States such as the rules on the validity, formation or effect of a contract in relation to a child*". It remains unclear at present what the actual impact of this particular paragraph will be in practice.

controller relies on consent as a legitimation ground, the processing of a child's personal data shall only be lawful if the child is at least 16 years old.[765] If the child is younger, parental consent needs to be obtained. A first essential question that arises is which services fall within the scope of this article. Information society services are defined as "*any service normally provided for remuneration, at a distance, by electronic means and at the individual request of a recipient of services.*"[766] As mentioned (*supra*), such services do not necessarily require payment by the users themselves, and services financed by advertising would also fall under this definition (i.e. the alleged 'free' services such as social media, search engines, news portals, etc.).[767] However, it is less clear whether online services for children provided by, for example, non-profit or educational organisations would or could in certain situations fall within the scope of article 8.[768]

Directly offered to a child. Second, it is unclear what is meant by a service 'directly offered to a child'. Is this limited to services such as YouTube Kids, for instance, which are targeted at children, or does this include all services that are actually used by children on a regular basis? In this regard, the Article 29 Data Protection Working Party has clarified that

> "*if an information society service provider makes it clear to potential users that it is only offering its service to persons aged 18 or over, and this is not undermined by other evidence (such as the content of the site or marketing plans) then the service will not be considered to be 'offered directly to a child' and Article 8 will not apply*".[769]

The margin of discretion concerning the age threshold. Article 8 does allow Member States to lower the age threshold of 16 years to a minimum of 13 years. If Member States use this option, it would mean that in practice

765 Note that in the Commission Proposal the age threshold was set at 13; for more information: see K. McCullagh, 'The General Data Protection Regulation: A Partial Success for Children on Social Network Sites?' in T. Bräutigam and S. Miettinen (eds), *Data protection, privacy and European regulation in the digital age* (Unigrafia 2016) <https://ueaeprints.uea.ac.uk/61415/4/Mc_Cullagh_2016_book_chapter_SNS.pdf> accessed 26 July 2018.

766 Article 4 (25) GDPR refers to 'information society service' as "*a service as defined in point (b) of Article 1(1) of Directive (EU) 2015/1535 of the European Parliament and of the Council*".

767 In its Guidelines on Consent, the Article 29 Working Party clarifies that "*Where a service has two economically independent components, one being the online component, such as the offer and the acceptance of an offer in the context of the conclusion of a contract or the information relating to products or services, including marketing activities, this component is defined as an information society service, the other component being the physical delivery or distribution of goods is not covered by the notion of an information society service.*" Article 29 Data Protection Working Party, 'Guidelines on Consent under Regulation 2016/679' 24 <http://ec.europa.eu/newsroom/article29/item-detail.cfm?item_id=623051> accessed 27 July 2018.

768 Macenaite and Kosta (n 760).

769 Article 29 Data Protection Working Party, 'Guidelines on Consent under Regulation 2016/679' (n 767) 25.

different age thresholds would apply throughout the European Union. This entails that companies providing online services in different Member States will have to respect different rules across the European Union, requiring extra efforts and investments, in particular for smaller players. The extent to which this will be necessary depends on whether Member States will require service providers to comply with the age threshold determined in the country in which they are established or in the country where their users reside.[770] Aside from this discussion, it is important to note that many of these providers (also) have establishments in the United States, where their services are subject to the rules of the Children's Online Privacy Protection Act (COPPA).[771] COPPA requires that websites and services that are specifically targeted at children or service providers who reasonably should know that they are collecting personal data of children under 13, obtain prior parental consent. In view of the implementation of the GDPR, national (draft) implementing acts, national consultations and guidance documents by the data protection authorities have been published in the different Member States. From these documents, it can be concluded that the implementation of article 8 is fragmented across the EU, and that all the options for the age limit (i.e. 13[772], 14[773], 15[774] and 16[775] years old) have been chosen by at least one Member State.[776]

Considerations on the age threshold from different fields of study. The implementation of article 8 and the setting of age thresholds has been discussed by scholars of different fields of study. First, social science studies have shown that children gradually become 'media literate' and 'commercially literate'

770 The first option entails that a company established in Member State A but offering its services in Member State B will need to comply with the age limit of the former. Exceptions could be made if the establishment is solely made for circumventing this rule. A second option implies that for services offered within Member State B the age threshold of that Member State will apply regardless of whether the provider is established in Member State A. Perhaps, other criteria might be considered as well. This question of private international law is being discussed in a group of experts of the Member States; cf. http://ec.europa.eu/transparency/regexpert/index.cfm?do=groupDetail.groupDetail&groupID=3461 and I. Milkaite and others, 'Roundtable Report: The General Data Protection Regulation and Children's Rights: Questions and Answers for Legislators, DPAs, Industry, Education, Stakeholders and Civil Society' (2017) <https://www.betterinternetforkids.eu/web/portal/practice/awareness/detail?articleId=2018677> accessed 26 July 2018. Furthermore, the Article 29 Working Party encourages the Member States to chose for a harmonised approach. Article 29 Data Protection Working Party, 'Guidelines on Consent under Regulation 2016/679' (n 767) 25.

771 Children's Online Privacy Protection Act of 1998, 15 U.S.C. 6501–6505.

772 For example: Belgium, Denmark, Latvia, Estonia, Finland, etc.

773 For example: Austria, Bulgaria, Cyprus.

774 For example: Czech Republic, France, Greece, Slovenia.

775 For example: Croatia, Germany, Hungary, Ireland, etc.

776 For an up-to-date overview of the national decisions concerning the implementation of article 8 of the GDPR see I. Milkaite and E. Lievens, 'GDPR: Updated State of Play of the Age of Consent across the EU, June 2018' <https://www.betterinternetforkids.eu/web/portal/practice/awareness/detail?articleId=3017751> accessed 31 August 2018.

as they age and become more mature (between the ages of 12 and 15 years).[777] As children grow older, research indicates that establishing an age threshold that is too high could encourage youngsters to circumvent protection mechanisms such as age-gating systems, considering the important role of online platforms in their lives (e.g. to communicate with their friends, express their creativity and access information).[778] Another crucial concern that is related to the age threshold and the requirement to obtain parental consent is related to the fact that companies might stop offering their services to children under the threshold. If children are excluded from information society services that matter to them, they will be denied important participation rights[779], such as the right to freedom of expression[780] and the right to freedom of assembly.[781] Finally, there is a risk that adolescents – i.e. minors above the established age threshold – are forgotten. This group of youngsters are equally awarded universal children's rights such as the right to privacy and freedom of expression. Considering the immense popularity of social networking services and mobile applications amongst this age group, as well as the sometimes-associated privacy-intrusive practices, it has been argued by Montgomery and Chester that guidelines and a policy on an appropriate level of protection for adolescents should also be developed.[782] Moreover, online service providers should, aside from the specific requirements of article 8, still take into account other provisions in the GDPR that are relevant for all 'children' (hence all under-18s), such as the necessity for transparent and 'child-friendly' information about data collection and processing (*infra*). In any case, it is essential that legislators carefully balance any decision in this context and adopt an age threshold that recognises the reality of children's daily digital lives.

1.3.3. Verification

The requirement of verification. If a data controller relies on consent as a legitimate ground for processing personal data of children under the age threshold in the context of the services mentioned above, the controller:

---

777 Livingstone and Olafsson (n 357).

778 According to Livingstone, research has demonstrated the benefits of formally including media education into the school curriculum of children and youngsters. The gap in the level of commercial literacy between 13 to 16-year-olds could be reduced by extending media education to all children, in particular from the age of 11, if not earlier, to learn them to critically reflect on and cope within the commercial digital environment, without the need for a parental consent requirement. Livingstone and Olafsson (n 357); McCullagh (n 765).

779 In this regard, van der Hof mentions that "*allowing children to develop their capacities by having their own space in which to enjoy their rights and freedoms creates more and more opportunities for participation in social life.*" S. van der Hof, 'I Agree, or Do I: A Rights-Based Analysis of the Law on Children's Consent in the Digital World' (2016) 34 Wis. Int'l LJ 409, 431.

780 Article 12 UNCRC.

781 Article 17 UNCRC.

782 Montgomery and Chester (n 483) 291.

> *"shall make reasonable efforts to verify in such cases that consent is given or authorised by the holder of parental responsibility over the child, taking into consideration available technology"*[783] *(emphasis added).*

Even though the GDPR explicitly introduces the concept of verification, article 8 does not include criteria to assess what constitutes 'verifiable consent' or a 'reasonable effort'. The Belgian DPA stresses that this does not imply a 'commitment of result' for the data controller.[784] Furthermore, it is not entirely clear what is meant with consent that "*is authorised*" instead of given.[785] Questions also arise as to whether the data controller needs to obtain 'fresh' consent for existing data processing practices concerning children's personal data, (1) if the prior obtained consent does not fulfil the GDPR-standard[786] or (2) when the child reaches the age of consent.[787] Additionally, it can be questioned whether the verification requirement also necessitates age verification. The Article 29 Working Party in its 2018 Guidelines on Consent clarified that controllers providing information society services to children on the basis of consent have to make reasonable efforts to verify whether the user is over the age of digital consent. Importantly, "*if a child gives consent while not old enough to provide valid consent on their own behalf, then this will render the processing of data unlawful.*"[788] The verification measures need to be proportionate to the nature and risks of the processing activities.[789]

---

783 Article 8, para. 2 GDPR.

784 Gegevensbeschermingsautoriteit, 'De Versterkte Toestemming' <https://www.gegevensbeschermingsautoriteit.be/de-versterkte-toestemming> accessed 27 July 2018.

785 For instance, in France this has led to the adoption of a provision requiring joint consent (i.e. minor and parents) for the processing of a minor's personal data, if the minor is under the age threshold (in France this is 15 years). Milkaite and Lievens point out that "*this is a very specific provision which is not found in other national implementation laws and it remains to be seen how exactly it will be implemented in practice.*" I. Milkaite and E. Lievens, 'GDPR: Updated State of Play of the Age of Consent across the EU, June 2018' <https://www.betterinternetforkids.eu/web/portal/practice/awareness/detail?articleId=3017751> accessed 31 August 2018.

786 Recital 171 GDPR provides in this regard that "*to allow the controller to continue such processing after the date of application of this Regulation, it is not necessary for the data subject to give his or her consent again if the manner in which the consent has been given is in line with the conditions of this Regulation*". (Emphasis added).

787 In this regard, the Article 29 Working Party provided that "*if the processing of a child's data began with the consent of their legal representative, the child concerned may, on attaining majority, revoke the consent. But if he wishes the processing to continue, it seems that the data subject need give explicit consent wherever this is required.*" Article 29 Data Protection Working Party, 'Opinion 2/2009 on the Protection of Children's Personal Data (General Guidelines and the Special Case of Schools). WP160.' (n 744) 5.

788 Article 29 Data Protection Working Party, 'Guidelines on Consent under Regulation 2016/679' (n 767) 25.

789 The WP29 also provides an example in its guidelines: "*An online gaming platform wants to make sure underage customers only subscribe to its services with the consent of their parents or guardians. The controller follows these steps:*

INSPIRATION FROM COPPA. Interesting to note is that article 40, para 2 (g) GDPR refers to the possibility of drafting codes of conduct on the manner in which parental consent is to be obtained. Inspiration can be found in the United States. The COPPA Rule provides that parental consent can be obtained by any means, if the method can reasonably ensure that the person providing consent is the parent of the child. Additionally, the COPPA Rule contains several non-exhaustive options from which companies can select.[790] The list mentions *inter alia* the 'print-and-send' method, by which parents can sign a consent form and send it back to the controller; the use of a credit card or other online paying system; mechanisms where parents can call a free telephone number or set up a video-conference with specially trained personnel. Selecting an appropriate method should be done on a case-by-case basis. For instance, different methods are recommended when companies share children's personal data with third parties or if children publish the data themselves (e.g. on social media, online fora)[791], than when the data is only used for internal purposes.[792] In addition to the listed methods, companies that develop new verification mechanisms can apply to the Federal Trade Commission to have them pre-approved.[793]

1.3.4. Transparent information

INFORMATION OBLIGATION. Considering the focus on specific and informed consent in the GDPR, the data controller's information obligation forms a crucial part of the specific protection that children merit. For consent to be valid it should be

---

Step 1: ask the user to state whether they are under or over the age of 16 (or alternative age of digital consent) If the user states that they are under the age of digital consent:
Step 2: service informs the child that a parent or guardian needs to consent or authorise the processing before the service is provided to the child. The user is requested to disclose the email address of a parent or guardian.
Step 3: service contacts the parent or guardian and obtains their consent via email for processing and take reasonable steps to confirm that the adult has parental responsibility.
Step 4: in case of complaints, the platform takes additional steps to verify the age of the subscriber. If the platform has met the other consent requirements, the platform can comply with the additional criteria of Article 8 GDPR by following these steps." Article 29 Data Protection Working Party, 'Guidelines on Consent under Regulation 2016/679' (n 767) 26.

790 Federal Trade Commission, 'Complying with COPPA: Frequently Asked Questions – A Guide for Business and Parents and Small Entity Compliance Guide.' (*Federal Trade Commission*, 20 March 2015) <https://www.ftc.gov/tips-advice/business-center/guidance/complying-coppa-frequently-asked-questions> accessed 26 July 2018.

791 Federal Trade Commission (n 790).

792 Including the methods mentioned above, but also the so-called 'e-mail plus method', where first the email address of the parent is asked and after a certain period a confirmation email is send.

793 For instance in 2015, a new method was approved by the FTC, which makes use of photographs and facial recognition technology ("Face Match to Verified Photo Identification", or FMVPI). Federal Trade Commission, 'FTC Grants Approval for New COPPA Verifiable Parental Consent Method' (*Federal Trade Commission*, 19 November 2015) <https://www.ftc.gov/news-events/press-releases/2015/11/ftc-grants-approval-new-coppa-verifiable-parental-consent-method> accessed 26 July 2018.

given freely and in an informed manner. The consent requirement thus goes hand in hand with the data subject's right to be informed. Article 12 GDPR determines that users should be provided with information concerning the processing of their personal data "*in a concise, transparent, intelligible and easily accessible form, using clear and plain language*". Recital 58 clarifies that, when provided to children, the information should be formulated in "*such a clear and plain language that the child can easily understand*". The manner in which this should be done in practice can be determined by means of a code of conduct (article 40 para 2 (g) GDPR).

Evidence-based approach. Furthermore, research insights into effective provision of information to users or consumers can be useful in this regard. Helberger, for instance, warns that providing information to users does not automatically lead to informed users. The process of providing information to users will only empower them if this happens in an efficient and effective way.[794] This is even more so when children are concerned. It requires a special effort to make information attractive and understandable to children of different ages, for example by visualisation or producing short video clips. In this context, co-creation methods where designers, lawyers and children work together to simplify information could be useful.[795]

The Article 29 Working Party recommendations. The Article 29 Working Party has recommended the use of layered-notices, offering a dual system consisting of (1) a shorter notice, containing the basic information to be provided when collecting personal data either directly from the data subject or from a third party, accompanied by a (2) more detailed notice, preferably via a hyperlink, where all relevant details are provided which are necessary to ensure a fair processing.[796] Of course, the notice needs to be posted in the right place and at the right time (i.e. they should appear directly on the screen, prior to the collection of information). The use of layered notices may be even more appropriate in the case of mobile apps, given the size of the screen of mobile devices. With regard to mobile apps, the Article 29 Working Party recommends to provide a clear overview of the collected data and, even further, request a granular consent for

794 N. Helberger, 'Form Matters: Informing Consumers Effectively – (Study Commissioned by BEUC)' 5–8 <www.beuc.eu/publications/x2013_089_upa_form_matters_september_2013.pdf.> accessed 26 July 2018.

795 E. Wauters, V. Donoso and E. Lievens, 'Optimizing Transparency for Users in Social Networking Sites' (2014) 16 info 8.

796 Article 29 Data Protection Working Party, 'Opinion 2/2009 on the Protection of Children's Personal Data (General Guidelines and the Special Case of Schools). WP160.' (n 744) 10; Article 29 Data Protection Working Party, 'Opinion 10/2004 on More Harmonised Information Provisions, WP 100' 8–9 <http://ec.europa.eu/justice/article-29/documentation/opinion-recommendation/files/2004/wp100_en.pdf> accessed 27 July 2018; Article 29 Data Protection Working Party, 'Guidelines on Transparency under Regulation 2016/679, Wp260' <http://ec.europa.eu/newsroom/article29/document.cfm?action=display&doc_id=51025> accessed 31 August 2018.

each type of data which is in particular accessed by mobile apps.[797] The use of cookies always requires additional text and consent (see also article 5(3) ePrivacy Directive, *infra*). Users need to be able to access all necessary information about the different types or purposes of cookies being used by the website or app, the qualification as a first or third party cookie and the expiry date. This could be achieved for example, by prominently displaying a link to a designated location where all the types of cookies used by the website are presented.[798]

1.3.5. Direct marketing

DIRECT MARKETING AS A LEGITIMATE GROUND FOR PROCESSING? Recital 38 emphasises that the processing of personal data of children for marketing purposes merits specific protection. Article 21 states that data subjects have the right to object at any time to processing of their personal data for direct marketing. Yet, according to recital 47 GDPR, direct marketing may constitute a legitimate interest of the controller under the GDPR, and hence offer a legitimation ground other than the consent of the data subject.[799] When this ground is relied upon, the controller must balance its own legitimate interest with the interests or the fundamental rights and freedoms of the data subject, taking into consideration the reasonable expectations of data subjects based on their relationship with the controller.[800] When the data subjects are children, article 6, 1) (f) GDPR indicates that the interests of children may override the interests of the data controller more easily.[801] Hence, when this legitimation ground is used in relation to children's personal data, it must be assumed that a heavier responsibility is imposed on the data controller. Yet, how data controllers must undertake this balancing exercise in practice remains a source of legal uncertainty.

---

797 Article 29 Data Protection Working Party, 'Opinion 02/2013 on Apps on Smart Devices, WP202' (n 730) 27.

798 Article 29 Data Protection Working Party, 'Opinion 02/2013 on Apps on Smart Devices, WP202' (n 730) 3–4.

799 Recital 47 GDPR: "*The processing of personal data for direct marketing purposes may be regarded as carried out for a legitimate interest*". Yet, according to the Belgian Privacy Commission obtaining consent of the data subject is a *best* practice, in the light of informational self-determination. Achieving a balance between the legitimate interest of the controller and interests or fundamental rights and freedoms of the data subject is very difficult in practice; when the balance is lost, the processing will need to be discontinued. Gegevensbeschermingsautoriteit, 'Aanbeveling Nr 02/2013 van 30 Januari 2013 Betreffende Direct Marketing En Bescherming van Persoonsgegevens [Recommendation No. 02/2013 of 30 January 2013 Regarding Direct Marking and the Protection of Personal Data]' 12.

800 Recital 47 GDPR. This balancing exercise must be undertaken continuously, and as soon as the interests of the controller do no longer outweigh the interests of the data subject the processing must be stopped: Gegevensbeschermingsautoriteit (n 799) 13–15.

801 Article 6, 1) (f) GDPR states that as a final legitimation ground that "*processing is necessary for the purposes of the legitimate interests pursued by the controller or by a third party, except where such interests are overridden by the interests or fundamental rights and freedoms of the data subject which require protection of personal data, in particular where the data subject is a child*".

1.3.6. Profiling

The concept. Children's activities in the digital environment reveal a significant amount of information on their lives, personal interests and preferences. Given today's advanced technologies and huge storage capacities this information can be continuously collected, processed and stored in detailed profiles, for instance by deploying cookies and other tracking tools.[802] Such profiles can be applied to categorise individuals and predict their preferences or future behaviour based on statistical methods.[803] In this way, profiles are very valuable to online service providers as well as to third parties (e.g. advertising networks) who will be able to offer targeted advertising to children or take other decisions in relation to those children with specific profiles.[804] This is a complex and largely opaque or 'invisible'[805] process which is very difficult to understand for children (or adults for that matter).

Provisions and recitals on profiling. Much attention is devoted to profiling in the GDPR.[806] The notion is defined in article 4 (4) as:

> "*any form of automated processing of personal data consisting of the use of personal data to evaluate certain personal aspects relating to a natural person, in particular to analyse or predict aspects concerning that natural person's performance at work, economic situation, health, personal preferences, interests, reliability, behaviour, location or movements*".[807]

Recital 75 GDPR finds that processing of personal data "*in order to create or use personal profiles*" may give rise to risks to the rights and freedoms of

802 F. J. Zuiderveen Borgesius, 'Improving Privacy Protection in the Area of Behavioural Targeting' (University of Amsterdam IViR 2015); Kosta (n 95). Recital 30 GDPR also mentions the use of internet protocol addresses or other identifiers such as radio frequency identification tags, "*leaving traces which, in particular when combined with unique identifiers and other information received by the servers, may be used to create profiles of the natural persons*".

803 Council of Europe, 'Recommendation CM/Rec(2010)13 on the Protection of Individuals with Regard to Automatic Processing of Personal Data in the Context of Profiling' <https://rm.coe.int/16807096c3> accessed 27 July 2018.

804 Y. Poullet, 'E-Youth before Its Judges – Legal Protection of Minors in Cyberspace' (2011) 27 Computer Law & Security Review 6, 11. An example of a decision or measure vis-à-vis a child in the commercial sphere is adapting the price of a specific product or service, based on the consumer profile of the child.

805 See the work of E. Keymolen, who has coined the notion 'invisible visibility' in relation to online interactions: E. Keymolen, 'Onzichtbare Zichtbaarheid. Helmuth Plessner Ontmoet Profiling' (2006); Keymolen (n 478).

806 The word 'profiling' appears 21 times in the GDPR.

807 Emphasis added by the author. For a similar definition see also Council of Europe, 'The Protection of Individuals with Regard to Automatic Processing of Personal Data in the Context of Profiling' (n 803).

natural persons.[808] The preamble of the GDPR provides a twofold protection for children in relation to profiling. First, circumstances in which personal data of children are processed in order to create personal or user profiles are explicitly acknowledged as requiring extra protection.[809] Second, according to recital 71, a decision that may include a measure evaluating personal aspects relating to a data subject that is based solely on automated processing should not concern children.[810] However, this is only prohibited as far as a decision produces legal effects for or similarly significantly affects the child.[811] Contrary to earlier interpretations of this recital[812], the GDPR does not prohibit the sole creation of personal or user profiles of children. This point of view is also underpinned by the debates in the process of the data protection reform, during which various Member States observed that profiling is a type or form of automated processing that does not necessarily result in the taking of decisions or measures that produce legal effects or similarly affect data subjects.[813] Moreover, in its recent guidelines on automated individual decision-making and profiling, the Article 29 Working Party confirms that there is no absolute prohibition on the profiling[814] of children in the GDPR.[815] Indeed, the Working Party recognises that under certain circumstances it may be necessary for controllers to carry out such decision-making, for instance to protect children's welfare.[816] In contrast to

808 Recital 75 GDPR underlines that the processing of personal data may result in a risk to the rights and freedoms of natural persons, in particular "*[...] where personal aspects are evaluated, in particular analysing or predicting aspects concerning performance at work, economic situation, health, personal preferences or interests, reliability or behaviour, location or movements, in order to create or use personal profiles*" (emphasis added).

809 Recital 38 GDPR.

810 Recital 71, first paragraph, final sentence GDPR.

811 Recital 71, first paragraph, final sentence GDPR.

812 See for instance: S. van der Hof, 'No Child's Play: Online Data Protection for Children' in S. van der Hof, B. van den Berg and B. Schermer (eds), *Minding Minors Wandering the Web: Regulating Online Child Safety* (TMC Asser Press, The Hague 2014) 137 <http://link.springer.com/chapter/10.1007/978-94-6265-005-3_7> accessed 27 July 2018; Macenaite (n 709) 7.

813 Council of the European Union, 'Presidency Note Concerning Profiling. Interinstitutional File: 2012/01(COD)' 5 <http://register.consilium.europa.eu/doc/srv?l=EN&f=ST%2010617%202014%20INIT> accessed 27 July 2018.

814 The ICO explained it well, by clarifying that "*the rules in Article 22 of the GDPR relate to solely automated decisions (which can include profiling) rather than to the process of profiling in itself*". ICO, 'What If We Want to Profile Children or Make Automated Decisions about Them?' (25 May 2018) <https://ico.org.uk/for-organisations/guide-to-the-general-data-protection-regulation-gdpr/children-and-the-gdpr/what-if-we-want-to-profile-children-or-make-automated-decisions-about-them/> accessed 30 July 2018.

815 However, the Working Party recommends data controllers not to rely upon the exceptions in Article 22 (2) GDPR to justify such profiling (i.e. necessary for the performance of a contract, authorised by law, consent of the data subject). Article 29 Data Protection Working Party, 'Guidelines on Automated Individual Decision-Making and Profiling for the Purposes of Regulation 2016/679' (2017).

816 Article 29 Data Protection Working Party, 'Guidelines on Automated Individual Decision-Making and Profiling for the Purposes of Regulation 2016/679' (n 815).

the preamble, the general 'profiling article' – article 22 GDPR – does not mention anything in relation to the specific protection that children deserve.[817]

PROFILING FOR DIRECT MARKETING PURPOSES. Finally, specific rules exist in relation to profiling for direct marketing purposes. Data subjects, including children, have the right to object at any time to profiling to the extent that it is related to direct marketing.[818] The data controller needs to clearly and explicitly inform the data subject of this right.[819]

1.3.7. Right to erasure ('right to be forgotten')

THE RIGHT TO ERASURE. In addition to the protection measures described above, the GDPR confirms data subjects' right to erasure of personal data. Recital 65 GDPR clarifies that this right is particularly relevant for children that have given their consent not being fully aware of the risks involved by the processing, and who later want to remove personal data, especially when being made public on the internet. According to article 17 GDPR, this right entails that data subjects may require the erasure of personal data when no longer necessary for the purposes for which they have been collected; when consent is withdrawn or they object to the processing; when the processing is unlawful; when the personal data have to be erased for compliance with a legal obligation; or when the personal data have been collected in relation to the direct offer of information society services to a child.[820] Yet, the right to erasure is not absolute. When considering whether a request should be granted, other interests such as the right to freedom of expression and information, and the public interest, must be taken into account.[821]

1.4. Other provisions with a potential impact on children

DATA PROTECTION BY DESIGN AND BY DEFAULT. Furthermore, the GDPR contains a number of provisions and recitals that could prove to be of particular importance from a children's rights perspective. The first two provisions can be framed within the responsibilities of data controllers. First, article 25 GDPR

---

817 Earlier case-law of the Court of Justice of the European Union (CJEU) has shown that recitals from the preamble must be used to interpret provisions in the legislation, and that courts may rely upon them to exercise their supervisory tasks. A recital, however, cannot be used as a ground to deviate from a provision of a directive or regulation. See *P Moskof AE v Ethnikos Organismos Kapnou* [1997] CJEU C-244/95, ECR I-06441; L. Humphreys and C. Santos, 'Mapping Recitals to Normative Provisions in EU Legislation to Assist Legal Interpretation' <http://icr.uni.lu/leonvandertorre/papers/jurix2015.pdf> accessed 27 July 2018.

818 Recital 70 and Article 21, (2) GDPR.

819 Recital 70 GDPR.

820 Article 17 GDPR.

821 Article 17, para 3 GDPR.

explicitly refers to the principles of data protection by design and data protection by default. It states that data controllers should implement appropriate technical and organisational measures to integrate necessary safeguards and protect the rights of data subjects and to ensure that, by default, only personal data that are necessary for each specific purpose of the processing are processed. Assessing which measures result in an appropriate level of protection should happen on a case-by-case basis, taking into account "*the state of the art, the cost of implementation and the nature, scope, context and purposes of processing as well as the risks of varying likelihood and severity for rights and freedoms of natural persons posed by the processing*".[822] This provision offers the data controller the possibility to build a specific level of protection for children into the technology or the offer of services, or to use different default settings for children.[823]

Data protection impact assessment. In addition, article 35 GDPR includes an obligation for data controllers to assess the impact of processing operations that are likely to result in a high risk to the rights and freedoms of data subjects, prior to the processing (i.e. a 'data protection impact assessment'; DPIA). Recital 91 states for instance that a DPIA must be carried out when personal data are processed for taking decisions regarding specific natural persons based on profiling. The processing of personal of data of children is not explicitly mentioned as a processing activity that carries a high risk[824], but in the light of recital 38, it could be considered a good practice to carry out a DPIA in such cases. Moreover, the Article 29 Working Party recognises the vulnerability of the data subject(s) as one of the criteria to be considered by national legislators when drafting a list of processing activities that require a DPIA.[825] When undertaking a DPIA a data controller should adopt a children's rights perspective that takes into account the full range of children's rights at stake as well as the best interests of the child.[826]

Awareness-raising. Finally, article 57 GDPR entrusts the supervisory authorities with the task of promoting public awareness and understanding of

822 Recital 83 GDPR.

823 S. van der Hof and E. Lievens, 'The Importance of Privacy by Design and Data Protection Impact Assessments in Strengthening Protection of Children's Personal Data under the GDPR' (2018) 23 Communications Law 33.

824 Note that in recital 75 in relation to the responsibility of the controller processing of "*personal data of vulnerable natural persons, in particular of children*" is considered a potential "*risk to the rights and freedoms of natural persons*".

825 Article 29 Working Party, Guidelines on Data Protection Impact Assessment (DPIA) and determining whether processing is "likely to result in a high risk" for the purposes of Regulation 2016/679

826 UNICEF has developed a children's rights impact assessment tool for companies; for more information; cf. https://www.unicef.org/csr/css/Children_s_Rights_in_Impact_Assessments_Web_161213.pdf.

the risks, rules, safeguards and rights in relation to processing. Specific attention should be paid to activities addressed specifically to children.

2. PROCESSING CHILDREN'S ELECTRONIC COMMUNICATIONS DATA – EPRIVACY FRAMEWORK

Specific rules for electronic communications. Another important legal instrument at the EU level is the ePrivacy Directive[827], which provides specific rules for the electronic communications sector and complements the General Data Protection Regulation. The ePrivacy Directive is the main legal instrument crystallising article 7 of the European Charter of Fundamental Rights (i.e. the right to respect for private life) into secondary EU law.[828] It provides specific rules for electronic communications services, including rules on the confidentiality of communications and on data breach notifications.[829] Over the years, the telecom sector has been undergoing significant changes, resulting in several updates of the rules in order to keep up with the new developments.[830]

2.1. ePrivacy Directive

Scope. In contrast to the GDPR, the scope of the ePrivacy Directive is not limited to personal data[831], as it protects communications from unwanted intrusions or interferences regardless of whether personal data is involved.[832] Furthermore, its main obligations only trigger responsibilities for traditional telecom operators.[833] Additionally, this Directive provides certain general rules on the use of location

827 Directive 2002/58/EC of the European Parliament and of the Council of 12 July 2002 concerning the processing of personal data and the protection of privacy in the electronic communications sector (Directive on privacy and electronic communications) 2002 (Official Journal L 201).

828 BEUC, 'Position Paper: Proposal for a Regulation on Privacy and Electronic Communications (e-Privacy)' 2 <www.beuc.eu/publications/beuc-x-2017-059_proposal_for_a_regulation_on_privacy_and_electronic_communications_e-privacy.pdf> accessed 3 April 2018.

829 Recital 10 of the ePrivacy Directive clarifies that the Data Protection Directive remains applicable "*to all matters concerning the protection of fundamental rights and freedoms which are not specifically covered by the provisions of this Directive, including the obligations on the controller and the rights of individuals*".

830 DLA Piper, 'European Telecommunications Network Operator's Association (ETNO) Study on the Revision of the EPrivacy Directive' (2016) 9–11 <https://etno.eu/datas/publications/studies/DPTS_Study_DLA_04082016_ePrivacy_Final.pdf> accessed 16 April 2018.

831 Recital 24 of the ePrivacy Directive states that "*Terminal equipment of users of electronic communications networks and any information stored on such equipment are part of the private sphere of the users requiring protection under the European Convention for the Protection of Human Rights and Fundamental Freedoms.*" (emphasis added).

832 BEUC (n 828) 2.

833 These were the main providers collecting electronic communications data at the time of the adoption of the Directive.

data or the storage of information on the devices of end-users (e.g. users of social media), which could be applicable when it comes to new advertising formats aimed at minors. The application of these general provisions is not limited to electronic communication services and include for instance article 5 (3) on cookies and spyware and article 13 on unsolicited communications.

Confidentiality of communications. One of the objectives of the ePrivacy Directive is to ensure confidentiality of communications. Accordingly, article 5 of the Directive contains a prohibition on intercepting or surveilling electronic communications as well as any storage of (or subsequent access to) information on the terminal equipment of end-users[834], unless (a) the users concerned have consented or (b) there exists an explicit legal authorisation.[835] The scope of application of this article is general and not limited to the electronic communications sector. Thus, this provision will apply to applications which run on mobile devices and on any other end-user devices and therefore be relevant for most online social network providers, website operators, application providers and trackers.[836]

Use of location data. Location data are often processed in digital mobile networks to enable the transmission of communications. This category includes all data indicating the geographic position of the terminal equipment of a user, like the latitude, longitude or altitude of the terminal equipment; the direction of travel of the user; or the time the location information was recorded.[837] Such data can be useful for advertisers who want to provide location-based direct marketing. The ePrivacy Directive contains specific requirements for the processing of location data in its article 9. However, according to the Article 29 Working Party, article 9 of the ePrivacy Directive only applies to providers of communication services and as such will not be applicable to advertisers.[838] Nevertheless, location data are generally regarded as personal data. Therefore, advertisers have to comply with the general requirements for the processing of personal data under the GDPR if they want to collect or use location data for advertising purposes.

2.2. *Proposal for an ePrivacy Regulation*

European Commission proposal. On January 10, 2017, the European Commission (EC) adopted its Proposal for a Regulation on Privacy and

834 Article 5 (3) ePrivacy Directive.

835 Article 5(1) ePrivacy Directive; See also Brendan Van Alsenoy, 'Rights and Obligations of Actors in Social Networking Sites' 33 <https://lirias.kuleuven.be/handle/123456789/453689> accessed 4 August 2017.

836 Van Alsenoy (n 835) 34.

837 Article 2 (c) ePrivacy Directive.

838 Article 29 Data Protection Working Party, 'Opinion 13/2011 on Geolocation Services on Smart Mobile Devices, WP 185' <http://ec.europa.eu/justice/article-29/documentation/opinion-recommendation/files/2011/wp185_en.pdf> accessed 27 July 2018.

Electronic Communications. The proposed Regulation contains new and more stringent privacy obligations that are said to have an important impact on online advertising and direct marketing (and on nearly all companies in the EU that are involved in online business).[839] The Commission considers the alignment of the ePrivacy rules with the GDPR as essential for ensuring a consistent EU framework on data protection and privacy. Furthermore, the review of the ePrivacy Directive was also triggered by the major advances in digital technologies of the last decade and the rise of over the top services including internet-based messaging and voice over IP which are currently not covered by the Directive. In the context of this book, t*he most important changes proposed by the EC's proposal relate to its scope, to existing rules on the use of cookies, direct marketing and the confidentiality of communications.*

Expanded scope. The proposed Regulation significantly expands its scope of application. First, regarding territorial scope, it does not only envisage entities in the EU, but any electronic communication service provided to end-users within the EU and devices located in the EU, regardless of the service provider's location. Second, the proposal now explicitly includes Over-the-Top communications services (OTTs) (i.e. online services that could to a certain extent substitute traditional media and telecom services, such as Skype, WhatsApp, Facebook Messenger).[840] As the user group of these services for a significant part consists of minors, it is important to see whether the proposed rules reflect their rights and interests, especially in the context of digital advertising.

Consent. The EC's proposal brings about some substantial changes for the online advertising industry. Most notably, it adapts existing rules on cookies, direct marketing and confidentiality of communications.[841] First, the Proposal introduces the application of the 'GDPR-grade of consent', also for the placement and accessing of cookies. Article 7(4) of the GDPR requires consent to be 'freely given, specific, informed and unambiguous' and must be expressed by way of a 'statement or by a clear affirmative action.' On top of that, it should be just as easy to withdraw as it is to give consent.

Cookies. The Proposal also adapts other aspects of the cookie rules (and broadens them to other tracking techniques, like device fingerprinting). First

---

839 S. Cadiot, 'Status Update on the EU E-Privacy Regulation Proposal Discussions' (*The WSGR Data Advisor*, 1 September 2017) <https://www.wsgrdataadvisor.com/2017/09/eu-e-privacy-regulation/> accessed 3 April 2018.

840 In line with the definition of an electronic communications service contained in the proposed Electronic Communications Code.

841 N. Johnson and G. Graham, 'The Draft EPrivacy Regulation and Its Impact on Online Advertising and Direct Marketing' <http://marketinglaw.osborneclarke.com/wp-content/uploads/sites/4/2017/04/DBL-January-2017-4-6.pdf>.

party functional cookies that are necessary to provide an information society service are already allowed without consent today. However, the Proposal broadens this approach: such cookies no longer need to be 'strictly' necessary, nor must the service be 'explicitly' requested by the end-user (e.g. form filling, language preference and shopping cart functionalities). Cookies for first party analytics are also allowed, even without consent. Additionally, the Commission wanted to tackle excessive cookie consent banners and consumer fatigue, by allowing consent to cookies through browser settings (when technically possible and feasible). For 'tracking cookies', however, the consent conditions are stricter: consent can only validly be granted if the user takes 'affirmative action' to actively select consent to tracking. It is even stipulated that all browsers should be configured to provide users with the ability to select options relating to cookies, fingerprinting etc. upon installation. The proposal places a burden on browser suppliers to equip all new software with this feature. When browser software is already installed, compliance would be required at the time of the first update of the software.

Direct marketing. Furthermore, the rules on direct marketing will apply to communications sent using a broader range of technologies, including instant messaging services and in-app notifications. All types of unsolicited electronic direct marketing communications would be prohibited by the proposed Regulation, unless the sender has obtained the end-user's consent in advance. However, there is an exception for the use of emails already collected during previous sales when it concerns direct marketing of similar goods and services to those already sold to these consumers and provided that the consumers have been clearly, distinctly and freely given the opportunity to object to such further use of their data.

No references to children. Finally, it is interesting to note that the proposed ePrivacy Regulation does not contain any reference to children. This is in contrast with the GDPR's explicit recognition of children as a vulnerable group of consumers that deserve specific protection, especially in the context of profiling and marketing.

Position of the European Parliament. Within the EP, the proposed ePrivacy Regulation was assigned to the Civil Liberties Committee (LIBE) and more than 800 amendments were submitted by mid-July 2017.[842] In October 2017, the EP adopted its position on the e-Privacy Regulation.[843] In general, the EP

842 See <www.europarl.europa.eu/legislative-train/theme-connected-digital-single-market/file-jd-e-privacy-reform> accessed 31 August 2018.

843 European Parliament (Committee on Civil Liberties, Justice and Home Affairs), 'Report on the Proposal for a Regulation of the European Parliament and of the Council Concerning the Respect for Private Life and the Protection of Personal Data in Electronic

proposes to tighten the rules of the EC's Proposal. A number of amendments are particularly relevant to the topic of this book. First, one of the main points of disagreement of the EP are the Commission's proposals on consent and preventing the further processing of data. The EP does not allow electronic communications service providers to (1) rely on their legitimate interest to process metadata, and (2) further process metadata for new purposes (e.g. big data, marketing) without the consent of the user, if the new purposes are considered compatible with the purposes for which the data was initially collected. Second, the EP proposes to expand the scope of the confidentiality principle to data related to or processed by devices (for instance cookies). Third, regarding the rules on direct marketing, the EP's amendments clarify that the right to withdrawal of consent must be available free of charge. Finally, the EP widened the scope of direct marketing communications to include any form of advertising, regardless of the form it takes.

Discussions in the Council. At the time of writing, the Member States had not reached a common position on the proposed e-Privacy Regulation. The main points of discussion amongst the Member States are the lawful grounds for processing electronic communications data (other than consent), introducing a possibility for further compatible processing of electronic communications metadata, protecting users' terminal equipment information and privacy settings.[844]

3. SELF-REGULATION

The advertising industry has also responded to the increased collection of consumer's personal data for targeted advertising purposes. Several industry organisations (international and European) have developed self-regulatory instruments or guidance documents, addressing the protection of children in this specific context.

3.1. ICC Code

The ICC Code. First, the International Chamber of Commerce Consolidated Code of Advertising and Marketing Practice contains – aside from provisions

---

Communications and Repealing Directive 2002/58/EC (Regulation on Privacy and Electronic Communications) (COM (2017)' (2017).

844 Council of the European Union, 'Presidency Text – Proposal for a Regulation of the European Parliament and of the Council Concerning the Respect for Private Life and the Protection of Personal Data in Electronic Communications and Repealing Directive 2002/58/EC (Regulation on Privacy and Electronic Communications)' <https://eur-lex.europa.eu/legal-content/EN/TXT/PDF/?uri=CONSIL:ST_10975_2018_INIT&from=EN> accessed 31 August 2018.

that are applicable to all forms of commercial communication[845] – provisions on the protection of (children's) personal data.[846]

GENERAL DATA PROTECTION PRINCIPLES. In this regard, article 19 of the ICC Code determines the requirements that need to be kept in mind when processing personal data. Personal data should only be collected for a specified and legitimate purpose; should be stored only for as long as needed to achieve the specified purpose; should be accurate and kept up to date; and should be adequate, relevant and not excessive in relation to the purpose for which they are collected. Furthermore, adequate security measures should be in place and any third party to which the data is transferred should respect an adequate level of security.

CHILDREN'S PERSONAL DATA. Aside from the general data protection principles, article 19 contains additional requirements for the collection of children's personal data. These requirements apply to children under 13 years. If, for example, a website provider (i.e. the data controller) collects children's personal data, he/she will have to offer guidance to parents or legal guardians about ways to protect their children's privacy (if feasible). Moreover, children should be stimulated to request their parents' permission before providing their personal data via digital interactive media. This requirement entails that a parental consent mechanism should be in place, with a reasonable degree of verifiability. However, the ICC Code does not mention any specific consent nor verification mechanisms. Accordingly, it will be up to each individual data controller to install an appropriate mechanism. The Code also requires parental consent for using children's data for addressing marketing communications to the parents or other family members as well as for any transfer of data to third parties. Furthermore, the Code also contains specific provisions concerning online behavioural advertising. In relation to children, the most important provision is article D7.4, which prohibits the creation of segments specifically designed to target children 12 and younger for OBA purposes.

3.2. *EASA Best Practice Recommendation on Online Behavioural Advertising*

THE ORGANISATION. At the EU level, a relevant initiative has been developed by the European Advertising Standards Alliance ("EASA"). As mentioned in the first part of this book, EASA was set up as a non-profit organisation promoting ethical standards in advertising through self-regulation in 1992.[847] It unites

845 For more information on the International Chamber of Commerce as an organisation and the general principles of the ICC Code see section 4.2 of this chapter.
846 International Chamber of Commerce (n 137).
847 For more information see www.easa-alliance.org/.

national self-regulatory organisations ("SROs") and organisations representing the advertising industry in Europe and beyond. The organisation has assisted in the setup of several self-regulatory mechanisms in Europe and it has promoted self-regulation as an alternative to detailed legislation at the EU policy level. In 2002, EASA's mission was expanded to include the adoption of Best Practice Recommendations to guide SROs, in order to strengthen and extend self-regulation in Europe.[848] EASA is funded by the membership fees paid by SROs and industry associations. In addition, EASA has become a member of the Commission on Marketing and Advertising, thereby taking up a more central role in the adoption and revision of the ICC Codes.[849]

3.2.1. Concept and definition

Best Practice Recommendations. EASA has a mandate to develop Best Practice Recommendations ("BPRs") for advertising practices. BPR's can be divided in two subcategories, (1) operational BPR's, which offer guidance regarding the operation, structure and procedures of SRO's, and (2) blueprint BPR's which provide guidance on the remit and codes of SRO's.[850] EASA developed a blueprint BPR on online behavioural advertising ("OBA"), which was agreed upon by the whole advertising eco-system and all SRO's at the European level. The BPR does not, however, constitute a European code and it is not formally binding. It merely presents a blueprint of guidance for a European implementation strategy. This means that the national SRO's are free to adopt the recommendations in their national self-regulatory codes and they may also go beyond that.[851]

Online behavioural advertising. The BPR defines online behavioural advertising as:

> *"the collection of data from a particular computer or device regarding web viewing behaviours over time and across multiple web domains not under Common Control for the purpose of using such data to predict web user preferences or interests to deliver online advertising to that particular computer or device based on the preferences or interests inferred from such web viewing behaviours. Online Behavioural Advertising*

[848] P. Verbruggen, 'Gorillas in the Closet? Public and Private Actors in the Enforcement of Transnational Private Regulation' 7 Regulation & Governance 512.

[849] Verbruggen, 'Case Study Report – Transnational Private Regulation in the Advertising Industry. Conducted within the Framework of the Research Project Constitutional Foundations of Transnational Private Regulation' (n 143).

[850] European Advertising Standards Alliance, 'Best Practice Recommendation on Online Behavioural Advertising' 7 <www.easa-alliance.org/sites/default/files/EASA%20Best%20Practice%20Recommendation%20on%20Online%20Behavioural%20Advertising_0.pdf> accessed 12 April 2018.

[851] European Advertising Standards Alliance (n 850) 7–8.

does not include the activities of Web Site Operators (First Party), Ad Delivery or Ad Reporting, or contextual advertising (e.g. advertising based on the content of the web page being visited, a consumer's current visit to a web page, or a search query)."[852] *(Emphasis added)*

3.2.2. Recommendations for best practices

Children and OBA. Similar to the ICC Code, the BPR standard requires that companies do not create segments that are specifically designed to target children using online behavioural advertising. However, what is not restricted is the collection of OBA data in order to market children's products to parents or other adults.[853]

Notice and choice. According to the BPR, third parties that are engaged in OBA should have a clear privacy notice on their website about their data processing practices and provide a link to the OBA Consumer Choice Platform (*infra*). Moreover, such companies have to provide an enhanced notice to internet users if they process data for OBA purposes on a website or mobile app that is not controlled by them.[854] Moreover, they should implement a user-friendly mechanism (i.e. an icon linking to the OBA Consumer Choice Platform) that allows internet users to exercise their choice with regard to the processing of their data for OBA purposes.

Easily accessible mechanisms for complaints. Finally, EASA recommends that easily accessible mechanisms for complaints should be developed, and these should be *inter alia* transparent, coordinated and consumers should be able to file complaints in their local language.[855] Moreover, as a minimum requirement, SROs should take appropriate action against persistent and repeated offenders, including the referral to appropriate legal authorities.

3.3. IAB Europe EU Framework for Online Behavioural Advertising

Interactive Advertising Bureau Europe ("IAB" Europe). Another self-regulatory initiative originates from the IAB Europe, a European business organisation that develops industry standards, offers legal advice, education and training and conducts research for the European digital advertising industry. Its members include a large number of players of the advertising industry.[856] IAB Europe promotes self-regulation and has laid down a structure for codifying

852 European Advertising Standards Alliance (n 850) 7–8. *Ibidem*, 10.
853 Principle III – Sensitive Segmentation, A. Children's Segmentation.
854 Principle I – Notice, A.2 Third Party Notice to Consumers.
855 Principle IV – Compliance and Enforcement Programmes.
856 For more information see www.iabeurope.eu/directory-member/adform/.

industry best practices on online behavioural advertising. Moreover, the framework establishes certain principles that aim at increasing transparency and choice for internet users within the EU.

3.3.1. Aim and scope of the Framework

AIM. The IAB Europe members that have worked jointly on and have signed the EU Framework for OBA commit to implementing the Framework's consumer-friendly standards, when making use of online behavioural advertising. The Framework is self-regulatory and creates obligations for any of the members that self-certify their compliance with the principles. The principles are intended to assist companies when designing their systems and contracts relating to online behavioural advertisements, to be compliant with the applicable law. The Framework does not, however, regulate the content nor the delivery of the online advertisements.[857]

SCOPE. The Framework is applicable to OBA, which is defined as follows:

> *"the collection of data from a particular computer or device regarding web viewing behaviours over time and across multiple web domains not under Common Control for the purpose of using such data to predict web user preferences or interests to deliver online advertising to that particular computer or device based on the preferences or interests inferred from such web viewing behaviours." (Emphasis added)*

Explicitly excluded from this definition are (1) the activities of website operators, (2) the actual advertising delivery or reporting or (3) contextual advertising (i.e. based on the content of the webpage that is currently visited by the consumer or a search query). The Framework establishes several principles and standards for OBA, which can be subdivided into one principle specifically applicable to children and the rest more general principles on data protection and privacy.

3.3.2. Principles for OBA

CHILDREN AND OBA. Important to note in the context of commercial communication aimed at children is that in line with the ICC Code, Principle 4.A of the Framework states that:

> *"companies agree not to create segments for OBA purposes that are specifically designed to target children. For the purposes of this provision, children refers to people age 12 and under." (Emphasis added)*

[857] IAB Europe, 'EU Framework for Online Behavioural Advertising.' <www.iabeurope.eu/wp-content/uploads/2016/05/2013-11-11-IAB-Europe-OBA-Framework_.pdf> accessed 27 July 2018.

Aside from this specific protection for children, the Framework also contains more general principles regarding data protection and privacy.

NOTICE AND CHOICE. The first two principles of the Framework deal with the concepts of notice and choice. Internet users must be given notice of the OBA data collection and use practices by the relevant third parties[858] as well as the website operator (i.e. of its OBA arrangements with third parties). Secondly, third parties have to provide internet users with a mechanism to exercise their choice regarding the use of their data for OBA purposes (Principle II). Important to note is that the minimum requirement is opt-out consent, with a more robust consent requirement for sensitive data.[859]

EDUCATION. Aside from the information that is required for the notice and choice mechanism, companies that employ OBA and are committed to the Framework should inform individuals and businesses about OBA, including *inter alia* on how data is collected, how the user may exercise his choice regarding OBA and how data is used for OBA purposes (Principle V).

SECURITY. According to the security principle, companies can only retain the data obtained and used for OBA purposes for as long as it is necessary to fulfil a legitimate business need (Principle III.B). Furthermore, companies should implement appropriate "*physical, electronic and administrative safeguards*" for the protection of the data collected and used for OBA purposes (Principle III.A).

SENSITIVE DATA. If companies want to collect and use sensitive data (other than children's data) for OBA purposes, they will have to obtain the prior explicit consent of the internet user, in accordance with data protection legislation (Principle IV.B). However, the OBA Principles do not address situations where profiling may be so unfair or discriminatory that it should not be allowed, apart from the profiling of under-13s.

---

858 The notice should include the following information of the third party: (a) their identity and contact details; (b) the types of data collected, (c) purposes for processing and recipients of the data, (d) an easy to use mechanism to exercise their choice, (e) the fact that the company commits to the Framework and finally (f) a link to the OBA User Choice Site. Accessed at www.iabeurope.eu/wp-content/uploads/2016/05/2013-11-11-IAB-Europe-OBA-Framework_.pdf on 06.09.2016.

859 N. King and P. Wegener Jessen, 'Profiling the Mobile Customer – Is Industry Self-Regulation Adequate to Protect Consumer Privacy When Behavioural Advertisers Target Mobile Phones? – Part II' (2010) 26 Computer Law & Security Review 595. With the adoption of the General Data Protection Regulation, these principles require an update as Recital 32 clarifies that "*consent should be given by a clear affirmative act establishing a freely given, specific, informed and unambiguous indication of the data subject's agreement to the processing of personal data relating to him or her*".

Audits. The Framework also requires companies to submit to independent audits of their self-certified commitments. Principle VI.C also establishes the minimum elements that should be demonstrated in an audit.

Complaint-handling. Finally, the OBA Principles also include requirements for complaint-handling mechanisms. First, consumers should be able to file complaints directly to the company. Second, consumers should have easy access to transparent and easily recognisable mechanisms for handling complaints through independent, alternative dispute resolution mechanisms (like national advertising self-regulatory organisations) in their own local language. To avoid multiple enforcement mechanisms, companies and alternative dispute resolution mechanisms should coordinate their efforts. Decisions of non-compliance should be published, including in the language of the country where the complaint was first launched.

3.4. *FEDMA Codes of conduct*

Finally, the Federation of European Direct Marketing also developed two relevant codes containing general data protection provisions and provisions containing specific protections for children.[860]

3.4.1. FEDMA European Code of Practice for the Use of Personal Data in Direct Marketing

Aim. The FEDMA Code of Practice for the Use of Personal Data in Direct Marketing is a European data protection code of practice for practitioners (i.e. direct marketers). More specifically, it is a self-regulatory initiative in the advertising sector to regulate data gathering for marketing purposes. The Code was drafted in collaboration with the Article 29 Working Party[861] and provides an interpretation of the European Data Protection Directive in the context of direct marketing.[862] The Article 29 Working Party is of the opinion that the FEDMA Code

---

860 For more information on the organisation, see section II of this chapter of the study.

861 Article 29 Data Protection Working Party, 'Opinion 4/2010 on the European Code of Conduct of FEDMA for the Use of Personal Data in Direct Marketing, WP 174' (2010) <http://ec.europa.eu/justice/data-protection/article-29/documentation/opinion-recommendation/files/2010/wp174_en.pdf> accessed 14 November 2017.

862 Article 29 Data Protection Working Party, 'Opinion 3/2003 on the European Code of Conduct of FEDMA for the Use of Personal Data in Direct Marketing' (2003) <http://ec.europa.eu/justice/article-29/documentation/opinion-recommendation/files/2003/wp77_en.pdf> accessed 31 July 2018. In this regard it should be kept in mind that article 27 of the Data Protection Directive required that any code of conduct submitted under this article (like the FEDMA Code and Annex) had to be of "*sufficient quality and internal consistency and must provide sufficient added-value, in terms of being sufficiently focussed on the specific data protection questions and problems in the organisation or sector to which it is intended to apply and offers sufficiently clear solutions for those questions and problems*".

and Annex fulfil these requirements. The FEDMA Data Protection Committee has to report annually to the Article 29 Working Party on the application of the Code. Additionally, for certain areas of practice, the Code recommends higher standards of practice than those established by the Directive. With the Code, FEDMA aims to create a general standard or custom and practice for the entire industry on the implementation of data protection rules in direct marketing.[863]

A. Scope and definitions

Scope. FEDMA's national members have agreed that their national codes of practice shall at least offer the same level of protection for data subjects as provided by the FEDMA Code (or offer a higher level of protection). The Code is an instrument of best practice that is to be interpreted in accordance with the framework of applicable data protection legislation. The Code is designed to be applied by direct marketers within the EU and those non-EU countries with data protection legislation similar to EU legislation, when using personal data for their marketing practices. As such, it is an instrument that could contribute to the spreading of the EU data protection standards across the globe.

Definition of direct marketing. According to the FEDMA Code, direct marketing is to be understood as:

> *"the communication by whatever means (including but not limited to mail, fax, telephone, on-line services etc...) of any advertising or marketing material, which is carried out by the Direct Marketer itself or on its behalf and which is directed to particular individuals".*

Definition of a child. The Code contains general principles on data protection applied to direct marketing, as well as specific provisions that apply to the processing of children's personal data. The Code defines children as "*any individual aged under 14 years old unless otherwise defined in national legislation/ self-regulation*". This subsection focuses on those provisions that specifically apply to children's personal data (i.e. Section 2.6 of the Code).

B. Principles regarding children's privacy and data protection

B.1. Direct Marketing – offline and online

Notice and choice. Direct marketers that collect children's personal data are required to make 'every reasonably effort' to ensure that the concerned child

[863] FEDMA, 'European Code of Practice for the Use of Personal Data in Direct Marketing' (n 709).

and/or the parent are properly informed about the purpose(s) for processing the data. Such a notice should be prominent, readily accessible and understandable by children. Direct marketers also have to obtain parental consent prior to the processing of the data, in accordance with applicable laws and self-regulation. Furthermore, they do not only have to obtain parental consent, but they also have to use every reasonable endeavour to verify whether the consent was actually given by the parent of the concerned child (and for instance not by the child himself).

Data subjects rights. According to the Code, parents should be able to exercise their children's rights as data subjects. More specifically these rights are – in line with EU data protection legislation – the right to object to the processing of their child's data or to the disclosure of that data to a third party, the right to access and rectification, and deletion of the data in case the processing does not comply with applicable data protection legislation.

Games. Finally, in relation to games, direct marketers should not demand more personal data than is strictly necessary when children want to participate in a game, when they may receive a prize or in relation to any other activity involving a promotional benefit.

B.2. Direct marketing – online

Electronic Communications Annex. Complementary to the provisions of the Code of Practice, FEDMA also adopted an Electronic Communications Annex that contains provisions specifically applicable to online direct marketing (or electronic mail marketing).[864] It aims at providing cross-border marketers with guidelines on how to behave when engaged in online marketing.[865] More specifically, the provisions of the Annex can be categorised as (1) general provisions for the processing of personal data and (2) provisions specific to the processing of children's personal data. This section only covers those provisions that specifically apply to children's personal data (Section 6 of the Annex).

Parental consent. Direct marketers will have to obtain prior parental consent for the processing of personal data of children who have not yet reached the age required by law to give their consent. Important to note is that parents may withdraw their consent at any point in time. For children that have reached this age, the Annex offers a model clause that direct marketers may use for obtaining the child's consent:

---

864 FEDMA, 'European Code of Practice for the Use of Personal Data in Direct Marketing – Electronic Communications Annex (the On-Line Annex)' <http://ec.europa.eu/justice/data-protection/article-29/documentation/opinion-recommendation/files/2010/wp174_annex_en.pdf> accessed 14 November 2017.

865 Article 29 Data Protection Working Party, 'Opinion 4/2010 on the European Code of Conduct of FEDMA for the Use of Personal Data in Direct Marketing, WP 174' (n 861).

Figure 1: Model clause for children's consent (Source: Annex p. 14, http://ec.europa.eu/justice/data-protection/article-29/documentation/opinion-recommendation/files/2010/wp174_annex_en.pdf)

3) Model Clause asking for the children's consent:

Here at [company name], we need your name and other details about you so that we can [purposes]. You can give us these details by filling out this form. Because you are under [x], we need to make sure that the people who look after you (like your parents or carer) are OK with us having information about you.

Remember, either you or someone who looks after you can ask us to see the information we have about you at any time. You can also ask us to correct it if it's wrong. You can also tell us to stop emailing you if you don't want to hear from us anymore.

If you want to email us about this (or anything else), use this email address (...@...).

Age verification mechanism. Direct marketers are also required to have an age verification mechanism in place. The mechanism should be able to guarantee that the age of the child as well as the authenticity of the parental consent has been effectively checked. The Annex does not provide any further guidance regarding the type of mechanism, but merely requires that direct marketers use "reasonable efforts". In this regard, FEDMA also recognises that at the moment there is no universally accepted age verification system.

Limitations. Furthermore, the Annex contains certain limitations direct marketers need to keep in mind:

- Data of family members: These data cannot be collected from the child, without the permission of the person to whom the data refer.[866]
- Sensitive data[867]: Direct marketers may not invite children to share this type of data without the prior consent of their legal representative.
- Incentivise children to share more data: Direct marketers may not incentivise children to provide their own personal data or personal data of a third party for marketing purposes, in exchange for a material or virtual reward.[868]

866 Nevertheless, data regarding the identity and address of the parent or legal representative may still be processed for authorisation and verification purposes. FEDMA, 'European Code of Practice for the Use of Personal Data in Direct Marketing – Electronic Communications Annex (the On-Line Annex)' (n 864).

867 Sensitive data are data revealing the racial or ethnic origin, political opinions, religious or philosophical beliefs, trade-union membership, or the processing of data concerning health or sex life of the child, as well as the financial situation of the child or any third party such as their friends or family. FEDMA, 'European Code of Practice for the Use of Personal Data in Direct Marketing – Electronic Communications Annex (the On-Line Annex)' (n 864).

868 This includes invitations to provide personal data in order to be able to participate in a game of chance, tombola or lottery. FEDMA, 'European Code of Practice for the Use of Personal

INFORMATION. Finally, direct marketers who want to process children's data will have to inform them about the processing. This information has to be expressed in easily understandable language.

C. COMPLAINT-HANDLING

COMPLAINT HANDLING AT THE NATIONAL LEVEL. As the FEDMA Code is a European initiative, the establishment of mechanisms to handle complaints regarding the application of the Code is left to the national DMA's. Complaints are usually handled by special compliance boards, ethics committees or similar commissions established at the national level.[869]

CROSS-BORDER COMPLAINTS. If a national DMA is unable to solve the problem due to cross-border aspects, FEDMA can investigate the complaint itself. For these situations, the Code foresees that the investigation is conducted by the Data Protection Committee, which is an internal body of representatives of (1) national DMA's, (2) FEDMA and (3) companies that are direct FEDMA members. However, no cross-border complaints have been filed with the Data Protection Committee. According to MACENAITE, this may be due to practical difficulties related to the complaint mechanism.[870] When individuals want to file a complaint concerning online direct marketing, it may be difficult for them to prove that the advertisement was served to them and that it constitutes a violation of the FEDMA Code.[871]

3.4.2. FEDMA Code of Conduct on E-Commerce & Interactive Marketing

Aside from the Code on Direct Marketing, FEDMA's Code on e-Commerce (*supra*) also contains certain provisions that specifically apply to the processing of children's personal data (i.e. Section 6 of the Code).[872] As a general principle, the Code guarantees that direct marketers:

> *" will respect the sensibilities of children and shall protect the privacy of children, for example by demanding parental consent for any personal data-collection."*

Thus, direct marketers should obtain prior parental consent for the processing of children's personal data. The Code uses the terms 'minor' and 'child'

Data in Direct Marketing – Electronic Communications Annex (the On-Line Annex)' (n 864).

869 Macenaite (n 709).

870 Macenaite (n 709).

871 Verbruggen, 'Gorillas in the Closet?' (n 848).

872 In addition, Section 5 of the FEDMA Code on e-Commerce contains general provisions on consumer privacy and data protection (in relation to information obligations and data subject rights).

interchangeably and notes that as long as there is no consensus on an age limit across the EU, marketers should respect the applicable national regulations.

Educating parents. Aside from the parental consent requirement, marketers have to educate parents on current software tools and technologies, for instance in relation to privacy enhancement or the supervision of online activities. Parents should be encouraged to be more involved in their children's online activities. Moreover, the Code recommends that marketers attempt to monitor the extent to which children use their websites.

Verifiable parental consent. The FEDMA Code requires marketers to verify whether the consent given in reality stems from the parent/guardian/teacher.[873] The Code requires that before any personal data of children is collected by a website, they first have to supply their age. However, the Code does not contain any further guidance on what verification mechanisms would be appropriate, or what features they recommend.

Information requirements. Marketers also have to comply with certain information requirements under the FEDMA Code. First of all, they should provide a clear notice of their request for data collection, with easy-to-understand explanations of the purposes of collection. Moreover, marketers should use awareness notices for children that encourage them to ask for parental consent before entering personal data.[874] Parents should also be informed and have the right to object to the disclosure of their children's personal data to third parties.[875]

Protection against unsolicited email. Marketers have to take the necessary steps to avoid that children are targeted with unsolicited commercial email communication which does not relate to their interests.[876]

Limitations. Finally, the Code contains a number of limitations to the collection of children's personal data. Indeed, marketers may not collect more data from the child than is necessary for his/her participation in the website activities.[877] Furthermore, the child's access to a website must not be depending on the collection of detailed personal data. Other incentives such as prize offers and games should also not be used to encourage children to share more of their data.

873 In line with article 8 GDPR.
874 "Such notices should be displayed at the point where the information is requested, be clear, prominent and easily understandable by young children." See Article 6.8.3 of the FEDMA Code on E-Commerce.
875 Article 6.8.4 of the FEDMA Code on E-Commerce.
876 Article 6.8.6 of the FEDMA Code on E-Commerce.
877 Article 6.8.2 of the FEDMA Code on E-Commerce.

SECTION V. INTERIM CONCLUSION

Piecing together the regulatory puzzle. The aim of this chapter was twofold. The first objective was to piece together the puzzle of instruments regulating advertising at the EU level. To achieve a balanced and future-proof regulatory framework for commercial communication in line with children's rights, it is crucial to be aware of the existing regulatory context. This descriptive-analytical outline focused on four different contexts of EU legislation, combined with ARIs at the European or international level that are relevant to the specific context.

The consumer protection context. The starting point of the mapping exercise was the consumer protection framework. First, the UCP Directive was analysed, which contains general rules that advertisers need to keep in mind. More specifically, the Directive prohibits any unfair commercial practice, including misleading or aggressive commercial communication. These rules are applicable regardless of the form or delivery of the commercial message and, as such, provide an important safety net for children. Likewise, the ICC Code contains general provisions and specific protections for children in relation to advertising and marketing. It was found that the ICC Code also applies to both traditional and new advertising formats and that it is based on the general principles of honesty, legal compliance, truthfulness and decency of advertisements.

The audiovisual media services context. Second, the revised Audiovisual Media Services Directive was analysed, as the cornerstone of media regulation in the EU. It was found that this Directive contains the general rules and principles for audiovisual commercial communication, such as television advertising or advertising in on-demand services like Netflix. These rules and principles include most importantly the identification principle, a prohibition of direct exhortations to children to buy, a prohibition to the use of harmful content in advertising and specific rules for product placement and sponsoring. Moreover, it was concluded that the revised Directive recognises the evolutions in the market of audiovisual media services, for instance by levelling the playing-field between traditional and new media services providers and broadening its scope to include video-sharing platforms (and to a certain extent social media platforms). The next chapter of this part of the book will analyse whether this broadened scope also impacts advertisements distributed through such platforms.

The e-commerce context. Third, it was explained that the e-Commerce Directive contains identification and information requirements for commercial communications which are part of or constitute an information society service (e.g. sponsored search results, advertisements on social media). In this context, FEDMA's self-regulatory initiative on e-Commerce and interactive marketing was discussed, which provides similar protection for consumers. In addition to the identification and information requirements, it was found that the FEDMA Code provides specific protections against misleading commercial communications.

The data protection context. Finally, with regard to advertising formats that collect and process children's personal data, it was found that different legislative and self-regulatory obligations and principles, which run in parallel, apply. The discussion continued on how the GDPR explicitly recognises that children need specific protection when it comes to the processing of their personal data, and especially when this happens for advertising purposes. Furthermore, there needs to be a legitimate ground for such processing, for instance consent, depending on the age of the child, by the parents or by the parents and the child. A number of important data protection principles must also be adhered to: for instance, the personal data of children need to be processed fairly and lawfully, the data can only be collected for specified, explicit and legitimate purposes and must not be further processed in a way incompatible with the initially specified purpose(s), and only adequate, relevant and non-excessive data can be collected and/or further processed. According to the ICC, IAB Europe and EASA, behavioural advertising should not be aimed at children 12 years or under. In addition, the ePrivacy Directive – which is currently under review – contains the provisions for the processing of consumer's communications data.

Preparation for the next chapter. As a second objective, this chapter aimed at laying the basis for the legal evaluation of how new forms of commercial communication fit within this regulatory framework, which will be conducted in the next chapter. All legal elements that could be relevant in this specific commercial context were listed and briefly described. In the next chapter, these legal elements will be further discussed and the provisions will be applied to specific use cases, in order to identify and describe the precise gaps or overlaps with regard to new forms of commercial communication aimed at children. Ultimately, it aims at answering the question as to whether the current framework needs new legal elements (substantive, procedural or organisational) to ensure that children are adequately protected against harmful or misleading advertising and are enabled to develop their advertising literacy skills.

CHAPTER II
EVALUATION OF THE CURRENT REGULATORY FRAMEWORK

Overview. After the presentation and clarification of the issues related to children and new forms of commercial communication and a detailed analysis of the role of children's rights in regulating such forms in the first part of the study, the first chapter of this second part provided a descriptive-analytical overview of the legal elements contained in the existing regulatory framework for commercial communication at the EU level. From these previous chapters, an important research question follows: how do new advertising formats and their specific features – i.e. integration, interaction, personalisation and emotional appeal – fit within the identified regulatory framework, while keeping in mind children's rights and principles? In short, this chapter aims to discover any gaps or overlaps and highlight what legal elements are needed to attain a future-proof regulatory framework for commercial communication.

Selection of advertising formats. The evaluation consists of three use cases, which were selected on the basis of two factors: (1) popularity and (2) the level of risk it poses to children's advertising literacy. The popularity of the formats was extracted from studies on children's and adolescent's media use[878] and the forms of commercial communication that are employed the most in these media.[879] The second factor was extracted from a risk assessment, to determine which of these advertising formats were perceived as highly risky for children and youngsters.[880] As a result, the following (both popular and risky) advertising formats were selected: (1) advergames, (2) personalised advertising and (3) digital influencers and vlogging advertising. These formats also reflect one or more of the features described in the first chapter of the first part of this book (i.e. 'emerging trends in the area of commercial communication'). Each section

878 Zarouali and others, 'Mediabezit En -Gebruik Bij Minderjarigen. Een Rapport in Het Kader van Het AdLit Onderzoeksproject' (n 46). The study showed for instance that 70% of 3–4 year olds is already active online, showing the relevance of assessing advertising techniques that are sent via the internet. Also, the popularity of gaming amongst young children, especially boys, was an element that was considered.

879 Daems and De Pelsmacker (n 63).

880 Vanwesenbeeck and others (n 6).

will first conceptualise the specific advertising format, the persuasive tactics employed and the impact thereof on children's advertising literacy. Reference is made to the children's rights and principles that were analysed in the second chapter of the first part of the book. Second, the regulatory framework that is applicable to the specific use case or advertising format is evaluated, in light of these rights and principles. More specifically, the evaluation consists of two steps: (1) evaluating whether the existing rules are applicable to the selected advertising format and (2) evaluating whether there are any gaps or overlaps that would hinder the effective realisation of children's rights and principles.

SECTION I. ADVERGAMES[881]

The concept. A prime example of an advertising format in which all four trends could potentially occur are 'advergames'. This is an online phenomenon wherein the commercial message is immersed into the digital gaming content through brand or product placement. Advergames are omnipresent in children's online environments as they are inexpensive and cost only a fraction of the expenses required to launch television advertisements. Once the game is created (e.g. a website or a mobile app), there are no further distribution costs unless the game is updated.[882] They are highly effective in capturing children's attention, which would otherwise be hard to reach these days.[883] More specifically, advergames present stimulating and motivating content, appealing lay-outs, fantasy-world aspects and gaming elements which are all attractive to children and especially suited to trigger an emotional response from them.[884] In addition, advergames may also be personalised, which may even increase their emotional impact on the child.[885] Such integrated, interactive, emotions-evoking and potentially personalised marketing techniques challenge the traditional boundaries set in the context of conventional advertising and will therefore be assessed in the context of the current regulatory framework to determine their legality, as well as in light of children's fundamental rights.[886]

---

881 This section of the book is an adaptation of the following article: Verdoodt, Clifford and Lievens (n 7).

882 A. E. Staiano and S. L. Calvert, 'The Influence of Advergames on Children's Consumer Choices and Behavior', *Advertising to Children* (Palgrave Macmillan, London 2014) <https://link.springer.com/chapter/10.1057/9781137313256_12> accessed 9 November 2017.

883 S. M. Grimes, 'Kids' Ad Play: Regulating Children's Advergames in the Converging Media Context' <www.academia.edu/183317/Kids_Ad_Play_Regulating_Childrens_Advergames_in_the_Converging_Media_Context> accessed 7 November 2017.

884 Nairn and Hang (n 87).

885 For instance, Game Pill, a marketing-design company phrases it as follows: "*Games offer individual users a personalised experience. It is this experience that gives users a high level of engagement and powerful recall that many brands desire.*" Available at http://gamepill.com/gamification-advergaming-transmedia-our-guide-to-game-marketing-terms/.

886 See also Verdoodt, Clifford and Lievens (n 7).

1. INTEGRATION, INTERACTION, EMOTIONAL APPEAL AND PERSONALISATION MAY ALL BE PART OF THE GAME

1.1. Persuasive tactics and children's rights implications

PERSUASIVE TACTICS. Advergames are first of all characterised by a strong interplay between commercial and non-commercial or editorial content.[887] As mentioned previously, such a mixture can prove to be confusing and children are often unable to distinguish between the commercial message (reference to the product or service, or even the brand) and the non-commercial content, *in casu* the gaming elements (e.g. 'story', moving from one level to another).[888] In this regard, RANEY et al. found that if game players are not aware of the advertisements that are embedded within the games they play, their defences would be lower and they process commercial communication in a different manner.[889] In addition, research on advergames promoting food brands showed that the immersive and interactive nature of the games had the potential to influence children's preferences for the specific brands, even when they understood the persuasive intent of the game.[890] Moreover, DE JANS et al. found that children especially requested the advertised product more after exposure to an advergame compared to other new formats such as sponsored content and they had less understanding of the persuasive intent of advergames compared to traditional advertising (i.e. television commercial or online banner).[891] Advergames as a technique may capitalise on the emotion of the games (i.e. that they are fun to play) by creating positive brand awareness[892] and attitude towards the product or service.[893] Games can improve moods and it was discussed above how those in positive moods (i.e. happy) are less likely to process information in a systematic and critical way in comparison to those in negative moods, thus leaving them more open to persuasion.[894] Indeed, it appears well established that mood or emotional state determines how individuals process information and influences whether they do so superficially or in detail, thereby having

---

887 See part I chapter I section 2.2.

888 Rozendaal and others (n 42).

889 A. A. Raney and others, 'At the Movies, on the Web: An Investigation of the Effects of Entertaining and Interactive Web Content on Site and Brand Evaluations' (2003) 17 Journal of Interactive Marketing 38.

890 V. Mallinckrodt and D. Mizerski, 'The Effects of Playing an Advergame on Young Children's Perceptions, Preferences, and Requests' (2007) 36 Journal of Advertising 87.

891 Vanwesenbeeck and others (n 6).

892 M. L. Gross, 'Advergames and the Effects of Game-Product Congruity' (2010) 26 Computers in Human Behavior 1259.

893 Cauberghe and De Pelsmacker (n 84).

894 Rozendaal and others (n 42).

consequences on the effect of advertising campaigns.[895] This effect is important considering that advergames have a positive effect on resulting intended[896] and actual behaviour.[897] Finally, as the advancements in technology allow for the personalisation of content (i.e. the targeting of certain games towards identified children), this may be particularly worrying given the positive effect of advergames on moods, the corresponding increasing effectiveness of advertising campaigns and the consequences for children's commercial decision-making.

A CHILDREN'S RIGHTS PERSPECTIVE. From the analysis of the children's rights and principles it followed that, in the context of commercial communication, a balance is required between protecting children against harmful or misleading advertising and educating them to be able to cope with advertising in the digital environment. In the context of advergames, of particular relevance are the child's right to development (article 6 UNCRC), linked with *inter alia* the protection against economic exploitation (article 32 UNCRC), the right to play (article 31 UNCRC), the freedom of thought (article 14 UNCRC) and the right to privacy (article 16 UNCRC). First, the fact that children do not recognise advergames as having a commercial persuasive intent undermines their ability to process the message critically. As a result, children face the risk of being manipulated. In relation to this, a broader notion of economic exploitation under the children's rights framework was advocated in chapter one of part one of this book, to include other forms of exploitation aside from child labour. Second, gaming and play have an important role in the development process of children. In this regard, new media technologies like mobile apps and online games can facilitate access to a variety of playful and social activities. However, as mentioned above, embedding commercial messages straight into children's gaming experience could lead children to normalise the commercialisation of play. In turn, this may have a significant impact on how they think, feel and act in the marketplace.[898] Finally, the (potential) collection of personal data through advergames presents a risk to children's fundamental rights of privacy and data protection.[899] The best interests of the child principle demands an adequate protection of children's privacy and personal data, by giving effect as far as possible to these fundamental rights.[900] These rights should be balanced with the interests of businesses and

895 Hullett (n 124).

896 Mallinckrodt and Mizerski (n 890).

897 F. Folkvord and others, 'The Effect of Playing Advergames That Promote Energy-Dense Snacks or Fruit on Actual Food Intake among Children' (2013) 97 The American Journal of Clinical Nutrition 239.

898 E. J. Arnould and C. J. Thompson, 'Consumer Culture Theory (CCT): Twenty Years of Research' (2005) 31 Journal of Consumer Research 868. And thus affect both children's rights to play and to freedom of thought.

899 This is further discussed in the second use case on targeted advertising.

900 And in which personal data has a broad scope, i.e. any information allowing an individual to be identified, directly or indirectly, ranging from a name over a birth date, e-mail address, IP

their right to freedom of commercial speech.[901] Nevertheless, the child's best interest principle requires advertisers to take into account a child's immaturity and vulnerability, which demands adequate protection and care.

1.2. *Blurred lines, mixed emotions and the existing regulatory framework*

CONCEPTUAL DISTINCTION. The analysis of the protections of the regulatory framework in the context of advergames can be subdivided according to the conceptual differences between on the one hand the use of emotions in advertising techniques, and on the other hand the actual influence of such emotions on decision making.[902] In relation to the latter, "a decision" (or contract) must be made in order to invoke the application of the legal protections (such as those found in the Unfair Commercial Practices Directive protecting consumers from being misled in transactional decisions). In contrast, the former focuses more on the emotional appeal of the advergame in itself and the potentially deceptive mixing of commercial and non-commercial content therein.

1.2.1. The mixing of commercial and non-commercial content and advergames' emotional appeal

ADVERGAMES AND THEIR EMOTIONAL APPEAL. The use of emotions in advertising campaigns has long been recognised as significant. Marketers aim to evoke emotional responses in order to create awareness and positive brand association, and an emotional desire for a product or service. In this regard, article 18 of the ICC Consolidated Code notes that specifically in relation to children

> *"Marketing communications should not suggest that possession or use of the promoted product will give a child or young person physical, psychological or social advantages over other children or young people, or that not possessing the product will have the opposite effect."*

This appears to restrict advergames' use of emotion to create a desire for a product or service in order to advance in the game (e.g. requiring the purchase of a particular product in order to get to the next level in the game). However, it is also important to note that advergames as a technique may capitalise on the emotion of the games (i.e. that they are fun to play) by creating positive brand

address or photo. Article 29 Data Protection Working Party, 'Opinion 4/2007 on the Concept of Personal Data. WP 136.' (2007) 29 <http://ec.europa.eu/justice/data-protection/article-29/documentation/opinion-recommendation/files/2007/wp136_en.pdf> accessed 21 November 2017.

901 *X and Church of Scientology v. Sweden* (n 428).

902 Verdoodt, Clifford and Lievens (n 7).

awareness. Accordingly, the identification of such content needs to be made clear in order to allow the consumer to make informed choices in decision making without being unwittingly influenced.

Identification is the key requirement for advertisers. Although the importance of emotions and moods has long been empirically established by marketers and investigated by communication science researchers, the legal approach to advertising and emotion manipulation has been somewhat mute. According to Reed and Coalson, traditional protections in the context of advertising have focused on deceptive practices and misrepresentations by marketers.[903] The mapping exercise in the previous chapter showed that there are several protections against misleading advertisements and deception in both legislative[904] and alternative regulatory instruments.[905] In particular, the identification principle (i.e. commercial communication needs to be recognisable as such) was discovered as the common thread in all of these instruments. However, first, it should be questioned whether these instruments apply to advergames.

Information society services. At the EU level, it was found that the e-Commerce Directive[906] contains certain provisions relating to commercial communications[907], which are applicable to advergames. More specifically, the Directive stipulates that commercial communications "*which are part of, or constitute, an information society service*" must clearly identify promotional competitions or games and present the conditions for participation in a clear and unambiguous way and make them easily accessible.[908] As mentioned[909], services financed by advertising[910] could also fall within the definition of information

903 Reed and Coalson (n 112).

904 The e-Commerce Directive, AVMS Directive, UCP Directive.

905 E.g. the ICC Consolidated Code.

906 The main objective of this legal instrument is to establish an internal market for information society services. One of the topics that required regulation and is necessary to achieve this objective is commercial communications in online services. Directive 2000/31/EC of the European Parliament and of the Council of 8 June 2000 on certain legal aspects of information society services, in particular electronic commerce, in the Internal Market (Directive on electronic commerce).

907 Under Article 2(f) of the e-Commerce Directive, commercial communication is defined as "*any form of communication designed to promote*". This definition should be interpreted broadly and entails both direct and indirect promotion, as a way to prevent circumvention of the ban on commercial communications for certain products (e.g., tobacco, alcohol).

908 Article 6(d) Directive 2000/31/EC of the European Parliament and of the Council of 8 June 2000 on certain legal aspects of informa- tion society services, in particular electronic commerce, in the Internal Market (2000) OJ L 178. Article 6(a) e-Commerce Directive also requires commercial communication in general to be clearly identifiable as such.

909 *Supra* part II, chapter I, section III of the book.

910 Recital 18 e-Commerce Directive.

society services[911] and services do not necessarily require payment by the users themselves.[912]

Audiovisual media services. In addition to the e-Commerce Directive, the AVMS Directive was outlined, which contains certain principles and substantive requirements that are applicable to 'audiovisual commercial communication'. However, the application of this legal instrument to advergames is unlikely. Although advergames in theory could be interpreted as falling within the definition of an audiovisual commercial communication as defined by article 1(h) AVMS Directive[913], recital 22 stipulates that the definition of an audiovisual media service

> *"should exclude all services the principal purpose of which is not the provision of programmes, i.e. where any audiovisual content is merely incidental to the service and not its principal purpose."*

The recital goes on to note that

> *"games of chance involving a stake representing a sum of money, including lotteries, betting and other forms of gambling services, as well as online games and search engines (…) should also be excluded from the scope of this Directive."*

As such, the precise scope of application of the Directive is somewhat unclear as although advergames are games *per se*, one could argue that the game itself is merely the means for the delivery of the audiovisual commercial communication.[914] In this regard, certain authors have argued in favour of the applicability of the AVMS Directive to advergames, but their arguments are hardly concrete and convincing.[915] Of particular significance for advergames would be article 9(1)(a) which bans surreptitious advertising and thus promotes the principle of transparency. The final text of the revised Directive does not

---

911 As a reminder, these services can be "*any service normally provided for remuneration, at a distance, by electronic means and at the individual request of a recipient of services.*" Recital 18 e-Commerce Directive.

912 *Giuseppe Sacchi. Reference for a preliminary ruling: Tribunale civile e penale di Biella v Italy* (n 689); *Bond van Adverteerders v the Netherlands* (n 689).

913 As a reminder: "*Images with or without sound that are designed to promote, directly or indirectly, the goods, services or image of a natural or legal entity pursuing an economic activity. Such images accompany or are included in a programme in return for payment or for similar consideration or self-promotional purposes. Forms of audiovisual commercial communication include, inter alia, television advertising, sponsorship, teleshopping and product placement.*"

914 Verdoodt, Clifford and Lievens (n 7).

915 Steiner for instance claims that the blanket exemption in the Recital is merely a means of interpretation, and not part of the enforceable text of the Directive. Thomas Steiner, 'Advertising in Online Games and EC Audiovisual Media Regulation' (Social Science Research Network 2008) SSRN Scholarly Paper ID 1101363 <https://papers.ssrn.com/abstract=1101363> accessed 22 November 2017.

provide a clear answer to the matter, but the explicit mentioning of games has been deleted.

SELF-REGULATION. Similarly, the ICC Consolidated Code in article 9 emphasises the fact that marketing communications "*should be clearly distinguishable as such, whatever their form and whatever the medium used*". This article goes on to state that "*when an advertisement appears in a medium containing news or editorial matter, it should be so presented that it is readily recognisable as an advertisement and the identity of the advertiser should be apparent*". Particularly relevant to advergames is article 18 of the Code, which provides that marketers should not make it difficult for children and young people to distinguish between reality and fantasy and the marketing communications aimed at children should be easily distinguishable to them as such.

ADVERTISING CUES AND ADVERTISING LITERACY. Thus, it can be concluded that marketers are legally required to identify advergames as commercial content, so that consumers are able to make informed decisions without being unwittingly influenced. In practice, the principle of identification has led certain advertisers to use a type of labelling[916] or 'cues' to make commercial content recognisable. According to van REIJMERSDAL *et al.*, disclosing the commercial nature of advergames allows those in a positive mood to become more critical of the advertising message following disclosure of the commercial intent.[917] More specifically,

> "*the disclosure made them more aware of the persuasive nature of the advergame as indicated by higher persuasion knowledge, which in turn led to more brand recall and more negative game and brand attitudes than without a disclosure. These results seem to indicate that, with a disclosure, people in a positive mood process the advergame on a more elaborate and critical level than without a disclosure. In this situation, disclosures activate people's persuasion knowledge; that is, their knowledge about the commercial source and persuasive intent of the advergame.*"[918]

The authors found that as those in negative moods were already critical of the advergame they were more aware and, as a result, the disclosure of the

916 For instance, Facebook uses the term 'sponsored' for advertising messages that appear in the newsfeed of Facebook users. A 'Sponsored Story' is a mix between user-generated content and pro- motional content. A user's action related to a promotional message is shown with a promotional message in 'News Feed', see B. Van Alsenoy and others, 'From Social Media Service to Advertising Network – A Critical Analysis of Facebook's Revised Policies and Terms' <https://www.law.kuleuven.be/citip/en/news/item/facebooks-revised-policies-and-terms-v1-2.pdf>.

917 E. A. van Reijmersdal and others, 'Disclosing the Persuasive Nature of Advergames: Moderation Effects of Mood on Brand Responses via Persuasion Knowledge' (2015) 34 International Journal of Advertising 70.

918 Reijmersdal and others (n 917).

advergame's commercial nature failed to have a discernible impact in contrast to those in positive moods. The link between emotions and decision making is therefore significant and it seems apparent that disclosing the commercial intent of advergames and adequately identifying the commercial content, can allow the consumer to become more aware and critical of the marketing message.[919] In line with these findings, De Pauw *et al.* found that children can be empowered by explaining them where to look for advertising tactics and how they operate (e.g. by an advertising cue). The authors argued that an increased tactic awareness and comprehension of new forms of commercial communication would allow children to make a conscious decision about commercial products or services.[920] According to Hudders *et al.*, identification of the commercial message is a necessary precondition for advertising literacy to have an effect.[921]

Limits to the identification principle. From a substantive perspective, the integration of the commercial and non-commercial content presents a clear challenge in relation to the identification principle. Although the industry has created several labels and tools to signpost commercial content and enhance transparency, these tools will only be effective if all factors are considered. This includes elements such as cross-media use (where uniform labels are used across different media and different advertising formats), adoption processes by users or viewers, specific cognitive characteristics and levels of advertising literacy of specific user groups (such as minors) and regular monitoring of efficiency.[922] Recent studies on the effectiveness of the current standard of implementation of this requirement showed that disclosure characteristics may have an important impact on visual attention of individuals and in turn visual attention on advertising recognition. Roozendaal and Van Reijmersdal stress that disclosures can only contribute to increased transparency if viewers see the disclosure, understand it and are given the opportunity to process it (i.e. store it in their memory).[923] In order for this process to be successful, the disclosure needs to be formulated in clear and understandable language and designed and placed in such a manner that viewers easily spot it. In addition, Wojdynski and

[919] Verdoodt, Clifford and Lievens (n 7).

[920] More specifically, children were able to take into account the perspective of other children, which is essential to form a well-balanced moral judgement about advertising. De Pauw and others (n 60).

[921] Hudders and others, 'Shedding New Light on How Advertising Literacy Can Affect Children's Processing of Embedded Advertising Formats' (n 1).

[922] D. Clifford and V. Verdoodt, 'Integrative Advertising: The Marketing'dark Side'or Merely the Emperor's New Clothes?' (2017) 8 European Journal of Law and Technology <http://ejlt.org/article/view/547> accessed 8 August 2017.

[923] Esther Rozendaal and Eva A van Reijmersdal, 'Hoe Kan de Transparantie van Reclame in Online Video's Vergroot Worden Voor Minderjarigen? Een Literatuuronderzoek Naar de Effecten van Vermeldingen' <https://www.cvdm.nl/wp-content/uploads/2017/11/Literatuur onderzoek-Transparantie-Rozendaal-Van-Reijmersdal.pdf> accessed 23 November 2017.

Evans discovered that the often used words 'sponsored' or 'advertising' led in fact to greater advertising recognition, compared to vague disclosure language. However, in a second study, the authors analysed the actual placement of the advertising cue and found that the technique often used by industry (i.e. the top-placed disclosure) was seen as relatively ineffective in attracting the visual attention of the consumer.[924] Conversely, a middle-positioned disclosure or a disclosure within the content could be more effective in garnering attention and increasing consumer awareness.[925] These studies highlight the need for a more structured, standardised and evidence-based approach to the implementation of the identification requirement. The lack of qualitative criteria and standards for assessing advertising disclosures or cues in practice allows for a wide berth of interpretation by the advertising industry.

1.2.2. Deception, personalisation and influenced decision making

Advergames and the UCP Directive. In addition, it is important to discuss advergames in light of the consumer protection mechanisms that were described in the previous chapter. More specifically, the UCP Directive protects consumers – including children – from unfair business-to-consumer commercial practices. As described above such commercial practices include advertising and marketing by a trader, if the commercial message causes the consumer to take a decision that he or she would not otherwise have taken.[926] The Directive stipulates that commercial communication needs to be "*directly connected with the promotion, sale or supply of a product to consumers*".[927] In this regard, it could be questioned whether branding (e.g. promoting a brand's image rather than a specific product) would also fall under the definition, as it does not directly promote a product. According to Trzaskowski, this exclusion does not seem to be intended by the EU legislators, yet it does complicate marketing regulation unnecessarily.[928] The average consumer will be the benchmark for assessing if an advergame aimed at children is unfair.[929] Especially in relation to vulnerable consumers[930] such as children, who are particularly susceptible to advertising, the assessment would be carried out from the perspective of the average member of that particular

924 B. W. Wojdynski and N. J. Evans, 'Going Native: Effects of Disclosure Position and Language on the Recognition and Evaluation of Online Native Advertising' (2016) 45 Journal of Advertising 157.

925 Wojdynski and Evans (n 924).

926 Art. 2(d) in conjunction with Art. 5 UCPD.

927 Article 2 (e) UCP Directive.

928 J. Trzaskowski, 'User-Generated Marketing – Legal Implications When Word-of-Mouth Goes Viral' (2011) 19 International Journal of Law and Information Technology 348.

929 European Commission, 'Commission Staff Working Document – Guidance on the Implementation/Application of Directive 2005/29/EC on Unfair Commercial Practices, SWD(2016) 163 Final.' (n 545).

930 Chiarella (n 557).

group.[931] The actual assessment of determining what a typical reaction of a child would be in relation to a specific advergame is left up to the national courts and authorities, while taking into account the case law of the CJEU.

Providing advergames without disclosure. The UCP Directive protects consumers against deception (either through a misleading practice or an omission) by traders. If an advertiser targets an advergame to children, deliberately without providing information on the commercial nature of the game (e.g. a label or disclosure), this could perhaps qualify as an omission. Moreover, in the previous chapter, it was discussed how the UCP Directive has a blacklist of commercial practices which are under all circumstances prohibited. One of these practices are advertisements that use editorial content for the promotion of a product, where a trader has paid for the promotion but does not make this clear in the content or by accompanying images or sounds that would be clearly identifiable for the user.[932] Thus, it is argued that providing an advergame without some sort of labelling of its commercial intent could also fall within the black-listed misleading practice.

Children and traditional contractual protections. Aside from general consumer protection mechanisms protecting informed commercial decision-making, it should be noted that traditionally there are additional legal protections for children. More specifically, protections for children have focused on their capacity to contract. For instance, in common law only certain contracts with minors are entirely valid, namely contracts for necessaries and beneficial contracts of service. All other contracts are voidable at the option of the minor reflecting their vulnerable status and restricted capacity to contract. Similar protections have evolved in civil law jurisdictions, the extent of which is dependent on whether or not the minor has reached the necessary level of discernment.[933] However, it should be noted that such protections fail to adequately deal with the emotional conditioning nature of advergames as they focus on the actual purchasing rather than the establishing of the particular desire for a product or service. As a result they may have restricted application

931 Recital 19 UCP Directive. We have also seen that there is a two-step criterion for determining the unfairness of a particular advertising technique: first, the lack of professional diligence of the trader and second, the influence on the economic behaviour of the consumer. Henning-Bodewig (n 546).

932 Annex I, point 28 and 11 of the Unfair Commercial Practices Directive.

933 For instance, according to the Belgian Civil Code, if a minor has not reached the necessary level of discernment (i.e. 12 years old), any legal actions would be invalid. This means that the court is obliged to declare the agreement invalid on request of the parents or the concerned minor, whereas the contracting party cannot request invalidation (Article 1125 Belgian Civil Code). If the minor has reached the necessary level of discernment, it will depend on the impact of the legal action, as well as on whether or not the action prejudiced the minor (Article 410 Belgian Civil Code).

as the mere provision of advertising does not in itself create a contractual relationship as it would constitute an offer.

PERSONALISATION. Advergames can also be used as mechanisms for gathering personal data with access to the game potentially conditional upon the provision of this information thus forming an agreement. As such, it can be argued that the contractual protections mentioned above could be applicable in such a context. Advergames could present a means of gathering children's valuable personal data in exchange for the accessing of content services. Such data gathering and its application present additional risks to children given the increase in computing capacity. With the proliferation of digital technologies, children are increasingly gaining access to the internet where they act as consumers thereby engaging in contractual agreements on a much more frequent basis. Although online contracts involving monetary consideration should practically necessitate adult participation (i.e. as children generally do not have access to online payment methods), contracts involving non-monetary consideration (e.g. access to social media in exchange for personal data as consideration) often slip under the radar. This reflects the general public's lack of awareness of the underlying legal significance associated with online browsing. Such data gathering invokes the application of the data protection and privacy framework and allows for the personalised targeting of marketing campaigns. Targeting children with personalised advertising forms a second use case, which will be discussed in the next section.

2. IDENTIFIED GAPS OR OVERLAPS

LEGALLY COMPLIANT, BUT NOT CHILD-FRIENDLY? From the analysis, it can be concluded that a myriad of provisions apply in the context of advergames, presenting a number of legal issues. This jigsaw reflects the complex nature of the area and the various competing interests involved. Having traced and applied the framework, it appears difficult to conclude that advergames in their current form as a mechanism for advertising are *de facto* compliant. Given their reliance on the merging and blurring of commercial and non-commercial content, there is a misalignment between modern advertising practices and traditional consumer protection standards. However, it remains unclear why such practices have escaped scrutiny. Scalability *vis-à-vis* investigations on the enforcement of legal requirements in an online environment remains an issue in this regard. This may provide some explanation, nevertheless it does not provide a justification to not truly assess the legality of this practice and to legislate for the social implications associated with such invasive means of advertising. Moreover, given the importance of data-driven business models and the emergence of increased personalisation, the gathering of children's personal data and the potential for the personalisation of advergames raises concerns which need to be addressed. This is not to conclude, however, that advergames are invariably in violation of the legal requirements. Indeed it may be possible to satisfy the requirements from a purely legal perspective, but from a children's rights perspective regard must be had for best practice recommendations.

Need for standard disclosures and qualitative requirements. Advergames present clear challenges as they involve the mixing of commercial and non-commercial content, rendering it difficult for consumers in general, and children in particular, to adequately recognise the marketing purpose. The identification principle requires that even integrated advertisements need to be recognisable as such. However, a consistent interpretation of how to implement this identification requirement is currently missing. The creation of labels or cues indicating the commercial nature of an advergame and enhancing transparency about commercial motives could be a possible solution. However, the development of such techniques would need to take into account all the different elements, including findings from social science studies. Moreover, such qualitative advertising standards should be adopted in a collaborative manner, by various responsible regulatory authorities and the advertising industry.

Advertising literacy. In order to adequately deal with these issues, a comprehensive and collaborative solution is required. It is crucial to ensure that the next generation of internet users is better educated and prepared for coping with new advertising techniques. In this regard, it should be noted that advertising literacy does not end with identification. Users must also be aided in order to help them understand the persuasive intent of commercial communications. Such advertising-literacy development would allow users to critically evaluate commercial communications and understand their persuasive intent.[934]

Precaution is better than cure. From an ethical point of view, it has been questioned whether it is acceptable or responsible to target young consumers with commercial messages, if they do not recognise them as such.[935] Even though there is currently little evidence for a causal link between the emergence of new means of advertising and targeting (such as advergames) and negative sociological developments (e.g., obesity amongst children), it is necessary to consider a precautionary approach in the context of children. Hence, the importance of this matter extends beyond a purely legal analysis and requires a balancing of socio-economic interests, which a legislative framework should reflect, in order to align itself with children's rights and the child's best interests principle.

934 Clifford and Verdoodt (n 922).
935 Austin and Reed (n 217).

SECTION II. TARGETING CHILDREN WITH PERSONALISED ADVERTISING[936]

The concept. Increased computing capabilities allow commercial entities to track children's online behaviour and preferences, on the basis of which they are then profiled and targeted with tailored marketing campaigns.[937] While the advertising industry argues that personalised advertising (e.g. online behavioural advertising or location-based advertising) is more relevant and efficient[938], the tracking, profiling and targeting of children may raise significant questions from a children's rights perspective.

1. PERSONALISATION: TRACKING, PROFILING AND TARGETING, THREE DIFFERENT STEPS

Before personalised advertisements are targeted at children, a chain of events takes place.

Tracking. First, children's personal data are collected, on the basis of which the commercial message may be tailored. For instance, for online behavioural advertising[939] – a specific form of personalised advertising – this would be the tracking or monitoring of children's online behaviour.[940] It may consist *inter alia* of tracking their search history, media consumption (e.g. videos, songs, news articles) and communication data.[941] The majority of existing online tracking technologies

936 This section of the book is an adaptation of the following book chapter: Verdoodt and Lievens (n 3).

937 Pew Internet and American Life Project, 'Teens, privacy and online social networks – How teens manage their online identities and personal information in the age of MySpace' (2007).

938 H. Beales, 'The Value of Behavioral Targeting' (2010) 1 Network Advertising Initiative <https://pdfs.semanticscholar.org/e2eb/6726f5a29d9c14dafaf056be9a3ade877b0a.pdf> accessed 24 October 2017; Boerman, Kruikemeier and Zuiderveen Borgesius (n 102).

939 Boerman et al. define online behavioural advertising as: "*the practice of monitoring people's online behaviour and using the collected information to show people individually targeted advertisements*". Boerman, Kruikemeier and Zuiderveen Borgesius (n 103). According to the IAB Europe Framework, OBA is "*the collection of data from a particular computer or device regarding web viewing behaviours over time and across multiple web domains not under common control for the purpose of using such data to predict web user preferences or interests to deliver online advertising to that particular computer or device based on the preferences or interests inferred from such web viewing behaviours.*" See also: Article 29 Working Party, 'Opinion 2/2010 on online behavioural advertising' (2010) WP171.

940 Other forms include location-based advertising or for instance social ads including friends' names, or advertising based on other elements such as a person's age, sex, etc.

941 Frederik J Zuiderveen Borgesius, 'Mensen Aanwijzen Maar Niet Bij Naam Noemen: Behavioural Targeting, Persoonsgegevens En de Nieuwe Privacyverordening' [2016] Tijdschrift voor Consumentenrecht en handelspraktijken <https://www.ivir.nl/publicaties/download/1786> accessed 17 October 2017.

are based on cookies, or use cookies as the backbone.[942] KOSTA clarifies that cookies are files that contain certain information on specific users and their interests and preferences.[943] The information is transmitted via the cookie from a server to the web browser of the user and back each time the user accesses a server's page using the same browser. As a result, KOSTA explains, the website 'knows' what language or the type of advertising specified users prefer.[944] Other popular technologies include plugins and device fingerprinting.[945] In 2015, an international network of data protection authorities conducted a privacy sweep of 1494 children's websites and apps, which showed that 67% of the websites and apps were in fact collecting children's personal data and 50% shared this personal data with third parties.[946]

PROFILING. A second step that forms part of the serving of personalised advertising consists of profiling. Profiling can be understood as a data mining method, which involves data harvesting and conversion of data into profiles. More specifically, BOSCO *et al.* describe profiling as an (semi-)automated process to examine large data sets in order to create classes or categories of characteristics.[947] The categories can be used to generate profiles (i.e. sets of correlated data) of *inter alia* individuals, groups or places. Subsequently, statistical methods can be used to generate analytical information regarding future trends or to predict future behaviours or developments. In other words, profiling transforms data into a new form of knowledge, by identifying patterns that are invisible to the human eye.[948] A similar definition was adopted in the Recommendation of the Committee of Ministers of the Council of Europe on the protection of individuals with regard to automatic processing of personal data in the context of profiling.[949] According to that Recommendation, profiling

---

942 G. Skouma and L. Léonard, 'On-Line Behavioral Tracking: What May Change after the Legal Reform on Personal Data Protection', *Reforming European Data Protection Law* (Springer 2015) <http://link.springer.com/chapter/10.1007/978-94-017-9385-8_2> accessed 11 August 2017; Zuiderveen Borgesius, 'Personal Data Processing for Behavioural Targeting' (n 95); Kosta (n 95).

943 Kosta (n 95).

944 Kosta (n 95).

945 I. Altaweel, N. Good and C. J. Hoofnagle, 'Web Privacy Census' [2015] Technology Science <https://papers.ssrn.com/sol3/papers.cfm?abstract_id=2703814> accessed 25 October 2017.

946 Global Privacy Enforcement Network (n 96).

947 F. Bosco and others, 'Profiling Technologies and Fundamental Rights and Values: Regulatory Challenges and Perspectives from European Data Protection Authorities', *Reforming European Data Protection Law* (Springer 2015) <http://link.springer.com/chapter/10.1007/978-94-017-9385-8_1> accessed 11 August 2017., 4.

948 M. Hildebrandt, 'Profiling: From Data to Knowledge' (2006) 30 Datenschutz und Datensicherheit-DuD 548; Claude Castelluccia, 'Behavioural Tracking on the Internet: A Technical Perspective' in Serge Gutwirth and others (eds), *European Data Protection: In Good Health?* (Springer Netherlands 2012) <www.springerlink.com/index/10.1007/978-94-007-2903-2_2> accessed 16 October 2017.

949 Council of Europe, 'The Protection of Individuals with Regard to Automatic Processing of Personal Data in the Context of Profiling' (n 803).

is an automatic data processing technique that consists of applying a 'profile' to an individual, particularly in order to take decisions concerning her or him or for analysing or predicting her or his personal preferences, behaviours and attitudes.[950] This Recommendation specifies that profiling entails that data on individual behaviour or characteristics are collected, are then analysed to correlate certain behaviour(al characteristics), with this correlation subsequently applied to an identified or identifiable person in order to deduct previous, current or future characteristics.[951]

TARGETING. Third, on the basis of a specific consumer profile, advertisers tailor their commercial messages to have a more persuasive effect. Messages are targeted at persons, including children, who have been profiled as potentially interested in or receptive to the products or services that are promoted.

1.1. Persuasive tactics and children's rights implications

PERSUASIVE TACTICS. In the first part of the book, the emerging trends in the area of commercial communication and the persuasive tactics employed under each of these trends were analysed. One of these trends was the emergence of personalised advertising formats, such as online behavioural targeting or location-based targeting. It was concluded that advertisements that correspond with the interests and behaviours of consumers lead to more positive brand attitudes.[952] In addition, consumers – and in particular children and youngsters – are mostly unaware of the data processing practices behind the advertisements and have a really low understanding of the persuasion tactics used. As a result, children are unable to make a critical commercial decision or decision related to their privacy, making personalised advertising formats particularly effective.[953]

A CHILDREN'S RIGHTS PERSPECTIVE. From the analysis of the children's rights framework[954], it was concluded that the largely opaque practices and techniques employed, paired with children's low level of advertising literacy *vis-à-vis* personalised advertising affects a number of children's rights.[955] First, the creation of profiles may negatively impact children's development, as the collection and use of personal data for the purpose of profiling may undermine

950 Council of Europe, 'The Protection of Individuals with Regard to Automatic Processing of Personal Data in the Context of Profiling' (n 803). We

951 This definition also corresponds to the definition provided by article 4 (4) of the GDPR as discussed *supra*.

952 Calvert (n 67).; Cauberghe and others (n 28).

953 Boerman, Kruikemeier and Zuiderveen Borgesius (n 103).

954 Part I, Chapter II, Section II, 2.4.

955 Including *inter alia* children's right to development (article 6 UNCRC), right to privacy (article 16 UNCRC) and right to protection against economic exploitation (article 32 UNCRC).

their rights to experiment with and critically reflect upon their interactions.[956] Moreover, the lack of control by children over their personal data may harm their capacities to develop, get to know and experiment with their own identity. Second, children have difficulties understanding the concept of commercial privacy and targeted advertising techniques.[957] In this regard, personalised advertisements may shape children's preferences and interests, which essentially affects their development, autonomy and freedom of thought.[958] Third, the collection of children's personal data and using it or reselling it for advertising purposes can be perceived as a form of economic exploitation.[959] Finally, in all actions concerning children their best interests should be the primary consideration (article 3 UNCRC).[960] The principle also requires that States must ensure that the best interests of the child are taken as a primary consideration in decisions and actions undertaken by the private sector. In the context of personalised advertising, this could be interpreted as requiring that the parties involved in the advertising chain must consider the best interests of children when profiling children, and tailoring and targeting their advertisements to this particular group of consumers.

ADVERTISERS' INTERESTS. These considerations should be offset against the fact that advertising revenues allow for the development of children's media content and digital platforms. At the moment, the dominant business model for online services remains advertising-based. Users often do not have to pay for the services, but in exchange personal information is collected and advertisements are part of the environment. As such, the creation of content and online spaces enables the exercise of other children's rights, including *inter alia* their right to information, to access and to participation in digital media. Moreover, for children to grow up to be critical, informed consumers, within these spaces they should have the opportunity to develop and practice advertising literacy skills which are needed to make balanced commercial decisions. The regulatory framework in place, encompassing both self-regulation and legislation, should enable the reconciliation of the interests of children and advertisers in relation to personalised advertising.

---

956 Ariely and Berns (n 119). For instance, there may be chilling effects if they know they are being 'watched', which limits them in their communication with friends and their participation online.

957 Ofcom Office of Communications (n 472); Lievens and others (n 16); Zarouali and others, 'Adolescents' Advertising Competences and Institutional Privacy Protection Strategies on Social Networking Sites: Implications for Regulation' (n 110).

958 Savirimuthu (n 475).

959 S. van der Hof, 'I Agree, or Do I: A Rights-Based Analysis of the Law on Children's Consent in the Digital World' (2016) 34 Wis. Int'l LJ 409, 123.

960 UN Committee on the Rights of the Child, 'General Comment No. 5 (2003) General Measures of Implementation of the Convention on the Rights of the Child (Arts. 4, 42 and 44, Para. 6)' (n 243) para 45.

1.2. *Personalised advertising in the current regulatory framework*

1.2.1. Collecting and processing of children's personal data under the GDPR and the proposed ePrivacy Regulation

Two EU instruments. In the previous chapter, it was found that at the EU level, the collection and processing of children's data is covered by the General Data Protection Regulation and the ePrivacy Directive. The GDPR pays particular attention to children and acknowledges that they merit 'specific protection' regarding their personal data and that the processing of children's personal data may result in risks to their rights and freedoms.[961] Such specific protection should be awarded to children especially when their personal data are processed in the context of marketing and profiling, or in relation to services offered directly to a child.[962] Advertisers that want to process children's personal data for the delivery of personalised advertising[963] will have to comply with the principles and requirements for data controllers and the specific protections for children in the GDPR.[964]

Legitimate ground for processing. One of these requirements entails that personal data may only be processed to the extent that there is a 'legitimate ground' justifying the processing.[965] In the context of personalised advertising, the consent of the data subject[966] or the legitimate interest of the controller are possible legitimation grounds. If the former is relied upon as a legitimate ground for processing children's personal data, article 8 of the GDPR requires verifiable parental consent for the processing of personal data of children under 16 (or lower[967]) in the context of 'information society services'[968] directly

961 Recital 75 GDPR.

962 Recital 38 GDPR.

963 It has been argued by behavioural targeting companies that, as long as they do not tie names to data they hold about individuals, they do not process any personal data, and that, therefore, the data protection framework does not apply to them. Zuiderveen Borgesius, however, argues that when data is used to single out an individual to target him or her with tailored advertising, the data protection legislation should apply: Zuiderveen Borgesius, 'Mensen Aanwijzen Maar Niet Bij Naam Noemen: Behavioural Targeting, Persoonsgegevens En de Nieuwe Privacyverordening' (n 941).

964 See *supra*: Part II, Chapter I, Section III, 1.2–1.3.

965 Article 6 GDPR.

966 The consent has to be freely given, specific, informed and unambiguous. The definition of consent can be found in recital 32 GDPR and article 4 (11) GDPR.

967 In the previous chapter, we have seen that Member States may lower this threshold to a minimum of 13 years. For a mapping of the recent national guidance and proposals in this context, see Eva Lievens and Milda Milkaite, 'Better Internet for Kids – Age of Consent in the GDPR: Updated Mapping' (2017) <https://www.betterinternetforkids.eu/web/portal/practice/awareness/detail?articleId=2019355> accessed 26 July 2018.

968 Information society services (e.g. social media, search engines, apps) often rely on personalised advertising as an essential element of their business model.

offered to a child.[969] Regarding the latter ground, recital 47 GDPR specifies that 'direct marketing' may constitute a legitimate interest for the controller and hence offer a legitimation ground other than the consent of the data subject.[970] This, however, must entail a careful balancing of the legitimate interest of the controller against the interests, fundamental rights and freedoms of children.[971] If children are involved, the GDPR clarifies that their interests may override those of the controller more easily, implying a heavier responsibility for controllers using this ground for processing (article 6, 1) (f) GDPR). Yet, in relation to direct marketing it has been argued by the Belgian data protection authority that obtaining consent remains a best practice.[972] Also in relation to online behavioural advertising it has been argued by scholars that consent is the only appropriate legitimation ground for the processing of personal data.[973]

PROCESSING CHILDREN'S COMMUNICATIONS DATA. Advertisers that employ tracking technologies such as cookies[974] and process children's communications data also have to take into account the rules of the ePrivacy framework. As analysed in the previous chapter, this legal framework is currently being reviewed and it is expected that the proposed ePrivacy Regulation (which will replace the ePrivacy Directive) will bring about important changes for the players involved in targeted advertising. More specifically, it was highlighted that the proposed Regulation will require the same type of consent as in the GDPR for the placement and accessing of cookies or the use of other tracking technologies (e.g. device finger printing).[975] In this regard, the European Parliament has

969 For more information see E. Lievens and V. Verdoodt, 'Looking for Needles in a Haystack: Key Children's Rights Issues in the General Data Protection Regulation' [2017] Computer Law & Security Review.

970 Recital 47 GDPR.

971 In this regard, MACENAITE and KOSTA argue that this processing ground potentially protects children more than relying on consent, should data controllers fully consider all factors of data processing and ensure children's interests and fundamental rights are duly taken into account. Macenaite and Kosta (n 760).

972 Belgian Privacy Commission, 'Recommendation No. 02/2013 of 30 January 2013 Regarding Direct Marketing and the Protection of Personal Data' (2013) 12 <https://www.privacycommission.be/sites/privacycommission/files/documents/aanbeveling_02_2013.pdf> accessed 14 November 2017.

973 Zuiderveen Borgesius, 'Personal Data Processing for Behavioural Targeting' (n 95).

974 Article 5(3) of the Directive provides that the installation of and access to cookies on users terminal equipment (e.g. smartphones, laptops) is only allowed with their consent, except for 'functional cookies' or 'similar technologies'.

975 Art. 7(4) of the GDPR requires consent to be 'freely given, specific, informed and unambiguous' and must be expressed by way of a 'statement or by a clear affirmative action.' Recital 20 of the Parliament's draft legislative resolution requires in relation to tracking that "*users should receive all information about the intended processing in clear and easily understandable language.*" EUROPEAN PARLIAMENT, Draft legislative resolution on the proposal for a regulation of the European Parliament and of the Council concerning the respect for private life and the protection of personal data in electronic communications and repealing Directive 2002/58/EC (Regulation on Privacy and Electronic Communications),

proposed an amendment requiring that users are to be provided with granular settings for consent, distinguishing between different categories: (1) tracking for commercial purposes or for direct marketing for non-commercial purposes (e.g. behavioural advertising); (2) tracking for personalised content; (3) tracking for analytical purposes; (4) tracking of location data; (5) providing personal data to third parties (including providing unique identifiers to match with personal data held by third parties).[976] Furthermore, one of the other amendments explicitly states that the Regulation should prevent the use of tracking or cookie walls (i.e. a barrier that users can only pass if they consent to tracking by third parties).[977] According to the EP, "*tracking walls do not help users to maintain control over their personal information and privacy or become informed about their rights*".[978]

No specific protection for children in the ePrivacy framework. Yet, whereas the GDPR explicitly recognises children as a vulnerable group of individuals that deserve specific protection when it comes to the processing of their personal data, especially in the context of profiling and marketing, the analysis above highlighted the fact that neither the European Commission's proposal for an ePrivacy Regulation, nor the EP's amendments contained any references to children.[979] With children being increasingly targeted directly by services tailored to a young audience it would only make sense to align the proposed Regulation with the GDPR, by recognising that children need specific protection when it comes to the processing of their communications data.[980] As mentioned above, research has shown that children have little or no knowledge or understanding of the tracking technologies used and the extent and sensitivity of the data collected for personalised advertising.[981] These findings resonate in the viewpoint of the Article 29 Working Party, who argued in 2013 that in the best interest of the child companies "*should not process children's personal data for behavioural advertising purposes, neither directly nor indirectly, as this will be outside the scope of a child's understanding and therefore exceed the boundaries of lawful processing*".[982] Moreover, it has been argued in this context, for instance by BEUC, that specific limitations on the collection and use of children's

23 October 2017, www.europarl.europa.eu/sides/getDoc.do?type=REPORT&reference=A8-2017-0324&language=EN (hereafter "EP Draft Legislative Resolution").

976 Recital 23 EP Draft Legislative Resolution.

977 F. J. Zuiderveen Borgesius and others, 'Tracking Walls, Take-It-Or-Leave-It Choices, the GDPR, and the EPrivacy Regulation' (2017) 3 European Data Protection Law Review 353.

978 Recital 22 EP Draft Legislative Resolution.

979 Most notably, article 8 GDPR is not reflected in the proposal.

980 Verdoodt and Lievens (n 3).

981 This includes a reference to the specific standard of consent as introduced by article 8 GDPR.

982 Article 29 Data Protection Working Party, 'Opinion 02/2013 on Apps on Smart Devices, WP202' (n 730) 26; Article 29 Data Protection Working Party, 'Opinion 2/2010 on Online Behavioural Advertising WP 171' (n 753).

communication data are needed.[983] In the Opinion of the EP Committee on the Internal Market and Consumer Protection[984], these ideas were integrated in a proposal for a new recital 16a:

> *"Regulation (EU) 2016/679 of the European Parliament and of the Council explicitly recognises the need to provide additional protection to children, given that they may be less aware of the risks and consequences associated with the processing of their personal data. This Regulation should also grant special attention to the protection of children's privacy. They are among the most active internet users and their exposure to profiling and behaviourally targeted advertising techniques should be prohibited."*

Parallel to the consideration included in recital 38 of the GDPR, a new recital 23a was proposed confirming the need for specific protection with regard to children's online privacy, as they are less aware of the risks and consequences associated to their online activities, as well as less aware of their rights. For that reason, the IMCO Opinion stresses that specific safeguards are necessary in relation to the use of children's data, notably for the purposes of marketing and the creation of personality or user profiles. As a result of these considerations, the Opinion proposed a new paragraph 1 to be added to article 6 asserting that

> *"Electronic communications data that is generated in the context of an electronic communications service designed particularly for children or directly targeted at children shall not be used for profiling or behaviourally targeted advertising purposes".*

In addition, a new paragraph 4a to article 8 was proposed stating that "*[t]erminal equipment that is intended particularly for children's use shall implement specific measures to prevent access to the equipment's storage and processing capabilities for the purpose of profiling of its users or tracking their behaviour with commercial intent.*" However, in the end, these amendments, which would have had a significant impact on current advertising practices that target and personalise commercial messages to and for children, were not included in the EP's Draft Legislative Resolution.

Profiling of children under the GDPR. In the previous chapter, the recitals and provisions of the GDPR that regulate the profiling of children were also analysed. It was found that the GDPR explicitly recognises that processing

983 BEUC, 'Data Collection, Targeting and Profiling of Consumers Online' (2010) BEUC discussion paper <www.beuc.eu/publications/2010-00101-01-e.pdf> accessed 26 October 2017.

984 European Parliament Committee on the Internal Market and Consumer Protection, Opinion on the proposal for a regulation of the European Parliament and of the Council concerning the respect for private life and the protection of personal data in electronic communications and repealing Directive 2002/58/EC (Regulation on Privacy and Electronic Communications), 23 October 2017, www.europarl.europa.eu/sides/getDoc.do?type=REPORT&reference=A8-2017-0324&language=EN.

personal data "*in order to create or use personal profiles*" may give rise to risks to the rights and freedoms of natural persons.[985] Furthermore, as profiling is a complex and invisible process, which is very difficult to understand for adults, let alone children, the GDPR did aim to introduce specific protection for children.[986] There is no further guidance, though, as to how this protection should be put into practice. In any case, data subjects must be informed about the fact that profiling is being deployed and the potential consequences thereof.[987] Especially when this occurs *vis-à-vis* children, the information provided will need to be clear and understandable for them.[988] In relation to profiling for direct marketing purposes, data subjects, including children, also have the right to object at any time to profiling to the extent that it is related to direct marketing.[989] The data controller needs to clearly and explicitly inform the data subject of this right.[990] Furthermore, according to recital 71, a decision which may include a measure evaluating personal aspects relating to a data subject, which is based solely on automated processing and produces legal effect for or similarly significantly[991] affects the data subject, should not concern children.[992] The Article 29 Working Party has confirmed that there is no absolute prohibition on the profiling of children in the GDPR.[993]Nevertheless, the Working Party stresses that targeted advertising may, depending on the particular characteristics of the case, have a 'similarly significant' effect on individuals. Especially in relation to children, the Working Party recognises that they

> *"can be particularly susceptible in the online environment and more easily influenced by behavioural advertising" and, therefore, "organisations should, in general, refrain from profiling them for marketing purposes."*[994]

Interestingly, one should keep in mind the lack of definition of a 'child' in the GDPR. The question thus arises whether this statement by the Working Party refers to all those under 18 years or alternatively the age thresholds adopted within the respective national implementing measures.

---

985 Recital 75 GDPR.

986 Recital 38 GDPR also explicitly recognises that circumstances in which personal data of children are processed in order to create personal or user profiles require extra protection.

987 Recital 60 GDPR.

988 Article 12 GDPR. Lievens and Verdoodt (n 969).

989 Recital 70 and Article 21, (2) GDPR.

990 Recital 70 GDPR.

991 In general, if advertising standards prohibit or limit the marketing of certain types of products to children, this should give you a good indication that influencing a child's choices in this area could potentially have a similarly significant effect on them.

992 Recital 71, first paragraph, final sentence GDPR.

993 Article 29 Data Protection Working Party, 'Guidelines on Automated Individual Decision-Making and Profiling for the Purposes of Regulation 2016/679' (n 815).

994 Article 29 Data Protection Working Party, 'Guidelines on Automated Individual Decision-Making and Profiling for the Purposes of Regulation 2016/679' (n 815) 26.

1.2.2. Personalised advertising in the Unfair Commercial Practices Directive?

Consumer protection. In the previous chapter, it was outlined how the UCP Directive forms an important safety net for children against harmful or misleading commercial communications. In the context of personalised advertising, the Directive may also provide protection for children. More specifically, the UCP Directive protects consumers against so-called 'aggressive' commercial practices. It was argued that while actual harassment or coercion (e.g. the use of physical force) is unlikely to occur, undue influence could perhaps arise in an advertising context[995], and especially when advertisers target children with personalised advertisements. The first element that needs to be present is the exploitation of "*a position of power in relation to the consumer so as to apply pressure*".[996] The European Consumer Organisation (BEUC) has argued that advertisers hold a position of power as they collect a lot of personal information of consumers (including children) without them being aware of what is happening.[997] The repetitive aspect of targeted advertising (e.g. through retargeting on social media) may qualify as applying pressure on consumers. Second, the pressure must be applied "*in a way which significantly limits the consumer's ability to make an informed decision*". In this regard, it can be argued that the selection of advertisements based on the presumed consumer choice may prevent the display of other advertisements thereby restricting the comparison with other advertisements and, hence, making an informed commercial decision.[998] The qualification of 'undue influence' will always depend on the specificities of the particular case, and when children are involved, their vulnerability should be taken into account.

1.2.3. Relevant protection for children in the revised AVMS Directive

Limitation to the use of children's personal data for advertising purposes. A final legislative protection for children in the context of personalised advertising can be found in the revised AVMS Directive. More specifically, it was mentioned that media service providers and providers of video-sharing platforms are required to take appropriate measures for the protection of children in relation to harmful content and commercial communication, such as age verification mechanisms, parental control tools, or other technical measures. In this regard, the Directive prohibits the use children's personal data

---

995 As a reminder: article 8 UCP Directive determines that marketing techniques are deemed aggressive if they "*by harassment, coercion or undue influence significantly impair the freedom of choice or conduct of the average consumer*".

996 Article 2 (j) of the UCP Directive.

997 BEUC (n 983).

998 BEUC (n 983).

for commercial purposes such as profiling an behavioural targeting which are generated pursuant to the implementation of such measures.[999]

1.2.4. Self-regulation and targeting children with personalised advertising

ADVERTISING SELF-REGULATION. In addition to the legislative instruments already discussed, advertisers have committed to observing a number of standards laid down in self-regulatory codes.[1000] The previous chapter discussed how these codes also contain provisions in relation to advertising aimed at children, direct marketing and behavioural advertising.

CHILDREN AND ONLINE BEHAVIOURAL ADVERTISING. Section D7.4 of the ICC Consolidated Code[1001], for instance, states that children of 12 years and younger should not be targeted by a behavioural advertising campaign. Along the same lines, in the Framework for OBA, created by the Interactive Advertising Bureau Europe (IAB Europe), companies agree not to create segments for OBA purposes that are specifically designed to target children, meaning people aged 12 and under. In this regard, KING and JESSEN argue that the framework does not sufficiently protect vulnerable consumers above the age of 12 (such as teenagers), even though such profiling practices may have significant privacy implications for this category of internet users.[1002]

THE OBA ICON. This Framework is also guiding the activities of the European Interactive Digital Advertising Alliance, which has been set up by a coalition of the European advertising industry, including advertisers, the advertising agency sector, the direct marketing sector, the advertising network sector and the media sector. Its main objective is to licence the "Online Behavioural Advertising Icon" to companies that are involved in the OBA business across Europe. This

999 Article 6a(2), juncto recital 9-b (for audiovisual media service providers) and article 28a(3), last subpara.) revised AVMS Directive.

1000 It has been argued before that drawbacks of self-regulation are a lack of effective enforcement and often mild sanctions; however, the advertising sector is one of the sectors where – depending on the self-regulatory body in question – decisions on violations of the codes of conduct are often complied with. Lievens, 'Is Self-Regulation Failing Children and Young People?' (n 362).

1001 International Chamber of Commerce (n 137).

1002 The framework also contains obligation related to notice and choice, including the principles that internet users must be given notice of the OBA data collection and use practices by the relevant third parties as well as the website operator (i.e. of its OBA arrangements with third parties), and that third parties have to provide internet users with a mechanism to exercise their choice regarding the use of their data for OBA purposes. It has been argued, for instance, by KING and JENSEN that in general the IAB principles do not offer consumers sufficient transparency nor do they ensure meaningful access to the information contained in the consumer profiles that are used for behavioral advertising purposes; King and Wegener Jessen (n 859).

icon notifies consumers of data collection for OBA purposes and the delivery of OBA advertising to them, and refers consumers to an online portal: 'www.youronlinechoices.eu', which intends to offer information on the practice of OBA and where consumers can turn off OBA by some or all companies.[1003] Research into the effectiveness of the OBA icon, however, has found that only a quarter of the respondents remembered OBA disclosure icons, and only 12% remembered seeing a tagline (e.g., "Why did I get this ad?" or "AdChoices") and correctly selected the tagline they had seen from a list. Also, none of the taglines were understood to be links to pages where you can make choices about OBA, nor did they increase knowledge about OBA.[1004] However, it has been argued that the standard icon could effectively increase OBA awareness and understanding when accompanied by an explanatory label stating, "*This ad is based on your surfing behavior*".[1005] It remains to be seen whether this finding is also valid *vis-à-vis* children.

(Online) Direct marketing. With regard to direct marketing, it was mentioned that FEDMA – the organisation representing the Direct and Interactive Marketing sector at the European Level – adopted two relevant instruments: (1) a Code of Practice for the Use of Personal Data in Direct Marketing in collaboration with the Article 29 Working Party[1006] and (2) an Electronic Communications Annex that contains provisions specifically applicable to online direct marketing (or electronic mail marketing).[1007] The Code and its Annex contain a number of protections[1008] for children (i.e. any

1003 When accessing the portal, the user will be asked to select his or her location. The user must then navigate to "Your Ad Choices", at which point the site collects the users' "status" from the participating companies. Once complete, the individuals can either "turn off" individual companies one by one or scroll down to the setting "turn off all companies". Van Alsenoy and others (n 916) 39. However, according to the Article 29 Data Protection Working Party, such an opt-out approach "*is not an adequate mechanism to obtain average users informed consent*" for purposes of online behavioural advertising. Article 29 Data Protection Working Party, 'Opinion 2/2010 on Online Behavioural Advertising WP 171' (n 753) 15.

1004 Boerman, Kruikemeier and Zuiderveen Borgesius (n 103).

1005 G. van Noort, E. G. Smit and H.A.M. Voorveld, 'The Online Behavioural Advertising Icon: Two User Studies', *Advances in Advertising Research (Vol. IV)* (Springer Gabler, Wiesbaden 2013) <http://link.springer.com/chapter/10.1007/978-3-658-02365-2_28> accessed 31 July 2018.

1006 Article 29 Data Protection Working Party, 'Opinion 4/2010 on the European Code of Conduct of FEDMA for the Use of Personal Data in Direct Marketing, WP 174' (n 861).

1007 FEDMA, 'European Code of Practice for the Use of Personal Data in Direct Marketing – Electronic Communications Annex (the On-Line Annex)' (n 864). FEDMA (2010). European Code of Practice for the Use of Personal Data in Direct Marketing – Electronic Communications Annex (the On-line Annex), http://ec.europa.eu/justice/data-protection/article-29/documentation/opinion-recommendation/files/2010/wp174_annex_en.pdf, accessed on 17 October 2017.

1008 The FEDMA codes go beyond the legal requirements defined by the data protection framework at the time (these initiatives were adopted under the EU Data Protection Directive), and already contained a number of protections which are now explicitly in the GDPR (i.e. verification, parental consent).

individual under 14 years): information obligations (in easily understandable language), the requirement for age and parental consent verification, requirements for the collection of special categories of data[1009] and the prohibition to incentivise children to share more personal data. Moreover, marketers are required to educate parents on parental control tools and how they can supervise and monitor their children's online behaviour.

2. IDENTIFIED GAPS OR OVERLAPS

While the current data protection and privacy laws and policies cover existing tracking, profiling and targeted advertising practices, certain improvements may be proposed.

THE GDPR. First, the GDPR foresees in specific protection for children, which is laudable, but it remains problematic that the text does not contain a definition of a 'child'. This leads to uncertainty regarding the age group(s) to which certain protection measures should apply. This could be clarified by data protection authorities and the European Data Protection Board. Furthermore, default limitations on the collection of personal data of children for both the development and application of user profiles could be considered. In this regard, the advertising industry should take up their responsibility[1010], and carry out an in-depth data protection impact assessment, with attention for the best interests and rights of children, when setting up digital marketing campaigns.[1011] The age and level of maturity of the child will also play an important role in such an assessment. In addition, information society service providers (such as social networking sites) could make a distinction between users based on the age information given upon registration, thereby offering an alternative child-friendly service incorporating the same features minus the tracking for personalised commercialisation.[1012]

THE PROPOSED EPRIVACY REGULATION. Second, the ePrivacy Regulation should be aligned with the GDPR, as was proposed in the IMCO Opinion of October 2017, by recognising that children require specific protection when it comes to the processing of their communications data. Adding specific limitations on the collection and use of children's communications data and special protection for terminal equipment or software that is developed for children would be a step forward. Finally, a prohibition for services specifically targeted towards children

1009 Such as data of family members or sensitive data. However, these data may still be processed with the consent of respectively the family members concerned or of their legal representative.
1010 Montgomery and Chester (n 483) 291.
1011 Article 35 and recital 91 GDPR.
1012 This is a highly debated issue and one should refer to Van Alsenoy and others (n 916).

to use profiling and behavioural marketing techniques would be beneficial for the protection of children's rights (e.g. the right to privacy and to protection against economic exploitation). However, the same concern regarding the fact of whether this applies or should apply to all under 18-year olds arises.

The UCP Directive. Third, the UCP Directive may provide additional protection for children against personalised advertising, as this advertising practice may qualify as a form of undue influence. It could even be considered to add behavioural advertising practices aimed towards children to the blacklist of practices, which are under all circumstances deemed unfair.

Self- and co-regulation. Fourth, the industry has been very active in self-regulating personalised advertising practices (i.e. direct marketing and online behavioural advertising). While it could be argued that the commitment not to create segments targeting children aged 12 and under is laudable, it does not provide any protection for children above the age of 12, even though these targeted advertising practices may also have significant privacy implications for 12 to 18-year olds.[1013] Moreover, different ages can be found in different self-regulatory instruments (e.g. 12 and under, under 14s), which could lead to confusion. Existing self-regulatory initiatives focus mostly on information provision and transparency (e.g. notice requirements, labelling), as well as on the requirement of (verifiable) parental consent for personalised advertising, rather than on actual limitations on the processing of children's personal data for marketing and advertising practices. Whereas such limitations might go against commercial interests of advertisers, the best interests of children might require this, also taking into account the fact that for advertising to be innovative and fun for children, collecting and using children's personal data is not a precondition.

Concluding remark. Finally, the evaluation shows that several legislative and alternative regulatory instruments are applicable to personalised advertising. As a result, both the substantive provisions and the competences of the respective regulatory authorities may overlap.

SECTION III. DIGITAL INFLUENCERS AND VLOGGING ADVERTISING

The concept. Nowadays, people can participate online, create and share their own content in all kinds of applications such as blogs, social media and

[1013] King and Wegener Jessen (n 859).

video-sharing platforms. Children and adolescents are increasingly consuming media content online, where their favourite digital influencers upload videos on a regular basis (e.g. on YouTube). Content creators like vloggers (i.e. video bloggers) have over time become extremely popular amongst the younger audiences and even in some instances gained celebrity status among their thousands of followers.[1014] The influence these people may exert over their loyal followers is significant and brings with it certain responsibilities, especially when commercial interests become involved. The popularity of these digital influencers is already shaping advertising and marketing techniques and vlogging advertising may take many forms: (1) online marketing by a brand with vlogger collaboration, (2) an advertorial, (3) a commercial break within a vlog, (4) product placement, (5) the promotion of the vlogger's own merchandise, (6) sponsorship and (7) free items.[1015] These integrated advertising techniques form an important source of revenue for vloggers. Vloggers may be rewarded *inter alia* on the basis of 'pay per acquisition or download' (i.e. earn rewards whenever a viewer purchases a product or service via the link within the vlog); product compensation; pay per post or a system of flat rate pricing; pay per click.[1016] Professional internet creator has become just another job and vloggers may be tied to agents and production companies, just like actors.[1017] However, it should be noted that not all vlogs contain commercial messages. Indeed, lots of vloggers merely present their honest opinions about a certain product or service, without receiving any financial benefits (i.e. without being sponsored by the brand or without receiving the product or service for free). Conversely, if a brand has a certain amount of control over the content of the post and rewards the influencer in any way, the post should be considered a form of commercial communication.[1018]

1014 For instance, Industry research has shown that 59% of 13 year-olds follows YouTubers on social media versus only 32% following television and movie stars. 'Acumen Report: Youth Video Diet' (Defy Media) <http://defymedia.com/wp-content/uploads/2017/11/Acumen_DL_booklet_16_12_04.pdf> accessed 29 November 2017.

1015 This list is not exhaustive and stems from the CAP Guidelines, a UK self-regulatory initiative, see *infra*. J. Ward, 'CAP Guidance on Vlogging Advertising' [2016] Entertainment Law 49. However, it does not include video pre-rolls that are placed around uploaded content by the video-sharing platform itself. For more information on such video pre-rolls, see *infra*.

1016 Influencers often use their vlogs as springboards to launch other projects that bring income, such as ebooks, books, speaking assignments, clothing lines, other products, etc. F.J. Cavaliere, 'People Can Make More Money on YouTube than Most Lawyers Earn – Is That Even Legal' <www.webwiselawyer.com>.

1017 In the US, YouTubers even have united in the Internet Creators Guild, which provides YouTubers with support to help them develop a rigorous business sense and avoid exploitation. C. Stokel-Walker, 'Vloggers Unite: Youtubers Are Getting Organized after a Decade of Exploitation' *Newsweek* (8 October 2016) <www.newsweek.com/vloggers-youtube-organized-decade-exploitation-507592> accessed 11 December 2017.

1018 Conversely, the practice of consumers that merely share or produce content containing *inter alia* brand references or the advertised product without receiving rewards in any way

1. INTEGRATION: PRODUCT PLACEMENT, SPONSORSHIPS, EDITORIALS AND OTHER FORMS OF VLOGGING ADVERTISING

1.1. Persuasive tactics and children's rights implications

PERSUASIVE TACTICS. Viewers or followers seek guidance from media personalities or influencers, see them as friends or imagine that they are part of a programme's social world.[1019] According to PERSE and RUBIN, viewers "*feel that they know and understand the influencer in the same intimate way they know and understand flesh and blood friends*".[1020] Followers will turn to influencers for advise and regard them as a trusted source of information. As a result, digital influencers have become an important intermediary between advertisers and consumer-followers. The two-way communication between the media personality (i.e. the vlogger) and the fans (i.e. the followers) is facilitated by social media. LEE and WATKINS argue that social media allows consumers to quickly and easily access user-generated content (i.e. video blogs or vlogs), which often contains product reviews and information.[1021] Research has shown that user-generated content generally has a significant influence on consumers' brand perspective, brand choices[1022] and new consumer acquisition.[1023] Children in particular perceive digital influencers as more relatable than traditional celebrities and they can identify themselves more with the former.[1024] Similarly, LIM *et al.* found that user-generated content is considered trustworthy.[1025] Vlogging advertising allows targeted exposure to the right consumers and repeated exposure to a vlogger can elicit enhanced feelings of connectedness with the advertised brands. As humans are social creatures, they tend to copy the behaviours and beliefs of people

(no discounts, no free products, no financial rewards) is not considerd a form of commercial communication and, therefore, falls outside the scope of this study.

1019 J. Eun Lee and Brandi Watkins, 'YouTube Vloggers' Influence on Consumer Luxury Brand Perceptions and Intentions' (2016) 69 Journal of Business Research 5753.

1020 E. M. Perse and R. B. Rubin, 'Attribution in Social and Parasocial Relationships' (1989) 16 Communication Research 59.

1021 Lee and Watkins (n 1019).

1022 T. W. Gruen, T. O. and A. J. Czaplewski, 'EWOM: The Impact of Customer-to-Customer Online Know-How Exchange on Customer Value and Loyalty' (2006) 59 Journal of Business Research 449.

1023 M. Trusov, R. E. Bucklin and K. Pauwels, 'Effects of Word-of-Mouth versus Traditional Marketing: Findings from an Internet Social Networking Site' (2009) 73 Journal of marketing 90.

1024 'Acumen Report: Youth Video Diet' (n 1014).

1025 Y. Lim, Y. Chung and P. A. Weaver, 'The Impact of Social Media on Destination Branding: Consumer-Generated Videos versus Destination Marketer-Generated Videos' (2012) 18 Journal of Vacation Marketing 197.

they like.[1026] In this regard, LEE and WATKINS refer to social comparison theory[1027], which entails that as consumer-followers view themselves as sharing similar opinions and preferences as digital influencers, a positive review of a brand from their preferred vlogger may lead to a positive review from the consumer.[1028]

A CHILDREN'S RIGHTS PERSPECTIVE. Considering the often hidden nature of vlogging advertising and the highly entertaining videos, digital influencers can have a direct impact on children's consumption behaviour without them being aware of the commercial nature of the communications.[1029] In the analysis of the children's rights framework, it was discussed that such mechanisms potentially have an impact on children's rights such as the right to development, the right to freedom of thought and the right to protection from economic exploitation (similar to the previously discussed use cases). This of course may need to be offset with the freedom of expression of the digital influencers themselves.[1030] Furthermore, as vlogging forms an important part of popular youth culture, it also enables children to participate online and exercise their rights to freedom of expression and culture.

1.2. Digital influencers and the current regulatory framework

IDENTIFICATION IS THE KEY REQUIREMENT. The mapping exercise showed that the current framework regulating commercial communications contains important requirements that are also applicable in the online environment, the key requirement being the identification principle. In the context of vlogging advertising, it is again important to analyse the scope of the instruments previously discussed (the AVMS Directive, the e-Commerce Directive and the UCP Directive). Furthermore, the responsibilities of the different parties involved for the implementation of these requirements in practice need to be clarified. Finally, certain specific guidelines and best practices have emerged from the industry that should be kept in mind.

1026 A. R. Bentley, M. Earls and M. O'brien, *I'll Have What She's Having – Mapping Social Behavior* <https://mitpress.mit.edu/books/ill-have-what-shes-having> accessed 29 November 2017.

1027 This theory was developed in the 1950s by personality theorists, including N.E. Miller and J. Dollard, *Social Learning and Imitation* (Yale University Press 1941); A. Bandura and R. H. Walters, *Social Learning and Personality Development* (Holt, Rinehart and Winston 1963).

1028 Lee and Watkins (n 1019).

1029 For instance, a risk assessment of new advertising formats conducted in the frame of the AdLit Project showed that the advertising literacy level for brand integration, advertiser funded programs, social media advertising and advergaming is rather low, posing a greater risk for children and teenagers. See Vanwesenbeeck and others (n 6).

1030 For examples of cases where commercial speech is balanced against other interests see *Casado Coca v. Spain* (n 432); *Barthold v Germany* [1985] ECtHR App No 8734/79.

1.2.1. Vlogging advertising: audiovisual or commercial communication?

A. Scoping the applicable legal framework and untangling the vlogging advertising chain

Scoping and untangling. A first question that needs to be answered is whether vlogging as a service would fall under the definition of an audiovisual media service (AVMS Directive) or an information society service (e-Commerce Directive) and subsequently whether vlogging advertising could fall under the notion 'audiovisual commercial communication' (AVMS Directive) or rather under the more general e-Commerce notion of 'commercial communication' (e-Commerce Directive).[1031] The distinction is significant considering the more stringent requirements for audiovisual commercial communication. As the vlogging advertising chain may consist of several parties, it needs to be clarified who is responsible for the implementation of the requirements in practice.

Commercial communication under the e-Commerce Directive. First of all, it is argued that vlogging may qualify as an information society service under the e-Commerce Directive. As mentioned, these services can be "*any service normally provided for remuneration, at a distance, by electronic means and at the individual request of a recipient of services.*"[1032] The service provided here entails the provision of videos and making them available to the public on video-sharing platforms like YouTube. In return, the influencer receives a reward, be it in the form of a financial remuneration, free products or services, promotion for their own products, etc. As the videos are uploaded on digital platforms, the requirement of 'by electronic means' is also fulfilled. Lastly, the video is shown at the individual request of the viewer, therefore fulfilling all requirements. Accordingly, the e-Commerce Directive requires digital influencers engaging in vlogging advertising to comply with several information requirements as well as with the identification principle.[1033]

Audiovisual media service and audiovisual commercial communication. The more difficult question, however, is whether vlogging and vlogging advertising could fall within the scope of the AVMS Directive. The central definition determining the scope of the AVMS Directive is the notion of audiovisual media service.[1034] From this definition, certain elements can be extracted that need to be present for vlogging advertising to fall within the scope of the Directive.

1031 This is a similar evaluation like the one in the context of advergames, *supra*.

1032 Recital 17 e-Commerce Directive.

1033 Article 6 of the e-Commerce Directive requires digital influencers to disclose their identity and in case they launch any promotional competition or game the conditions for participation shall be easily accessible and be presented clearly and unambiguously.

1034 Article 1(1)(h) AVMS Directive.

Pursuing an economic activity and images designed to promote. First, the Directive comprises economic activities, an element that can only be found with the more professional digital influencers, as the rewards they receive for vlogging advertising may be regarded as remuneration.[1035] For instance, if digital influencers promote products or services in the style of a review for their followers, a clear indicator of a commercial intent can be found if the video is made in return for financial compensation or if there are other financial ties between the vlogger and the advertiser (product owner).[1036] As mentioned, vloggers may also be tied to agents who receive a part of the advertising revenue generated by the vlogger. Conversely, the Directive does not apply to activities that are primarily non-economic, including *inter alia* the provision of user-generated content for the sole purpose of sharing and exchanging within communities of interest or to private websites or blogs.[1037] Thus, this first element will depend on the intent of the digital influencer and/or the platform provider and the commercial influence on or interference with the content of the vlogs.

Accompany or be included in a programme. As a second requirement, the commercial communication needs to accompany or be included in a programme[1038] (i.e. a television broadcast or an on-demand service[1039]), established by a media service provider. Valcke and Lievens clarify that the notion of a programme needs to be interpreted in a dynamic way, taking into account the developments in television broadcasting.[1040] Translated to the context of digital influencers and vlogging advertising, it means that the form and content of the vlogs needs to be sufficiently comparable to the form and content of television broadcasting. Furthermore, the nature and means of accessing the vlogs (e.g. via the influencer's YouTube channel) could lead the user to reasonably expect a regulatory protection within the scope of the AVMS Directive. In this regard, one should take into account that the viewing habits of children and adolescents have changed significantly over time, as they increasingly consume audiovisual content via tablets and smartphones.[1041]

1035 For instance the YouTube star PewDiePie, who started with uploading silly (and often crude) snippets of himself playing videogames, now has 50 million subscribers and earns approximately $15 million a year of commercial collaborations. M. Berg, 'The Highest-Paid YouTube Stars 2016: PewDiePie Remains No. 1 With $15 Million' (*Forbes*) <https://www.forbes.com/sites/maddieberg/2016/12/05/the-highest-paid-youtube-stars-2016-pewdiepie-remains-no-1-with-15-million/> accessed 15 December 2017.

1036 Verdoodt, Lievens and Hellemans (n 9).

1037 Chavannes and Castendyk (n 36).

1038 Article 1 (b) AVMS Directive.

1039 Excluded are those services which are audio-only and not sufficiently television-like services such as radio, electronic versions of newspapers and magazines, blogs.

1040 Valcke and Lievens (n 615).

1041 For instance, research by Ofcom, the UK media regulator, showed that children are watching less broadcast television as they turn to online activities and services such as YouTube. J.

Children and adolescents arguably may find certain vlogs or series of vlogs similar to traditional television broadcasting, depending on the format[1042] and content of the videos (e.g. episodes in the life of a digital influencer). The professionalism of some of these digital influencers and their 'channels', the regular upload of edited vlogs (e.g. daily, weekly) and the fact that the channels are accessible on the same screen as traditional broadcasts may contribute to such a finding. The Directive also requires that the programme should be aimed to inform, entertain or educate the general public and the service should be provided by electronic communications networks. With regard to vlogging, these elements may be present, as the videos of digital influencers may have an entertaining, informative or educational purpose[1043] and viewers or followers can access the content online via the video-sharing platform.

EDITORIAL RESPONSIBILITY IN A VLOGGING CONTEXT. The requirement of 'accompanying or being included in a programme' also links to another element, namely editorial responsibility, which requires the exercise of effective control over both the selection and the organisation of the programmes.[1044] This entails that a professional media service provider is responsible for the editorial design and final compilation of a programme for broadcasting in accordance with a fixed programme schedule or for viewing on-demand for a catalogue.[1045] In other words, the AVMS Directive provides regulatory standards for professionally created mass media content.[1046] Applying this criterion in a vlogging context is not straightforward considering many new players have entered the value chain. First, SCHOEFS underlines that video-sharing platforms like YouTube play a crucial role in providing access to users to both user-generated content and edited professional content. YouTube hosts a massive amount of content, which

Jackson, 'Children Spending Less Time in Front of the TV as They Turn to Online Media' *The Guardian* (6 August 2015) <www.theguardian.com/media/2015/aug/06/children-spending-less-time-in-front-of-tv-ofcom> accessed 7 December 2017.

1042 In this regard, the Belgian media regulator of the French-speaking community underlines that more and more high quality short forms of content are appearing on audiovisualplatforms which can have a high impact on the public opinion and they are competing with the same audience as TV broadcasts. Jerome Dheur, 'Belgian CSA Conference – The Platform Is the Message' (2016) <www.csa.be/system/documents_files/2591/original/CI_20160310_The%20Platform%20is%20the%20Message_report.pdf?1458160565> accessed 11 December 2017.

1043 Accordingly, the case of digital influencers differs from the *Peugeot Deutschland* case, in which the CJEU decided that a YouTube channel of Peugeot containing short promotional videos for new passenger car models did not have as its principal purpose the provision of programmes in order to inform, entertain or educate the general public and thus excluding it from the scope of the AVMS Directive. *Peugeot Deutschland GmbH v. Deutsche Umwelthilfe eV* (n 611) para 28.

1044 Article 1 (1) (c) AVMS Directive.

1045 Verdoodt, Lievens and Hellemans (n 9).

1046 W. Closs, S. Nikoltchev and European Audiovisual Observatory (eds), *The Regulation of On-Demand Audiovisual Services: Chaos or Coherence?* (European Audiovisual Observatory : Council of Europe 2011).

it organises into different categories depending on the topic of the uploaded video.[1047] While it seemed well established that the AVMS Directive (prior to its review) did not apply to amateur user-generated content[1048], the same cannot be said for professional content which has been provided and/or edited by the platform provider or a professional third party provider before the upload.[1049] Indeed, several Member States accept that such professional content and channels do fall within the scope of the AVMS Directive and, as such, assign the responsibility wherever the editorial power rests.[1050] Second, the segregation of content produced by professional and amateur vloggers forms a major borderline case. On the one hand, the content that some of these professional vloggers create could arguably be considered 'television-like' (e.g. reality shows with episodes airing every week), especially for children and adolescents who watch less traditional broadcasts.[1051] Furthermore, vloggers' capacity to influence social trends, the ubiquity of integrated commercial messages and the significant financial rewards they gain in return call for more stringent requirements or even restrictions. On the other hand, making such a distinction is extremely complicated and would require a case-by-case analysis taking into account all relevant characteristics and evidence.[1052] Important to note is that the revised AVMS Directive provides some clarity on the matter, with recital 3 of the final text stating that:

> "*channels or any other audiovisual services under the editorial responsibility of a provider may constitute audiovisual media services in themselves, even if they are offered in the framework of a video-sharing platform which is characterised by the*

1047 R. Schoefs, 'Connected TV: Editorial Responsibility in a Converged Media Environment' (2014) 5 Droit des médias – Mediarecht 346.

1048 Chavannes and Castendyk (n 36).

1049 Schoefs (n 1047); Clifford and Verdoodt (n 922).

1050 Schoefs (n 1047). Austria, Belgium, Finland, Italy, The Netherlands and Slovenia. For example, the author mentions BBC's Top Gear YouTube channel. Video sharing platform providers will be directly responsible for their own placement of commercial communications on the platform (e.g. banners, personalised advertising). Hence, the platform itself will be responsible for satisfying the identification requirements in these situations. However, it is important to note that the platform provider will only be editorially responsible for its own content. This means that the provider of the third party content on that platform should comply with the AVMS Directive if he in his turn can be held editorially responsible for his content.

1051 For instance research by Ofcom showed that are supplementing their TV viewing by turning to sites such as YouTube, Vimeo and Vine, as well as watching clips posted on Facebook or Twitter and news websites. Ofcom, 'Children's Content Review: Update Assessing the Current Provision of Children's Programmes on TV and Online' (2018) 9 <https://www.ofcom.org.uk/__data/assets/pdf_file/0023/116519/childrens-content-review-update.pdf> accessed 2 August 2018.

1052 Criteria to take into account could include *inter alia* the type of vlogs provided, the amount of videos uploaded and the consistency of uploads, the editorial work performed, the financial rewards gained by the influencer.

absence of editorial responsibility. In such cases, it will be up to the providers with editorial responsibility to abide by the provisions of this Directive."[1053]

UNTANGLING THE VLOGGER-PLATFORM RELATIONSHIP. Attributing responsibility to platform providers in the context of digital influencers would alter the generally accepted interpretation of 'selection' as a way to exercise control.[1054] Several European media regulators found that in the case of video-sharing platforms like YouTube or DailyMotion, there is neither any selection of videos as everyone can upload them, nor any organisation of the videos in function of their content by the platform provider.[1055] This is supported by the fact that these providers often remain outside the specific vlogging advertising revenue chain as they merely facilitate the delivery of the videos to the influencer's audience and usually generate an income through other forms of digital advertising (e.g. banners, personalised pre-rolls)[1056] accompanying the influencer's videos.[1057] However, if the platform provider is the one who engages the services of such professional influencers, the interpretation of editorial responsibility, selection and effective control becomes even more complex.[1058] Furthermore, the increased use of automated means of selection and organisation (e.g. algorithmic recommender systems[1059]) potentially decreases the role of the digital influencers uploading videos and strengthens that of the platform provider, thereby having a *de facto* influence on viewers' choice.[1060] For these reasons, the Belgian[1061] and German media regulators called for a special category under EU law for large audiovisual platforms that is subject to the (or some of the core[1062]) provisions of the AVMS Directive.[1063] In this regard, it is important to point out the broadened scope of the revised AVMS Directive, which also includes video-sharing platforms and (under certain circumstances) even social media platforms.

1053 Recital 3 of the AVMS Directive.
1054 Clifford and Verdoodt (n 922).
1055 Schoefs (n 1047).
1056 Hellemans, Lievens and Valcke (n 75).
1057 Clifford and Verdoodt (n 922); Schoefs (n 1047).
1058 YouTube recently launched a premium subscription-only version.
1059 YouTube's recommendations system helps users discover personalised content from an ever-growing corpus of videos. It takes as input *inter alia* user's watch history, implicit feedback of video watches by users and explicit feedback such as a thumbs up or a thumbs down and through filtering selects videos in the range of hundreds. P. Covington, J. Adams and E. Sargin, 'Deep Neural Networks for YouTube Recommendations' (ACM Press 2016) <http://dl.acm.org/citation.cfm?doid=2959100.2959190> accessed 7 December 2017.
1060 Schoefs (n 1047); Clifford and Verdoodt (n 922).
1061 More specifically, the media regulator of the French-speaking Community, Conseil Superieur de l'Audiovisuel (www.csa.be/).
1062 SCHOEFS for instance refers to the obligations in relation to commercial communication and the protection of minors under the AVMS Directive. Schoefs (n 1047).
1063 Dheur (n 1042).

B. Broadening the audiovisual playground

Video-sharing platforms officially enter the audiovisual playground. In the previous chapter, it was explained how the European Commission recognised the lack of a level-playing field for traditional and new audiovisual media providers, and the lack of consumer protection in relation to the latter in its 2016 REFIT evaluation of the AVMS Directive.[1064] Furthermore, considering that these new digital providers increasingly offer audiovisual content online and research has shown that video viewing is one of the earliest internet activities preferred by young children, it made sense to include them in the scope of the AVMS Directive, especially in relation to the protection of minors. The revised AVMS Directive, therefore, explicitly refers to a new category of 'video-sharing platform services' ("VSPs"), which will be subject to specific rules. To fall within the scope of the definition, several cumulative conditions need to be fulfilled[1065]:

- First, it needs to be a service normally provided for remuneration, which entails an economic activity, and its principal purpose needs to be of interest to the general public. As mentioned, this may also include services financed by advertising like a vlogger's YouTube channel.[1066]
- Second, the platform service must consist of the provision of programmes or user-generated videos to the general public, for which the service provider does not have editorial responsibility. However, it is up to the national legislator to determine the exact meaning of the concept of editorial responsibility.[1067]
- Third, the service provider must determine the organisation of the stored content. This includes the organisation by automatic means, such as displaying, tagging and sequencing. Video-sharing platforms like YouTube and Dailymotion (or at the very least specific parts or sections of these platforms) will most likely fulfil the conditions.
- Fourth, the principal purpose of the service or a dissociable section thereof or an essential functionality of the service must be devoted to providing

1064 DG CONNECT, 'REFIT Evaluation and Impact Assessment of the EU Audiovisual Media Services Directive 2010/13/EU (AVMSD)' <http://ec.europa.eu/smart-regulation/roadmaps/docs/2015_cnect_006_cwp_review_avmsd_iia_en.pdf> accessed 6 December 2017.

1065 Art. 1 (aa) AVMS Directive.

1066 Conversely, more private websites where video-sharing takes place within certain communities or groups (e.g. a website of the dancing school for children where videos are uploaded exclusively for parents) would be excluded.

1067 The same margin of appreciation has led in the past to different interpretations. For instance, Hermanns and Matzneller are of the opinion that the extensive cataloguing and composing of programmes would fall under editorial responsibility and the media regulator of the French-speaking Community of Belgium ruled that the sole possibility of exercising control over the content of programmes would be sufficient. O. Hermanns, P. Matzneller and S. Nikoltchev, 'The Regulation of On-Demand Audiovisual Services : Chaos or Coherence?' [2011] IRIS Special : The regulation of on-demand audiovisual services : chaos or coherence ?

programmes and user-generated videos to the general public, in order to inform, entertain or educate.
- Finally, the service needs to be made available through electronic communications networks.

As is clear for these cumulative criteria, the revised Directive aims to overcome the difficulties described above associated with the interpretation of editorial responsibility.[1068]

The legal qualification of social media platforms. An interesting question that arises is whether or not social media platforms such as Facebook are included in the VSP definition. The revised Directive strongly emphasises the role of social media services in young people's lives, recognising that they "*have a considerable impact in that they facilitate the possibility for users to shape and influence the opinions of other users*".[1069] Furthermore, such services also compete for the same audiences and the revenues as audiovisual media services and, therefore, are included in the scope of the Directive. However, social media services are only covered by the Directive insofar as they fall under the definition of a VSP. The Directive clarifies that social media services are included when the provision of programmes or user-generated videos could be considered an essential functionality of that service, meaning '*not merely ancillary or a minor part of its activities*'. Therefore, it needs to be assessed to what extent social media services revolve around providing user-generated audiovisual content.[1070] This assessment will need to be decided on a case-by-case basis, and may change over time when these services evolve.[1071] It is up to the European Commission to provide guidelines on the practical application of this criterion of essential functionality.

Responsibilities for VSP providers concerning commercial communications. The actual impact of the introduction of VSPs into the AVMS Directive on digital influencers and vlogging advertising depends on

1068 The second and third requirement aim to specifically cater for these problems and the increased usage of automated means of selection and organisation by platforms. Clifford and Verdoodt (n 922).

1069 Recital 4 of the AVMS Directive.

1070 I. Lambrecht, V. Verdoodt and J. Bellon, 'Platforms and Commercial Communications Aimed at Children: A Playground under Legislative Reform?' [2018] International Review of Law, Computers and Technology.

1071 K. Ehle, 'Digital Single Market Update: The European Commission's Proposal to Revise the Audiovisual Media Services Directive' (*Lexology*) <https://www.lexology.com/library/detail.aspx?g=dc9d66d9-f916-4f0b-b0cc-f3b6e2f45de4> accessed 15 December 2017. Facebook, for instance, has been increasingly investing in audiovisual content (e.g. Facebook Watch application). J. Costine, 'Facebook Launches Watch Tab of Original Video Shows' (*Techcrunch*, 9 August 2017) <https://techcrunch.com/2017/08/09/facebook-watch/> accessed 15 December 2017.

whether or not the provisions on commercial communication are applicable to such platforms. In this regard, article 28a of the revised Directive requires VSP providers to take appropriate measures to protect:

> (a) *minors from programmes, user-generated videos and audiovisual commercial communications which may impair their physical, mental or moral development in accordance with Article 6a(1);*
> (b) *the general public from programmes, user-generated videos and audiovisual commercial communications containing incitement to violence or hatred directed against a group of persons or a member of a group based on any of the grounds referred to in Article 21 of the Charter of the Fundamental Rights of the European Union;*
> (ba) *the general public from programmes, user-generated videos and audiovisual commercial communications containing content the dissemination of which constitutes an activity which is a criminal offence under Union law, namely public provocation to commit a terrorist offence within the meaning of Article 5 of Directive (EU) 2017/541, offences concerning child pornography within the meaning of Article 5(4) of Directive 2011/93/EU and offences concerning racism and xenophobia within the meaning of Article 1 of Council Framework Decision 2008/913/JHA on combating certain forms and expressions of racism and xenophobia by means of criminal law. (Emphasis added)*

Thus, VSP providers are required to take measures to protect minors from harmful audiovisual commercial communications and the general public from audiovisual commercial communications containing hate speech or illegal content. In addition, VSP providers also have to ensure compliance with article 9(1) of the Directive, which requires *inter alia* that audiovisual commercial communications should be recognisable as such (i.e. the identification principle) and should not directly exhort minors to buy or hire a product or service by exploiting their inexperience.[1072] However, this requirement only applies to those audiovisual commercial communications that are marketed, sold or arranged by the VSP provider. In contrast, for those that are not (for instance vlogging advertising arranged by a digital influencer), the revised Directive recognises the limited control exercised by VSP providers over such commercials and requires that VSP providers take appropriate measures. In order to determine what measures are appropriate, VSP providers have to take into account the

> *"nature of the content in question, the harm it may cause, the characteristics of the category of persons to be protected as well as the rights and legitimate interests at stake, including those of the video-sharing platform providers and the users having created and/or uploaded the content as well as the public interest."*[1073]

1072 Article 28 (1a) of the AVMS Directive.
1073 Article 28 (2) of the AVMS Directive.

Additionally, the measures have to be practicable and proportionate, in light of the actual size of the VSP service and the nature thereof. Important to note is that the Directive explicitly states that such measures may not lead to any type of ex-ante control or a filtering of uploaded content, as this would not comply with article 15 of the e-Commerce Directive.[1074] The revised Directive also provides a list of potential measures, including *inter alia* adding the identification requirement in the VSPs terms and conditions; installing flagging, age verification, parental control and rating mechanisms; and media literacy measures.[1075] For the implementation of these measures, Member States are required to encourage the use of co-regulation.

1.2.2. Vlogging advertising in the Unfair Commercial Practices Directive

Scope. In the previous chapter – but also in the evaluation of the previous use cases – it was mentioned that the UCP Directive is a horizontal Directive containing rules for commercial communications regardless of the form or delivery used. It applies to unfair business-to-consumer practices, including commercial communications directly connected with the promotion, sale or supply of a product to consumers. Because of its general scope, it will be applicable to many commercial practices that are also regulated by other general or sector-specific EU legislation.[1076] In this regard, the more specific requirements laid down under other EU legislation usually add to the general requirements of the UCP Directive, thus offering complementary protection (unless the aspect is specifically regulated by the sector-specific rules).[1077]

A. Unfair commercial practices by digital influencers and third-party traders

Responsibilities of digital influencers and third-party traders. Video-sharing platforms like YouTube have become platforms for commercial communication, in the form of advertising, product placement reviews, etc. In this regard, digital influencers promoting brands, products or services of a company (or their own) could qualify as traders under the UCP Directive. As

1074 Article 15 of the e-Commerce Directive states that "*Member States shall not impose a general obligation on providers, when providing the services covered by Articles 12, 13 and 14, to monitor the information which they transmit or store, nor a general obligation actively to seek facts or circumstances indicating illegal activity.*"

1075 Article 28 (2) of the AVMS Directive. In relation to the age verification and parental control mechanisms, the Directive prohibits that any personal data of minors collected in this context is used or resold for commercial purposes (e.g. behavioural advertising, direct marketing).

1076 European Commission, 'Commission Staff Working Document – Guidance on the Implementation/Application of Directive 2005/29/EC on Unfair Commercial Practices, SWD(2016) 163 Final.' (n 545).

1077 In this regard, article 3 (4) of the UCP Directive clarifies that "*in case of conflict between the provisions of this Directive and other Community rules regulating specific aspects of unfair commercial practices, the latter shall prevail and apply to those specific aspects.*"

noted above a trader is "*anyone (including legal persons) who is acting for the purposes relating to his trade, business, craft or profession, and anyone acting on behalf of another trader*".[1078] This means that both the brand or company that wants to promote their goods or services and the digital influencer that is hired to engage in the promotion could qualify as traders under the UCP Directive.

Hidden traders and advertising. In the context of social media and VSPs, the European Commission (2016) has warned for increased risks to hidden and misleading advertising, as commercial elements are often mixed with social and cultural user-generated content.[1079] Moreover, consumers experience these platforms just as services for exchanging information or communicating with other consumers. As such, they are often unaware of traders employing these platforms for advertising and marketing purposes. Regulatory authorities of several Member States found the practice of companies paying bloggers to promote and advertise their products on a blog aimed at teenagers without disclosing the commercial nature of the blogs to be a hidden commercial practice.[1080] By analogy, the same reasoning could be applied in the context of vlogging. Other examples of commercial practices by third party traders (e.g. brands) and/or digital influencers include:

- A third party trader encourages users to share marketing material with other users by offering price reductions on its marketed products as a reward.
- A blogger is given a free vacation by a tour operator in exchange for posting positive reviews on the vacation and the tour operator.
- A celebrity (music, sports) is given an endorsement deal in exchange for posting pictures of bought products such as sneakers.[1081]

The UCP Directive has specifically tackled the problem of hidden traders, by explicitly forbidding in all circumstances the practices of

> "*falsely claiming or creating the impression that the trader is not acting for purposes relating to his trade, business, craft or profession, or falsely representing oneself as a consumer*". *(Emphasis added)*

[1078] Article 2(b) UCP Directive.

[1079] European Commission, 'Commission Staff Working Document – Guidance on the Implementation/Application of Directive 2005/29/EC on Unfair Commercial Practices, SWD(2016) 163 Final.' (n 545).

[1080] European Commission, 'Commission Staff Working Document: Guidance on the Implementation/Application of Directive 2005/29/Ec on Unfair Commercial Practices' (2009) <http://ec.europa.eu/justice/consumer-marketing/files/ucp_guidance_2009_en.pdf> accessed 16 January 2018.

[1081] European Commission, 'Commission Staff Working Document – Guidance on the Implementation/Application of Directive 2005/29/EC on Unfair Commercial Practices, SWD(2016) 163 Final.' (n 545).

For example, traders are not allowed to post fake reviews in the name of consumers or by using e-reputation agencies. Furthermore, digital influencers and traders should refrain from "*using editorial content in the media to promote a product where a trader has paid for the promotion without making that clear in the content or by images or sounds clearly identifiable by the consumer (advertorial)*". Thus, the UCP Directive clearly requires that digital influencers disclose the commercial nature of their vlogs to their consumer-followers. Important to note is that the Directive does not provide further details on what such a disclosure should look like. With regard to advertorials, this could be either 'by images or sounds', and it has to be 'clearly identifiable'.

Fake likes could qualify as misleading commercial practices. Also relevant for digital influencers is article 6 of the UCP Directive which protects consumers against misleading commercial practices involving the use of systems such as 'likes'. The EC clarifies that by presenting fake 'likes' to consumers, a digital influencer or third party trader may mislead consumers about its own reputation or the reputation of its products or services. In turn, this could potentially influence consumers' purchasing behaviour, causing them to take transactional decisions they would not have taken otherwise.[1082] Significant to note in this regard is the practice of so-called 'pods', which entail (mostly hidden) collaborations on social media between a group of digital influencers. Members of a pod agree to like and comment on each other's videos in a specific manner (e.g. using a minimum amount of words, using enough hashtags), with the aim of being prioritised by the algorithm of the platform and appear more often in consumers' search results or newsfeeds.[1083] Considering that these collaborations are largely unknown to the public, it may constitute a misleading commercial practice. Therefore, it could be argued that digital influencers participating in pods should disclose this to their consumer-followers.

Additional protections for children. Finally, as mentioned, digital influencers are particularly popular amongst children and adolescents. Accordingly, article 5(3) of the UCP Directive could provide a legal basis of protecting "*a clearly identifiable group of consumers who are particularly vulnerable*". The EC explains that this legal basis reinforces the general

1082 European Commission, 'Commission Staff Working Document – Guidance on the Implementation/Application of Directive 2005/29/EC on Unfair Commercial Practices, SWD(2016) 163 Final.' (n 545).

1083 For instance, regarding pictures or vlogs on Instagram, the more likes and comments a post receives shortly after posting, the better it will perform in the algorithm. High initial engagement signals to Instagram that quality, engaging content is posted and as a result, the post can move higher up in people's feeds (and potentially go viral through the Instagram Explore page). G. Barkho, 'Inside Instagram Pods: The Secret Trick to Increase Your Engagement' (*Later Blog*, 23 February 2017) <https://later.com/blog/instagram-pods/> accessed 18 January 2018.

identification requirements (i.e. clearly indicating the marketing purpose).[1084] Furthermore, digital influencers need to keep in mind that their vlogs cannot contain a direct exhortation to children to buy a certain product or persuade their parents or other adults to buy such a product for them. For instance, statements of vloggers such as "Go buy my sweaters now" or "Tell your mom to order it in my webshop" would be prohibited under the UCP Directive. As mentioned, this does not imply an outright ban on advertising, but merely aims at providing protection to children against direct exhortations to purchase.[1085]

B. Unfair commercial practices by the video-sharing platform

Platforms as traders. The VSP provider can also qualify as a trader under the UCP Directive in certain instances. In its 2016 guidance document on the application of the UCP Directive, the European Commission explains that it must be assessed on a case-by-case basis whether a platform service provider is acting as a trader, whether it is engaging in a commercial practice and whether this practice is aimed towards consumers.[1086] In particular, the Commission stresses that platform service providers may be acting as traders when they draw revenues from targeted advertising.[1087] In addition, the VSP provider may put in place commercial practices such as facilitating and selling paid 'likes' and sponsored reviews, blogs and accounts to third-party traders. Conversely, for third-party advertising, the VSP provider will not have direct obligations under the UCP Directive.[1088] The VSP provider also needs to inform users about any processing of their personal data for commercial purposes, otherwise this could be considered an omission of material information necessary for informed commercial decision-making. Article 7 of the UCP

1084 European Commission, 'Commission Staff Working Document – Guidance on the Implementation/Application of Directive 2005/29/EC on Unfair Commercial Practices, SWD(2016) 163 Final.' (n 545).

1085 M. Capello, 'Article 13 TWFD' in Olivier Castendyk, Egbert Dommering and Alexander Scheuer (eds), *European Media Law* (Kluwer Law International 2008).

1086 European Commission, 'Commission Staff Working Document – Guidance on the Implementation/Application of Directive 2005/29/EC on Unfair Commercial Practices, SWD(2016) 163 Final.' (n 545).

1087 European Commission, 'Commission Staff Working Document – Guidance on the Implementation/Application of Directive 2005/29/EC on Unfair Commercial Practices, SWD(2016) 163 Final.' (n 545) 122. Also supported by the CJEU in the Papasavvas case: *Sotiris Papasavvas v O Fileleftheros Dimosia Etaireia Ltd and Others* [2014] CJEU C-291/13.

1088 For instance with regard to advertorials, the CJEU held that the prohibition was applicable to the trader whose products or services were advertised, rather than for instance the provider of a newspaper via which the advertisement is published. In other words, the Court found that there was no direct obligation on the newspaper in EU law. CJEU RLvS Verlagsgesellschaft v Stuttgarter Wochesblatt. *RLvS Verlagsgesellschaft mbH v Stuttgarter Wochenblatt GmbH* [2013] CJEU C-391/12; Geraint Howells, Christian Twigg-Flesner and Thomas Wilhelmsson, *Rethinking EU Consumer Law* (Routledge 2017).

Directive prohibits such an omission if it is shown that it is likely to cause the average consumer to take a transactional decision he would not have taken otherwise.[1089]

1.2.3. Further guidance for vloggers in self- and co-regulation – National best practices

LACK OF QUALITATIVE DISCLOSURE REQUIREMENTS IN LEGISLATION. Although the general identification requirement is applicable to digital influencers, it was discussed that the means of practically implementing this requirement are not specified in the current legislative framework. The same requirement can also be found in self-regulation, for instance in the International Chambers of Commerce Code of Advertising and Marketing Communication Practice.[1090] Recently, however, several national self-regulatory authorities, as well as groups of digital influencers themselves, have issued or pledged to follow guidelines on how to disclose commercial relationships.

UNITED KINGDOM: ASA "OREO RULING". A first example can be found in the United Kingdom, where the self-regulatory body for the advertising industry – the Advertising Standards Authority ("ASA")[1091] – had received a complaint in 2014 from a BBC journalist regarding vlogging advertising of Mondelez's Oreo cookie. The journalist claimed that the Oreo advertisements were not obviously identifiable as marketing communications. The case involved so-called 'Lick Race videos' on different YouTube Channels, owned by popular vloggers, which portrayed the vloggers eating an Oreo in a particular way.[1092] The videos were part of a marketing project by Mondelez UK Ltd, in cooperation with the vloggers concerned. The ASA ruled that the references used by the vloggers at the end of the videos – "*Thanks to Oreo for making this video possible*" – did not sufficiently make clear to the audience that the vloggers were collaborating with Mondelez. More specifically, the ASA highlights that the identification requirement is applicable to the general audience of the advertisement. Since the video advertisements were uploaded on a video-sharing platform that is usually editorial-based, viewers might perceive the video advertisements as a form of sponsorship, where the vlogger retains the editorial responsibility over

---

[1089] Again, article 5 (3) UCP Directive could present a legal basis for the protection of children in this regard, and as such, reinforces the information requirement and lowers the threshold when it comes to defining whether or not the omission has influences the consumer's transactional decision-making (i.e. the average consumer will be a child).

[1090] International Chamber of Commerce (n 137).

[1091] For more information on the ASA, see part III chapter II of the book.

[1092] P. Matzneller, 'GB-United Kingdom:ASA Upholds Complaint about Oreo Biscuit Ad in YouTube Videos' [2015] IRIS – Legal Observations of the European Audiovisual Observatory.

its content despite receiving financial support.[1093] The video advertisements were very similar to the editorial content on the respective channels, and as such, the ASA ruled that the commercial intent would not have been immediately clear from the style alone. In addition, the references in some of the videos were only made at the end of the video, or merely in the video description. According to the ASA, this entails that viewers have already interacted with the video, undermining the protective aim of the identification requirement.

CAP Guidelines for vloggers. Following the ruling, the ASA's sister body – Committee of Advertising Practice ("CAP")[1094] – launched guidelines for vlogging advertising, which clarify the responsibilities for the different parties involved. The principle remains the same: advertising by vloggers needs to be recognisable as such to the audience. If influencers receive any benefits from brands, they will have to disclose this commercial relationship. According to the CAP Guidelines, there are two ways in which a vlogger may clarify the commercial intent of a vlog: (1) by making it clear within the overall context of the communication or (2) by labelling a vlog as an advertisement.[1095] The CAP provides specific guidelines for several forms of vlogging advertising and clarifies for each of these who is responsible for complying with the identification requirement. For instance, advertorials (i.e. the video is in the usual style of the vlogger but the content is controlled by the brand and the vlogger has been reimbursed in some way) need to be labelled upfront so that viewers are aware of the nature of the video before engaging with it. In this context, both the vlogger (i.e. publisher) and the brand (i.e. marketer) are considered responsible for this labelling requirement.[1096] For each type of vlogging advertising, the CAP provides guidance on how to fulfil the identification requirement. These guidelines are meant to provide "*a non-exhaustive overview of vlogging scenarios with practical advice on how and when the rules kick in*".[1097] Although the scenarios and means of labelling are non-exhaustive, digital influencers that do not follow the CAP guidelines are at risk of being subject of a ruling by the ASA.

1093 Matzneller (n 1092).

1094 For more information on the CAP, see part III chapter II of the book.

1095 Advertising Standards Authority, 'Video Blogs: Scenarios' <www.asa.org.uk/advice-online/video-blogs-scenarios.html> accessed 13 February 2018.

1096 Rule 2.4 CAP Guidance.

1097 Advertising Standards Authority, Committees of Advertising, 'New Vlogging Advertising Guidance' <www.asa.org.uk/news/new-vlogging-advertising-guidance.html> accessed 15 February 2018.

Table 1: Vlogging scenarios and how to deal with them. (Source: https://www.asa.org.uk/advice-online/video-blogs-scenarios.html#.Vq9PWGdF2Uk).

Type of vlogging advertising	**Label**	**Who is responsible for the labelling?**
Online marketing by a brand	No label needed: commercial intent is likely to be clear from the context	/
Advertorial vlogs *(the whole vlog is paid for and controlled by a brand)*	Use: "advertisement feature", "ad", "ad feature", "advertorial" or similar Where: in the title or thumbnail Do not use: "sponsored", "Supported by", " Funded by" and "Thanks to X for making this possible"	The vlogger as 'publisher' and the brand as 'marketer'
Commercial breaks within vlogs *(a dedicated section of the editorial content is paid for and controlled by a brand)*	Make clear when the ad starts: Onscreen text stating "ad", "ad feature", holding up a sign, incorporating the brand's logo, or by the vlogger simply explaining that they've been paid to talk about the product. In addition (so not necessary) vloggers may add in the description box: "this video includes advertising for specific products which is indicated by [...]"	Vlogger
Product placement	No label needed for the entire vlog; onscreen text stating "ad", "product placement", holding up a sign, or the vlogger explaining that they've been paid to talk about the product.	Vlogger
A vlogger's video about their own product	The video title should make clear that the video is promoting the vlogger's products: "I'm excited about my promotional/book/album tour", "new product news" or "Let me show you how to use my new make-up line" would be sufficient.	Vlogger
Editorial video referring to a vlogger's own products	No label needed if the marketing communication is clear within the context: e.g. a gaming vlogger may say "I'm currently using the new headphones I've just released; you can purchase them through the link below". In addition (so not necessary) vloggers may add in the description box: "this video includes advertising for my new [...]", especially where they haven't advertised to their followers before.	Vlogger
Sponsorships *(A brand sponsors a vlogger to create a video but has no control of the content)*	No label needed under the CAP Guidance However: a nod to the sponsorship is required under consumer protection law.	Vlogger
Free items *(A brand sends a vlogger items for free without any control of the content (or any conditions attached))*	No label needed under the CAP Guidance However: vloggers are required under consumer protection law to tell consumers if an item was given on the condition that it is talked about.	Vlogger

Norway. Similarly, the Norwegian Media Authority ("NMA") has issued a very specific guide for Video Bloggers and YouTubers in 2017, on the labelling of advertisements. Interestingly, the Norwegian Broadcasting Act contains rules for hidden advertising, product placement and sponsorships, which also apply to digital influencers posting videos on video-sharing platforms. Influencers that do not follow these rules risk financial penalties, coercive fines or time-limited prohibitions on sending advertisements in their videos.[1098] The NMA's guide aims at helping digital influencers to comply with these rules. Similar to the CAP Guidelines, the NMA Guide contains certain scenarios or forms of vlogging advertising and provides for each of these different qualitative requirements for the labelling.

Table 2: Guide for YouTubers and Video Bloggers about Labelling of Advertisements. (Source: https://www.medietilsynet.no/globalassets/engelsk/engelsk-youtube-veileder.pdf).

Type of vlogging advertising	Label	Who is responsible for the labelling?
Advertisement *(you are paid to present a product in a video, the product is the main focus of the video)*	Labelled in writing on-screen, either before you present the product or at the beginning of the video. In addition (so not necessary): mention the collaboration verbally Do's: - Use the term "reklame" or "annonse" ("advertisement") - The label must be clear enough, large enough and must appear long enough on-screen for the viewers to acknowledge it - The label must be clearly visible against the background - The title of the video or the video's information field should also state that the video contains advertising Don'ts: - It is not enough to merely refer to the fact that the video was produced in "cooperation with..." - You cannot use the expression "sponsored by...". Read more about sponsorships below	Vlogger
Product placement *(you are paid to present a product in a video, the product is not the main focus of the video)*	Label the video in writing "P- Inneholder produktplassering" ("P – Contains product placement") both at the start and end of the video - The label must be visible for at least four continuous seconds - The label must be sufficiently large and entirely clear against the background so that it can be easily read	Vlogger
Including links to sales outlets = advertising	Use the term "reklame" or "annonse" ("advertisement") in connection with the links If you receive a share of the profits every time anyone buys the product via the relevant link, you could also make this clear to your viewers	Vlogger

1098 Medietilsynet, 'Advertisement, Sponsorship and Product Placement' (*Medietilsynet*) <www.medietilsynet.no/en/for-media-businesses/advertisement-sponsorhip-and-product-placement/> accessed 15 February 2018.

Type of vlogging advertising	**Label**	**Who is responsible for the labelling?**
Sponsorship *(the sponsor does not have any influence on the content of the video, and you do not discuss or demonstrate the sponsor's products or services)*	The sponsor must be identified in a clear manner at the start and/or end of the programme. - E.g.: "Sponset av X" ("Sponsored by X"), or "Takk til X for bidraget" ("Thanks to X for the contribution"). - Verbally or in writing.	Vlogger

THE NETHERLANDS. A third interesting example of self-regulation was set up by several Dutch YouTubers in 2017 called 'Social Code: Guidelines for advertising in online video' ("Social Code: YouTube").[1099] The Code was developed in collaboration with *inter alia* the Dutch Media Authority and the self-regulatory body for advertising – Stichting Reclame Code ("SRC"). The latter enforces the Dutch self-regulatory code for advertising, which also contains rules for social media advertising (including identification of commercial messages). The new Social Code: YouTube contains labelling requirements specifically for vlogging advertising on YouTube.[1100] Compliance with the Code will also entail compliance with the rules for social media advertising of the self-regulatory code of the SCR. Digital influencers pledging compliance to the Code can only collaborate with advertisers that accept the Code's labelling requirements.

Table 3: Social Code: YouTube. (Source: https://www.cvdm.nl/wp-content/uploads/2017/11/Social_Code_YouTube.pdf).

Type of vlogging advertising	**Label**	**Who is responsible for the labelling?**
Advertising paid by a brand	The label can either be: - An image before the video starts, screen-filling, minimum of 3 seconds - The vlogger mentions that the video includes an advertisement Add in the description box: "This video includes a paid collaboration with …"	Vlogger
Advertising paid by charity	Idem	Vlogger

1099 YouTube Vloggers, 'Social Code: Richtlijnen Voor Reclame in Online Videos' (2017) <https://www.cvdm.nl/wp-content/uploads/2017/11/Social_Code_YouTube.pdf> accessed 15 February 2018.

1100 According to MEINDERSMA, the rules are platform-dependent and do not apply to other video-sharing platforms. C. Meindersma, 'Nieuwe Regels Voor YouTubers, de Social Code' (*Marketingfacts*, 21 November 2017) <https://www.marketingfacts.nl/berichten/nieuwe-regels-voor-youtubers-de-social-code> accessed 15 February 2018.

Type of vlogging advertising	Label	Who is responsible for the labelling?
Free goods or services or discounts	Statement at the bottom of the description box.	Vlogger
Products paid by the vlogger (so no advertising)	Add in the description box: This video does not contain any paid collaborations or free products…	Vlogger

BELGIUM. As a final example, guidelines for influencer-marketing have also been released in Belgium. First, the Belgian Federal Public Service Economy (FPS Economy) – a governmental body – provided a set of guidelines for influencer advertising on social media on May 15th, 2018. The guidelines contain a specific subsection that is dedicated to YouTube. More specifically, vloggers are required to add a disclosure to their videos (i.e. the word 'reclame' in writing) when commercial statements are made. The disclosure should be shown at regular intervals of at least every fifteen seconds; should be visible for at least three seconds each time; may not be hidden between hashtags or at the end of the video. The company or brand that is behind the advertisement should also be identified. However, the FPS Economy already had to withdraw the guidelines, as they had been published before being validated. Interesting to note is that the guidelines would be legally enforceable and that non-compliance could lead to fines.

Secondly, the Jury for Ethical Practices in Advertising ("JEP") had to handle a complaint concerning questionable statements made by a digital influencer, in and accompanying one of his vlogs.[1101] In its decision, the JEP requested the influencer involved to either change or remove the contested vlog, based on the national implementation of the UCP Directive and the self-regulatory ICC Code. Following this decision, the Belgian Council for Advertising (*infra*) together with the JEP published their own guidelines on commercial practices by digital influencers.[1102] These guidelines aim to assist digital influencers, advertising companies, agencies, media and platforms with regard to consumer protection

1101 In the contested video, the vlogger addresses his young audience while elaboratly praising a sweater that is for sale on his website. A number of questionable statements are used in and around the video. For example, the title of the vlog reads: 'GRATIS ECHTE BROER TRUIEN' (freely translated: 'free sweaters for real fans'). While watching the video, however, it becomes clear that the sweaters in fact cost € 30. Besides this, the vlogger calls upon his (mostly underage) public to steal their parents' credit card in case they are not allowed to buy his merchandising. In addition, the vlogger also regularly emphasises that only when viewers buy one of his sweaters, they are considered to be 'real fans'. JEP, 'Acid Apparel', 12 September 2018, <https://www.jep.be/nl/nieuws/acid-apparel-12-09-2018-beslissing-tot-wijzigingstopzetting> accessed 29 October 2018.

1102 Aanbevelingen van de Raad voor de Reclame inzake online influencers, October 2018, <https://www.jep.be/sites/default/files/rule_reccommendation/aanbevelingen_van_de_raad_voor_de_reclame_online_influencers_nl.pdf> accessed 29 October 2018. For a

and legal certainty. The document is built upon the principles of identification, fairness and transparency, which have been formed into four concrete guidelines. First, online influencers have to disclose any commercial relationship with a brand in a visual or audible way. This can be done by stating one of the following words: "reclame, advertentie, sponsoring, promotie, gesponsord door, in samenwerking met, …" or hashtags: "#spon, #adv, #prom, #reclame, #recl, #sample, #…". Furthermore, the words or hashtags disclosing the commercial intent of the vlog will need to be adjusted in function of the language of the message or target audience, as social media does not have (linguistic) boundaries (*publicité, advertising, promoted, ad, paid, …*). Third, the disclosing words should be mentioned in such a way and place that the recipient immediately understands the correct nature of the message. Finally, the words should not be hidden: the average consumer will have to be able to take notice of the disclosure in normal circumstances. Important to note is that the scope of application of the guidelines is limited as it only applies if two conditions are fulfilled: (1) a remuneration was received, (2) the advertising company exercises control over the commercial communication. The latter envisages the situation where the advertiser and online influencers have agreed upon guidelines concerning the commercial message. This second condition implies that cases where a vlogger would receive a product for free under the condition to make a video about that product, will not be covered by the guidelines unless the advertiser has explicitly ordered how the promotion of the product will have to take place.

2. IDENTIFIED GAPS OR OVERLAPS

TOWARDS A COORDINATED, EVIDENCE-BASED APPROACH FOR LABELLING. It is clear from the analysis that digital influencers need to identify commercial communications that are integrated in their videos. Although the regulatory framework currently requires that certain information needs to be made visible to the consumer, it leaves a wide berth for interpretation and implementation. At the national level, this has led to a variety of self-regulatory initiatives, providing guidelines for the labelling of vlogging advertising. These self-regulatory instruments contain very clear and specific instructions for the implementation of the legal identification requirement in the context of vlogging, making it easy for digital influencers to comply. However, the lack of a coordinated approach at the EU level and the resulting distributed nature of labelling requirements could raise practical questions regarding enforcement. Furthermore, as digital influencers are highly popular amongst children, it could be questioned whether the labelling guidelines and current industry practices were developed with a

complete overview of events see V Verdoodt and N Feci, 'Digital Influencers and Vlogging Advertising: Calling for Awareness, Guidance and Enforcement' (2018) 1 Auteurs en Media.

children's audience in mind. For instance, research by Zarouali *et al.* indicates that adolescents do not comprehend that the word 'sponsored' refers to the persuasive intent of a message. In other words, the current practice of several social media platforms – i.e. the signposting of commercial communication with the word "sponsored" or "sponsored posts" – is not effective when it comes to adolescents and, as such, fails to fulfil the aim of the identification principle. Accordingly, it is argued that a coordinated, evidence-based approach to labelling, also taking into account the specific needs of children, could be useful for the proper implementation of the identification principle. The European Advertising Standards Alliance could take up a coordinating role in this regard.

Video-sharing platforms need to take up their share of responsibility. Aside from digital influencers, VSP providers also have important responsibilities for commercial communications distributed via their platforms. The legal framework distinguishes between those advertisements that are marketed, sold or arranged by the platform and third-party advertisements. With regard to the first category, both the AVMS and the UCP Directive require VSP providers to identify them as commercial communications. Furthermore, the VSP provider has a number of other responsibilities concerning the protection of minors specifically (e.g. protect them against harmful advertising content) and the public in general (i.e. protect them against hate speech, illegal content). The VSP provider must also refrain from unfair commercial practices such as facilitating and selling paid 'likes' and sponsored reviews, blogs and accounts to third-party traders. With regard to the second category, both the AVMS and UCP Directives recognise that VSP providers have limited control over content and commercial communications uploaded by third parties. Accordingly, rather than having a general obligation to monitor or filter uploaded content for harmful commercial communications, the revised AVMS Directive requires platform providers to foresee appropriate measures to ensure the protection of minors and the general public (e.g. flagging mechanisms, age verification mechanisms, parental control systems). It has also been described how the European Commission has encouraged the development of co-regulatory mechanisms for appropriate measures in the revised AVMS Directive. In this regard, it is argued that the EC should ensure that they take into account social science studies and that these co-regulatory mechanisms are evaluated and updated on a regular basis.

The safety net of consumer protection law. Finally, the analysis showed that certain provisions of the UCP Directive could form an important layer of protection for consumer-followers against certain types of 'unfair' vlogging advertising practices. Due to its broad scope of application, the Directive can also cover new commercial practices such as fake likes, hidden traders, Instagram pods or any other persuasive tactic emerging in the future.

CONCLUSION

GAPS AND OVERLAPS IN THE CURRENT REGULATORY FRAMEWORK FOR COMMERCIAL COMMUNICATION AIMED AT CHILDREN

ASSESSMENT OF THE REGULATORY FRAMEWORK FOR COMMERCIAL COMMUNICATION IN LIGHT OF CHILDREN'S RIGHTS. From the assessment, it can be concluded that at the EU level there are several legislative and self-regulatory initiatives imposing a myriad of obligations on advertisers first and foremost with regard to the identification of commercial communications, but also with regard to the content of the commercial message or the use of personal data for advertising purposes. However, the multitude of rules and obligations does not mean that, automatically, the level of protection and empowerment of children is high. Indeed, in the first part of this book, it was argued that the emerging trends in the area of commercial communication create difficulties for children to make carefully considered and critical commercial decisions or decisions concerning their privacy and personal data. This finding was confirmed in the second part of the book, and more specifically in the assessment of the persuasive tactics used in each of the three use cases and the impact thereof on children's advertising literacy. Furthermore, it was found that the advertising formats discussed affect several children's rights, such as their rights to development, privacy, protection against economic exploitation and freedom of thought. In this regard, the current regulatory framework provides specific protections for children across different regulatory instruments related to their autonomy and commercial decision-making, such as *inter alia* the principle of identification, information requirements and the reliance on (parental) consent as one of the main grounds legitimising the processing of children's personal data. However, the effectiveness of these advertising formats calls the existing protections and their enforcement into question. From the above mapping and evaluation it can be concluded that there are a number of gaps in the current regulatory framework for commercial communication aimed children.

1. Problems caused by the fragmentation of the regulatory framework

From the evaluation, a first general finding is that the fragmented regulatory framework leads to confusion among the different stakeholders involved. Both the legislative and self-regulatory principles are often formulated in a general or abstract manner ("commercial communications must be recognisable as such" or "marketing communications should not be intended to primarily appeal to minors"), and guidelines for the implementation in practice thereof are often lacking. Furthermore, the application and enforcement of the existing legislative and self-regulatory provisions will always be assessed on a case-by-case basis: first, it will be determined whether a specific provision is applicable to a certain message, and second, it will be determined whether the commercial message – the content, the identification or other elements – infringes the provision in question. However, as described above certain definitions in legislative or self-regulatory instruments are formulated in a manner that leads to uncertainty as to their scope of application for new, digital advertising formats. Moreover, no uniform definition on what constitutes a 'child' exists. Indeed, children are regarded *inter alia* as 'anyone under 18', 'anyone under the legal purchase age as regards alcohol advertisements' or '12 years or under in relation to online behavioural advertising'. Whereas of course different commercial messages may be inappropriate for children of different ages, the variety of ages that are relevant for the application of different provisions may lead to confusion, not only for advertisers, but also for parents and children. In light of these findings, it is contended that emerging trends in the area of commercial communication require a comprehensive approach and dynamic interpretation of all applicable frameworks in an intertwined manner. In other words, rather than looking at instruments in isolation, a holistic interpretation of the existing regulatory framework on commercial communication is needed.

2. The empowerment-protection scales of the regulatory framework are out of balance

A second gap that was discovered refers back to the analysis of the children's rights framework. Here, it was concluded that in the context of commercial communication a balance is need between (1) empowering children as young consumers and allowing them to practice their commercial decision-making skills and (2) protecting them against harmful or misleading commercial practices, especially considering the sophistication and persuasiveness of certain trends in commercial communication. It is up to the State to ensure that the regulatory framework is structured to achieve such a balance. At the moment, however, the existing protections for children in the context of new forms of commercial communication often revolve around identification and transparency requirements, essentially allocating much of the responsibility with children and their parents (e.g. advertisers have to label commercial messages but it is up to children and parents to recognise and understand the meaning of these labels). In light of this, it is concluded that the empowerment-protection scales are tipped out of balance. Considering the impact and effectiveness of emerging trends in the area of commercial communication on children, it is argued that a deresponsabilisation of the child (and parent) is required in the regulatory framework.

3. The limitations of the identification principle

Third, the identification principle was highlighted as a common thread throughout the regulatory framework. In this regard, it was discovered that there is a lack of structure and coherence with regard to its implementation. More specifically, it was found that a variety of labels exists to indicate the commercial nature of advertisements, which may lead to confusion among consumers. Therefore, it is argued that a more structured and coherent approach is needed in order to protect children's consumer interests. In addition, even though existing industry disclosures might be legally compliant, in some situations it could be argued that they are not in line with children's rights (e.g. for some advertising formats disclosures do not activate children's advertising literacy). In this regard, it is important to recognise the limitations of children's advertising literacy and empowerment and, as such, the effectiveness of the identification principle in today's online market reality.

4. The data protection framework is undergoing significant changes and guidance on its implementation is urgently needed

Another finding relates to the EU data protection framework, which has been undergoing significant changes (i.e. the adoption of the GDPR, the proposal for an ePrivacy Regulation). It was found that the GDPR provides specific protection for children, especially in the context of advertising, but it remains unclear what the specific protection for children will entail in practice. Furthermore, the framework does not contain a definition of a 'child', leading to uncertainty regarding the age group(s) to which certain protection measures should apply. Aside from this, the advertising industry has been very active in developing self-regulation, however, the focus lies too often on transparency and information, rather than on limitations to the collection and use of children's personal data. In this regard, it was argued that a children's rights inspired interpretation of the data protection framework is needed.

5. Need for better distribution of responsibilities in the advertising chain

The evolving role of platform providers such as video-sharing platforms in relation to commercial communications was also assessed. In this regard, it was concluded that increased responsibilities for platform providers could be a more practical means of ensuring compliance (e.g. regarding the identification requirements). The discussion is also reflected in the broadened scope and the increased responsibilities for video-sharing platform providers in the revised AVMS Directive.

6. Lack of coordination between regulatory authorities

Finally, considering the myriad of instruments regulating commercial communication, it was concluded that different regulatory bodies (i.e. both government regulatory bodies, such as media regulators, data protection authorities, consumer protection authorities, and self-regulatory bodies) are competent to enforce the existing provisions. As illustrated, in practice the application of these frameworks to emerging trends of commercial communication – and, hence, the competences of the regulators – may overlap, which may lead to uncertainty not only for the regulators themselves but also for consumers who want to file digital advertising-related complaints. In this regard, it was concluded that increased coordination and collaboration between the different regulatory authorities involved is needed.

Remainder of the book. This part of the book focused on the substantive legal elements of the regulatory framework for commercial communication. In the next part, the focus shifts to procedural and organisational elements of advertising regulation. As illustrated in the mapping exercise, the advertising industry has been very active in developing ARIs that play an important role in regulating commercial communication. The remainder of this book aims at finding best practice recommendations for the structuring and organisation of such ARIs.

PART III

ASSESSMENT OF NATIONAL ARIS IN THE AREA OF COMMERCIAL COMMUNICATION

CHAPTER I
THE INTERPLAY BETWEEN ALTERNATIVE REGULATORY INSTRUMENTS AND THE LEGAL FRAMEWORK FOR COMMERCIAL COMMUNICATION

Recap. The mapping of the current regulatory framework for commercial communication aimed at children showed that a myriad of provisions contained in both legislative and self-regulatory instruments may apply. These provisions are enforced at the national level by different regulatory authorities (i.e. media regulators, self-regulatory bodies, data protection authorities and consumer protection authorities). However, the evaluation of this fragmented framework revealed that the high number of applicable provisions and the existence of several regulatory authorities does not automatically mean that children are protected and empowered (cfr. the remaining gaps).

Procedural and organisational elements. As the previous part of the book provided a detailed evaluation of the substantive elements of the regulatory framework, this part focuses on procedural (i.e. monitoring, enforcement and remedial measures) and organisational (i.e. the attribution of regulatory power, organisational structures) elements and, more specifically, within existing alternative regulatory instruments. The mapping showed that the advertising industry has been very active in the development of self-regulatory initiatives. Moreover, self-regulation and private rule-making has been promoted by the European Commission as an important part of the regulatory process of protecting children online since the very beginning.[1103] For these reasons this part of the research will be limited to a selection of existing ARIs in the area of commercial communication at the national level and explore their strengths and shortcomings.[1104] The aim of the comparative analysis is to distinguish

1103 Macenaite (n 709) 2.

1104 Academic research has already focused on enforcement (or aspects thereof) of the separate legal instruments such as for data protection law see for instance F. Bieker, 'Enforcing Data Protection Law – The Role of the Supervisory Authorities in Theory and Practice', *Privacy*

those procedural or organisational elements that could improve the quality and effectiveness of ARIs to protect children in the context of commercial communication. The analysis also takes into account children's procedural rights.

Introduction. As an introduction to the comparative assessment, this chapter aims to situate ARIs within the broader legal framework for commercial communication. In relation to the interplay between legislation and ARIs, it is argued by Lievens that

> *"the use of ARIs does not occur in a legal vacuum. On the contrary, there are fundamental rights and other legal requirements – stemming from conventions, constitutions, laws, jurisprudence and soft law instruments – that need to be respected when creating, implementing and enforcing ARIs."*[1105]

A comprehensive analysis of those legal provisions that need to be taken into account for the construction and structuring of ARIs has already been addressed by Lievens.[1106] Her research showed that there are no legal obstacles which lead to an *a priori* exclusion of the use of ARIs to protect children – a finding that could be extended to the protection of children against harmful and misleading advertising. Therefore, this chapter focuses on a number of aspects that are of particular relevance to the context of commercial communication and/or for the comparative assessment of the procedural and organisational elements in the next chapter. First, it discusses the role and responsibilities of the advertising industry under the children's rights framework and analyses where ARIs come in. Second, it briefly touches upon how the EU legislators have promoted ARIs throughout the legal framework for commercial communication. Third, specific attention is given to children's procedural rights and safeguards, which form the basis for the comparative assessment. Finally, this section briefly describes

---

and Identity Management. Facing up to Next Steps (Springer, Cham 2016) <http://link.springer.com/chapter/10.1007/978-3-319-55783-0_10> accessed 5 July 2018.; for media law see for instance 'INDIREG – Indicators for Independence and Efficient Functioning of Audiovisual Media Services Regulatory Bodies for the Purpose of Enforcing the Rules in the AVMS Directive' (Hans Bredow Institute for Media Research 2011) <http://ec.europa.eu/archives/information_society/avpolicy/docs/library/studies/regulators/final_report.pdf> accessed 5 July 2018.; and for consumer protection law see for instance F. Weber, *The Law and Economics of Enforcing European Consumer Law: A Comparative Analysis of Package Travel and Misleading Advertising* (Routledge 2016).

1105 E. Lievens, 'The Use of Alternative Regulatory Instruments to Protect Minors in the Digital Era: Applying Freedom of Expression Safeguards' (2011) 29 Netherlands Quarterly of Human Rights 164, 49.

1106 Interested readers may take notice of the Phd research of Eva Lievens, which provides an extensive overview of both substantive and procedural requirements for the use of ARIs for the protection of children against harmful content. Lievens, *Protecting Children in the Digital Era: The Use of Alternative Regulatory Instruments* (n 12) 379–498.

a number of relevant procedural and/or organisational principles for ARIs stemming from EU policy and the industry itself, which are also relevant for the comparative assessment.

SECTION I. THE USE OF ARIS AND THE LEGAL FRAMEWORK

1. CHILDREN'S RIGHTS

State responsibility for regulating business activities. The UNCRC Committee underlines that States have important obligations regarding the impact of business activities and operations on children's rights, arising from the Convention.[1107] First, the obligation to respect entails that States "*should not directly or indirectly facilitate, aid and abet any infringement of children's rights*".[1108] Second, States have a duty to ensure that the activities and operations of businesses do not have an adverse impact on children's rights (i.e. protect). The Council of Europe has also explicitly recognised this duty in its 2016 Recommendation on human rights and business.[1109] Considering the important impact of new forms of commercial communication on children's lives, States must ensure that effective regulation and monitoring of businesses' advertising and marketing practices aimed at children are in place. Moreover, children's best interests should be central to the development of such legislation and policies. Third, States should take positive actions to facilitate the realisation of and promote the enjoyment of children's rights (i.e. fulfil).[1110] In this regard, supportive, stable and predictable legal and regulatory environments should be created for businesses to support children's rights. States should also strengthen regulatory agencies responsible for the oversight of standards that are relevant in the context of children's rights, such as with respect to advertising and marketing. More specifically, the UNCRC Committee stresses that these agencies require sufficient resources for the monitoring and investigation of complaints,

---

1107 UN Committee on the Rights of the Child, 'General Comment No. 16 (2013) on State Obligations Regarding the Impact of the Business Sector' (n 148).

1108 UN Committee on the Rights of the Child, 'General Comment No. 16 (2013) on State Obligations Regarding the Impact of the Business Sector' (n 148) 8.

1109 According to the Council of Europe, "*Member States should require that business enterprises respect the rights of children when operating within their territorial jurisdiction and, as appropriate, throughout their operations abroad when domiciled in their jurisdiction*". Council of Europe, Committee of Ministers, 'Recommendation CM/Rec(2016)3 on Human Rights and Business' 25 <http://edoc.coe.int/en/fundamental-freedoms/7302-human-rights-and-business-recommendation-cmrec20163-of-the-committee-of-ministers-to-member-states.html> accessed 28 June 2018.

1110 UN Committee on the Rights of the Child, 'General Comment No. 16 (2013) on State Obligations Regarding the Impact of the Business Sector' (n 148) 9.

but also to enforce remedies for abuses of children's rights.[1111] Finally, States must ensure that children whose rights have been infringed by businesses have access to effective remedy (i.e. remedy).[1112] In this regard, the Council of Europe underlines that *"accessible, affordable and child-friendly avenues to submit complaints and seek remedies, both judicial and non-judicial, should be ensured for children and their representatives"*.[1113]

Business responsibilities regarding children's rights. Although the UNCRC does not specifically refer to the responsibilities of the business sector for realising children's rights, the UNCRC Committee recognises the sector's increasing impact on children's rights. This is especially true in the digital era, where children's access and use of technologies becomes ever more reliant on internet companies that operate on a global scale.[1114] The impact of the sector can be positive, as such businesses may strengthen the realisation of children's rights (particularly their participation rights) through for instance technological advancements and investments, however, this is not always the case.[1115] Accordingly, the UN Committee on the Rights of the Child recognises that:

> *"duties and responsibilities to respect the rights of children extend in practice beyond the State and State-controlled services and institutions and apply to private actors and business enterprises. Therefore, all businesses must meet their responsibilities regarding children's rights and States must ensure they do so."*[1116]

For instance, businesses are recommended to take voluntary initiatives in the framework of their corporate social responsibility strategy, including the development of self- and/or co-regulatory instruments.[1117]

Corporate social responsibility for respecting children's rights. Promoting corporate social responsibility for human rights has been on the

1111 UN Committee on the Rights of the Child, 'General Comment No. 16 (2013) on State Obligations Regarding the Impact of the Business Sector' (n 148) 15.
1112 UN Committee on the Rights of the Child, 'General Comment No. 16 (2013) on State Obligations Regarding the Impact of the Business Sector' (n 148) 15.
1113 Council of Europe, Committee of Ministers, 'Recommendation CM/Rec(2018)7 of the Committee of Ministers to Member States on Guidelines to Respect, Protect and Fulfil the Rights of the Child in the Digital Environment' (n 170).
1114 Lievens and others (n 16).
1115 The Committee mentions the example of marketing harmful products such as cigarettes, alcohol and fatty foods, which can have a long-term impact on children's health. UN Committee on the Rights of the Child, 'General Comment No. 16 (2013) on State Obligations Regarding the Impact of the Business Sector' (n 148) 3.
1116 UN Committee on the Rights of the Child, 'General Comment No. 16 (2013) on State Obligations Regarding the Impact of the Business Sector' (n 148) 2. (Emphasis added by author).
1117 UN Committee on the Rights of the Child, 'General Comment No. 16 (2013) on State Obligations Regarding the Impact of the Business Sector' (n 148) 2.

policy agenda for quite some time.[1118] An important milestone in the business and human rights debate is the unanimous endorsement by the United Nations Human Rights Council of the 'Guiding Principles on Business and Human Rights'.[1119] This instrument contains a set of guidelines for States and companies to prevent, address and remedy human rights abuses committed in business operations.[1120] However, certain academics[1121] and children's rights organisations felt the need for stronger visibility of children's rights. According to Collins, the challenge was to articulate values and develop policies and practices that respect children's rights in business in a meaningful, convincing and effective way.[1122] In response to this need, several children's rights organisations joined forces to develop a similar instrument from a children's rights perspective.[1123] In 2012, the 'Children's rights and business principles' ("CRBP") were released, which form the basis of actions companies can take in terms of their corporate social responsibility to respect children's rights.[1124] The CRBP were an important precursor to the UNCRC Committee's General Comment 16.[1125]

Children's Rights and Business Principles. The CRBP were designed to guide companies *"on the full range of actions they can take in the workplace, marketplace and community to respect and support children's rights"*.[1126] They were developed in light of existing standards and best practices in relation to business and human rights, but from a children's rights perspective.[1127] The

1118 T. M. Collins, 'The Relationship between Children's Rights and Business' (2014) 18 The International Journal of Human Rights 582, 583.

1119 The development process of this instrument marks a shift towards a new "rights-based approach", supporting the human rights principle of participation. More specifically, according to Collins, the guiding principles "*were developed following long consultations and tested extensively before release to ensure effectiveness. There were 47 international consultations on all continents and site visits to businesses and local stakeholders in over 20 countries by January 2011 as well as practical testing of the non- judicial grievance mechanisms in five different sectors in five countries, and the due diligence provisions by 10 companies and involvement of corporate law experts from over 20 countries.*" This participatory development process was then taken up by the UN Committee in its General Comment 16 (2013) On State obligations regarding the impact of business on children's rights. See Collins (n 1118) 588.

1120 For more information see https://business-humanrights.org/en/un-guiding-principles.

1121 A. Crane and B. A. Kazmi, 'Business and Children: Mapping Impacts, Managing Responsibilities' (2010) 91 Journal of Business Ethics 567, 567.

1122 Collins (n 1118) 583.

1123 The principles were developed through consultations led by UNICEF, Save the Children and the United Nations Global Compact.

1124 UNICEF, UN Global Compact and Save the Children (n 412).

1125 For more information see Verdoodt, Lievens and Hellemans (n 9).

1126 UNICEF, UN Global Compact and Save the Children (n 412).

1127 P. Gerber, J. Kyriakakis and K. O'Byrne, 'General Comment 16 on State Obligations Regarding the Impact of the Business Sector on Children's Rights: What Is Its Standing, Meaning and Effect?' [2013] Melbourne Journal of International Law 123 <https://papers.ssrn.com/abstract=2319537> accessed 14 November 2017.

Principles, however, do not create new international legal obligations, but are derived from the internationally recognised human rights of children.[1128] While instruments such as the Guiding Principles and the CRBP have been described as the authoritative UN normative documents on business and human/children's rights, scholars have clarified that their normative contribution predominantly lies in elaborating the implications of existing standards and practices for States and businesses.[1129] Against this background, certain authors have commented upon the CRBP and their potential lack of effectiveness. For instance, Collins stresses that while recognising the value of articulating the commitments for business, there is the danger that the CRBP will not be fully appreciated or respected considering that it does not create new international legal obligations.[1130] According to Gerber *et al.* the CRBP are ultimately a private initiative, without the authoritative status enjoyed by General Comments.

No adverse effect on children's rights. The CRBP contains 10 principles, which each have their own set of criteria for reviewing critical areas of potential or actual impacts on children's rights. Of particular importance in the context of commercial communication is Principle 6, which states the following:

> *"All businesses should use marketing and advertising that respect and support children's rights".*

This principle entails that businesses have to ensure that the marketing and communication of their products or services does not have an adverse impact on children's rights. This entails that commercial communication may not reinforce discrimination and must offer children and parents clear and accurate information so that they can make informed decisions. To assess whether commercial communication has an adverse impact on children's rights, certain factors may be considered, such as children's greater susceptibility to manipulation, and the effects of using unrealistic or sexualised body images and stereotypes.[1131] Furthermore, the corporate responsibility to respect this principle requires compliance with the standards of business conduct in World Health Assembly instruments related to marketing and health. Finally, companies are also encouraged to raise awareness of and promote children's rights, positive self-esteem, healthy lifestyles and non-violent values through their own communication and marketing channels.

1128 W. Vandenhole and others, *Routledge International Handbook of Children's Rights Studies* (Routledge 2015) 397 <https://www.book2look.com/book/rUPT8r8gaE> accessed 14 November 2017.

1129 Gerber, Kyriakakis and O'Byrne (n 1127) 125.

1130 Collins (n 1118) 583.

1131 UNICEF, UN Global Compact and Save the Children (n 412).

Implementation of the principles. A key element for the implementation of the corporate responsibility to respect children's rights is conducting a children's rights impact assessment. In this regard, UNICEF has developed a guide for companies, for the implementation of the principle in practice and for the integration of children's rights into impact assessments.[1132] This tool contains the primary and supplementary criteria for assessment as well as recommended actions for companies. The criteria are subdivided into three categories: (1) policy, (2) due diligence and (3) remediation criteria. An important aspect of the assessment tool relates to the impact of marketing and advertising on children's rights. In this context, the tool defines several primary and supplementary criteria that companies need to keep in mind when they decide to market or advertise their services to children.

Policy criteria. First, the assessment tool defines a checklist of primary and secondary criteria for marketing and advertising policies. In addition, the tool offers practical guidance to companies by providing concrete action points. These action points are real structural decisions or measures that companies can make or implement. The policy criteria require companies to have *inter alia* a global responsible marketing and advertising policy in place that prohibits harmful and unethical advertising related to children. This would entail considering the appropriateness of their advertising campaigns for different age groups, addressing the adverse impact of digital media, taking adequate security measures to protect children in all internet-marketing venues (e.g. social media), etc.[1133]

Due diligence criteria. A second category of criteria for companies that market and advertise their products or services to children are due diligence criteria.[1134] These criteria require a certain standard of care from the company when defining their advertising or marketing strategies. The concept of due diligence also plays an important role in the Framework of the Special Representative, where it is defined as "*the steps a company must take to become aware of, prevent and address adverse human rights impacts*".[1135] In this regard, Parker and Howe have argued that there is a need for a sufficiently coercive legal environment for due diligence policies to be effective. Otherwise there may

---

1132 UNICEF, 'Children's Rights in Impact Assessments' (2013) <https://www.unicef.org/csr/css/Children_s_Rights_in_Impact_Assessments_Web_161213.pdf> accessed 14 November 2017.

1133 UNICEF (n 1132).

1134 Examples include conducting a regularly assessment of the impact of the company's marketing content on children, taking into account different age groups; conducting assessments on discrimination in advertising and marketing; disseminating messages to children and parents that promote healthy behaviours and products. UNICEF (n 1132).

1135 United Nations General Assembly, 'Protect, Respect, and Remedy: A Framework for Business and Human Rights Doc A/HRC/8/5' 56 <https://documents-dds-ny.un.org/doc/UNDOC/GEN/G08/128/61/PDF/G0812861.pdf?OpenElement> accessed 6 August 2018.

be a risk that due diligence policies will merely be a sort of "greenwashing" of corporate action on human rights.[1136]

REMEDIATION CRITERIA. Finally, the Children's Rights and Business Principles require that a formal complaint mechanism is in place, which should be accessible to children or their representatives. In this regard, UNICEF's children's rights impact assessment contains certain remediation criteria that companies should consider.[1137] For instance, companies should inform consumers, employees and other stakeholders about the mechanism and available channels to report concerns. The mechanism should also be accessible to children (e.g. a hotline or online channel for reporting).

CONCLUDING REMARK. To sum up, the advertising industry does have certain responsibilities for the realisation of children's rights, such as developing advertising campaigns that respect or promote children's rights, or develop advertising self-regulation. Regarding the latter, it is important to note that any self- or co-regulatory mechanism has to be in compliance with the children's rights framework, including children's procedural rights.

2. EU LEGISLATIVE INSTRUMENTS ON COMMERCIAL COMMUNICATION AND ARIS

The European legislator has recognised the potential of ARIs to regulate different forms and aspects of commercial communication aimed at minors, by specifically encouraging the Member States to consider or adopt such mechanisms in a number of legislative instruments or review procedures thereof.[1138]

AVMS DIRECTIVE. First, ARIs are explicitly mentioned in the revised Audiovisual Media Services Directive as a means to regulate the fields coordinated by the Directive. More specifically, article 4 (a) of the AVMS Directive obliges Member States to encourage the development of co-regulatory and/or self-regulatory mechanisms to the extent permitted by their legal systems. Such mechanisms

1136 C. Parker and J. Howe, 'Ruggie's Diplomatic Project and Its Missing Regulatory Infrastructure' in Radu Mares (ed), *The UN Guiding Principles on Business and Human Rights* (Martinus Nijhoff 2012) 279.

1137 UNICEF and The Danish Institute for Human Rights, 'Children's Rights in Impact Assessments: A Guide for Integrating Children's Rights into Impact Assessments and Taking Action for Children' (2013) <https://www.unicef.org/csr/css/Children_s_Rights_in_Impact_Assessments_Web_161213.pdf> accessed 6 August 2018.

1138 E. Lievens and Directorate-General for Internal Policies of the Union, *Research for CULT Committee Solutions and Policy Dilemmas Regarding Minors' Protection Online: In-Depth Analysis.* (2018) 10.

have to fulfil four major requirements: (1) representativeness, meaning that the main stakeholders should broadly accept them, (2) they must clearly and unambiguously set out their objectives, (3) provide for regular, transparent and independent monitoring and evaluation of the achievement of the objectives aimed at; and (4) effectiveness, meaning that the Member States should provide for effective enforcement.[1139] The rationale for this support for ARIs in relation to audiovisual media services is explained in recital 13 of the AVMS Directive:

> *"experience has shown that both co-regulatory and self-regulatory instruments, implemented in accordance with the different legal traditions of the Member States, can play an important role in delivering a high level of consumer protection".*

The idea is that measures aimed at achieving public interest objectives in the audiovisual media services sector would be more effective if they are supported by the service providers themselves. However, it should be noted that the EU legislators do not see self-regulation as a substitute for the obligations of the national legislator. It is rather a complementary mechanism to the legislative, judicial and/or administrative mechanisms in place.[1140] As such, any ARI regulating audiovisual commercial communication should be in line with the national legal framework implementing the AVMS Directive. Aside from the general encouragement for ARIs in the revised AVMS Directive, article 9 (4) obliges Member States to encourage media service providers to develop codes of conduct regarding inappropriate advertising of unhealthy foods.

E-COMMERCE DIRECTIVE. Second, the E-Commerce Directive explicitly mentions codes of conduct at Community level as the best means to regulate professional ethics in relation to commercial communication in an online environment. As such, Member States, the European Commission and professional associations and bodies are encouraged to develop codes of conduct for instance regarding the practical implementation of the information requirements for advertisers.[1141] Immediately after the adoption of the Directive, several associations developed sector-specific codes and trustmark schemes at both the European (e.g. Fedma Code for Direct Marketing, *supra*) and national level. However, after this initial boom the activity in this area appeared to slow down.[1142] The E-Commerce

---

1139 Article 4 (1) (a-d) of the AVMS Directive.

1140 Recital 7a of the AVMS Directive defines that "*However, while self-regulation might be a complementary method of implementing certain provisions of this Directive, it should not constitute a substitute for the obligations of the national legislator. Co-regulation provides, in its minimal form, a legal link between self-regulation and the national legislator in accordance with the legal traditions of the Member States.*"

1141 Article 8 §2 E-Commerce Directive.

1142 'First Report on the Application of Directive 2000/31/EC of the European Parliament and of the Council of 8 June 2000 on Certain Legal Aspects of Information Society Services, in Particular Electronic Commerce, in the Internal Market (Directive on Electronic Commerce)'

Directive also defines certain obligations for Member States in relation to the implementation of enforcement mechanisms. Member States are required to ensure that their national legislation does not hamper the use of out-of-court schemes for dispute settlement, including appropriate electronic means.[1143] Furthermore, the court actions available under national law in relation to information society services need to allow for the rapid adoption of measures (e.g. interim measures), in order to cease the alleged infringement and allow the prevention of further impairment of interests.[1144] Finally, Member States need to define effective, proportionate and dissuasive sanctions for infringements of the national measures implementing the E-Commerce Directive.[1145]

Unfair Commercial Practices Directive. Third, the EU legislators have recognised that codes of conduct are a means to promote fair business practices. Article 10 of the Directive states that Member States may encourage the use of code of conducts, and allows recourse to code owners (i.e. self-regulatory organisations) by consumers against unfair commercial practices such as misleading or aggressive advertisements. Important to note, however, is that such a complaint mechanism should not be deemed the equivalent of foregoing a means of judicial or administrative recourse.[1146]

General Data Protection Regulation. Finally, in the context of the processing of personal data, the EU legislators have explicitly recognised in the GDPR that codes of conduct can be a means to contribute to the proper application of the data protection principles.[1147] Considering the broad variety of processing sectors and the specific needs of micro, small and medium-sized enterprises, codes of conduct could provide more specific and concrete guidance on the application of the Regulation. In the context of commercial communication, this could for instance lead to the development of a specific code of conduct on the collection of children's personal data for behavioural advertising purposes, guidelines for the implementation of parental consent and verification mechanisms.

Concluding remark. Thus, the legislative instruments at EU level encourage the development of advertising ARIs. However, this does not necessarily mean

---

16–17 <www.europarl.europa.eu/RegData/docs_autres_institutions/commission_europeenne/com/2003/0702/COM_COM(2003)0702_EN.pdf> accessed 6 August 2018.

1143 Article 17 E-Commerce Directive.

1144 Article 18 E-Commerce Directive.

1145 Article 20 E-Commerce Directive.

1146 Article 10, second paragraph UCP Directive.

1147 Article 40 GDPR. For instance, article 40 (g) of the GDPR states that codes of conduct can be developed "*for the purpose of specifying the application of this Regulation, such as with regard to the information provided to, and the protection of, children, and the manner in which the consent of the holders of parental responsibility over children is to be obtained*".

that the complaint mechanisms provided by such instruments are an equivalent of judicial or administrative recourse

SECTION II. PROCEDURAL AND ORGANISATIONAL ELEMENTS FOR ARIS

1. CHILDREN'S PROCEDURAL RIGHTS AND THE USE OF ARIS

The first part of this book showed that a broad variety of children's rights are at stake in the context of new forms of commercial communications. When decisions are made that might interfere with these fundamental rights (e.g. a self-regulatory body deciding on a complaint against a hidden or misleading advertisement), it can be expected from the decision-making body that a number of procedural safeguards are adhered to.[1148] These safeguards can be found in the right to a fair trial and the right to an effective remedy.[1149]

1.1. *Right to a fair trial*

RIGHT TO A FAIR TRIAL. In the analysis of the children's rights framework, article 6 of the ECHR, which defines that everyone (including children) is entitled to a right to a fair and public hearing before an independent and impartial tribunal established by law when a dispute concerning their civil rights arises, was discussed.[1150] This might for instance be the case when children's rights to development, privacy or the protection against economic exploitation are interfered with by an ARI in the area of commercial communication aimed at children.[1151] LIEVENS clarifies that if the ARI concerned allows children to raise the issue with an alternative regulatory body, it should be assessed whether the body qualifies as a 'tribunal established by law'.[1152] If this is the case, then all the requirements put forward by article 6 ECHR must be complied with. If this is not the case, judicial review needs to be available.

1148 Lievens, 'The Use of Alternative Regulatory Instruments to Protect Minors in the Digital Era' (n 1105) 49.

1149 See also *supra* part I, chapter II, section II of the book.

1150 Similarly, article 47 of the EU Charter of Fundamental Rights determines that "*Everyone is entitled to a fair and public hearing within a reasonable time by an independent and impartial tribunal previously established by law.*"

1151 By analogy see E. Lievens, *Protecting Children in the Digital Era: The Use of Alternative Regulatory Instruments*, vol 105 (Martinus Nijhoff Publishers 2010) 417.

1152 E. Lievens, *Protecting Children in the Digital Era: The Use of Alternative Regulatory Instruments*, vol 105 (Martinus Nijhoff Publishers 2010) 417–418.

TRIBUNAL ESTABLISHED BY LAW. The first requirement entails that cases need to be dealt with by an independent and impartial tribunal established by law. This does not necessarily have to be a traditional court of law.[1153] The essential criterion is the function of the body concerned, which should be "*to determine matters within its competence on the basis of rules of law, following proceedings conducted in a prescribed manner*".[1154] LIEVENS examined whether recourse to an alternative regulatory body that would exercise functions which are determinative of civil rights could fulfil the requirement of 'a trial before a tribunal established by law'. As the ECtHR's requirements are relatively strict, LIEVENS argues that it can be assumed that self-regulatory bodies will not meet the standards of the court and that it is also doubtful that co-regulatory bodies would qualify as tribunals.[1155] Therefore, if a dispute concerning a civil right occurs, and the alternative regulatory body does not meet this first requirement, then the dispute must be "*subject to subsequent control by a judicial body that has full jurisdiction*" and which does fully comply with the requirements of article 6 ECHR.[1156] Nevertheless, article 6 ECHR contains a number of procedural safeguards which should be adhered to by alternative regulatory bodies, regardless of whether the first requirement is fulfilled.

INDEPENDENCE AND IMPARTIALITY. The right to a fair hearing under article 6 §1 requires that a case be heard by an "*independent and impartial tribunal*".[1157] Bodies which are not courts may also exercise functions determinative of civil rights, but MOLE and HARBY clarify that this is acceptable only if these bodies comply with the requirements of independence and impartiality.[1158] First, the independence requirement refers to independence *vis-à-vis* the other powers (i.e. the executive[1159] and the parties[1160]). In the assessment of independence, several criteria are taken into account, such as (1) the manner of appointment of the members, (2) the duration of their appointment[1161], (3) the existence of

1153 Directorate of the Jurisconsult of the European Court of Human Rights (n 532) 28.

1154 *Campbell and Fell v The United Kingdom* [1984] ECtHR 7819/77; 7878/77 para 76.

1155 Lievens, *Protecting Children in the Digital Era: The Use of Alternative Regulatory Instruments* (n 12) 414.

1156 Lievens, *Protecting Children in the Digital Era: The Use of Alternative Regulatory Instruments* (n 12) 414–415. This is required by the doctrine of full review.

1157 As there is a close interrelationship between the two requirements, the ECtHR usually considers them together. *Kleyn and others v The Netherlands* [2003] ECtHR 39343/98, 39651/98, 43147/98 and 46664/99.

1158 N. Mole and C. Harby, *The Right to a Fair Trial, A Guide to the Implementation of Article 6 of the European Convention on Human Rights* (Council of Europe 2006) 30; Lievens, *Protecting Children in the Digital Era: The Use of Alternative Regulatory Instruments* (n 6) 415.

1159 *Beaumartin v France* [1994] ECtHR 15287/89.

1160 *Sramek v Austria* [1984] ECtHR 8790/79.

1161 The case law of the ECtHR does not specify a particular term of office, but irremovability of members during their term of office should generally be considered as a result of their independence. Directorate of the Jurisconsult of the European Court of Human Rights (n 532) 34.

sufficient safeguards against the risk of outside pressure and (4) whether the body presents an appearance of independence.[1162] Second, impartiality requires that the court or decision-making body is not biased regarding the decision to be taken, does not allow itself to be influenced by information from outside or popular sentiment or by any pressure. Instead, decisions must be made on the basis of objective arguments grounded on what was put forward during the trial.[1163] The existence of impartiality must be determined on the basis of two tests: (1) a subjective test, focusing on the personal behaviour and convictions of the judges and (2) an objective test, focusing on the tribunal or decision-making body itself to see whether *inter alia* its composition offers enough guarantees for the exclusion of any legitimate doubt of partiality.[1164]

Right to a fair and public hearing. In addition, article 6 ECHR requires that the trial or hearing conducted by the tribunal (or decision-making body) is fair and public. First, the fairness requirement refers to the "*duty to conduct a proper examination of the submissions, arguments, and evidence adduced by the parties, without prejudice to its assessment of whether they are relevant to its decision*".[1165] Lievens clarifies that the requirement also links with a number of other rights, such as the right to participate effectively at the hearing[1166] and the right to a reasoned judgment.[1167] Second, the requirement of a public hearing "*protects litigants against the administration of justice in secret with no public scrutiny*" and is "*one of the means whereby confidence in the courts, superior and inferior, can be maintained*".[1168]

1.2. *Right to an effective remedy*

Right to a remedy. It was also mentioned that children have the right to an effective remedy before a national authority if their rights or freedoms under

1162 *Campbell and Fell v The United Kingdom* [1984] ECtHR 7819/77; 7878/77, para 78.

1163 P. van Dijk and others (eds), *Theory and Practice of the European Convention on Human Rights: Fourth Edition* (4th edition edition, Intersentia Publishers 2006) 614; Lievens, *Protecting Children in the Digital Era: The Use of Alternative Regulatory Instruments* (n 12) 416.

1164 Directorate of the Jurisconsult of the European Court of Human Rights (n 532) 39.

1165 *Ternovskis v Latvia* [2014] ECtHR 33637/02, para 66.

1166 In the context of children, this could also be linked with the child's right to be heard under article 12 of the UNCRC.

1167 The right to a reasoned judgment entails that "*a judicial decision should state clear and complete reasons and the arguments of the decision-making body should be legally valid and convincing*". M. Kuijer, *The Blindfold of Lady Justice: Judicial Independence and Impartiality in Light of the Requirements of Article 6 ECHR* (M Kuijer 2004) 167 as cited by E. Lievens, *Protecting Children in the Digital Era: The Use of Alternative Regulatory Instruments* (Brill 2010) 417.

1168 *Axen v Germany* [1983] ECtHR 8273/78, para 25. If an alternative regulatory body does not comply with this last requirement, it may be remedied if the decision of that body is subject to review by a judicial body that has full jurisdiction – on the law and the facts – and that provides a public hearing. Lievens, *Protecting Children in the Digital Era: The Use of Alternative Regulatory Instruments* (n 12) 417.

the ECHR have been violated, as enshrined by article 13 ECHR.[1169] The remedy should lead to the prevention of the suspected violation or if appropriate to the obtainment of adequate redress (e.g. compensation) and should be effective in practice and in law.[1170] The effectiveness of a remedy is assessed on the basis of the concrete circumstances of the case. With regard to children, article 13 ECHR is complied with if a legal representative of a child that is involved in a violation of Convention rights has recourse to a remedy.[1171] In this regard, States should remove social, economic and juridical barriers, so that children can have access to effective judicial mechanisms without discrimination of any kind.[1172]

Alternative regulatory instruments. In the context of this chapter, it could be questioned whether a remedy provided by an alternative regulatory body qualifies as a remedy before a national authority under article 13 ECHR. The ECtHR has confirmed in its case law that remedies do not necessarily have to be judicial:

> "*The "effectiveness" of a "remedy" within the meaning of Article 13 does not depend on the certainty of a favourable outcome for the applicant. Nor does the "authority" referred to in that provision necessarily have to be a judicial authority; but if it is not, its powers and the guarantees which it affords are relevant in determining whether the remedy before it is effective. Also, even if a single remedy does not by itself entirely satisfy the requirements of Article 13, the aggregate of remedies provided for under domestic law may do so.*"[1173]

Ovey and White explain that non-judicial remedies could also be considered adequate (e.g. an ombudsman procedure).[1174] In such a case, the ECtHR will assess the "*powers and the procedural guarantees an authority possesses*", when determining whether a remedy can be considered accessible, adequate and

---

1169 Similarly, article 47 of the EU Charter of Fundamental Rights determines that "*Everyone whose rights and freedoms guaranteed by the law of the Union are violated has the right to an effective remedy before a tribunal in compliance with the conditions laid down in this Article.*"

1170 Lievens, *Protecting Children in the Digital Era: The Use of Alternative Regulatory Instruments* (n 12) 418.

1171 Indeed, the ECtHR has stated that "*It was common ground that Article 13 (art. 13) did not require that a 12 year-old child be able to institute and conduct such proceedings on his own; it was sufficient for the purposes of this provision that a legal representative was able to do so on the child's behalf*". *Margareta and Roger Andersson v Sweden* (ECtHR), para 101.

1172 UN Committee on the Rights of the Child, 'General Comment No. 16 (2013) on State Obligations Regarding the Impact of the Business Sector' (n 148) 16.

1173 *Kudla v Poland* [2000] ECtHR 30210/96, para 156.

1174 C. Ovey and R. White, *Jacobs and White, the European Convention on Human Rights* (4th ed., Oxford university press 2006) 463 as cited by Eva Lievens, *Protecting Children in the Digital Era: The Use of Alternative Regulatory Instruments* (Brill 2010) 419.

effective.[1175] More specifically, it will analyse whether the body is independent, impartial and provides a number of minimal procedural guarantees. Furthermore, the body should be competent to receive complaints, investigate the merits of the complaint and take binding decisions concerning redress.[1176] Therefore, Lievens stresses that

> *"when alternative regulatory bodies are involved in the protection of Convention rights, such as the freedom of expression, in the framework of a system to protect minors from harmful content, the availability of remedies should be carefully considered".*[1177]

It is argued that the same reasoning is valid for alternative regulatory bodies that decide on compliance with advertising rules, as such decisions may also affect children's fundamental rights (*supra* part I, chapter II and part II chapter II).

Non-judicial mechanisms at company-level. Finally, non-judicial mechanisms such as mediation, conciliation and arbitration can also be useful alternatives for resolving disputes concerning children and businesses. According to the UNCRC Committee, such mechanisms can play an important role alongside judicial mechanisms if they are in conformity with the UNCRC Convention and should be available without prejudice to the right to judicial remedy. Such grievance mechanisms should also comply with a number of standards, such as effectiveness, promptness and due process and fairness. Furthermore, the UNCRC Committee requires these mechanisms to comply with a number of criteria, including accessibility, legitimacy, predictability, equitability, rights compatibility, transparency, continuous learning and dialogue.[1178] Nonetheless, children's access to courts or judicial review of administrative remedies and other procedures should still be available.

1175 In this regard, one should note the ECtHR ruling in Peck v the United Kingdom 28 January 2003, No. 44647/98, a case in which the applicant had been able to assert and vindicate his claims before self- or co-regulatory bodies. However, the ECtHR found that these bodies could not provide an effective remedy for the applicant to have his right of privacy protected, resulting in the finding of a violation of Article 13 in conjunction with Article 8. Reasons for this finding were the lack of legal power to award damages of the bodies involved and the lack of power to prevent a publication or broadcast. P. Valcke, D. Voorhoof and E. Lievens, 'Independent Media Regulators: Condition Sine qua Non for Freedom of Expression?' in W. Schulz, P. Valcke and K. Irion (eds), *The Independence of the Media and Its Regulatory Agencies* (INTELLECT LTD; Bristol, UK; Chicago, USA 2013) 66.

1176 Lievens, *Protecting Children in the Digital Era: The Use of Alternative Regulatory Instruments* (n 12) 419.

1177 Lievens, *Protecting Children in the Digital Era: The Use of Alternative Regulatory Instruments* (n 12) 421.

1178 J. Ruggie, 'Report of the Special Representative of the Secretary-General on the Issue of Human Rights and Transnational Corporations and Other Business Enterprises, A/HRC/8/5'.

2. GENERAL PRINCIPLES FOR SELF-AND CO-REGULATION AT EU LEVEL

2.1. The EU Principles for Better Self- and Co-regulation

Establishment of a community practice for self- and co-regulation. As part of its Strategy for Corporate Social Responsibility, the European Commission developed a benchmark for self- and co-regulation in collaboration with enterprises and other stakeholders. More specifically, the aim of the EU Principles for Better Self- and Co-regulation is to help actors involved in self- and co-regulation to improve recognition, respect and credibility for their efforts. Any initiative must always be in line with applicable law and fundamental rights as enshrined in EU and national law.[1179] The Principles contain a number of procedural safeguards which are relevant for the analysis of national ARIs.

Monitoring. First, the monitoring of the ARI should be conducted in a way that is sufficiently open and autonomous. Each participant to the ARI must monitor its performance against agreed targets and indicators, share the results with the other participants, and make them public (in an aggregated manner where possible in an objective and transparent way).[1180]

Evaluation. Second, the ARI should be subject to regular evaluation, not only regarding output commitments but also regarding the actual impact. This leaves scope for improvement in case any shortcomings are identified.[1181]

Resolving disagreements. Furthermore, regard must be had for resolving disagreements both among participants and non-participants. On the one hand, this entails having in place (confidential) procedures, which address any disputes involving participants in a timely fashion. On the other hand, it means having a complaint-mechanism in place, whereby complaints of non-participants are submitted to a panel of independent assessors which consist of a majority of non-participants. The outcome of these decisions should be made public. In case of non-compliance, the ARI should foresee in "*a graduated scale of sanctions, with exclusion included and without prejudice to any consequences of non-compliance under the terms of the Unfair Commercial Practices Directive*".[1182]

1179 European Commission, 'EU Principles for Better Self- and Co-Regulation' <https://ec.europa.eu/digital-single-market/en/news/principles-better-self-and-co-regulation-and-establishment-community-practice> accessed 24 May 2018.

1180 European Commission, 'EU Principles for Better Self- and Co-Regulation' (n 1179) 2.

1181 European Commission, 'EU Principles for Better Self- and Co-Regulation' (n 1179) 2.

1182 European Commission, 'EU Principles for Better Self- and Co-Regulation' (n 1179) 2.

FINANCING. Finally, the participants to the ARI should foresee in the means that are necessary for the realisation of the commitments. Civil society organisations that do not have fully adequate means themselves may be aided by public funders or others. Any support in this regard must be made public.[1183]

2.2. *EASA Charter principles for self-regulation*

EASA CHARTER PRINCIPLES FOR SELF-REGULATION. Finally, the European advertising industry has also agreed to adhere to a number of principles for self-regulation, some of which are procedural in nature. More specifically, the members of EASA (*supra* part II, chapter I) are all signatories to the Advertising Self-Regulatory Charter, which contains certain principles and standards of best practice for self-regulatory mechanisms in the area of commercial communication. By signing the Charter, the members confirm their commitment to implement these principles and standards in the practical operation of self-regulatory mechanisms. In that sense, it is not a code of conduct for marketers, but rather a guiding document for industry players that want to set up self-regulatory initiatives. The aim of EASA is to create a level playing field for advertisers across the EU while safeguarding a high level of consumer protection.

CHARTER PRINCIPLES. The Charter contains the following 10 principles (the principles relating to procedural elements have been underlined):

1. *Comprehensive coverage by self-regulatory systems of all forms of advertising and all practitioners;*
2. *Adequate and sustained funding by the advertising industry proportionate to advertising expenditure in each country;*
3. *Comprehensive and effective codes of advertising practice-based on the globally accepted codes of marketing and advertising practice of the International Chamber of Commerce (ICC) applicable to all forms of advertising;*
4. *Broad consultation with interested parties during code development;*
5. *Due consideration of the <u>involvement of independent, non-governmental lay persons in the complaint adjudication process</u>;*
6. *Efficient and resourced administration of codes and handling of complaints thereon in an <u>independent and impartial manner by a self-regulatory body set up for the purpose</u>;*
7. *<u>Prompt and efficient complaint handling at no cost to the consumer</u>;*
8. *Provision of advice and training to industry practitioners in order to raise standards;*

1183 European Commission, 'EU Principles for Better Self- and Co-Regulation' (n 1179) 2.

9. *Effective sanctions and enforcement, including the publication of decisions, combined with efficient compliance work and monitoring of codes;*
10. *Effective awareness of the self-regulatory system by industry and consumers.*

SECTION III. INTERIM CONCLUSION

The aim of this introductory chapter to this final part of the thesis was to situate advertising ARIs in the context of the broader legal framework for commercial communication and examine the responsibilities of the advertising industry for the development of such ARIs.

First, it was discussed that under the UNCRC framework, States have important obligations regarding the impact of business activities and operations on children's rights. More specifically in the context of commercial communication, the UNCRC Committee recommends States to encourage the advertising industry to develop ARIs for the protection of children against certain types of advertising. In line with this, the European legislators have recognised ARIs as an important means to protect children online, also in the context of advertising, as the development of ARIs is encouraged throughout the EU legislative framework for commercial communication (i.e. the AVMS Directive, the e-Commerce Directive, the UCP Directive and the GDPR).

Second, it has been established in academic literature that ARIs do not operate in a legal vacuum, but have to be in compliance with the broader legal framework, including children's rights, the EU secondary legal framework on commercial communication, other internal market legislation etc. This chapter analysed children's procedural rights (i.e. the right to a fair trial and the right to an effective remedy), which need to be taken into account when developing ARIs to protect children against certain forms of commercial communication. It was found that decision-making bodies must adhere to certain procedural safeguards (i.e. fairness, impartiality, independence, competence to receive complaints, competence to investigate the merits and take binding decisions) whenever decisions are made concerning (children's) fundamental rights.

Finally, this chapter examined a number of general principles or benchmarks for the procedural and organisational aspects of ARIs at the EU level. It was found that ARIs should: be subject to regular evaluation; have an open and autonomous oversight and monitoring mechanism in place; allow consumers to file complaints at no cost, which will be handled promptly and effectively, and consumers should be made sufficiently aware of this possibility; have a number of procedural safeguards in place such as the independence of assessors and public decisions; have effective sanctions in place; and finally receive sufficient funding to ensure a proper and independent functioning.

CHAPTER II

FUNCTIONAL COMPARATIVE ASSESSMENT OF NATIONAL ARIS

Introduction. After identifying a number of procedural safeguards and general principles or benchmarks for ARIs in the previous chapter, this chapter studies the procedural and organisational elements of three national ARIs, in order to extract best practices for ARIs aimed to protect and empower children in the context of new advertising formats. The selection of national ARIs is explained in a first subsection and the second subsection contains the actual comparative assessment.

SECTION I. SELECTION OF NATIONAL ARIS AND QUESTIONS FOR THE COMPARATIVE ANALYSIS

Selection of national systems. There are two principal factors that are decisive in determining the structure or form that ARIs may take in any country. First of all, it is the countries' tradition (i.e. the combination of cultural, commercial and legal traditions) that influences the self-regulatory system. According to Durovic and Micklitz, consumers in different countries and regions will respond differently to the same advertising practices.[1184] Consequently, the regulation of advertising is supposed to take into account the cultural dimension. Second, it depends on the opportunity of ARIs to exist next to legislation. ARIs are (usually) complementary to legislation. Accordingly, in countries where detailed and extensive legislation on commercial communication exists, the role of ARIs will be smaller than in those countries in which the legal framework exists only of broad principles.[1185] Considering these two decisive factors, it can be said that advertising ARIs across the EU have taken different forms, which differ significantly. Indeed, while certain countries have opted for the use and promotion of self-regulation, others only foresee a limited role for self-regulatory organisations, or the co-regulatory structure dominates the

1184 Durovic and Micklitz (n 142) 26.

1185 EASA, *Blue Book: Advertising Self-Regulation in Europe and Beyond* (2010). EASA (2010). Blue Book: Advertising self-regulation in Europe and beyond.

system. In light of this, Belgium, the Netherlands and the United Kingdom have been selected after a preliminary study, as their systems are well-developed but significantly different. More specifically, in Belgium and the Netherlands, rules are integrated in self-regulatory instruments, whereas in the United Kingdom the rules on commercial communication are integrated in a complex co-regulatory framework which includes elements of statutory legislation and self-regulation.

Questions guiding the comparative analysis. The assessment can be divided into three sub questions, for which a number of elements of assessment have been defined, based on the analysis conducted in the previous chapter (i.e. the analysis of children's procedural rights and the general principles or benchmarks for the procedural and organisational aspects of ARIs at the EU level).

Questions guiding the assessment	Elements to take into consideration
1. How is the ARI organised, in what form and how broadly is it supported?	a. Attribution of regulatory powers b. Coverage c. Complaint procedure d. Procedural safeguards
2. How effective is each of the ARIs discussed?	e. Amount of complaints / cases dealing with new advertising formats f. Arrangement of monitoring and oversight g. Availability of remedies and enforcement powers
3. On the basis of the answers provided to the two questions above and taking into consideration the characteristics that set apart advertising ARIs from ARIs in other sectors, what best practices can be extracted?	

SECTION II. COMPARATIVE STUDY

1. COUNTRY REPORTS

1.1. Belgium

Jury for Ethical Practices in Advertising. The Belgian self-regulatory organisation of the advertising industry is the Jury for Ethical Practices in Advertising (hereafter "JEP", *Jury voor Ethische Praktijken inzake Reclame*). The decisions of the JEP are based on (1) legislation and (2) the self-regulatory codes that complement the legislation (in particular the ICC Code, but also a number of thematic covenants, etc).[1186] The JEP examines whether advertising messages are in conformity with these frameworks.

1186 For an overview of the substantive provisions of these self-regulatory codes, see Verdoodt, Lievens and Hellemans (n 9).

1.1.1. Attribution of regulatory power

Self-regulatory mechanism. The JEP was established in 1974 by the Council for Advertising (*Raad voor de Reclame*), the organisation representing the Belgian advertising industry, which aims at improving, valorising and defending commercial communication and the commercial freedom of expression.[1187] The mechanism is dependent on the voluntary commitment of the advertisers, communication bureaus and advertising media.[1188] Indeed, decisions of the JEP are in nature non-binding, but the industry commits voluntarily to bring their advertisements in compliance with these decisions without the government having a supervisory or sanctionary role. In situations where a case concerning an advertisement has been brought before a judicial or administrative instance, the JEP may decide to temporarily or permanently abstain from a decision in this case.[1189]

Competences. The JEP is responsible for watching over the correct and fair nature of commercial messages aimed at the public. The task of the JEP is limited to researching content of advertising messages that are spread via mass media – such as daily or weekly magazines, radio, television, movie theatres but also the internet and social media – as well as via emailing or direct mail. Furthermore, the JEP is competent to examine personalised advertising, regardless of the medium used.[1190] The JEP does not, however, have competence for (1) buyer-seller disputes, (2) other forms of media like brochures in a shop or packaging and (3) commercial practices such as sales promotions, contests, product placement, etc.[1191]

Prior consultation. Advertisers, advertising agencies and media have the possibility to request a preliminary examination by the JEP, prior to the publication of the advertisement.[1192] However, this is not an obligation,

1187 The Council for advertising consists of and is financed by different partners in the commercial communication industry, (1) advertisers, (2) communication bureaus and (3) advertising media. The members of the Council are responsible for the creation and dissemination of more than 80% of Belgian commercial communication.

1188 P. Valcke and D. Voorhoof, 'Hoofdstuk 20 – De Reclamecode En de Jury Voor Ethische Praktijken Inzake Reclame', *Handboek mediarecht* (Editions Larcier 2014) 725.

1189 Article 2 'Rules of the JEP [Reglement van de JEP]' <https://www.jep.be/sites/default/files/inline-media/reglement_jep_nl_-_februari_2017.pdf> accessed 8 June 2018. In this regard, Article 2 also determines that if the Jury on appeal decides to abstain from a decision, that the decision taken by the Jury in first instance will not be executed.

1190 Article 2 'Rules of the JEP [Reglement van de JEP]' (n 1189). However, excluded are all elements that do not relate to the content of the advertisement, such as privacy aspects, techniques of behavioural targeting etc.

1191 Article 2 'Rules of the JEP [Reglement van de JEP]' (n 1189).

1192 In 2016, the JEP conducted a preliminary examination of 15 advertisements. JEP, 'Yearly report 2016' <https://www.jep.be/sites/default/files/year_report/jaarverslag_2016_nl_-_hyperlinks.pdf> accessed 6 June 2018.

advertisers remain responsible for the ads they use. The JEP is there to help interpret and respect the applicable legal and self-regulatory rules.

Examination of advertisements at its own initiative. The President of the Jury in the first instance may submit an advertisement at his/her own initiative or at the request of one or more members of the Jury to the examination of the Jury, with the aim of defending consumer interests or the image of commercial communication.[1193]

Transboundary advertisements. The JEP is a member of EASA and even a member of its Board of Directors and the Executive Committee.[1194] Accordingly, the JEP can intervene in cases where commercial communications are spread in a transboundary manner. In this regard, the following distinction needs to be kept in mind:

- **For traditional media**: as a basic principle of the procedure, the competent institution will be the one of the country of origin of the media outlet that disseminates the advertising. This could also be the country where the advertiser is located. As such, a Belgian consumer could file a complaint about a commercial communication that is spread in Belgium by for instance a foreign newspaper. This complaint will then immediately be transferred to the self-disciplinary body of the country involved, which will handle the complaint according to its own procedures and on the basis of the applicable national rules.
- **For non-traditional media (direct mail, websites):** other rules or procedures may be applicable (such as those of the country of origin of the advertiser).

Evaluation. There is no formal procedure for the evaluation of the self-regulatory mechanism in place.

1.1.2. Complaint procedure and consumer awareness

Complaints. The following natural or legal persons may file advertising complaints with the Jury, in so far as they aim at defending the interests of consumers and/or the image of advertising: consumers, consumer organisations, sociocultural organisations, professional associations and representatives of an official body or public authority. Complaints can be filed free of charge. The formal requirements entail that complaints must be submitted in writing

1193 However, in 2016, the President of Jury in First Instance submitted only one advertisement to the Jury. JEP (n 1192).

1194 Raad voor de Reclame, 'De Raad Voor de Reclame Wil de Europese Verankering van de JEP Versterken' (2016) <www.raadvoordereclame.be/nl/dossiers/115-de-raad-voor-de-reclame-wil-de-europese-verankering-van-de-jep-versterken> accessed 7 August 2018.

and accompanied by a motivation. Complaints cannot be anonymous, but the identity of the complainant is not made public by the JEP.[1195]

Review of decisions. Both the advertisers and the complainants can appeal against the decisions taken by the Jury in first instance. It is the Jury on Appeal that will review the decision.

Awareness. The JEP received 186 complaints in 2016, of which 167 originated from consumers, 3 from consumer organisations, 1 from a professional organisation, 1 from the President of the Jury in First Instance and 14 from a public authority.[1196]

Timing. The JEP treats a complaint within a period of (approximately) ten days.[1197] The Jury convenes on a weekly basis and the Jury on appeal whenever necessary (in principle monthly).

1.1.3. Enforcement and procedural safeguards

Enforcement. In case of non-conformity, the JEP reaches out to the advertiser or if needed the involved professional associations, and shares its recommendation on whether or not the advertiser needs to make adjustments or has to stop using the advertisement. If the person or company responsible for the advertisement refuses to follow the JEP's decision, the latter can also directly contact the media or the professional associations concerned to recommend to stop spreading the contested advertisement. Aside from decisions to stop or adjust advertisements, the JEP may also confine itself to communicating a reservation to the advertiser.[1198] However, the JEP does not have sanctionary powers.

Incentives for compliance. After closing a complaint, a summary of the complaint and decision is published on the website of the JEP.[1199]

JEP Label. Furthermore, the organisations and media that financially support the JEP and commit to abide by the JEP's decisions may reproduce the JEP Label. However, this label does not imply that the JEP has monitored all commercial

---

1195 JEP (n 1192).

1196 JEP (n 1192).

1197 The yearly report of 2016 showed that 3/5 of the complaints filed was treated within two weeks. JEP (n 1192) 19.

1198 However, the JEP does not have the intention to censor or to promote a particular ideology or taste. If the JEP is of the opinion that an advertisement only requires a reservation, then it will not issue a decision to change or stop the advertising campaign but confine itself to an opinion of reservation which is shared with the advertiser, or the concerned media or professional organisations if needed. 'Rules of the JEP [Reglement van de JEP]' (n 1189) 2.

1199 Article 12 'Rules of the JEP [Reglement van de JEP]' (n 1189).

messages that are being spread via that medium. Nevertheless, it is useful for the public, as it allows them to easily find the contact details of the JEP and it confirms at the same time that the organisation or medium has committed to comply with the decisions of the JEP.

Independence and impartiality. The advertising sector and civil society are equally represented in the JEP, both in first instance and on appeal. The Presidents of the Jury in first instance and on appeal are elected among honorary magistrates or public figures of the Bar, academia or the advertising industry. This equal representation aims to ensure the independence of the JEP *vis-à-vis* the government, the advertising sector, political organisations, etc. Furthermore all members are appointed in a personal capacity. The Jury deliberates in secret and decisions are made by majority vote. Members that are unable to make a decision freely will refrain from participating in the deliberations.[1200]

Funding. The JEP was established and is financed by the Council for Advertising (*Raad voor de Reclame)*[1201] as a private body.[1202]

Transparency. As mentioned, the decisions of the JEP are published on their website. The JEP also publishes a yearly report of its activities.

Analysis of existing case law. Already in 2010, Cannie and Voorhoof argued that the JEP has developed a rich and strong advisory practice concerning the protection of children and minors against radio and television advertising, set benchmarks, delivered important decisions and interpreted numerous advertising rules intended to protect minors.[1203] An analysis of a selection of the more recent decisions of the JEP[1204] has shown that although there are several

---

1200 Article 8 'Rules of the JEP [Reglement van de JEP]' (n 1189).

1201 The organisation representing the Belgian advertising industry, which aims at improving, valorising and defending commercial communication and the commercial freedom of expression. It consists of and is financed by different partners in the commercial communication industry, (1) advertisers, (2) communication bureaus and (3) advertising media. The members of the Council are responsible for the creation and dissemination of more than 80% of Belgian commercial communication. In 1974, the Council established the Jury for Ethical Practices in Advertising, the self-disciplinary body of the advertising sector in Belgium.

1202 Raad voor de Reclame, 'Reglementering van En Controle Op de Reclame – Repertorium Op 1 Januari 2013. 8th Edition.' 11.

1203 H. Cannie and D. Voorhoof, 'Audiovisuele media, reclame en minderjarigen: Veel regels, maar weinig toezicht, Etmaal van de Communicatiewetenschap' (2010) 8.

1204 The inventory was developed as follows: first of all, a search through the JEP's database (in July 2018) using filters 'Internet' as type of media and 'child' as keyword resulted in 37 cases, of which 7 actually dealt with children and new advertising formats (i.e. the commercial communication was aimed at children). Second, a search using 'Internet' as type of media and 'minor' as keyword resulted in 26 hits, of which 5 were new and relevant for the case law inventory.

cases involving new advertising formats (e.g. internet banners[1205], Facebook pages and events), the identification of the commercial message is not the point of discussion.[1206] More specifically, the majority of the cases concerned breaches of the rules on alcohol advertising (e.g. no age warning[1207], no educational slogans[1208]). Hence, from these decisions, it is difficult to deduct further guidelines on how to implement certain general principles (e.g. the identification requirement) or mechanisms (e.g. age verification) with regard to new, digital advertising formats.

1.2. The United Kingdom

Complex regulatory landscape. The regulatory landscape for commercial communication in the UK consists of a patchwork of governmental acts and self-regulatory codes drafted by mostly independent bodies. Some of these bodies are attributed with statutory powers, while others form part of a purely self-regulatory mechanism.[1209] Furthermore, a distinction is made between broadcast advertising, for which a co-regulatory mechanism was developed and non-broadcast advertising (such as digital advertising), which is regulated by self-regulation.

1.2.1. Attribution of regulatory power

The Advertising Standards Authority as the single regulator for advertising across all media. Broadcast advertising in the UK was traditionally covered by legislation and subject to statutory control.[1210] In the sixties, the advertising industry recognised the importance of consumer trust in advertisements, including in non-broadcast media. Accordingly, the industry formed the Committee of Advertising Practice ("CAP") and drafted the first edition of what is now the Code of Non-broadcast Advertising, Sales Promotion and Direct Marketing ("CAP Code"). In addition, CAP established the Advertising Standards Authority ("ASA"), as the independent advertising

1205 *AB INBEV, 5/08/2009* (JEP).

1206 One case dealt with the use of drawings or characters popular with minors: *DELHAIZE, 19/08/13* (JEP). Nevertheless, the 2016 yearly report shows that misleading advertising does remain an important criterion for the Jury.

1207 *BOCKOR BROUWERIJ, 05/08/2010* (JEP).

1208 *SALITO BEACH – HAVANA DISTRIBUTION, 7/07/16* (JEP).

1209 For more information on the regulatory landscape in the UK, see: L. Senden and others, 'Mapping Self- and Co-Regulation Approaches in the EU Context' (Utrecht Centre for Shared Regulation and Enforcement in Europe 2015) 21–24 <https://ec.europa.eu/digital-single-market/en/content/mapping-self-and-co-regulation-approaches-eu-context> accessed 7 August 2018.

1210 Advertising Standards Authority, 'About the ASA and CAP' <www.asa.org.uk/about-asa-and-cap/about-regulation/about-the-asa-and-cap.html> accessed 7 June 2018.

regulator supervising the working of the new self-regulatory system in the public interest. Over time, the ASA has become the one-stop-shop for advertising complaints and its competences were extended to include broadcast advertising. More specifically, in 2004 the UK Communications Regulator ("Ofcom") – supported by the Parliament – decided to contract-out the responsibility for broadcast advertising to the ASA system in a co-regulatory partnership.[1211] A new industry committee was established, the Broadcast Committee of Advertising Practice ("BCAP"), to draft and maintain the Code of Broadcast Advertising ("BCAP Code"), and an ASA (Broadcast) was launched to administer the Codes. Thus, the ASA is a hybrid body, with statutory powers in relation to broadcasted advertising materials[1212] and non-statutory powers regarding non-broadcast advertising. Considering that this book is focused on digital advertising, the following sections will only cover the CAP and the CAP Code.

Competences. The ASA is competent to proactively monitor compliance of advertisements across all media and take action against misleading, harmful or offensive advertisements, sales promotions and direct marketing where necessary.[1213] The ASA may also initiate an investigation into potential code breaches, on the back of complaints they receive. The advertising codes and the ASA rulings have universal coverage across the entire advertising industry, meaning that advertisers cannot opt out of them.[1214]

Prior consultation. Advertisers can also turn to the copy advice team when developing digital advertising campaigns. The team provides an informed view of the likely acceptability of non-broadcast marketing communications under the CAP Code. However, such an advice is ultimately not binding on the ASA.

Proactive monitoring. Another part of the system is the compliance team, which regularly monitors advertisements in the national and regional press, consumer magazines, posters, direct mailings and internet advertisements. If the team discovers a breach of the CAP Code, it will contact the responsible business and seek assurance that the marketing message will be changed. Furthermore,

---

1211 Advertising Standards Authority, 'About the ASA and CAP' (n 1210).

1212 The ASA still functions in close cooperation with Ofcom with regard to broadcasted advertising. Ofcom has delegated some powers to the ASA, including limited statutory powers of pre-clearance and enforcement. However, Ofcom has retained the most imposing enforcing powers, such as fines and retentions of license.

1213 More specifically, a CAP compliance team regularly monitors advertisements in the national and regional press, consumer magazines, posters, direct mailings and internet advertisements. Committee on Consumer Policy, 'Industry Self-Regulation: Role and Use in Supporting Consumer Interest' (OECD 2015) 46 <www.oecd.org/officialdocuments/publicdisplaydocumentpdf/?cote=DSTI/CP(2014)4/FINAL&docLanguage=En>.

1214 Advertising Standards Authority, 'About the ASA and CAP' (n 1210).

the compliance team also monitors particular media or industry sectors to check the compliance rate within and uncover potential sectoral problems.[1215]

Legal backstop. When non-broadcast materials incessantly breach ASA rules and decisions, the ASA can refer them to Trading Standards for misleading or unfair advertising.[1216] Broadcasting advertisers that breach the Broadcasting Code can be referred to the Ofcom, which has statutory powers to impose fines or withdraw broadcasting licenses.[1217] For sector-specific scenario's, the ASA works in close cooperation with statutory sector regulators, such as the Financial Conduct Authority, the Food Standards Agency, the Gambling Commission and the Medicines and Healthcare products Regulatory Agency.[1218]

Decision-making process: interaction BCAP – CAP. Both the Broadcasting Advertising Code and the non-Broadcast Advertising Code are very similar in its content aside from those few provisions specifically related to the technical characteristics of the regulated medium.[1219] Accordingly, the different investigative cells (BCAP and CAP) have the explicit permission to take into account decisions made in relation to other media before delivering their findings to the ASA Council for the final decision.[1220]

Transboundary advertisements. The ASA is a founding member of and plays an important role in two networks: (1) EASA (cf. *supra*) and (2) the International Council for Advertising Self-Regulation (ICAS) which promotes effective advertising self-regulation globally. As a result, the ASA will handle cross-border complaints under the same conditions as national complaints.[1221]

1215 Advertising Standards Authority, 'Our Proactive Work' <www.asa.org.uk/about-asa-and-cap/the-work-we-do/our-proactive-work.html> accessed 8 August 2018.

1216 Trading Standards are the local authority departments that enforce consumer protection legislation. Trading Standards officials will investigate the complaints referred by the ASA and have the power to take legal action against those traders who break the law.

1217 Aside from a regulatory framework, the ASA also provides parents with a specific page with not only information regarding Children and Advertising, including case law and how to file a complaint, but also including links to other social organisations helping parents and children alike in a variety of ways, eg. Lobbying connections, practical help, children's society and so on. Visit the parents' page at: https://www.asa.org.uk/Consumers/Parents-Page.aspx (accessed on: 18/10/2016).

1218 Advertising Standards Authority, 'Working with Others' <www.asa.org.uk/about-asa-and-cap/the-work-we-do/working-with-others.html> accessed 7 August 2018.

1219 For a more detailed overview of the relevant provisions on commercial communications aimed at children in these instruments, see V. Verdoodt, I. Lambrecht and E. Lievens, 'Mapping and Analysis of the Current Self- and Co-Regulatory Framework on Commercial Communication Aimed at Minors. A Report in the Framework of the AdLit SBO Project.' <www.adlit.be> accessed 20 November 2017.

1220 For example when assessing an advertisement contained in an online video stream, taking into account a previous, related assessment for a broadcast advertisement.

1221 L. Conway, 'The Role of the Advertising Standards Authority' 11 <https://researchbriefings.parliament.uk/ResearchBriefing/Summary/SN06130> accessed 8 August 2018.

Evaluation. There are different forms of evaluations. First, the ASA conducts quarterly customer satisfaction surveys from complainants about non-broadcast and broadcast advertisements.[1222] Second, Ofcom evaluated the co-regulatory arrangements for broadcast with the ASA for their renewal in 2014.[1223] Third, for updates to the codes, open consultations are held.

1.2.2. Complaint procedure and consumer awareness

Asa complaint mechanism. As mentioned, the ASA is the one-stop-shop for consumers that want to file advertising complaints. Consumers can file complaints with the ASA in most scenario's. The ASA will direct the complainant to either the CAP or BCAP investigative cells, depending on the advertising format (i.e. broadcasted or non-broadcasted).[1224] The designated investigative cell will then assess the complaint in light of their respective codes, whilst taking into account other relevant self-regulatory provisions. These cells will call upon the ASA for the enactment of the final decision and the enforcement thereof. If the point at issue is subject of simultaneous legal action, the ASA will normally not pursue the complaint.

Review of decisions. If a party does not agree with the decision of the ASA, he or she can address the Independent Reviewer of the Rulings of the ASA Council.[1225]

Limitations. There are certain limitations that consumers need to keep in mind. First, there is a limitation in time, as complaints must be made within three months of the advertisement's appearance.[1226] Second, there is a limitation in points of complaints that the complainant may bring to the discussion. More specifically, complaints should focus on no more than three issues.[1227]

Awareness. Although it is composed of a number of essential parts, the system operates as a single regulator for advertising across all media. The yearly report

1222 Committee on Consumer Policy (n 1213) 47.

1223 Ofcom, 'Renewal of the Co-Regulatory Arrangements for Broadcast Advertising' (2014) <https://www.ofcom.org.uk/__data/assets/pdf_file/0028/58942/statement.pdf> accessed 7 August 2018.

1224 The complaint-handling mechanisms operate mostly the same, with the main difference being the absence of competence for Ofcom in complaints against non-broadcasted materials.

1225 For more information on how to file a complaint, visit: https://www.asa.org.uk/Consumers/How-to-complain.aspx (accessed 07.08.2018).

1226 However, the ASA notes that in exceptional circumstances older advertisements will still be considered.

1227 If a complaint contains more than three issues, the investigation will only focus on the three most important ones (although again, the ASA notes that in exceptional circumstances they may investigate more than three points).

of the ASA shows that in 2017 the internet overtook TV as the most complained about medium. The ASA received 16365 non-broadcast complaints, of which 4313 were further investigated. Of these non-broadcast complaints, 3,709 were investigated and 353 were upheld or upheld in part, however it is unclear from the annual report how many of these cases dealt with children and new advertising formats.

Timing. The ASA is committed to acknowledging complaints within five days of receiving them.[1228] Furthermore, complaints are resolved 'as quickly as possible' and straightforward issues can be resolved 'in days'. However, for more complex cases it may take longer, the most complex ones can even take up to six months or more (for instance if independent experts are appointed).[1229] In its yearly report, the ASA provides some insights into the duration of the procedure:

Figure 3: Duration of the ASA procedure for complaints concerning non-broadcast advertisements (source https://www.asa.org.uk/uploads/assets/uploaded/34872c48-106e-4f5f-a92983c95e92c84b.pdf)

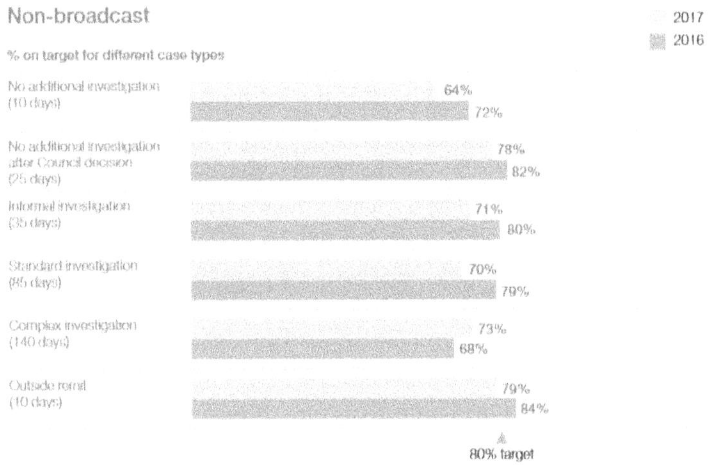

1.2.3. Enforcement and procedural safeguards

Enforcement. In case there is a minor or clear-cut breach of the Advertising Codes, the ASA may resolve the issue informally in the form of an advice on how to be compliant or seek assurance that the advertiser will adapt or withdraw the

1228 Advertising Standards Authority, 'Non-Broadcast Complaint Handling Procedures' 2 <https://www.asa.org.uk/asset/171EB506-B4EF-4FEC-BDCEC62DC49E0BE2.1759E419-AD92-452B-865FC913C62CE312/> accessed 8 August 2018.

1229 Advertising Standards Authority, 'Making a Complaint' <https://www.asa.org.uk/asset/8C4ECE0C-1EFA-43B9-885C0D18480E3F94/> accessed 8 August 2018.

advertisement immediately.[1230] However, if there is a more serious breach of the Advertising Codes or ASA Rulings, the ASA Council (i.e. the jury deciding on potential breaches) may require advertisers to withdraw or adapt their advertisement. Advertisers that do not comply with the codes in their non-broadcast advertising practices can become subject to a number of sanctions, including bad publicity[1231], disqualification from industry awards, advertising alerts[1232], withdrawal of trading privileges[1233] and requiring serious offenders to have their marketing material vetted before publication.[1234] In relation to online advertising, the ASA can also request search engines to remove a marketer's paid-for search advertisements when those advertisements link to a page on the marketer's website containing material that is not compliant with advertising regulation. The ASA, however, does not have powers to impose fines or bring advertisers to court. In the situation of persistent breaches of the advertising rules, the ASA may refer advertisers to (1) Trading Standards for non-broadcast advertisements and (2) Ofcom for broadcast advertising.[1235]

INCENTIVES FOR COMPLIANCE. All parties involved in a complaint-procedure are made aware of the collective decision of the ASA Council, and these decisions need to contain a detailed reasoning. This information is also shared publicly on the website of the ASA.

INDEPENDENCE AND IMPARTIALITY. The ASA Council consists of 13 members, of which two-thirds are independent of the industry and the remaining members have a recent or current knowledge of the advertising or media sectors. If a position opens up, it is advertised and members will have to follow an open recruitment process.

FUNDING. The ASA is funded by advertisers through arm's length levy arrangements that guarantee its independence. More specifically, in 1974,

1230 Advertising Standards Authority and Committees of Advertising Practice, 'Annual Report 2017' (2017) 18 <https://www.asa.org.uk/uploads/assets/uploaded/34872c48-106e-4f5f-a92983c95e92c84b.pdf> accessed 19 June 2018.

1231 For instance, marketers name and details of the problem may be featured on a 'blacklist' (i.e. a dedicated section of the ASA website), which is designed to appear in search engine results when a consumer searches for a company's website.

1232 CAP can issue alerts to its members, including the media, advising them to withhold services such as access to advertising space.

1233 CAP members can revoke, withdraw or temporarily withhold recognition and trading privileges. For example, the Royal Mail can withdraw its bulk mail discount, which can make running direct marketing campaigns prohibitively expensive.

1234 When dealing with complaints concerning broadcast advertising, the ASA can take certain actions against or with the broadcaster. For example, the ASA can require the broadcaster to withdraw, amend or suspend an advertisement even before the result of a formal investigation is published. These decisions by the ASA Council are based on their own interpretation of the BCAP and are published on a weekly basis on the ASA website.

1235 Ofcom can (1) present the advertiser with a formal warning, (2) suspend, shorten or revoke licenses to a broadcast and (3) impose fines when and to the extent deemed necessary.

the industry set up the Advertising Standards Board of Finance (Asbof) to provide secure funding for the system through a levy of 0,1% on advertising space cost.[1236] In addition, they receive a small income from the organisation of seminars, from premium industry advice service and from the European Interactive Digital Advertising Alliance for regulating online behavioural advertising.[1237]

Transparency. The rulings of the ASA are published on their website.[1238] As mentioned, the ASA also publishes a yearly report of its activities.[1239]

Analysis of existing case law. From a search through the database of the ASA Rulings, a small number of cases dealing specifically with children and digital advertising were found. While most of these cases concerned the content of the advertisements (e.g. containing offensive language on social media[1240], the promotion of alcohol[1241] or unhealthy foods[1242], misleading information or false claims[1243]), few cases analysed the delivery of the commercial communication. Nevertheless, from these cases some guidelines for advertisers in relation to the implementation of the identification principle and the requirement of age verification could be derived. First, as described in the previous part of the book, the ASA delivered a landmark ruling in the case concerning the Oreo Lick Race. From this ruling, it can be concluded that vloggers are forced to be upfront with their followers regarding paid promotions of products in their videos. Second, some guidance on the implementation of age verification in relation to alcohol advertising on YouTube (more specifically regarding prerolls) can be distilled.[1244] Thus, it can be concluded that the ASA Rulings do contain limited guidelines for advertisers on how to comply with existing rules, in the context of children and new advertising formats.

1236 The Broadcast Advertising Standards Board of Finance (Basbof) was established to collect the 0.1% levy on broadcast advertising space costs. Advertising Standards Authority, 'Our History' <www.asa.org.uk/about-asa-and-cap/our-history.html> accessed 8 August 2018.

1237 Advertising Standards Authority and Committees of Advertising Practice (n 1230).

1238 The rulings can be accessed via <https://www.asa.org.uk/codes-and-rulings/rulings.html> (accessed 8 August 2018).

1239 The yearly reports can be accessed via <https://www.asa.org.uk/advice-and-resources/resource-library/annual-reports.html> (accessed 8 August 2018).

1240 *Stomp Racing Ltd t/a Rocker BMX* (Advertising Standards Authority).

1241 *Flava Bar Ltd* (Advertising Standards Authority).

1242 *Ferrero UK Ltd* (Advertising Standards Authority).

1243 *Westland Horticulture Ltd t/a westland garden health* (Advertising Standards Authority).

1244 *ILLVA SARONNO SPA* (Advertising Standards Authority). Regarding the age verification: "*However, we noted that the ad in question would only have been seen by YouTube users who were registered as aged 18 or over and were logged into their accounts. We therefore considered that the advertisers had taken reasonable steps to prevent those who were under 18 from viewing the ad and we concluded that it did not breach the Code.*"

1.3. *The Netherlands*

The Advertising Code Authority. In the Netherlands, the institution dealing with the advertising self-regulating system is the Advertising Code Authority ("AC Authority", in Dutch: *'Stichting Reclame Code'*.[1245] The institution is based on the voluntary agreement of the advertising industry. The rules for advertisers are contained in the Dutch Advertising Code, which includes a specific Code for Advertising directed at Children and Young People. The rules of the Code are formulated by the advertising industry itself (i.e. the advertisers, advertising agencies and media). This code applies to all forms of commercial communication, regardless of the medium used, unless explicitly stated otherwise.[1246]

1.3.1. Attribution of regulatory power

The Advertising Code Authority and the Advertising Code Committee. The AC Authority was set up in 1963 as an independent private organisation financed by the advertising industry, in response to at least two events. First, the ICC Code of Advertising Practice that got a foothold in European countries in the sixties and second, the increasing political pressure to regulate commercial communication in the Netherlands.[1247] The main players in the field of advertising and marketing have subscribed to the self-regulatory mechanism. Within the AC Authority, the advertising industry is represented in three columns, being the Advertisers, Channel (or media) and Creation. Additionally, consumers are represented in the column Consumer and Society.[1248] The Dutch self-regulatory mechanism is monitored by the Advertising Code Committee (hereafter "AC Committee"), an independent body handling complaints against advertisements that do not comply with the Dutch Advertising Code.

Competences. The AC Committee and the Board of Appeal are competent to deal with advertising-related complaints. All the major players in the advertising and marketing industry have subscribed to the mechanism.[1249] Furthermore,

---

1245 Dutch Advertising Code Authority, 'The Dutch Advertising Code – Information about the Working Procedures of the Advertising Code Committee and the Board of Appeal' 4 <https://www.reclamecode.nl/bijlagen/20120701_NRC_Engels.pdf> accessed 29 June 2018.

1246 Dutch Advertising Code Authority (n 1245) 3.

1247 W.H. Van Boom and others, 'Handelspraktijken, Reclame En Zelfregulering: Pilotstudy Maatschappelijke Reguleringsinstrumenten' (Ten verzoeke van: Wetenschappelijk Ond erzoek – en Documentatiecentrum Ministerie van Justitie 2009) 53 <www.professorvanboom.eu/pdf_files/2009_eindrapportage_Pilotstudy_zelfregulering.pdf> accessed 3 July 2018.

1248 Advertising Code Authority [Stichting Reclame Code], 'Yearly Report [Jaarverslag]' (2017) 3 <https://www.reclamecode.nl/bijlagen/SRC_JV2017_internet.pdf> accessed 3 July 2018.

1249 Van Boom and others (n 1247) 54. For instance, one of the participating organisations is the BVA, an organisation representing

in accordance with Dutch Media law, all organisations that provide radio or audiovisual commercial communications have to be registered at and subscribed with the AC Authority.[1250] This entails that the AC Committee has the competence to make recommendations to adapt or to stop specific broadcasts or distributions.

Prior consultation. The AC Authority also guides advertisers in the development of their advertising campaigns. First, the AC Authority has developed a digital tool for advertisers to check whether a certain commercial communication complies with the Dutch Advertising Code.[1251] The tool contains all the rules of the Code and the case law of the AC Committee and the Board of Appeal since 2007.[1252] Second, under certain conditions advertisers may also have access to copy advice on a draft commercial communication. Finally, branch organisations that want to know whether their members comply with the rules can ask the AC Authority to conduct a monitoring exercise. Such an exercise entails that during a certain period of time, commercial communications in different media are assessed in light of the advertising rules.[1253]

Cooperation agreements with other regulatory authorities. Important to note is that the AC Authority has cooperation agreements with a number of governmental bodies for the actual enforcement of the advertising codes. For monitoring and enforcement of the general codes, the AC Authority has cooperation agreements with both the Consumer Authority and the Media Commissariat, and for specific sectors there are cooperation agreements with the Dutch Food Authority[1254], the Authority Financial Markets[1255] and the Gaming Authority.[1256]

Transboundary advertisements. Similar to the JEP and the ASA, the AC Authority is affiliated with EASA (*supra*).[1257]

1250 But see for the whole list of relevant media organisations involved: https://www.reclamecode.nl/adverteerder/default.asp?paginaID=21&hID=1.

1251 The digital checklist can be accessed via www.checksrc.nl.

1252 Stichting Reclame Code, 'Stichting Reclame Code: Wie Zijn Wij?' <https://www.reclamecode.nl/adverteerder/default.asp?paginaID=1&hID=1> accessed 3 July 2018.

1253 Advertising Code Authority [Stichting Reclame Code], 'The Dutch Advertising Code and the Advertising Code Committee [De Nederlandse Reclame Code En de Reclame Code Commissie]' 6 <https://www.reclamecode.nl/bijlagen/SRC_brochure_totaal_sep17.pdf> accessed 5 July 2018.

1254 For more information see www.vwa.nl.

1255 For more information see https://www.afm.nl.

1256 For more information see https://www.kansspelautoriteit.nl/algemene-onderdelen/secundaire-navigatie/english/.

1257 For more information on their activities on a supranational and international level, see <https://www.reclamecode.nl/consument/default.asp?paginaID=167&hID=102> accessed

EVALUATION. The advertising codes developed by the AC Authority are subject to evaluation after a certain time period determined in the specific code or when there is a sufficient cause to do so.[1258]

1.3.2. Complaint procedure and consumer awareness

AC COMMITTEE COMPLAINT PROCEDURE. Complaints may be filed with the AC Committee by anyone who feels that specific advertisements are non-compliant.[1259] The complaint mechanism is the same for violations of the general Advertising Code as for the format- or sector-specific codes, or any combination thereof, including the Code related to minors. A complaint filed by a consumer is essentially free[1260], whereas the complaint by a professional party could be subject to certain costs.[1261] Complaints can be made via an online form or by mail. After a complaint is filed, there is a reversed burden of proof, which entails that the advertiser must show that the advertisement used is not in breach with the advertising codes.[1262] After the advertiser's written defence, a date is set for handling the complaint. If desired, the complainant and advertiser can explain their arguments during a hearing by the AC Committee or Board of Appeal. Experts or witnesses can also be called during this hearing. The hearing will be public and in so far as one or both parties give an oral explanation.[1263] The procedure then ends with a written recommendation to discontinue such a way of advertising.

REVIEW. Filing an appeal is possible with the Board of Appeal, which is composed of the same members as the AC Committee.

AWARENESS. According to the 2017 report of the AC Authority, there were 3619 complaints and notifications filed. The AC Committee and the Board of Appeal together decided on 1270 cases 418 of these dealt with digital marketing communications (i.e. 30%), of which 34 appeared on social media, 3 on search engines, 325 on websites, 3 were traditional online advertisements such as banners and pop-ups, and 54 were distributed via E-mail, SMS and MMS. Interestingly, only 2% of all cases dealt with the identification of the commercial message.[1264]

---

8 August 2018.

1258 Dutch Advertising Code Authority (n 1245) 41.

1259 However, there is no possibility to file mass claims. Weber (n 1104) 174.

1260 And there is no need to involve a lawyer or any other legal assistance.

1261 Submitting a complaint will usually cost a company 1000€. Dutch Advertising Code Authority (n 1245) 8. WEBER explains that this fee for businesses avoids the strategic use of the self-regulatory mechanism. Weber (n 1104) 180.

1262 Stichting Reclame Code (n 1252).

1263 However, parties can object to a public hearing. A hearing behind closed doors is only granted when there is a good reason for it. It is the chairman of the AC Committee or Board of Appeal who decides on such requests. Dutch Advertising Code Authority (n 1245) 7.

1264 Advertising Code Authority [Stichting Reclame Code] (n 1248) 24–26.

Timing. Advertisers have fourteen days to respond to a complaint. The AC Committee will then issue its decision within a 'short frame of time'. The 2017 report shows that in 69% of the cases, a decision is made within 4 weeks and in 23% within 6 to 8 weeks.[1265] It then takes approximately 25 days before the decision is ready to be send to the parties. Thus, it takes a little more than 8 weeks after a complaint has been filed to decide whether an advertisement is in breach with the advertising rules or not.

1.3.3. Enforcement and procedural safeguards

Monitoring and enforcement. In case the AC Committee finds that an advertisement violates the Advertising Code (or one of the specific Codes), it can only impose a legally non-enforceable individual or public recommendation.[1266] The advertiser has the option to either adapt the advertisement or stop its distribution. The compliance department of the AC Committee will then monitor whether the advertiser has complied with the recommendation.[1267] If needed, the AC Committee can rely on its cooperation agreements with other regulatory authorities to enforce its decisions. First, if collective damage to consumers occurs due to misleading or comparative advertising, the Committee can rely on the Consumer Authority.[1268] Second, in case of radio or audiovisual commercial communications breach the advertising codes, the Committee may refer to the Media Commissariat, which has strong enforcement powers. More specifically, the Commissiariat may revoke licences and impose fines on traditional media players (e.g. television broadcasters, radio stations).[1269] Third, if the AC Committee deems it necessary due to the sensitive nature of the advertisement to increase awareness of the advertisement's unsuitability, the Commission can also send out an "ALERT". This means that the AC Authority will make sure that the recommendation will be brought to the public's attention by way of an official press release.[1270] Finally, the AC Authority has

---

1265 Advertising Code Authority [Stichting Reclame Code] (n 1248) 29.

1266 These recommendations are generally followed by the industry. Dutch Courts also tend to follow such recommendations when court proceedings are initiated.

1267 The AC Authority has found that some 96% of advertisers comply with these recommendations.

1268 This cooperation constitutes a mutually beneficial relationship where the Consumer Authority can rely on the expertise and swift procedures of the Committee and the Committee can rely on the Authority to use their legal competences when enforcement is required. For more information about this cooperation see their agreement (in Dutch) <https://www.reclamecode.nl/bijlagen/11-7-2011_13_46_12.PDF> accessed 5/07/2018.

1269 For more information on the tasks and competences of the Media Commissariat, see <www.cvdm.nl/over-het-commissariaat-voor-de-media/bevoegdheden/#> accessed 5/07/2018.

1270 See for an example of an alert published on the 20th of June, 2016 <https://www.reclamecode.nl/consument/default.asp?nieuwsID=537&terugURL=%2Farchiefnieuwsberichten%2Easp%3FhID%3D7> accessed 5/07/2018.

made agreements with certain sectors about financial sanctions, for instance in relation to alcohol advertising.[1271]

Other incentives for compliance. Advertisers who refuse to comply, are mentioned on an online non-compliance list[1272], open for consultation by the supervisory authorities. Furthermore, the decisions of both the AC Committee and the Board of Appeal are published on the AC Authority's website.

Level of compliance. The Dutch self-regulatory mechanism has a very high compliance rate. More specifically, the 2017 report of the AC Authority showed that 96% of the advertisers who were found to be in breach of the advertising rules had adapted or stopped distributing the commercial communication concerned.[1273]

Independence and impartiality. Both the Commission and its Board of Appeal consist of 5 members, which are appointed by each of the following stakeholders: (1) the organisations of advertisers that are affiliated with the AC Authority; (2) the Association of Communication consultancies, (3) the participating media organisations, (4) the Consumers' Association and finally (5) a chairman with legal qualifications appointed by the AC Authority. Important to note is that the evaluation by the members of the Committee is independent of the organisation that appointed them (i.e. decisions are made without (prior) consultation of people outside the Committee or Board. The Board of Appeal consists of the same members.[1274]

Funding. The mechanism is financed by the advertising industry itself, the government does not provide any funding. All advertisers with a total annual gross media spending of € 1 million or more will receive a request for payment.[1275]

Transparency. As mentioned, the complaint-procedure entails a public hearing and all decisions are published on the website of the AC Authority and alert decisions appear in press releases.

Analysis of existing case law. From the AC Authority's yearly report it can be concluded that there are numerous complaints and cases, of which 30% dealt with

---

1271 Such a fine can amount up to 50 000€. Weber (n 1104) 174.

1272 The non-compliance list can be accessed at <https://www.reclamecode.nl/adverteerder/default.asp?paginaID=92&hID=3> accessed 8 August 2018.

1273 Advertising Code Authority [Stichting Reclame Code] (n 1248).

1274 Advertising Code Authority [Stichting Reclame Code] (n 1253).

1275 The contribution is based on the gross media spending drawn up annually by Nielsen. The AC Authority developed a website that specifically focuses on the financial contributions (in Dutch) which can be accessed via www.srcbijdrage.nl/home.asp?paginaID=9&hID=7.

digital marketing communications. However, the report also showed that only in 2% of all cases (not just those dealing with digital marketing) the AC Committee had to make a decision on the identification of the commercial message. From a search of the database of the AC Committee's rulings, it was found that only a handful of cases specifically concerned children and new advertising formats. For instance, a case concerning vloggers, which provides some guidelines on the implementation of the identification principle when it comes to vlogs aimed at children was found.[1276] Additionally, cases dealing with promotional statements made by a child[1277], harmful content[1278] and misleading information were also discovered.[1279] Therefore, it can be concluded that – at the time of writing – the existing case law only provides limited guidance for advertisers on new advertising techniques.

1.4. *Table of comparison*

Procedural and Organisational Elements		**National Alternative Regulatory Mechanisms**		
		JEP (BE)	ASA (UK)	**Stichting Reclamecode (NL)**
Attribution of regulatory power	Type of ARI	Self-regulation	Hybrid mechanism: self-regulation for non-broadcast ads and co-regulation for broadcast ads	Self-regulation
	Government involvement	None	Formal cooperation agreement with governmental body for non-broadcast ads Delegation of statutory powers by governmental body for broadcast ads	Formal cooperation agreement with governmental bodies

1276 For instance, in relation to a vlog published on a YouTube Channel named 'Little ones' [Kleintjes], the disclosure "This video contains PP" was included in the description of the video. The AC Committee decided that the disclosure did not uncover in a sufficiently clear way to children that the video contains advertising and, as such, is in breach of the rules for advertising aimed at children and youngsters. *Decision No 2017/00494* (Advertising Code Committee [Reclame Code Commissie)).

1277 This case concerned a video of a five year old who – in the presence of his mother – tries different types of sweets and comments whether or not he likes them. The AC Committee held that it did not constitute a form of advertising. *Decision No 2018/00214* (Advertising Code Committee [Reclame Code Commissie]).

1278 The video contained animated people who are shot by various weapons and explode. The AC Committee held that this content was contrary to good taste and decency. *Decision No 2015/00972* (Advertising Code Committee [Reclame Code Commissie]).

1279 The case concerned a vlog, which was in fact an advertorial but the vlogger did not disclose the commercial relationship (i.e. the vlogger received a discount when purchasing the advertised product) with the brand. The AC Authority held that this was in breach with the Advertising Code on Social Media. *Decision No 2016/00079* (Advertising Code Committee [Reclame Code Commissie)).

Procedural and Organisational Elements		National Alternative Regulatory Mechanisms		
		JEP (BE)	ASA (UK)	Stichting Reclamecode (NL)
Attribution of regulatory power	Competences	Act on complaint	Act on a complaint	Act on complaint
		Submit an ad for examination (only by the Jury of First Instance)	Proactive monitoring, launch an investigation	Monitoring of compliance with decisions made, proactive monitoring only at the request of a sector organisation
	Coverage	Supported by the Council for Advertising, which represents (almost) the entire advertising industry (80% of Belgian ads)	The Advertising Codes and the ASA rulings have universal coverage across the entire advertising industry, advertisers cannot opt out	The main players in the field of advertising and marketing have subscribed to the self-regulatory mechanism
Complaint procedure and consumer awareness	Complaint procedure at no cost, easy and accessible	Free of charge for consumers, online complaint form or in writing via mail	Free of charge for consumers, online complaint form, in writing or via telephone	Free of charge for consumers, online form or via mail Professionals have to pay a fee
	Review of decisions	The Jury on Appeal	Independent Review Procedure	Board of Appeal
	Awareness of consumers	N° of consumer complaints (in 2016): 167 N° of cases dealing with digital commercial communications (in 2016): 46	N° of consumer complaints (in 2017): 16365 N° of cases dealing with digital commercial communications (in 2017): 3709	N° of consumer complaints (in 2017): 3619 N° of cases dealing with digital commercial communications (in 2017): 418
	Timing	Aim is to deal with cases within 10 days. (Yearly report shows that 3/5 complaints is dealt with within 2 weeks).	Aim is to 'acknowledge' complaints within 5 days, but no further commitments regarding timing	Advertiser has to submit his defence within 14 days upon the complaint, AC Committee sets a meeting as soon as possible.

Procedural and Organisational Elements		National Alternative Regulatory Mechanisms		
		JEP (BE)	ASA (UK)	Stichting Reclamecode (NL)
Attribution of regulatory power	Independence and impartiality	Advertising sector and civil society are equally represented During decision-making procedure: Experts may be consulted	Two-thirds of the members are independent of industry	Representatives from 4 stakeholder groups, evaluations happen on an independent basis without prior consultation of the Board, president is not a representative of any of the 4 stakeholder groups During the decision-making procedure: Experts or witnesses may be called
Enforcement and procedural safeguards	Effective proportionate and dissuasive sanctions	No real sanctions by JEP (i.e. the JEP can issue decisions to stop or adjust advertisements, but it has no strong enforcement powers) Public decisions, taking away the JEP label	Various sanctions (for non-broadcast): bad publicity, mandatory preventing, withdrawal of trading privileges, ad alerts, ask internet search websites to remove a marketer's paid-for search advertisements. In addition legal backstop in the form of a formal cooperation agreement with Trading Standards	No real sanctions by AC Committee, but collaboration agreements with other regulators/ sectors
	Funding	Financed by the Council for Advertising as a private body.	Financed through a system of levy arrangements, collected by the Advertising Standards Board of Finance	Financed by advertising industry itself (a percentage).
	Public hearing and decision	Procedure in writing, extended summaries of each decision are published on the JEP's website.	Rulings of the ASA are published.	Public hearing if parties want to present their arguments orally, decisions are published.

2. DISCUSSION

2.1. Characteristics of commercial communications that influence the structuring of ARIs

Before going into the comparison of the national ARIs, it is questioned what characteristics set apart advertising ARIs from ARIs in other sectors. These aspects should be taken into account when extracting best practices for the structuring of the instrument and the selection of procedural guarantees. As described above, ARIs in the area of commercial communication are developed to achieve the objectives of protecting consumers, including children, from harmful or misleading advertising (in the digital environment) or protecting their privacy and data protection, in accordance with EU legislation. In relation to these objectives, the following characteristics should be kept in mind throughout our discussion: (1) characteristics of commercial communications and (2) characteristics related to children's advertising literacy in the digital area.

1. Characteristics of commercial communications.

First, as outlined in the first part of the book, the harm caused by advertisements is not always measurable. As a result, it is equally difficult to define what an effective remedy is: does this mean awarding damages or does the removal of the infringing advertisement suffice? Second, from the mapping and analysis of the regulatory framework, it was found that there are different regulatory authorities which have (sometimes overlapping) competences for enforcing provisions of the fragmented legal framework. Therefore, coordination and cooperation between different regulatory bodies is crucial and should be built in the ARI.

2. Characteristics related to children's advertising literacy in the digital era.

Furthermore, throughout this book, it has been highlighted that children (and their parents) have difficulties activating their advertising literacy skills in the context of new advertising formats. This should be kept in mind in the development of complaint mechanisms of ARIs. More specifically, a number of issues may need to be resolved: children and their parents may not be able to recognise infringements or it might be difficult to provide evidence of infringements as advertisements may appear and disappear in the blink of an eye.

2.2. Structure, organisation and coverage of the ARIs

Attribution of regulatory power. A first element for discussion is the structuring of the ARI and the form. One of the drawbacks of a purely self-regulatory mechanism that has received most criticism in academic literature is the lack of effective enforcement.[1280] Sanctions may be mild and reluctantly imposed. Furthermore, LIEVENS warns that certain protections of the legal framework (i.e. provisions that are in theory addressed at states or governments) are more likely to apply if there is some form of government involvement.[1281] Especially in the area of child protection, the use of a system where the government and other actors work together would provide greater guarantees to the actual realisation of the policy objective. This cooperation can take different forms. For instance, there could be an actual delegation of power from a governmental body with legal powers to a self-regulatory body (as in the UK system with Ofcom and the ASA), or the relationship could be established through formal cooperation agreements (e.g. the UK system with the ASA and Trading Standards, the Dutch system with the AC Authority and the Media Commissariat). Other forms of involvement of the governmental body could be through audits of the functioning of the ARI or funding. It is argued that especially in the area of advertising where different regulatory authorities may be involved, cooperation and consultation are crucial. This is to avoid confusion and certain practices remaining under the radar because of unclear competences.

COVERAGE. A second element of discussion relates to the question, how broadly is the ARI supported? In this regard, the OECD underlines that the higher the level of participation in an ARI, the greater the likely impact.[1282] From the research on the advertising industry and ARIs, it was found that the advertising industry has traditionally been very active and involved when it comes to the development of ARIs. This is in line with the results of the comparative study. With regard to the ASA (UK), it was shown that the system is binding for the entire advertising industry and that advertisers cannot opt out. For the other two instruments, it was found that the majority of the advertising industry supports the system.

ACCESS TO COMPLAINT-MECHANISMS. Another important aspect from a children's rights perspective is the access to complaint procedures. To reiterate, the UNCRC Committee requires that "*accessible, affordable and child-friendly avenues to submit complaints and seek remedies, both judicial and non-judicial*" are ensured for children and their parents.[1283] From the analysis, it can be concluded that all

1280 Lievens, *Protecting Children in the Digital Era: The Use of Alternative Regulatory Instruments* (n 12) 205; Macenaite (n 709).

1281 Lievens, 'The Use of Alternative Regulatory Instruments to Protect Minors in the Digital Era' (n 1105) 49.

1282 OECD, 'Industry Self Regulation: Role and Use in Supporting Consumer Interests' (2015) OECD Digital Economy Papers 247 22 <https://www.oecd-ilibrary.org/science-and-technology/industry-self-regulation_5js4k1fjqkwh-en> accessed 8 August 2018.

1283 UN Committee on the Rights of the Child, 'General Comment No. 16 (2013) on State Obligations Regarding the Impact of the Business Sector' (n 148).

three ARIs have a complaint mechanism in place which is accessible at no cost to consumers. Furthermore, complaints may be filed online as well as offline and the procedures do not require a lot of information. Aside from consumers, civil society organisations may also file complaints, which allows them to explore the limits of the ARI and demand accountability from the advertising industry.[1284] An interesting feature of the AC Authority system (NL) is that traders can file complaints but have to pay for using the system, in order to limit strategic use and anti-competitive behaviour. Another consideration links to the attribution of regulatory powers and the cooperation between regulatory bodies. From the analysis in the second part of this book, it was concluded that in some situations, different regulatory authorities may be competent to receive consumer complaints regarding the same advertising formats – for instance, a complaint against behavioural advertising targeted to children could be brought before the data protection authority, the consumer protection authority (for instance as an aggressive unfair commercial practice) or a self-regulatory authority (for instance for a breach of the FEDMA Code a complaint to the national Direct Marketing Association). In relation to this, there should be continuous efforts in raising awareness among citizens regarding the existing complaint mechanisms.[1285]

Procedural safeguards. From the analysis of children's procedural rights, it was concluded that whenever decisions are made that may affect children's rights, the least that can be expected from the decision-making body is adhere to a number of procedural safeguards. A first safeguard that was extracted from children's procedural rights was the independence of the decision-making body. The three ARIs all have an independent body for the monitoring or enforcing of the advertising rules. The members of these bodies are representatives from different stakeholder groups: the advertising sector, civil society, academia, honorary magistrates. This ensures independence *vis-à-vis* the government, the advertising sector, political organisations, etc. A second procedural safeguard is the impartiality of the decision-making body. In this regard, it can be argued that, again, the composition of the decision-making bodies offers guarantees for excluding partiality. Furthermore, it was discussed that certain ARIs allow for consultation with experts and witnesses during the decision-making procedure. Finally, regarding transparency, it was found that all decision-making bodies publish their rulings on their websites and also make their argumentations public. In turn, this provides other advertisers with guidance on the implementation of the rules.

1284 Van Boom and others (n 1247).

1285 An interesting initiative in relation to this is the Digital Clearing House, set up by the European Data Protection Supervisor, which aims at increased collaboration and coordination between different regulatory bodies. For more information see <https://edps.europa.eu/data-protection/our-work/subjects/big-data-digital-clearinghouse_en>, accessed 31 August 2018.

2.3. *Effectiveness of the ARIs*

AMOUNT OF COMPLAINTS, CASES DEALING WITH NEW ADVERTISING FORMATS. From the country-level analysis, it can be concluded that the ASA (UK) and the AC Authority (NL) dealt with significantly more cases concerning digital commercial communications, compared to the JEP (BE). However, of these cases only a few related to the protection of children against new advertising techniques (e.g. identification of the commercial message, age verification) and thus provided only limited guidance for advertisers. There are potentially a number of reasons for this, including the inherent qualities of such advertising techniques (i.e. they are designed in an immersive and interactive manner), the lack of awareness of consumers regarding complaint procedures and confusion concerning competences of regulatory bodies. Furthermore, while the ASA is competent to proactively monitor the internet for advertising breaches and launch investigations (and the AC Authority under certain conditions), the JEP is not, apart from the ability of the Jury of First Instance to submit an advertisement to the Jury. Nevertheless, it should be noted that the number of complaints can also be linked to the size of the country, as well as its media and advertising landscape.

MONITORING AND OVERSIGHT. The manner in which each of the ARIs organised monitoring and oversight of the rules was also analysed. The ASA proactively monitors advertisements across all media, in order to check the level of compliance of the advertising industry, and takes action against misleading, harmful or offensive advertisements, sales promotions and direct marketing where necessary. The AC Authority may, at the request of a certain sector organisation, proactively monitor advertisements across different media within that specific sector. In contrast, as illustrated above the JEP almost exclusively acts on complaints, potentially resulting in a significantly lower amount of cases.[1286] According to the OECD, regular monitoring of the operation and effectiveness of schemes can help to demonstrate whether objectives are being achieved and members of the scheme are complying.[1287] Such monitoring would also need to capture instances of non-compliance to help build credibility, and should evaluate the effects on consumers. Furthermore, considering that

---

1286 In relation to this, a question was asked in the Flemish Parliament about whether or not the JEP should act more on a proactive bases, by submitting advertisements to the Jury and, hence, initiate more cases. The Flemish Minister for Media responded that the JEP already works proactively, by offering advertisers copy advice. 'Schriftelijke Vraag Nr. 306 Door Katia Segers Aan Sven Gatz, Vlaams Minister van Cultuur, Media, Jeugd En Brussel: Jury Voor Ethische Praktijken – Klachtenbehandeling' <http://docs.vlaamsparlement.be/pfile?id=1287066> accessed 9 August 2018. However, in 2016, only 15 advertisements were filed with the JEP for a preliminary examination.

1287 OECD (n 1282).

consumers often do not recognise new forms of commercial communication as advertisements, it can be concluded that proactive monitoring is particularly useful for ARIs in this area.

Remedies and enforcement powers. Another question that can be asked is whether the ARI provides effective remedies in case of breaches of the advertising rules. In this regard, the OECD has stressed that "*well-established, transparent enforcement mechanisms are key to establishing the credibility of self-regulatory mechanisms, as are sanctions which are substantial enough to discourage non-adherence*".[1288] Furthermore, as mentioned, the EU Principles for Better Self- and Co-Regulation require that in case of non-compliance, the ARI has a graduated scale of sanctions in place.[1289] Faire *et al.* clarify that such sanctions could be multifaceted, ranging from mild reprimands to the actual expulsion from the system.[1290] In light of these findings, it can be concluded that both the ASA (UK) and AC Authority (NL) system foresee a graduated scale of sanctions. For instance, the ASA may choose between various sanctions ranging from bad publicity, to mandatory preventing, withdrawal of trading privileges and advertising alerts. Additionally, both the ASA and the AC Authority (NL) have formal cooperation agreements in place for the referral of violations to governmental agencies with legal powers. Of the three ARIs discussed, the Belgian system has the softest enforcement powers, as the JEP can only fall back on bad publicity and the withdrawal of a compliance label.

1288 OECD (n 1282) 24.

1289 European Commission, 'EU Principles for Better Self- and Co-Regulation' (n 1179) 2.

1290 M. Faure, A. Ogus and N. Philipsen, 'Curbing Consumer Financial Losses: The Economics of Regulatory Enforcement' (2009) 31 Law & Policy 161.

CONCLUSION

BEST PRACTICES FOR THE STRUCTURING OF ARIS IN THE AREA OF COMMERCIAL COMMUNICATION

ARIs AND THE BROADER LEGAL FRAMEWORK. The first chapter of this final part of the research explored the interplay between ARIs and the broader legal framework. It was concluded that the advertising industry has important responsibilities to respect and promote children's rights throughout their advertising and marketing practices. Relatedly, the EU legislative framework indirectly encourages them to develop advertising self-regulation, in light of children's rights. In this regard, several requirements for the structuring and development of advertising ARIs were distilled. First, it was concluded that children's procedural rights require that an ARI adheres to a number of procedural safeguards, such as impartiality, independence and transparency. Second, a number of general benchmarks at the EU level, which provide input for the best practices were analysed. Finally, the analysis explored how the advertising industry has developed its own benchmarks for advertising self-regulation.

COMPARATIVE ASSESSMENT. The second chapter of this part of the research examined three national ARIs in the area of commercial communication. On the basis of this comparison and the requirements and benchmarks found in the first chapter, a number of best practices for ARIs in the area of commercial communication can be extracted:

1. Proactive monitoring of advertisements online

A first best practice relates to the specific characteristics of commercial communication. More specifically, as illustrated, consumers (and especially children) have difficulties recognising the sophisticated and immersive advertising techniques that are being used in the digital environment. It was argued that this could be a reason for the low amount of consumer complaints concerning new advertising techniques and children. Accordingly, from the analysis of the monitoring and oversight mechanisms of the three ARIs, it was concluded that some form of proactive monitoring of advertisements online by the alternative regulatory body, which has the competence to launch investigations, is to be preferred over a purely complaint-based system.

2. Formal cooperation between alternative regulatory bodies and governmental agencies

A second best practice relates to the most frequent criticisms of a purely self-regulatory approach in academic scholarship, namely the lack of effective enforcement. From the comparative study, it was concluded that having some form of government involvement is recommended to obtain stronger enforcement. This involvement entails having a legal backstop in place in case of incessant breaches with the advertising rules, such as an actual delegation of powers from a governmental body or having formal cooperation agreements with governmental authorities that have stronger enforcement powers (e.g. awarding fines). In addition, from the second part of the research it was concluded that there are several regulatory bodies (both governmental agencies and alternative regulatory bodies) that have (to a certain extent overlapping) competences for enforcing the provisions of the regulatory framework for commercial communication. In relation to this, the need for coordination and collaboration between the regulatory bodies involved was underlined. To facilitate this, more research into the collaboration and coordination of self-regulatory organisations and governmental agencies in the context of commercial communication is needed.

3. A one-stop-shop for consumer complaints

Third, linked to the previous finding, the complaint-mechanisms of the ARIs in light of the right to an effective remedy and the other benchmarks discussed in the first chapter were analysed. It was found that in some situations, different regulatory bodies may be competent to receive consumer complaints regarding the same advertising formats. This may lead to confusion amongst consumers (and even the regulatory bodies themselves), resulting in a lack of complaints and cases. In this regard, a one-stop-shop for advertising-related complaints could solve consumer confusion and simplifies awareness-raising efforts. Such a one-stop-shop mechanism should have a low threshold, meaning that the procedure is free for consumers, complaints can be brought online and no lawyer needs to be involved. In contrast, a fee may be required from professional complainants, in order to avoid structural misuse of the complaint mechanism. Aside from this and as already mentioned, children (and their parents) might not even recognise certain advertising formats used in the digital environment. Consequently, allowing civil society actors to file complaints for consumers in general can also be considered a best practice. As a final consideration in relation to the complaint-mechanism of ARIs, it was argued that in practice it can be difficult to provide evidence of an online advertisement in breach of the regulatory framework. To overcome these difficulties, only limited information should be required when filing complaints.

4. Best practices for procedural safeguards

From the analysis of the children's rights framework it was concluded that it can be expected from alternative regulatory bodies to adhere to a number of procedural safeguards. First, in relation to the decision-making body's independence and impartiality, it is recommended that the members are representatives from different stakeholder groups (i.e. the advertising industry, civil society, academia). The consultation of experts or witnesses during the decision-making procedure could also be considered. Second, with regard to the requirement of transparency, it was concluded that alternative regulatory bodies should make their decisions and argumentations public. As illustrated this provides useful guidance for advertisers on the implementation of the advertising rules in practice. In addition, it was found that it is generally accepted that the effectiveness and working of ARIs (and regulation in general) is to be evaluated on a regular basis. These evaluations should also be made public.

5. A graduated scale of sanctions

A fifth best practice relates to the actual enforcement powers of the alternative regulatory body. From the analysis, a graduated scale of sanctions, which are substantial enough to discourage non-adherence can be recommended. This could start from bad publicity, taking away compliance labels and mandatory pre-vetting, to referring incessant violations to governmental agencies.

6. Ex ante compliance mechanism: copy advice

Another best practice relates to the prevention of advertising breaches. It is recommended that ARIs consider a copy advice feature as an ex ante compliance mechanism. Such a feature may reduce the need for complaint-handling and, hence, the costs related to decision-making procedures (it can even generate resources).

7. Raising awareness

Finally, all stakeholders should continue their efforts in raising awareness with consumers of complaint mechanisms and the regulatory framework.

CONCLUDING REMARKS AND RECOMMENDATIONS FOR THE FUTURE

CHAPTER I

RETROSPECTIVE OF THE RESEARCH UNDERTAKEN

Retrospective. Before presenting the recommendations for the regulatory framework for commercial communication aimed at children this section first looks back on the research findings.

PART I, CHAPTER I

Part I. The first chapter of the first part of the book aimed to gain a clearer understanding of the research issues. More specifically, an in-depth analysis was conducted of the constitutive elements of the study (i.e. children and new forms of commercial communication) and the need for a strong and empowering regulatory framework for commercial communication. It also introduced the children's rights perspective. A number of findings can be recalled:

1. As an introduction to the legal research, the advertising techniques and formats that advertisers employ to target children were analysed. Nowadays, children grow up as digital natives in a media landscape that is constantly evolving as a result of technological advancements and convergence. Traditional and new media are being consumed interchangeably and children split their attention between various screens and sources of media. The changes in the media landscape have driven advertisers to transform their approach to commercial communication. In the digital environment, commercial messages are being distributed through a variety of platforms and on numerous devices, such as tablets, game consoles, smartphones and connected televisions. The specific features of new forms of commercial communication – i.e. their integrated, interactive, personalised and emotions-evoking nature – make it difficult for children to apply their advertising literacy skills. These skills entail both identifying the commercial nature of these messages and being able to process the commercial message in a critical manner, as to allow them to make well-balanced commercial decisions and decisions related to their privacy. In this regard, it was concluded that it remains crucial for children to be educated

and enabled to understand the persuasive tactics of emerging trends in the area of commercial communication.

2. The protection of children against certain forms of commercial communication can be traced as an important objective throughout the policy history at the international and EU level from 2008 onwards. Three recurring themes were identified. First, the protection of children against the pressure of advertising and marketing in the digital environment. Second, policy makers have clearly recognised the issues related to the collection of personal data for advertising purposes and the need for the protection of children in this context. Third, aside from protecting children, policy makers have emphasised the importance of education and nurturing children's advertising literacy for their development and empowerment.

3. After analysing the policy objectives, the regulatory context was examined and the instruments that were developed to achieve these objectives were introduced. It was found that the regulatory framework is complex and fragmented into legislation and self- and co-regulation at the international, EU and national levels. Indeed, the advertising industry has been very active in developing alternative regulatory instruments, for various reasons: the sector is known for its high degree of organisation, its strong desire to avoid government regulation and its reliance on consumer trust in advertising and marketing. Considering the effectiveness of new advertising techniques on children, it is questioned whether the existing regulatory framework achieves the above mentioned policy goals.

4. There is no agreement in social science literature on the exact impact of children's increased exposure to commercial communication online (and offline). Moreover new trends are constantly emerging and research on the impact of advertising techniques on children's development is not moving at the same pace. In this regard, the precautionary principle might be considered as a justification for additional regulatory protections for children.

PART I, CHAPTER II

The second chapter examined the role of children's rights in regulating new advertising techniques. More specifically, it provided an interpretation of the fundamental rights framework in the specific context of commercial communication. The main research question this part of the study aimed to answer was: which children's rights and principles are at stake and what is their role in regulating new advertising formats aimed at children? From the analysis, a number of findings can be recalled:

1. Children are awarded a number of rights under the United Nations Convention on the Rights of the Child, which is the most highly ratified instrument in international law. Moreover, it can be considered the most powerful children's rights instrument in European law, considering that the fundamental rights instruments of both the Council of Europe and the European Union must be interpreted in light of the UNCRC. The underlying objective of the UNCRC is to contribute to children's personal or psychological development, a child being defined as every human under the age of 18 (unless under the law applicable to the child, majority is attained earlier). The UNCRC recognises that children, depending on the environments and culture in which they grow up, will develop and acquire competencies at different ages. Therefore, it was concluded that children require varying degrees of protection, participation and opportunities for autonomy and decision-making in accordance with their evolving capacities. Children's rights need to be protected and promoted in relation to all aspects of children's lives, also in the (digital) media environment. Indeed, as described, information and communication technologies affect not only the protection, but also the enjoyment of their rights. Moreover, children's rights are reconfigured not only by the internet, but also by the increased commercialisation of the digital environments in which children play, communicate and search for information. To address this reconfiguration and understand the role of children's rights in regulating new forms of commercial communication, it was decided that an interpretation of children rights in this context was needed.

2. It was concluded that several rights and principles are at stake in an advertising context. Furthermore, the issue of new forms of commercial communication aimed at children showcases the multi-dimensionality of children's rights (i.e. the objectives of protection, participation and provision). It was found that a balance is needed between on the one hand empowering children to cope with the commercial pressure online and on the other hand protecting them against those advertising practices for which empowerment and advertising literacy alone is insufficient. In relation to the former, it is crucial to ensure that the next generation of internet users is better educated and prepared to deal with digital advertising and marketing. Children's rights to development and education entail that from an early age they should be taught how to cope with (digital) advertising, in accordance with the child's evolving capacities as a 'consumer'. However, considering the effectiveness and sophistication of new advertising techniques, children also need to be protected from harmful and misleading advertisements to be in line with *inter alia* children's rights to development, to protection against economic exploitation and to freedom of thought. To attain such a balance, it is argued that all stakeholders, such as the government, the advertising industry (i.e. all parties involved in the advertising chain), schools and parents should take up their share of responsibility to enable

children to grow up to be critical, informed consumers who make their own conscious choices in today's media environment.

3. Children's digitised worlds are permeated with immersive, entertaining and personalised advertising. The commercialisation of nearly all aspects of their online lives (e.g. communication, play, information seeking) shapes children's thinking patterns and preferences as consumers and may negatively affect their rights to development and autonomy, to freedom of thought and to play. Furthermore, advertisers increasingly collect and use children's personal data for the purposes of profiling and targeted advertising. Children's rights to privacy and development, however, protect their self-determination and their ability to make autonomous commercial decisions or decisions related to their privacy.

4. In light of the need for a balance between protection and empowerment, it was illustrated that children are entitled to develop their abilities to think critically, make well-balanced decisions and to develop a healthy lifestyle, which are all essential when dealing with new forms of commercial communication. More specifically, children's rights to education and access to information requires the necessary opportunities for children to mature and practice their advertising-related knowledge, attitudes, and skills, such as their ability to recognise the commercial nature of communications online and offline and to critically reflect on them.

5. Aside from education and advertising literacy, it was argued that children also require protection against harmful or misleading forms of commercial communication. The emerging trends in advertising have specific features that are particularly effective when used on children (e.g. targeted advertising, playing on children's emotions). In relation to those practices, the limitations to education and advertising literacy, and the need for additional protections for children were expressed. More specifically, the adaption of the children's right to protection against economic exploitation to the online market reality was advocated. It was argued that the notion of economic exploitation can be broadened to include exploitative advertising (e.g. targeted or misleading advertising).

6. Finally, children's procedural rights in preparation of the third part of the research were explored. Children's rights to a fair trial and an effective remedy provide a number of procedural safeguards that are relevant for the structuring and development of self- and co-regulatory instruments in the area of commercial communication, such as independence, impartiality and transparency.

Thus, the first part of the book provided insights into the role of children's rights in regulating advertising and provided a number of procedural safeguards to consider when developing alternative regulatory instruments. It was concluded that the interpretation of the rights and principles should function as the comprehensive analytical framework in light of which the regulatory framework for commercial communication aimed at children should be evaluated.

PART II, CHAPTER I

Part II. In the second part of the book, the regulatory framework was mapped and evaluated, to examine whether the balance between empowerment and protection is attained. In chapter one of part two of this study, the current legislative and self-and co-regulatory framework for commercial communication aimed at children was mapped and analysed. This chapter aimed to provide a better understanding of the existing substantive protections for children against commercial communication in both legislative and alternative regulatory instruments, by presenting and analysing four relevant contexts. From this analysis, it was found that a myriad of provisions regulating commercial communication aimed at children at both national and EU level.

1. The consumer protection context

As a first context, the consumer protection framework was explored. The Unfair Commercial Practices Directive was first analysed and a number of provisions that are relevant in the context of the research were outlined. The Directive is applicable to commercial communications, regardless of their form or delivery and prohibits any unfair commercial practice, which includes misleading or aggressive commercial communication. Similarly, it was found that the ICC Code contains a number of general principles and specific protections for children in the context of advertising. The Code applies to both traditional and new advertising formats and is built on the general principles of honesty, legal compliance, truthfulness and decency of advertisements.

2. The audiovisual media services context

Second, the Audiovisual Media Services Directive, which determines the rules for audiovisual commercial communications, such as television advertising or advertising in on-demand services was analysed. This legislative instrument contains protections for children against several advertising practices. These include protections against misleading advertising (i.e. the identification principle), direct exhortations to buy, harmful messages, the promotion of harmful products and there are specific rules for sponsoring and product placement. Furthermore, the AVMS Directive has undergone an important review. From the analysis of the revised Directive, it was concluded that the EU legislators recognised the increased convergence of media services and addressed the evolutions in the market for audiovisual media services. More specifically, the revised Directive aims at levelling the playing-field between traditional and new media service providers. Furthermore, the scope of the Directive is broadened to include video-sharing platforms (and to a certain extent social media platforms if their service or part of their service qualifies as a video-sharing platform).

3. The e-commerce context

The third context analysed was that of the e-Commerce Directive. The Directive provides the rules for commercial communications that form part of or constitute information society services (e.g. advertisements on social media, advergames, online banners). Most important to our research, the Directive contains identification and information requirements. Furthermore, a self-regulatory initiative in the context of e-commerce, namely the FEDMA Code on E-Commerce was discussed. This instrument provides similar protections for consumers – in the form of identification and information requirements – but also contains more specific protections against misleading commercial communications.

4. The data protection context

The final context consisted of the data protection framework, which contains the rules for the processing of children's personal data and communications data for advertising purposes. In this particular context, there are applicable legislative and self-regulatory instruments, which run in parallel. First, the manner in which the General Data Protection Regulation explicitly recognises that children require specific protection in relation to the processing of their personal data, especially if this processing takes place in an advertising context. The GDPR requires a legitimate ground for such processing – which will most likely be (parental) consent – and that the data is processed in accordance with *inter alia* the principles of fairness, data minimisation, purpose specification and limited retention. Second, the ePrivacy Directive – which is currently under review – contains the provisions for the processing of children's communications data. Finally, several self-regulatory instruments at the international and EU level that contain provisions regulating privacy and data protection were explored. An interesting finding was that the ICC, IAB Europe and EASA all underlined that behavioural advertising should not be aimed at children aged 12 or younger.

PART II, CHAPTER II

The second chapter of the second part of the book proceeded with an in-depth evaluation of the mapped regulatory framework. More specifically, it examined how a selection of advertising techniques fits within the scope of this framework, while taking into account the children's rights and principles as discussed in the first part of the research. Based on the conclusions of this evaluation, a number of gaps were compiled:

1. Problems caused by the fragmentation of the regulatory framework

First, it was noted that the number of legislative and alternative regulatory rules is not necessarily indicative of a high level of protection and empowerment of children, in particular regarding new advertising formats (i.e. advergames, personalised advertising and vlogging advertising). Various points of confusion, which are caused by the fragmented nature of the regulatory framework for commercial communication, were exposed. Indeed, as illustrated the provisions contained in both legislative and self-regulatory instruments are often formulated in an abstract manner and guidance on their implementation is not always available. Furthermore, a number of definitions that were formulated in a manner leading to uncertainty regarding their scope of application for new forms of commercial communication were outlined. Another point of confusion is the lack of a uniform definition of a child in the regulatory framework. Although it was recognised that different commercial messages may be considered inappropriate for children of different ages, it was also found that the diversity of ages defining the application of the various provisions is confusing, not only for advertisers trying to comply with the advertising rules, but also for parents and children.

2. The empowerment-protection scales of the regulatory framework are out of balance

A second gap that was found relates to the need for a balance between protecting children against harmful or misleading advertisements and educating and allowing them to develop their commercial decision-making capacities. The State is responsible for ensuring that the regulatory framework is organised to attain this balance. However, from the evaluation, it was concluded that the empowerment-protection scales of the regulatory framework are tipped out of balance. The existing protections for children often revolve around identification and transparency requirements or the reliance on the legitimate ground for (parental) consent for the processing of children's data. These protections, in practice, allocate much of the responsibility with children and their parents (e.g. advertisers use different disclosures to clarify the commercial nature of communications, but it is up to children and parents to recognise and understand the meaning of the labels used). Accordingly, considering the difficulties children – and their parents for that matter – have with applying their advertising literacy skills to the emerging trends of commercial communication, it was concluded that a deresponsibilisation of the child and the parent is needed in the regulatory framework.

3. The limitations of the identification principle

A third gap relates to the common red thread of the regulatory framework for commercial communication: the identification principle. More specifically, from the evaluation, a lack of structure and coherence in the implementation of the principle was discovered. As mentioned, advertisers use a variety of labels to indicate the commercial nature of advertisements, which may lead to confusion among consumers. Moreover, it was noted that for certain advertising formats, disclosures do not aid children to recognise or critically reflect on the commercial nature of the formats. Thus, in light of children's rights and the empowerment-protection balance, the importance of recognising the limits of children's advertising literacy and, as a result, the effectiveness of the identification principle in the digital environment was underlined.

4. The data protection framework is undergoing significant changes and guidance on its implementation is urgently needed

As a fourth gap, issues related to the implementation of the data protection framework which has been undergoing significant changes were described. First, it is unclear what the specific protection for children under the GDPR will entail in practice. As the GDPR does not define children, it is also unclear to which age groups certain measures should apply. Second, the proposed e-Privacy Regulation is not aligned with the GDPR on recognising that children need specific protection for their communications data. In fact, children are not even mentioned in the text that is currently being debated. Third, although several self-regulatory organisations at international and EU level have developed instruments regulating the processing of children's personal data for advertising purposes, the focus lies too often on transparency and information instead of actual limitations to the collection of children's personal data. Accordingly, we argued that a children's rights inspired interpretation of the data protection framework is needed.

5. Need for better distribution of responsibilities in the advertising chain

Fifth, the role of platform providers such as video-sharing platforms in the context of commercial communication was examined. In this regard, it was argued that by increasing the responsibilities of platform providers it could be easier to achieve compliance with the advertising rules, for instance regarding the identification requirement. It was found that the revised AVMS Directive already addressed this need, by broadening its scope to include video-sharing platforms and by giving them certain responsibilities regarding the commercial communications that are distributed via their platforms.

6. Lack of coordination between regulatory authorities

As a final gap, it was found that although different regulatory bodies – both government agencies, like media regulators, data protection authorities, consumer protection authorities, and self-regulatory bodies – are competent to enforce the mapped provisions, few decisions related to children and new advertising formats have been issued up until the time of writing. As a result, there is little guidance for advertisers on how to interpret these provisions in practice, when they use or develop new advertising techniques. In this respect, it was argued that there is a need for further coordination and collaboration between the regulatory bodies concerned and to raise awareness amongst consumer-citizens regarding complaint-mechanisms.

PART III

Part III. Following the detailed mapping and evaluation of the substantive elements of the regulatory framework, the final part of the study proceeded with an analysis of the organisational and procedural elements. First of all this entailed an exploration of the advertising industry's responsibilities under the children's rights framework, the role of ARIs in this regard and existing requirements and benchmarks for the structuring of such ARIs. Second, a comparative analysis of three national ARIs was conducted. The aim of this part of the research was to distinguish those procedural or organisational elements that could improve the quality and effectiveness of ARIs to protect children in the context of commercial communication. From this analysis, a number of findings can be recalled:

1. First, it was argued that the advertising industry has important responsibilities for respecting and promoting children's rights throughout their advertising practices, and are encouraged to develop ARIs. In this regard, a number of requirements and benchmarks for the structuring of advertising ARIs in children's procedural rights, in instruments at the EU level, and benchmarks developed by the industry itself were extracted. These requirements and benchmarks were taken into account in the development of the best practice recommendations.

2. Second, from the comparative assessment of three national ARIs in the area of commercial communication, several best practices were identified for (1) the monitoring and oversight of ARIs, (2) the attribution of regulatory powers and the involvement of governmental agencies, (3) the complaint-mechanism and procedures, (4) the procedural safeguards that the decision-making body must adhere to, (5) the enforcement and remedial measures in case of breaches of the industry commitments, (6) *ex ante* compliance mechanisms and finally (7) consumer awareness of the existence of ARIs. These best practices are discussed in more detail in the recommendations below.

CHAPTER II
CONCLUSIONS

From the above listed research results, a number of final conclusions can be drawn.

THE ROLE OF CHILDREN'S RIGHTS IN REGULATING COMMERCIAL COMMUNICATION. First of all, with regard to the research question at the heart of this book, it can be concluded that children's rights and principles – as interpreted in the specific context of commercial communication in the digital environment – constitute the analytical framework in light of which legislation and alternative regulatory instruments in the area of commercial communication need to be evaluated. This analytical framework requires a balance between empowering children to cope with advertising (i.e. by educating them and providing them with the necessary opportunities to practice their commercial decision-making skills) and protecting them against harmful or misleading advertising (i.e. by recognising the limitations to advertising literacy and providing additional protections). States are responsible for structuring the regulatory framework in such a way that the balance is attained.

SUBSTANTIVE GAPS IN THE EXISTING REGULATORY FRAMEWORK FOR COMMERCIAL COMMUNICATION AIMED AT CHILDREN. From the mapping and evaluation, it can be concluded that such a balance is not achieved in the existing regulatory framework. Several gaps were identified that need to be addressed in order to stabilise the empowerment-protection scales. First, a number of issues which need to be resolved, resulting from the fragmented nature of the regulatory framework, including uncertainties regarding definitions and the scope of application of provisions to new advertising formats were mentioned. In relation to this, the need for a holistic approach to the regulatory framework was discussed. Second, as described, the provisions containing protections for children in the context of commercial communication allocate too much responsibility to children and their parents. In this regard, the need for a deresponsibilisation was underlined. The deresponsibilisation consists of a number of aspects: recognising the limitations of the identification principle and improving its implementation in practice, implementing the data protection framework in light of children's rights and emphasising platform responsibilities.

To overcome these significant gaps, several recommendations have been included in the following section.

Structuring of ARIs in the area of commercial communication. Finally, with regard to the procedural and organisational elements of ARIs, it was concluded that they need to be structured in accordance with the broader legal framework, including children's procedural rights, but also the benchmarks developed by the advertising industry itself. The comparative analysis of three national ARIs provided valuable insights into the working and effectiveness of ARIs. To improve the quality of existing ARIs in the area of commercial communication, the best practices extracted are included in the next section.

CHAPTER III
RECOMMENDATIONS

A HOLISTIC APPROACH TO CHILDREN'S RIGHTS AND ADVERTISING LITERACY IN THE DIGITAL ERA. In relation to the fragmentation of and confusion surrounding the regulatory framework for commercial communication, it was concluded that a holistic interpretation is needed. First, this entails that the multi-dimensionality of children's rights is considered and respected. As described, the reconfiguration of children's rights in the context of commercial communication in the digital era necessitated an interpretation into this specific context. Such an exercise consists of a careful balancing of the objectives of protection, participation and provision. More specifically, it was concluded that from a children's rights perspective, a balance is needed in the context of commercial communication between children's right to protection against harmful or misleading advertising and their right to be empowered, educated and provided with the necessary opportunities to develop their commercial decision-making skills. Moreover, throughout the research it has become apparent that many rights in the digital environment are actually multi-dimensional and should be considered and acknowledged in such a manner at different levels.

Second, it was found that the protections for children in the context of new forms of commercial communication are spread across different instruments (both legislative and self-regulatory). In this regard, it is recommended that emerging advertising trends are evaluated in light of all applicable frameworks in order to attain meaningful protection for children. Furthermore, the different regulatory bodies with competences to enforce advertising-related provisions (both governmental agencies and alternative regulatory bodies) should coordinate their efforts and work collaboratively on guidance for the implementation of the rules in relation to new advertising formats. Additionally, raising awareness amongst consumers and advertisers of their rights and obligations in this context is also crucial, as it could lead to more consumer complaints, more cases and, hence, more guidelines for advertisers on how to comply with the rules for advertising.

Third, instead of focusing on finding the perfect legal elements for the protection of children in relation to emerging advertising formats, it is suggested that combining all the elements of the regulatory toolbox is the only way to bring the empowerment-protection scales in balance. This toolbox includes *inter alia* the enhanced enforcement of the regulatory framework, stimulating the collaboration between regulatory bodies and improving the effectiveness of advertising ARIs. Furthermore, advertisers should carry out children's rights impact assessments that respect the multi-dimensionality of rights, when developing advertising and marketing campaigns. In addition, further research should be conducted on emerging trends in the area of advertising and their impact on children's advertising literacy. Advertising literacy should form part of the school curriculum and the development of new technology solutions for the protection of children (e.g. privacy-friendly verification mechanisms, new means of information provision) should also be stimulated.

Deresponsibilisation of the child and parent throughout the regulatory framework. The research has focused on examining whether the current regulatory framework is able to attain the balance between protection and empowerment of children in the context of commercial communication. Currently, the framework puts too much emphasis on empowerment with much of the responsibility resting on the shoulders of children and their parents, thereby tipping the empowerment-protection scales out of balance. In light of this and considering the impact and effectiveness of the emerging trends in commercial communication, the deresponsabilisation of the child and parent in the regulatory framework is recommended. First, the importance of recognising the limits of children's advertising literacy in relation to new advertising techniques and, hence, to the effectiveness of the identification principle in the digital environment was stressed. Aside from this, a more structured and coherent approach to the implementation of the principle is needed for the protection of children's consumer interests. This could include harmonised, evidence-based, qualitative requirements for disclosure cues, for instance through alternative regulatory mechanisms.

Second, the deresponsabilisation of the child and parent in the data protection framework was recommended. Data processing and targeted advertising are sophisticated and obscure practices, very difficult to understand for both children and parents. As described, the General Data Protection Regulation pays particular attention to children and acknowledges that they merit 'specific protection' regarding their personal data. However, as the actual implementation of the GDPR in practice is not entirely clear, the practical meaning of this specific protection remains to be seen. As part of the deresponsabilisation of the child and parent in the context of digital advertising, it is recommended that the focus should shift to actual limitations to the processing of children's personal data for marketing and advertising purposes, rather than solely or primarily focusing on information provision, transparency and the requirement of (verifiable) parental consent. In this regard, the advertising industry should take up their responsibility, and carry out in-depth data protection impact assessments, with attention for the best interests and rights of children, when setting up digital marketing campaigns. The age and level of maturity of the child will also play an important role in such an assessment. More specifically, as described children's advertising literacy gradually develops when they grow older. Therefore, it is important that the protection of children's personal data is adapted to their level of maturity. Relatedly, service providers that target their services to children (e.g. social networking sites, mobile apps) should acknowledge the evolving capacities of children by adapting their privacy policies and providing alternative child-friendly services incorporating the same features but without the collection and use of children's personal data for advertising purposes. Finally, it is recommended that a prohibition for services specifically targeted towards children to use profiling and behavioural marketing techniques, as this would be beneficial for the protection of children's rights (e.g. the right to privacy and to protection against economic exploitation).

Third, it has been argued that increased responsibilities for platform providers in relation to the advertisements that are distributed on their platforms could be a more practical means of ensuring more effective compliance. The Audiovisual Media Services Directive also embraces this approach, by expanding its scope to cover video-sharing platforms and by requiring them to foresee appropriate measures to ensure the protection of minors and the general public (e.g. flagging mechanisms, age verification mechanisms, parental control systems). It is argued that similar responsibilities could be included throughout the regulatory framework, in a way that all commercial communications would be covered.

Recommendations for the structuring of ARIs in the area of commercial communication. The advertising industry has traditionally been very active in the development of ARIs for a variety of reasons. As outlined above, the industry is greatly reliant on consumer trust in advertising and marketing, it is known for being highly organised and characterised by its strong desire to avoid government regulation. Considering the broad variety of ARIs in the area of commercial communication, procedural and organisational elements that would enhance their quality and effectiveness were explored. From the analysis of a selection of national ARIs, a number of best practice recommendations for the structuring of ARIs in the area of commercial communication were extracted:

Proactive monitoring of advertisements online. Consumers (and especially children) have difficulties recognising and critically reflecting on new advertising formats in the digital environment. This could be a reason for the low amount of consumer complaints concerning such formats and children. Accordingly, proactive monitoring of advertisements online and competences to launch investigations by the alternative regulatory body as a best practice were highlighted.

Formal cooperation between alternative regulatory bodies and governmental agencies. Second, it was argued that having some form of government involvement is needed to obtain effective enforcement. This could be achieved through an actual delegation of powers from a governmental body or by having formal cooperation agreements with governmental agencies.

A one-stop-shop for consumer complaints. Third, it was concluded that a one-stop-shop for advertising-related complaints would solve issues related to consumer confusion and simplify raising awareness amongst consumers. The complaint procedure should be free for consumers, allow complaints to be filed both online and in writing, only require limited information upon filing complaints, and should not require the involvement of a lawyer.

Best practices for procedural safeguards. Fourth, it was concluded that alternative regulatory bodies should adhere to a number of procedural safeguards when making decisions that impact children's rights (such as advertising-related issues), including independence, impartiality and transparency. In relation to independence and impartiality, it is recommended that the members of the decision-making body represent different stakeholder groups (i.e. the advertising industry, civil society, academia) and that at least more than half of the members are independent from the advertising industry. Furthermore, the consultation of independent experts or witnesses during the decision-making procedure could also be considered. Second, with regard to the requirement of transparency, it was concluded that decisions and argumentations of the alternative regulatory body should be made public, as well as regular evaluation reports on the working of the ARI.

A graduated scale of sanctions. Fifth, a graduated scale of sanctions, which are substantial enough to discourage non-adherence is recommended. It could range from bad publicity, taking away compliance labels and mandatory pre-vetting, to referring incessant violations to governmental agencies.

Ex ante compliance mechanisms. Sixth, it is recommended that ARIs invest in a copy advice feature as an *ex ante* compliance mechanism. Such a feature may reduce the need for complaint-handling and the costs related to decision-making procedures (it can even generate resources).

Raising awareness. Finally, all stakeholders should continue their efforts in raising awareness with consumers of complaint mechanisms and the regulatory framework.

BIBLIOGRAPHY

1. LEGISLATION AND POLICY DOCUMENTS

A. INTERNATIONAL

International Telecommunications Union, 'Guidelines for Industry on Child Online Protection.' <https://www.itu.int/en/cop/Documents/bD_Broch_INDUSTRY0809.pdf> accessed 19 July 2018

La Rue F, 'Report of the Special Rapporteur on the Promotion and Protection of the Right to Freedom of Opinion and Expression' (2011) <www2.ohchr.org/english/bodies/hrcouncil/docs/17session/A.HRC.17.27_en.pdf> accessed 10 November 2017

OECD, 'The Protection of Children Online – Recommendation of the OECD Council' (2012) <https://www.oecd.org/sti/ieconomy/childrenonline_with_cover.pdf> accessed 12 July 2018

—, 'Industry Self Regulation: Role and Use in Supporting Consumer Interests' (2015) OECD Digital Economy Papers 247 <https://www.oecd-ilibrary.org/science-and-technology/industry-self-regulation_5js4k1fjqkwh-en> accessed 8 August 2018

Ruggie J, 'Report of the Special Representative of the Secretary-General on the Issue of Human Rights and Transnational Corporations and Other Business Enterprises, A/HRC/8/5'

Shaheed F, 'Report of the Special Rapporteur in the Field of Cultural Rights' (2014) A/69/286 <https://digitallibrary.un.org/record/755488> accessed 19 July 2018

UN Committee on the Rights of the Child, 'General Comment No. 12 (2009) The Right of the Child to Be Heard'

—, 'General Comment No. 16 (2013) on State Obligations Regarding the Impact of the Business Sector' (2013)

—, 'General Comment No. 17 (2013) on the Right of the Child to Rest, Leisure, Play, Recreational Activities, Cultural Life and the Arts (Art. 31)' (2013)

—, 'General Comment No. 14 (2013) on the Right of the Child to Have His or Her Best Interests Taken as a Primary Consideration (Art. 3, Para.1)' (2013)

—, 'Report of the 2014 Day of General Discussion "Digital Media and Children's Rights"' (2014) <www.ohchr.org/Documents/HRBodies/CRC/Discussions/2014/DGD_report.pdf> accessed 26 October 2017

—, 'General Comment No. 20 (2016) on the Implementation of the Rights of the Child during Adolescence'

UN Committee on the Rights of the Child G, 'UNCRC Discussion Day 1993, Economic Exploitation of Children, CRC/C/20' (1993) <www.ohchr.org/EN/HRBodies/CRC/Documents/Recommandations/exploit.pdf>

—, 'General Comment No. 1 (2001) Article 29 (1): The Aims of Education'

—, 'General Comment No. 5 (2003) General Measures of Implementation of the Convention on the Rights of the Child (Arts. 4, 42 and 44, Para. 6)' (2003)

—, 'General Comment No. 13 (2011) The Right of the Child to Freedom from All Forms of Violence' (2011)

UNICEF, 'Children's Rights in Impact Assessments' (2013) <https://www.unicef.org/csr/css/Children_s_Rights_in_Impact_Assessments_Web_161213.pdf> accessed 14 November 2017

—, 'Main Principles – Child Rights Approach' (*UNICEF*) <https://www.unicef.org/tdad/index_55678.html> accessed 4 April 2018

UNICEF and The Danish Institute for Human Rig, 'Children's Rights in Impact Assessments: A Guide for Integrating Children's Rights into Impact Assessments and Taking Action for Children' (2013) <https://www.unicef.org/csr/css/Children_s_Rights_in_Impact_Assessments_Web_161213.pdf> accessed 6 August 2018

UNICEF, UN Global Compact and Save the Children, 'Children's Rights and Business Principles' (2012) <https://www.unglobalcompact.org/docs/issues_doc/human_rights/CRBP/Childrens_Rights_and_Business_Principles.pdf> accessed 14 November 2017

United Nations, 'Optional Protocol to the Convention on the Rights of the Child on a Communication Procedure' <https://treaties.un.org/doc/source/signature/2012/ctc_4-11d.pdf> accessed 12 July 2018

United Nations General Assembly, 'Resolution – A World Fit for Children, A/RES/S-27/2' (2004) 23 Refugee Survey Quarterly 225

—, 'Protect, Respect, and Remedy: A Framework for Business and Human Rights Doc A/HRC/8/5' <https://documents-dds-ny.un.org/doc/UNDOC/GEN/G08/128/61/PDF/G0812861.pdf?OpenElement> accessed 6 August 2018

World Health Organization (Regional Office for Europe), 'Tackling Food Marketing to Children in a Digital World: Trans-Disciplinary Perspectives – Children's Rights, Evidence of Impact, Methodological Challenges, Regulatory Options and Policy Implications for the WHO European Region' <www.euro.who.int/__data/assets/pdf_file/0017/322226/Tackling-food-marketing-children-digital-world-trans-disciplinary-perspectives-en.pdf> accessed 9 April 2018

B. EUROPEAN UNION

Article 29 Data Protection Working Party, 'Guidelines on Transparency under Regulation 2016/679, Wp260' <http://ec.europa.eu/newsroom/article29/document.cfm?action=display&doc_id=51025> accessed 31 August 2018.

—, 'Opinion 3/2003 on the European Code of Conduct of FEDMA for the Use of Personal Data in Direct Marketing' (2003) <http://ec.europa.eu/justice/article-29/documentation/opinion-recommendation/files/2003/wp77_en.pdf> accessed 31 July 2018.

—, 'Opinion 10/2004 on More Harmonised Information Provisions, WP 100' <http://ec.europa.eu/justice/article-29/documentation/opinion-recommendation/files/2004/wp100_en.pdf> accessed 27 July 2018.

—, 'Opinion 4/2007 on the Concept of Personal Data. WP 136.' (2007) <http://ec.europa.eu/justice/data-protection/article-29/documentation/opinion-recommendation/files/2007/wp136_en.pdf> accessed 21 November 2017.

—, 'Opinion 2/2009 on the Protection of Children's Personal Data (General Guidelines and the Special Case of Schools). WP160.' (2009) <http://ec.europa.eu/justice/policies/privacy/docs/wpdocs/2009/wp160_en.pdf> accessed 27 November 2017.

—, 'Opinion 1/2010 on the Concepts of "Controller" and "Processor", WP 169' <http://ec.europa.eu/justice/article-29/documentation/opinion-recommendation/files/2010/wp169_en.pdf> accessed 26 July 2018.

—, 'Opinion 2/2010 on Online Behavioural Advertising WP 171' (2010) http://ec.europa.eu/justice_home/fsj/privacy/index_en.htm.

—, 'Opinion 4/2010 on the European Code of Conduct of FEDMA for the Use of Personal Data in Direct Marketing, WP 174' (2010) <http://ec.europa.eu/justice/data-protection/article-29/documentation/opinion-recommendation/files/2010/wp174_en.pdf> accessed 14 November 2017.

—, 'Opinion 13/2011 on Geolocation Services on Smart Mobile Devices, WP 185' <http://ec.europa.eu/justice/article-29/documentation/opinion-recommendation/files/2011/wp185_en.pdf> accessed 27 July 2018.

—, 'Opinion 02/2013 on Apps on Smart Devices, WP202' (2013) <http://ec.europa.eu/justice/data-protection/article-29/documentation/opinion-recommendation/files/2013/wp202_en.pdf> accessed 14 November 2017.

—, 'Guidelines on Automated Individual Decision-Making and Profiling for the Purposes of Regulation 2016/679' (2017).

—, 'Guidelines on Consent under Regulation 2016/679' <http://ec.europa.eu/newsroom/article29/item-detail.cfm?item_id=623051> accessed 27 July 2018.

Council of the European Union, 'Presidency Note Concerning Profiling. Interinstitutional File: 2012/01(COD)' <http://register.consilium.europa.eu/doc/srv?l=EN&f=ST%2010617%202014%20INIT> accessed 27 July 2018

—, 'Proposal for a Directive of the European Parliament and of the Council Amending Directive 2010/13/EU on the Coordination of Certain Provisions Laid down by Law, Regulation or Administrative Action in Member States Concerning the Provision of Audiovisual Media Services (Audiovisual Media Services Directive) in View of Changing Market Realities – Analysis of the Final Compromise Text with a View to Agreement' (2018) <http://data.consilium.europa.eu/doc/document/ST-9817–2018-INIT/en/pdf> accessed 25 July 2018

Directive 95/46/EC of the European Parliament and of the Council of 24 October 1995 on the protection of individuals with regard to the processing of personal data and on the free movement of such data (OJ L 281) 31

Directive 95/46/EC of the European Parliament and of the Council of 24 October 1995 on the protection of individuals with regard to the processing of personal data and on the free movement of such data 1995

Directive 2000/31/EC of the European Parliament and of the Council of 8 June 2000 on certain legal aspects of information society services, in particular electronic commerce, in the Internal Market (Directive on electronic commerce) 2000

Directive 2002/58/EC of the European Parliament and of the Council of 12 July 2002 concerning the processing of personal data and the protection of privacy in the electronic communications sector (Directive on privacy and electronic communications) 2002 (OJ L 201) 37

Directive 2002/58/EC of the European Parliament and of the Council of 12 July 2002 concerning the processing of personal data and the protection of privacy in the electronic communications sector (Directive on privacy and electronic communications) 2002 (Official Journal L 201)

Directive 2005/29/EC of the European Parliament and the Council of 11 May 2005 concerning unfair business-to-consumer commercial practices in the internal market and amending Council Directive 84/450/EEC, Directives 97/7/EC, 98/27/EC and 2002/65 /EC of the European Parliament and of the Council and Regulation (EC) No 2006/2004 of the European Parliament and of the Council ('Unfair Commercial Practices Directive') 2005

Directive 2010/13/EU of the European Parliament and of the Council of 10 March 2010 on the coordination of certain provisions laid down by law, regulation or administrative action in Member States concerning the provision of audiovisual media services (Audiovisual Media Services Directive) 2010

Directive (EU) 2018/1808 of the European Parliament and of the Council of 14 November 2018 amending Directive 2010/13/EU on the coordination of certain provisions laid down by law, regulation or administrative action in Member States concerning the provision of audiovisual media services (Audiovisual Media Services Directive) in view of changing market realities

European Commission, 'Green Paper on Commercial Communications in the Internal Market' <http://europa.eu/documents/comm/green_papers/pdf/com96_192_1_en.pdf> accessed 15 March 2018

—, 'Communication of 18 April 1997: A European Initiative in the Sector of Electronic Commerce' (18 April 1997) <https://eur-lex.europa.eu/legal-content/EN/TXT/?uri=LEGISSUM%3Al32101> accessed 12 April 2018

—, 'Interpretative Communication on Certain Aspects of the Provisions on Televised Advertising in the "Television without Frontiers" Directive (2004/C 102/02)'

—, 'Towards an EU Strategy on the Rights of the Child, COM(2006) 367 Final' <https://eur-lex.europa.eu/legal-content/EN/TXT/PDF/?uri=CELEX:52006DC0367&from=NL> accessed 26 July 2018

—, 'Communication from the Commission to the Council, the European Parliament and the European Economic and Social Committee – EU Consumer Policy Strategy 2007–2013 – Empowering Consumers, Enhancing Their Welfare, Effectively Protecting Them' <https://eur-lex.europa.eu/legal-content/EN/TXT/PDF/?uri=CELEX:52007DC0099&from=EN> accessed 20 March 2018

—, 'Commission Staff Working Document: Guidance on the Implementation/Application of Directive 2005/29/Ec on Unfair Commercial Practices' (2009) <http://ec.europa.eu/justice/consumer-marketing/files/ucp_guidance_2009_en.pdf> accessed 16 January 2018

—, 'Communication from the Commission to the European Parliament, the Council, the European Economic and Social Committee and the Committee of the Regions: An EU Agenda for the Rights of the Child, COM (2011) 60' <https://eur-lex.europa.eu/legal-content/EN/TXT/PDF/?uri=CELEX:52010DC0245R(01)&from=EN> accessed 16 July 2018

—, 'Communication from the Commission to the European Parliament, the Council, the European Economic and Social Committee and the Committee of the Regions on a European Strategy for a Better Internet for Children' <https://eur-lex.europa.eu/legal-content/EN/TXT/PDF/?uri=CELEX:52012DC0196&from=EN> accessed 16 March 2018

—, 'Communication from the Commission to the European Parliament, the Council, the European Economic and Social Committee and the Committee of the Regions on a European Strategy for a Better Internet for Children' <https://eur-lex.europa.eu/legal-content/EN/TXT/PDF/?uri=CELEX:52012DC0196&from=EN> accessed 28 March 2018

—, 'Communication To The European Parliament, The Council And The European Economic And Social Committee On the Application of the Unfair Commercial Practices Directive – Achieving a High Level of Consumer Protection Building Trust in the Internal Market' (2013) <https://eur-lex.europa.eu/legal-content/EN/TXT/?uri=celex%3A52013DC0138> accessed 31 July 2018

—, 'EU Principles for Better Self- and Co-Regulation' <https://ec.europa.eu/digital-single-market/en/news/principles-better-self-and-co-regulation-and-establishment-community-practice> accessed 24 May 2018

—, 'Green Paper: Preparing for a Fully Converged Audiovisual World: Growth, Creation and Values, COM(2013) 231 Final.'

—, 'Executive Summary of Contributions to the Public Consultation – Green Paper Preparing for a Fully Converged Audiovisual World'

—, 'Principles for Better Self- and Co-Regulation' <https://ec.europa.eu/digital-single-market/sites/digital-agenda/files/CoP%20-%20Principles%20for%20better%20self-%20and%20co-regulation.pdf> accessed 12 July 2018

—, 'Communication from the Commission to the European Parliament, the Council, the European Economic and Social Committee and the Committee of the Regions on a Digital Single Market Strategy for Europe. [COM(2015)192 Final] 11'

—, 'REFIT Evaluation and Impact Assessment of the EU Audiovisual Media Services Directive 2010/13/EU (AVMSD)' <http://ec.europa.eu/smart-regulation/roadmaps/docs/2015_cnect_006_cwp_review_avmsd_iia_en.pdf> accessed 2 April 2018

—, 'Synopsis Report of the Public Consultation on Directive 2010/13/EU on Audiovisual Media Services (AVMSD) – A Media Framework for the 21st Century' <https://ec.europa.eu/digital-single-market/en/news/report-public-consultation-review-audiovisual-media-services-directive-avmsd> accessed 10 April 2018

—, 'Commission Staff Working Document – Guidance on the Implementation/Application of Directive 2005/29/EC on Unfair Commercial Practices, SWD(2016) 163 Final.' (2016) <http://ec.europa.eu/justice/consumer-marketing/files/ucp_guidance_en.pdf> accessed 9 October 2017

—, 'The Precautionary Principle – Summaries of EU Legislation' (30 November 2016) <https://eur-lex.europa.eu/legal-content/EN/TXT/?uri=LEGISSUM%3Al32042> accessed 9 April 2018

—, 'Commission Staff Working Document: Executive Summary of the Fitness Check Report, SWD(2017) 208 Final'

—, 'Contributions and Preliminary Trends of the Public Consultation on Audiovisual Media Services (AVMSD)' (*Digital Single Market*) <https://ec.europa.eu/

digital-single-market/en/news/contributions-and-preliminary-trends-public-consultation-audiovisual-media-services-avmsd> accessed 10 April 2018

European Data Protection Supervisor, 'Preliminary Opinion – Privacy and Competitiveness in the Age of Big Data: The Interplay between Data Protection, Competition Law and Consumer Protection in the Digital Economy' <https://edps.europa.eu/sites/edp/files/publication/14-03-26_competitition_law_big_data_en.pdf> accessed 25 July 2018

European Economic and Social Committee, 'Opinion of the European Economic and Social Committee on a Framework for Advertising Aimed at Young People and Children'

European Parliament, 'Report on the Proposal for a Directive of the European Parliament and of the Council Amending Council Directive 89/552/EEC on the Coordination of Certain Provisions Laid down by Law, Regulation or Administrative Action in Member States Concerning the Pursuit of Television Broadcasting Activities.' (2006)

—, 'Resolution of 15 December 2010 on the Impact of Advertising on Consumer Behaviour'

—, 'European Parliament Resolution of 22 May 2012 on a Strategy for Strengthening the Rights of Vulnerable Consumers (2011/2272(INI))'

—, 'European Parliament Resolution of 20 November 2012 on Protecting Children in the Digital World'

European Parliament and the Council, 'First Report on the Application of Directive 2000/31/EC of the European Parliament and of the Council of 8 June 2000 on Certain Legal Aspects of Information Society Services, in Particular Electronic Commerce, in the Internal Market (Directive on Electronic Commerce)' <www.europarl.europa.eu/RegData/docs_autres_institutions/commission_europeenne/com/2003/0702/COM_COM(2003)0702_EN.pdf> accessed 6 August 2018

—, 'Recommendation 2006/952/EC of 20 December 2006 on the Protection of Minors and Human Dignity and on the Right of Reply in Relation to the Competitiveness of the European Audiovisual and on-Line Information Services Industry'

European Parliament (Committee on Culture and Education), 'Report on Protecting Children in the Digital World (2012/2068(INI))' (2012) <www.europarl.europa.eu/sides/getDoc.do?pubRef=-//EP//NONSGML+REPORT+A7-2012-0353+0+DOC+PDF+V0//EN> accessed 8 November 2017

European Parliament (Committee on Women's Rights and Gender Equality), 'Report on How Marketing and Advertising Affect Equality between Women and Men (2008/2038(INI))' (2008) <www.europarl.europa.eu/sides/getDoc.do?pubRef=-//EP//NONSGML+REPORT+A6-2008-0199+0+DOC+PDF+V0//EN> accessed 8 November 2017

Proposal for a Regulation of the European Parliament and of the Council concerning the respect for private life and the protection of personal data in electronic communications and repealing Directive 2002/58/EC (Regulation on Privacy and Electronic Communications) 2017

Regulation (EU) 2017/2394 of the European Parliament and of the Council of 12 december 2017 on cooperation between national authorities responsible for the enforcement of consumer protection laws and repealing Regulation (EC) No 2006/2004.

C. COUNCIL OF EUROPE

Convention on the Protection of Children against Sexual Exploitation and Sexual Abuse (Lanzarote Convention), CETS No. 201. 2012

Council of Europe, 'Recommendation Rec(2006)12 of the Committee of Ministers to Member States on Empowering Children in the New Information and Communications Environment' (2006) <https://www.coe.int/en/web/freedom-expression/committee-of-ministers-adopted-texts/-/asset_publisher/aDXmrol0vvsU/content/recommendation-rec-2006-12-of-the-committee-of-ministers-to-member-states-on-empowering-children-in-the-new-information-and-communications-environment> accessed 10 November 2017

—, 'Recommendation CM/Rec(2010)13 on the Protection of Individuals with Regard to Automatic Processing of Personal Data in the Context of Profiling' <https://rm.coe.int/16807096c3> accessed 27 July 2018

—, 'Recommendation CM/Rec(2014)6 of the Committee of Ministers to Member States on a Guide to Human Rights for Internet Users' (2014) <https://search.coe.int/cm/Pages/result_details.aspx?ObjectID=09000016804d5b31> accessed 19 July 2018

—, 'Recommendation CM/Rec(2019), Preventing and Combating Sexism, 27 March 2019 <https://rm.coe.int/prems-055519-gbr-2573-cmrec-2019-1-web-a5/168093e08c> accessed 17 September 2019.

—, 'Internet Governance – Council of Europe Strategy 2016–2019: Democracy, Human Rights and the Rule of Law in the Digital World' <https://rm.coe.int/16806aafa9> accessed 10 November 2017

—, 'Strategy on the Rights of the Child 2016–2021' (2016) <https://rm.coe.int/168066cff8> accessed 2 August 2017

—, 'Children's Rights Committee' (*Council of Europe Portal: Children's Rights*) <https://www.coe.int/en/web/children/cahenf> accessed 19 March 2018

—, 'Europe an Treaty Series – No. 132 Explanatory Report to the European Convention on Transfrontier Television' <https://rm.coe.int/16800cb348> accessed 25 July 2018

Council of Europe, Committee of Ministers, 'Recommendation No. R (84) 3 of the Committee of Ministers to Member States on Principles on Television Advertising.' <https://rm.coe.int/CoERMPublicCommonSearchServices/DisplayDCTMContent?documentId=09000016804dc8b4> accessed 25 July 2018

—, 'Declaration of the Committee of Ministers on Protecting the Dignity, Security and Privacy of Children on the Internet'

—, 'Recommendation CM/Rec(2016)3 on Human Rights and Business' <http://edoc.coe.int/en/fundamental-freedoms/7302-human-rights-and-business-recommendation-cmrec20163-of-the-committee-of-ministers-to-member-states.html> accessed 28 June 2018

—, 'Recommendation CM/Rec(2018)7 of the Committee of Ministers to Member States on Guidelines to Respect, Protect and Fulfil the Rights of the Child in the Digital Environment' <https://search.coe.int/cm/Pages/result_details.aspx?ObjectId=09000016808b79f7>

Council of Europe (Parliamentary Assembly, 'Recommendation 2092 (2016) – Fighting the over-Sexualisation of Children' (2016) <https://assembly.coe.int/nw/xml/XRef/Xref-XML2HTML-EN.asp?fileid=22938&lang=en> accessed 8 November 2017

European Convention on Human Rights. CETS No. 005 1950

European Social Charter. European Treaty Series – No. 163 1996

Geneva Declaration of the Rights of the Child 1924

D. BELGIUM

Belgian Privacy Commission, 'Recommendation No. 02/2013 of 30 January 2013 Regarding Direct Marketing and the Protection of Personal Data' (2013) <https://www.privacycommission.be/sites/privacycommission/files/documents/aanbeveling_02_2013.pdf> accessed 14 November 2017.

Gegevensbeschermingsautoriteit, 'Aanbeveling Nr 02/2013 van 30 Januari 2013 Betreffende Direct Marketing En Bescherming van Persoonsgegevens [Recommendation No. 02/2013 of 30 January 2013 Regarding Direct Marking and the Protection of Personal Data]'

—, 'De Versterkte Toestemming' <https://www.gegevensbeschermingsautoriteit.be/de-versterkte-toestemming> accessed 27 July 2018

E. THE UNITED KINGDOM

ICO, 'What If We Want to Profile Children or Make Automated Decisions about Them?' (25 May 2018) <https://ico.org.uk/for-organisations/guide-to-the-general-data-protection-regulation-gdpr/children-and-the-gdpr/what-if-we-want-to-profile-children-or-make-automated-decisions-about-them/> accessed 30 July 2018

Ofcom Office of Communications, 'Renewal of the Co-Regulatory Arrangements for Broadcast Advertising' (2014) <https://www.ofcom.org.uk/__data/assets/pdf_file/0028/58942/statement.pdf> accessed 7 August 2018

—, 'Children and Parents: Media Use and Attitudes Report 2017' (2017) <https://www.ofcom.org.uk/__data/assets/pdf_file/0020/108182/children-parents-media-use-attitudes-2017.pdf> accessed 11 July 2018

—, 'Children's Content Review : Update Assessing the Current Provision of Children's Programmes on TV and Online' (2018) <https://www.ofcom.org.uk/__data/assets/pdf_file/0023/116519/childrens-content-review-update.pdf> accessed 2 August 2018

—, 'Social Networking – A Quantitative and Qualitative Research Report into Attitudes, Behaviours and Use' (Ofcom 2008) <http://news.bbc.co.uk/2/shared/bsp/hi/pdfs/02_04_08_ofcom.pdf> accessed 19 July 2018

2. CASE LAW

A. CJEU

Artegodan GmbH and Others v Commission of the European Communities [2002] CJEU T-74/00 (Joined cases T-74/00, T-76/00, T-83/00, T-84/00, T-85/00, T-132/00, T-137/00 and T-141/00)
Bond van Adverteerders v the Netherlands [1988] CJEU C-352/85
Dynamic Medien Vertriebs GmbH v Avides Media AG CJEU C-244/06
Giuseppe Sacchi Reference for a preliminary ruling: Tribunale civile e penale di Biella v Italy [1974] CJEU C–155/73
P Moskof AE v Ethnikos Organismos Kapnou [1997] CJEU C-244/95, ECR I-06441
Parliament v Council [2006] CJEU C-540/03
Peugeot Deutschland GmbH v Deutsche Umwelthilfe eV [2018] CJEU C-132/17
RLvS Verlagsgesellschaft mbH v Stuttgarter Wochenblatt GmbH [2013] CJEU C-391/12
Sabam v Netlog [2012] CJEU C-360/10.
Sotiris Papasavvas v O Fileleftheros Dimosia Etaireia Ltd and Others [2014] CJEU C-291/13

B. ECTHR

Axen v Germany [1983] ECtHR 8273/78
Barthold v Germany [1985] ECtHR App No 8734/79
Beaumartin v France [1994] ECtHR 15287/89
Bohlen and Ernst August von Hannover v Germany [2015] ECtHR 53495/09.
Campbell and Fell v The United Kingdom [1984] ECtHR 7819/77; 7878/77
Casado Coca v Spain [1994] ECtHR Series A., No. 285
Golder v The United Kingdom [1975] ECtHR 4451/70
Harroudj v France [2013] ECtHR 43631/09
Keegan v Ireland [1994] ECtHR 16969/90
Kleyn and others v The Netherlands [2003] ECtHR 39343/98, 39651/98, 43147/98 and 46664/99
KT v Norway [2008] ECtHR 26664/03
Kudla v Poland [2000] ECtHR 30210/96
Margareta and Roger Andersson v Sweden [1992] ECtHR 12963/87
Markt Intern Verlag GmbH and Beermann v Germany [1989] ECtHR 10572/83
Maslov v Austria [2008] ECtHR 1638/0323
MTE v Hungary [2016] ECtHR 22947/13
Osman v the United Kingdom [1998] ECtHR 23452/94
Özgür Gündem v Turkey [2000] ECtHR 23144/93
Perna v Italy [2003] ECtHR 48898/99
Sahin v Germany [2003] ECtHR 30943/96
S and Marper v the United Kingdom [2008] ECtHR 30562/04
Sporrong and Lönnroth v Sweden [1982] ECtHR 7151/75; 7152/75

Sramek v Austria [1984] ECtHR 8790/79
Ternovskis v Latvia [2014] ECtHR 33637/02
X and Church of Scientology v Sweden [1979] ECtHR 7805/77

C. ALTERNATIVE REGULATORY BODIES

AB INBEV, 5/08/2009 (JEP)
ACID APPAREL, 12/09/2018 (JEP)
BOCKOR BROUWERIJ, 05/08/2010 (JEP)
Decision No 2015/00972 (Advertising Code Committee [Reclame Code Commissie])
Decision No 2016/00079 (Advertising Code Committee [Reclame Code Commissie))
Decision No 2017/00494 (Advertising Code Committee [Reclame Code Commissie))
Decision No 2018/00214 (Advertising Code Committee [Reclame Code Commissie])
DELHAIZE, 19/08/13 (JEP)
Ferrero UK Ltd (Advertising Standards Authority)
Flava Bar Ltd (Advertising Standards Authority)
ILLVA SARONNO SPA (Advertising Standards Authority)
SALITO BEACH – HAVANA DISTRIBUTION, 7/07/16 (JEP)
Stomp Racing Ltd t/a Rocker BMX (Advertising Standards Authority)
Westland Horticulture Ltd t/a westland garden health (Advertising Standards Authority)

3. DOCTRINE

A. BOOKS AND BOOK CHAPTERS

Abramson B, Article 2: The Right of Non-Discrimination (BRILL 2008).
Bakan J, Childhood Under Siege: How Big Business Ruthlessly Targets Children (Random House 2012).
Bentley AR, Earls M and O'brien M J, I'll Have What She's Having – Mapping Social Behavior <https://mitpress.mit.edu/books/ill-have-what-shes-having> accessed 29 November 2017.
Bieker F, 'Enforcing Data Protection Law – The Role of the Supervisory Authorities in Theory and Practice', Privacy and Identity Management. Facing up to Next Steps (Springer, Cham 2016) <http://link.springer.com/chapter/10.1007/978-3-319-55783-0_10> accessed 5 July 2018.
Bosco F and others, 'Profiling Technologies and Fundamental Rights and Values: Regulatory Challenges and Perspectives from European Data Protection Authorities', Reforming European Data Protection Law (Springer 2015) <http://link.springer.com/chapter/10.1007/978-94-017-9385-8_1> accessed 11 August 2017.
Böttcher K and others, 'Directive 2007/65/EC "Audiovisual Media Services" Directive. Article 3 e AVMSD' in O Castendyk, E Dommering and A Scheuer (eds), European Media Law (Kluwer Law International 2008).

boyd, D 'Social Network Sites as Networked Publics: Affordances, Dynamics, and Implications' in Z Papacharissi (ed), Networked self: Identity, community, and culture on social network sites (Routledge) <https://www.danah.org/papers/2010/SNSasNetworkedPublics.pdf> accessed 9 November 2018.

Brems E, A Commentary on the United Nations Convention on the Rights of the Child – Article 14: The Right to Freedom of Thought, Conscience and Religion (Martinus Nijhoff Publishers 2006).

Bueren GV, International Law on the Rights of the Child (Springer Netherlands 1995).

Capello M, 'Article 13 TWFD' in Olivier Castendyk, Egbert Dommering and Alexander Scheuer (eds), European Media Law (Kluwer Law International 2008)

Castelluccia C, 'Behavioural Tracking on the Internet: A Technical Perspective' in Serge Gutwirth and others (eds), European Data Protection: In Good Health? (Springer Netherlands 2012) <www.springerlink.com/index/10.1007/978-94-007-2903-2_2> accessed 16 October 2017

Castendyk O, 'Directive 89/552/EEC "Television without Frontiers" Directive.' in O Castendyk, EJ Dommering and A Scheuer (eds), European Media Law (Kluwer Law International 2008)

Castendyk O and Schaar O, 'Directive 2007/65/EC "Audiovisual Media Services" Directive. Article 10 AVMSD' in O Castendyk, EJ Dommering and A Scheuer (eds), European Media Law (Kluwer Law International 2008)

Castendyk O and Woods L, 'Part 2 – European Media Law' in Olivier Castendyk, Egbert Dommering and Alexander Scheuer (eds), European Media Law (Kluwer Law International 2008)

Chavannes R and Castendyk O, 'Directive 2007/65/EC "Audiovisual Media Services Directive"' in Oliver Castendyk, Egbert Dommering and Alexander Scheuer (eds), European Media Law (Kluwer Law International 2008)

Couzens M, 'Autonomy Rights versus Parental Autonomy' in André Alen (ed), The UN Children's rights Convention: theory meets practice (Intersentia 2006)

Daly A, A Commentary on the United Nations Convention on the Rights of the Child, Article 15: The Right to Freedom of Association and to Freedom of Peaceful Assembly (Brill 2016) <http://booksandjournals.brillonline.com/content/books/9789004258839> accessed 14 November 2017

David P, A Commentary on the United Nations Convention on the Rights of the Child, Article 31: The Right to Leisure, Play and Culture (Brill 2006)

De Pelsmacker P, Geuens M and Van Den Bergh J, Marketing Communications: A European Perspective, 6/E (Pearson 2017) <http://catalogue.pearsoned.co.uk/educator/product/Marketing-Communications-A-European-Perspective/9781292135762.page> accessed 15 March 2018

Detrick S, A Commentary on the United Nations Convention on the Rights of the Child (Martinus Nijhoff Publishers 1999)

Dijk P van and others (eds), Theory and Practice of the European Convention on Human Rights: Fourth Edition (4th edition, Intersentia Publishers 2006)

Dommering EJ, 'General Introduction Towards a European Media Law' in Olivier Castendyk, EJ Dommering and Alexander Scheuer (eds), European Media Law (Kluwer Law International 2008)

Durovic M and Micklitz HW, Internationalization of Consumer Law: A Game Changer (Springer 2017) <https://kclpure.kcl.ac.uk/portal/en/publications/internationalization-of-consumer-law(6cab25a6-6b64-4837-ab12-523c9a8dfe53)/export.html> accessed 12 July 2018

Fortin J, Children's Rights and the Developing Law (Cambridge University Press 2003)

Freeman M, Article 3 : The Best Interests of the Child (2007)

Freeman M, Human Rights (EPZ ed edition, Polity Press 2002).

Garde A, 'The Best Interests of the Child' in James Devenny and Mel Kenny (eds), European Consumer Protection: Theory and Practice (Cambridge University Press 2012)

Groothuis MM, 'The Right to Privacy for Children on the Internet: New Developments in the Case Law of the European Court of Human Rights', Minding Minors Wandering the Web: Regulating Online Child Safety (TMC Asser Press, The Hague 2014) <https://link.springer.com/chapter/10.1007/978-94-6265-005-3_8> accessed 13 November 2017

Grover SC, Children Defending Their Human Rights Under the CRC Communications Procedure (Springer Berlin Heidelberg 2015)

Gunter B, Kids and Branding in a Digital World (Manchester University Press 2016)

Harremoes P and others, The Precautionary Principle in the 20th Century: Late Lessons from Early Warnings (Routledge 2013)

Henning-Bodewig F, 'Directive 2005/29/EC & Directive 2006/114/EC.' in O Castendyk, E Dommering and A Scheuer (eds), European Media Law (Kluwer Law International 2008)

Hodgkin R and Newell P, 'Implementation Handbook for the Convention on the Rights of the Child: Fully Revised Third Edition' (UNICEF 2007) <https://www.unicef.org/publications/index_43110.html> accessed 10 November 2017

Howells G, Twigg-Flesner C and Wilhelmsson T, Rethinking EU Consumer Law (Routledge 2017)

Hudders L and others, 'Children's Advertising Literacy for New Advertising Formats: The Mediating Impact of Advertising Literacy on the (Un)Intended Effects of Advergames and Advertising Funded Programs.' in Peeter Verlegh, Hilde Voorveld and Martin Eisend (eds), Advances in Advertising Research (Vol. VI) (Springer Fachmedien Wiesbaden 2016) <http://link.springer.com/10.1007/978-3-658-10558-7_19> accessed 29 March 2018

Hutchby I and Moran-Ellis J, Children, Technology, and Culture: The Impacts of Technologies in Children's Everyday Lives (Routledge 2001)

Irwin SO, Digital Media: Human–Technology Connection (Rowman & Littlefield 2016)

Keymolen E, Trust on the Line: A Philosophical Exploration of Trust in the Networked Era (Wolf Legal Publishers 2016)

—, 'Onzichtbare Zichtbaarheid. Helmuth Plessner Ontmoet Profiling' (2006)

Kilkelly U, 'The Right to Respect for Private and Family Life: A Guide to the Implementation of Article 8 of the European Convention on Human Rights, Human Rights Handbooks, No 1' (Council of Europe 2003) Human rights handbooks, No 1 <www.refworld.org/docid/49f17e212.html> accessed 13 November 2017

Kuijer M, The Blindfold of Lady Justice: Judicial Independence and Impartiality in Light of the Requirements of Article 6 ECHR (M Kuijer 2004)

Lansdown G, The Evolving Capacities of the Child (Florence 2005)
Laureckis E and Martínez Miralpeix A, 'Ethical and Legal Considerations in Research Subject and Data Protection' in Andrew R Thomas and others (eds), Ethics and Neuromarketing: Implications for Market Research and Business Practice (Springer International Publishing 2017) <https://doi.org/10.1007/978-3-319-45609-6_5> accessed 27 August 2018.
Lievens E, Protecting Children in the Digital Era: The Use of Alternative Regulatory Instruments, vol 105 (Martinus Nijhoff Publishers 2010)
—, 'Children's Rights and Media : Imperfect but Inspirational', Children's rights law in the global human rights landscape isolation, inspiration, integration? (Routledge 2017) <http://hdl.handle.net/1854/LU-8532067> accessed 10 November 2017
—, 'Children's Rights and Digital Technologies' in Ursula Kilkelly and Ton Liefaard (eds), International human rights of children (Springer 2018)
Lodder AR and Murray AD, EU Regulation of E-Commerce: A Commentary (Edward Elgar Pub 2017)
Lundy L and McEvoy L, 'Childhood, the United Nations Convention on the Rights of the Child and Research: What Constitutes a Rights-Based Approach' in M Freeman (ed), Law and Childhood (Oxford University Press) <https://www.qub.ac.uk/research-centres/CentreforChildrensRights/ChildrensRights-BasedResearch/> accessed 29 August 2018.
Mansell R and Raboy M, The Handbook of Global Media and Communication Policy (John Wiley & Sons 2011)
McCullagh K, 'The General Data Protection Regulation: A Partial Success for Children on Social Network Sites?' in T Bräutigam and S. Miettinen (eds), Data protection, privacy and European regulation in the digital age (Unigrafia 2016) <https://ueaeprints.uea.ac.uk/61415/4/Mc_Cullagh_2016_book_chapter_SNS.pdf> accessed 26 July 2018
Meuwese S, Blaak M and Kaandorp M, Handboek Internationaal Jeugdrecht (Ars Aequi Libri 2005)
Miller NE and Dollard J, Social Learning and Imitation (Yale University Press 1941)
Mole N and Harby C, The Right to a Fair Trial, A Guide to the Implementation of Article 6 of the European Convention on Human Rights (Council of Europe 2006)
Nowak M, Article 6: The Right to Life, Survival, and Development (Martinus Nijhoff Publishers 2005)
Oster J, European and International Media Law (Cambridge University Press 2016)
Ovey C and White R, Jacobs and White, the European Convention on Human Rights (4th ed., Oxford university press 2006)
Parkes A, Children and International Human Rights Law: The Right of the Child to Be Heard (Routledge 2013)
Price ME and Verhulst S (eds), Routledge Handbook of Media Law (Routledge 2013)
Rainey B, Wicks E and Ovey C, Jacobs, White and Ovey: The European Convention on Human Rights (Oxford University Press 2017)
Richards N, Intellectual Privacy: Rethinking Civil Liberties in the Digital Age, vol 6 (Oxford University Press 2016)
Riordan J, The Liability of Internet Intermediaries (Oxford University Press 2016)
Rouvroy A and Poullet Y, 'The Right to Informational Self-Determination and the Value of Self-Development: Reassessing the Importance of Privacy for Democracy',

Reinventing Data Protection? (Springer, Dordrecht 2009) <https://link.springer.com/chapter/10.1007/978-1-4020-9498-9_2> accessed 13 November 2017

Narayanan A, Huey J and Felten EW, 'A Precautionary Approach to Big Data Privacy' in Serge Gutwirth, Ronald Leenes and Paul De Hert (eds), Data Protection on the Move, vol 24 (Springer Netherlands 2016) <http://link.springer.com/10.1007/978-94-017-7376-8_13> accessed 6 April 2018

Noort G van, Smit EG and Voorveld HAM, 'The Online Behavioural Advertising Icon: Two User Studies', Advances in Advertising Research (Vol. IV) (Springer Gabler, Wiesbaden 2013) <http://link.springer.com/chapter/10.1007/978-3-658-02365-2_28> accessed 31 July 2018

O'Neill B, Staksrud E and McLaughlin S (eds), Towards a Better Internet for Children? Policy Pillars, Players and Paradoxes (Nordicom 2013)

Opree SJ, Consumed by Consumer Culture? Advertising's Impact on Children's Materialism and Life Satisfaction (9789462590335 2014) <http://dare.uva.nl/search?arno.record.id=467433> accessed 30 March 2018

Parker C and Howe J, 'Ruggie's Diplomatic Project and Its Missing Regulatory Infrastructure' in Radu Mares (ed), The UN Guiding Principles on Business and Human Rights (Martinus Nijhoff 2012)

Peleg N, 'The Child's Right to Development' (UCL (University College London) 2012)

Sacino SW, A Commentary on the United Nations Convention on the Rights of the Child, Article 17: Access to a Diversity of Mass Media Sources (Brill 2011)

Scaife L, Handbook of Social Media and the Law (Informa Law from Routledge 2015)

Schaar O, 'Directive 89/552/EEC "Television without Frontiers" Directive. Article 1 TWFD' in O Castendyk, EJ Dommering and A Scheuer (eds), European Media Law (Kluwer Law International 2008)

—, 'Television Advertising, Sponsorship and Teleshopping' in O Castendyk, EJ Dommering and A Scheuer (eds), European Media Law (Kluwer Law International 2008)

Siegert G, Rimscha B von and Grubenmann S (eds), Commercial Communication in the Digital Age: Information or Disinformation? (1 Edition, Walter de Gruyter 2017)

Skouma G and Léonard L, 'On-Line Behavioral Tracking: What May Change after the Legal Reform on Personal Data Protection', Reforming European Data Protection Law (Springer 2015) <http://link.springer.com/chapter/10.1007/978-94-017-9385-8_2> accessed 11 August 2017

Smith L, 'Convention on the Rights of the Child: Freedom of Expression for Children' in Tarlach McGonagle and Yvonne Donders (eds), The United Nations and Freedom of Expression and Information: Critical Perspectives (Cambridge University Press 2015)

Staiano AE and Calvert SL, 'The Influence of Advergames on Children's Consumer Choices and Behavior', Advertising to Children (Palgrave Macmillan, London 2014) <https://link.springer.com/chapter/10.1057/9781137313256_12> accessed 9 November 2017

Strasburger VC and Wilson BJ, Children, Adolescents, and the Media (SAGE Publications 2002)

Sunde IM, 'Enforcing Legal Protection against Online Violation of Privacy' in DJB Svantesson and S Greenstein (eds), Nordic Yearbook of Law and Informatics

2010–2012, Internationalisation of Law in the Digital Information Society (Ex Tuto Publishing 2013) <https://brage.bibsys.no/xmlui/handle/11250/174974> accessed 13 November 2017

Swepston L, A Commentary on the United Nations Convention on the Rights of the Child, Article 32: Protection from Economic Exploitation (Brill 2012) <http://booksandjournals.brillonline.com/content/books/9789004231467> accessed 13 November 2017

Valcke P and Dommering E, 'Directive 2000/31/EC-'e-Commerce' Directive' in Olivier Castendyk, Egbert Dommering and Alexander Scheuer (eds), European Media Law (Kluwer Law International 2008)

Valcke P and Voorhoof D, 'Hoofdstuk 20 – De Reclamecode En de Jury Voor Ethische Praktijken Inzake Reclame', Handboek mediarecht (Editions Larcier 2014)

Valcke P, Voorhoof D and Lievens E, 'Independent Media Regulators: Condition Sine qua Non for Freedom of Expression?' in W Schulz, P Valcke and K Irion (eds), The Independence of the Media and Its Regulatory Agencies (INTELLECT LTD; Bristol, UK; Chicago, USA 2013)

van der Hof S, 'No Child's Play: Online Data Protection for Children' in Simone van der Hof, Bibi van den Berg and Bart Schermer (eds), Minding Minors Wandering the Web: Regulating Online Child Safety (TMC Asser Press, The Hague 2014) <http://link.springer.com/chapter/10.1007/978-94-6265-005-3_7> accessed 27 July 2018

S. van der Hof and M. Groothuis (eds), Innovating Government, Normative, policy and technological dimensions of modern government, (The Hague: T M C Asser, Berlin/Heidelberg: Springer, 2011).

van der Hof S and Prins C, 'Personalisation and Its Influence on Identities, Behaviour and Social Values', Profiling the European Citizen (Springer, Dordrecht 2008) <https://link.springer.com/chapter/10.1007/978-1-4020-6914-7_6> accessed 8 November 2017

Vandenhole W, Non-Discrimination and Equality in the View of the UN Human Rights Treaty Bodies (Intersentia nv 2005)

—, Routledge International Handbook of Children's Rights Studies (Routledge 2015) <https://www.book2look.com/book/rUPT8r8gaE> accessed 14 November 2017

Verbruggen P, 'Enforcement of Transnational Private Regulation of Advertising Practices: Decentralization, Mechanisms and Procedural Fairness' in Fabrizio Cafaggi (ed), Enforcement of Transnational Regulation: Ensuring Compliance in a Global World (Edward Elgar Publishing 2012)

Verdoodt V and Lievens E, 'Targeting Children with Personalised Advertising: How to Reconcile the Best Interests of Children and Advertisers' in Gert Vermeulen and Eva Lievens (eds), Privacy and Data Protection under Pressure: Transatlantic tensions, EU surveillance, and big data (Maklu 2017)

Verhellen E, Convention on the Rights of the Child – Background, Motivation, Strategies, Main Themes (Garant 2005)

Verheyde M, Article 28: The Right to Education (Martinus Nijhoff Publishers 2006)

Voorhoof D, Media(Recht) En Kinder(Recht)En (Mys & Breesch 1994)

—, 'Vrijheid van meningsuiting' in Yves Haeck and Johan Vande Lanotte (eds), Handboek EVRM : deel 2 : artikelsgewijze commentaar, vol 1 (Intersentia 2004)

Voorhoof D and Valcke P, Handboek mediarecht (Larcier 2014) <http://hdl.handle.net/1854/LU-5766382> accessed 25 July 2018

Waschefort G, International Law and Child Soldiers (Bloomsbury Publishing 2014)

Weijers I, 'Grondslagen van Jeugdstrafrecht', Jeugdstrafrecht in internationaal perspectief (3de edn, Boom Lemma uitgevers 2014) <https://www.jongbloed.nl/boek/9789089740212/jeugdstrafrecht-ido-weijers> accessed 16 November 2017

Wheaterill S, EU Consumer Law And Policy (2nd ed. edition, Edward Elgar Pub 2005)

Willems J, Developmental and Autonomy Rights of Children (2007) <http://intersentia.be/nl/developmental-and-autonomy-rights-of-children.html> accessed 8 November 2017

Williams A, 'Human Rights in the EU' in Damian Chalmers and Anthony Arnull (eds), The Oxford Handbook of European Union Law (Oxford University Press 2015) <www.oxfordhandbooks.com/view/10.1093/oxfordhb/9780199672646.001.0001/oxfordhb-9780199672646-e-10> accessed 17 July 2018

Weber F,, The Law and Economics of Enforcing European Consumer Law: A Comparative Analysis of Package Travel and Misleading Advertising (Routledge 2016)

B. ARTICLES IN JOURNALS

Altaweel I, Good N and Hoofnagle CJ, 'Web Privacy Census' [2015] Technology Science <https://papers.ssrn.com/sol3/papers.cfm?abstract_id=2703814> accessed 25 October 2017.

An S, Seung Jin H and Hae Park E, 'Children's Advertising Literacy for Advergames: Perception of the Game as Advertising' (2014) 43 Journal of Advertising 63.

An S and Stern S, 'Mitigating the Effects of Advergames on Children: Do Advertising Breaks Work?' (2011) 40 Journal of Advertising 43.

Ariely D and Berns GS, 'Neuromarketing: The Hope and Hype of Neuroimaging in Business' (2010) 11 Nature Reviews Neuroscience 284.

Arnould EJ and Thompson CJ, 'Consumer Culture Theory (CCT): Twenty Years of Research' (2005) 31 Journal of Consumer Research 868.

Austin MJ and Reed ML, 'Targeting Children Online: Internet Advertising Ethics Issues' (1999) 16 Journal of Consumer Marketing 590.

Auty S and Lewis C, 'Exploring Children's Choice: The Reminder Effect of Product Placement' (2004) 21 Psychology and Marketing 697.

Baarsma BE, 'Afwegingskader Bij Het Gebruik van Zelfreguleringsinstrumenten' (2010) 1 Tijdschrift voor Toezicht <https://dare.uva.nl/search?identifier=4dfccb8b-1f3e-41d3-898a-fcab1453b4f0> accessed 22 March 2018.

Bandura A and Walters RH, Social Learning and Personality Development (Holt, Rinehart and Winston 1963).

Banerjee R and Dittmar H, 'Individual Differences in Children's Materialism: The Role of Peer Relations' (2008) 34 Personality & Social Psychology Bulletin 17.

Besson S, 'The Principle of Non-Discrimination in the Convention on the Rights of the Child' (2005) 13 International Journal of Children's Rights 433.

Blume P, 'The Data Subject' (2015) 1 European Data Protection Law Review 258.

Boddewyn JJ, 'Advertising Self-Regulation: True Purpose and Limits' (1989) 18 Journal of Advertising 19.

Boerman SC, Kruikemeier S and Zuiderveen Borgesius FJ, 'Online Behavioral Advertising: A Literature Review and Research Agenda' (2017) 46 Journal of Advertising 363.

Borgesius FJZ and others, 'Tracking Walls, Take-It-Or-Leave-It Choices, the GDPR, and the EPrivacy Regulation' (2017) 3 European Data Protection Law Review 353.

Boush DM, Friestad M and Rose GM, 'Adolescent Skepticism toward TV Advertising and Knowledge of Advertiser Tactics' (1994) 21 Journal of Consumer Research 165.

Brasel SA, 'How Focused Identities Can Help Brands Navigate a Changing Media Landscape' (2012) 55 Business Horizons 283.

Bright LF and Daugherty T, 'Does Customization Impact Advertising Effectiveness? An Exploratory Study of Consumer Perceptions of Advertising in Customized Online Environments' (2012) 18 Journal of Marketing Communications 19.

Buijzen M and Valkenburg PM, 'The Effects of Television Advertising on Materialism, Parent–Child Conflict, and Unhappiness: A Review of Research' (2003) 24 Journal of Applied Developmental Psychology 437.

Buijzen M, Van Reijmersdal EA and Owen LH, 'Introducing the PCMC Model: An Investigative Framework for Young People's Processing of Commercialized Media Content' (2010) 20 Communication Theory 427.

Burleton E, 'The Self-Regulation of Advertising in Europe' (1982) 1 International Journal of Advertising 333.

Calvert SL, 'Children as Consumers: Advertising and Marketing' [2008] Journal of Consumer Research 205.

Castendyk O, 'Werbeintegration Im TV-Programm – Wann Sind Themen Placements Schleichwerbung Oder Sponsoring?' [2005] ZUM

Cauberghe V and De Pelsmacker P, 'Advergames: The Impact of Brand Prominence and Game Repetition on Brand Responses' (2010) 39 Journal of Advertising 5

Cheyne AD and others, 'Marketing Sugary Cereals to Children in the Digital Age: A Content Analysis of 17 Child-Targeted Websites' (2013) 18 Journal of Health Communication 563

Clark S, 'Child Rights and the Movement from Status to Agency: Human Rights and the Removal of the Legal Disabilities of Vulnerability' (2015) 84 Nordic Journal of International Law 183

Clifford D, 'EU Data Protection Law and Targeted Advertising: Consent and the Cookie Monster – Tracking the Crumbs of Online User Behaviour' (2014) 5 JIPITEC <www.jipitec.eu/issues/jipitec-5-3-2014/4095>

Clifford D and Verdoodt V, 'Integrative Advertising: The Marketing'dark Side'or Merely the Emperor's New Clothes?' (2017) 8 European Journal of Law and Technology <http://ejlt.org/article/view/547> accessed 8 August 2017

Collins TM, 'The Relationship between Children's Rights and Business' (2014) 18 The International Journal of Human Rights 582

Costa L, 'Privacy and the Precautionary Principle' (2012) Vol. 28 Computer Law & Security Review, 14

De Pauw P and others, 'From Persuasive Messages to Tactics: Exploring Children's Knowledge and Judgement of New Advertising Formats' [2017] New Media and Society 1

Eekelaar J, 'The Interests of the Child and the Child's Wishes: The Role of Dynamic Self-Determinism' (1994) 8 International Journal of Law, Policy and the Family 42

Etzioni A, 'On Protecting Children from Speech' (2004) 79 Chicago-Kent Law Review

Faure M, Ogus A and Philipsen N, 'Curbing Consumer Financial Losses: The Economics of Regulatory Enforcement' (2009) 31 Law & Policy 161

Folkvord F and others, 'The Effect of Playing Advergames That Promote Energy-Dense Snacks or Fruit on Actual Food Intake among Children' (2013) 97 The American Journal of Clinical Nutrition 239

Garde A, 'Advertising Regulation and the Protection of Children-Consumers in the European Union: In the Best Interests of … Commercial Operators?' [2011] International journal of children's rights 523

Garnett K and Parsons DJ, 'Multi-Case Review of the Application of the Precautionary Principle in European Union Law and Case Law' (2017) 37 Risk Analysis 502

Gerber P, Kyriakakis J and O'Byrne K, 'General Comment 16 on State Obligations Regarding the Impact of the Business Sector on Children's Rights: What Is Its Standing, Meaning and Effect?' [2013] Melbourne Journal of International Law <https://papers.ssrn.com/abstract=2319537> accessed 14 November 2017

Ghose A and Yang S, 'An Empirical Analysis of Search Engine Advertising: Sponsored Search in Electronic Markets' (2009) 55 Management Science 1605

Grimes SM, 'Kids' Ad Play: Regulating Children's Advergames in the Converging Media Context' (2008) 8 International Journal of Communications Law and Policy 162

Gross ML, 'Advergames and the Effects of Game-Product Congruity' (2010) 26 Computers in Human Behavior 1259

Gruen TW, Osmonbekov T and Czaplewski AJ, 'EWOM: The Impact of Customer-to-Customer Online Know-How Exchange on Customer Value and Loyalty' (2006) 59 Journal of Business Research 449

Hang H, 'Online Game Advertising and Children: A Literature Review', Advances in Advertising Research (University of Bath 2015) <http://opus.bath.ac.uk/45052/> accessed 7 November 2017

Harris JL, Bargh JA and Brownell KD, 'Priming Effects of Television Food Advertising on Eating Behavior' (2009) 28 Health Psychology: Official Journal of the Division of Health Psychology, American Psychological Association 404

Helberger N, Borgesius FJZ and Reyna A, 'The Perfect Match? A Closer Look at the Relationship between EU Consumer Law and Data Protection Law' (2017) 5 28

Hellemans L, Lievens E and Valcke P, 'Playing Hide-and-Seek? A Legal Perspective on the Complex Distinction between Commercial and Editorial Content in Hybrid Advertising Formats' (2015) 17 info 19

Henley N, Donovan RJ and Moorhead H, 'Appealing to Positive Motivations and Emotions in Social Marketing: Example of a Positive Parenting Campaign' (1998) 4 Social Marketing Quarterly 48

Hermanns O, Matzneller P and Nikoltchev S, 'The Regulation of On-Demand Audiovisual Services : Chaos or Coherence?' [2011] IRIS Special : The regulation of on-demand audiovisual services : chaos or coherence ?

Hildebrandt M, 'Profiling: From Data to Knowledge' (2006) 30 Datenschutz und Datensicherheit-DuD 548

Hudders L and others, 'Shedding New Light on How Advertising Literacy Can Affect Children's Processing of Embedded Advertising Formats: A Future Research Agenda' (2017) 46 Journal of Advertising 333

Hullett CR, 'The Impact of Mood on Persuasion: A Meta-Analysis' (2005) 32 Communication Research 423

Kabel J, 'The Search for Consistency in European Advertising Law' [2003] IRIS Plus, Legal Observations of the European Audiovisual Observatory 8

Kilkelly U, 'The Best of Both Worlds for Children's Rights? Interpreting the European Convention on Human Rights in the Light of the UN Convention on the Rights of the Child' (2001) 23 Human Rights Quarterly 308

King N and Wegener Jessen P, 'Profiling the Mobile Customer – Is Industry Self-Regulation Adequate to Protect Consumer Privacy When Behavioural Advertisers Target Mobile Phones? – Part II' (2010) 26 Computer Law & Security Review 595

Kirsch MS, 'Do-Not-Track: Revising the EU's Data Protection Framework to Require Meaningful Consent for Behavioral Advertising' (2011) 18 Rich. JL & Tech. 1

Koops BJ, 'The Trouble with European Data Protection Law.' [2014] International Data Privacy Law

Kosta E, 'Peeking into the Cookie Jar: The European Approach towards the Regulation of Cookies' (2013) 21 International Journal of Law and Information Technology 380

Kramera AD, Guillory JE and Hancock JT, 'Experimental Evidence of Massive-Scale Emotional Contagion through Social Networks' (2014) 111 PNAS 8788

Kuczerawy A, 'Intermediary Liability & Freedom of Expression: Recent Developments in the EU Notice & Action Initiative' (2015) 31 Computer Law & Security Review 46

Lambrecht I, Verdoodt V and Bellon J, 'Platforms and Commercial Communications Aimed at Children: A Playground under Legislative Reform?' [2018] International Review of Law, Computers and Technology

Lee JE and Watkins B, 'YouTube Vloggers' Influence on Consumer Luxury Brand Perceptions and Intentions' (2016) 69 Journal of Business Research 5753

Lerner JS and others, 'Emotion and Decision Making' (2015) 66 Annual Review of Psychology 799

Liefaard T and others, 'Het belang van het kind en de hooggespannen verwachtingen van het IVRK' (Boom Criminologie 2016) <http://hdl.handle.net/1887/45678> accessed 16 November 2017

Lievens E, 'The Use of Alternative Regulatory Instruments to Protect Minors in the Digital Era: Applying Freedom of Expression Safeguards' (2011) 29 Netherlands Quarterly of Human Rights 164

—, 'A Children's Rights Perspective on the Responsibility of Social Network Site Providers' (2014) <https://www.econstor.eu/bitstream/10419/101441/1/795276834.pdf> accessed 7 November 2017

—, 'Is Self-Regulation Failing Children and Young People? Assessing the Use of Alternative Regulatory Instruments in the Area of Social Networks', European media policy for the twenty-first century : assessing the past, setting agendas for the future (Routledge 2016)

Lievens E and Verdoodt V, 'Looking for Needles in a Haystack: Key Children's Rights Issues in the General Data Protection Regulation' [2017] Computer Law & Security Review

Lim Y, Chung Y and Weaver PA, 'The Impact of Social Media on Destination Branding: Consumer-Generated Videos versus Destination Marketer-Generated Videos' (2012) 18 Journal of Vacation Marketing 197

Little V, 'Audiovisual Media Services Directive: Europe's Modernization of Broadcast Services Regulations' [2008] Journal of Law, Technology & Policy 14

Livingstone S and Helsper EJ, 'Does Advertising Literacy Mediate the Effects of Advertising on Children? A Critical Examination of Two Linked Research Literatures in Relation to Obesity and Food Choice' (2006) 56 Journal of Communication 560

Lupton D and Williamson B, 'The Datafied Child: The Dataveillance of Children and Implications for Their Rights' (2017) 19 New Media & Society 780

Lynskey O, The Foundations of EU Data Protection Law (Oxford University Press 2015)

Macenaite M, 'Protecting Children's Privacy Online: A Critical Look to Four European Self-Regulatory Initiatives' (2016) 7 European Journal of Law and Technology <http://ejlt.org/article/view/473> accessed 21 June 2018

Macenaite M and Kosta E, 'Consent for Processing Children's Personal Data in the EU: Following in US Footsteps?' (2017) 26 Information & Communications Technology Law 146

Mallinckrodt V and Mizerski D, 'The Effects of Playing an Advergame on Young Children's Perceptions, Preferences, and Requests' (2007) 36 Journal of Advertising 87

Martin MC, 'Children's Understanding of the Intent of Advertising: A Meta-Analysis' [1997] Journal of Public Policy & Marketing 205

Mascheroni G, Jorge A and Farrugia L, 'Media Representations and Children's Discourses on Online Risks: Findings from Qualitative Research in Nine European Countries' (2014) 8 Cyberpsychology: Journal of Psychosocial Research on Cyberspace <https://cyberpsychology.eu/article/view/4310> accessed 18 July 2018

Matzneller P, 'GB-United Kingdom:ASA Upholds Complaint about Oreo Biscuit Ad in YouTube Videos' [2015] IRIS – Legal Observations of the European Audiovisual Observatory

McDermott L and others, 'International Food Advertising, Pester Power and Its Effects' (2006) 25 International Journal of Advertising 513

McGonagle T, 'A Survey and Critical Analysis of Council of Europe Strategies for Countering "Hate Speech"', The Content and Context of Hate Speech: Rethinking Regulation and Responses (Cambridge University Press 2012) <http://dare.uva.nl/search?metis.record.id=385322> accessed 8 November 2017

McMillan SJ and Hwang J-S, 'Measures of Perceived Interactivity: An Exploration of the Role of Direction of Communication, User Control, and Time in Shaping Perceptions of Interactivity' (2002) 31 Journal of Advertising 29

Metzdorf J, 'The Implementation of the Audiovisual Media Services Directive by National Regulatory Authorities National Responses to Regulatory Challenges' (2014) 5 JIPITEC <www.jipitec.eu/issues/jipitec-5-2-2014/3998>

Milkaite I and others, 'Roundtable Report: The General Data Protection Regulation and Children's Rights: Questions and Answers for Legislators, DPAs, Industry, Education, Stakeholders and Civil Society' (2017) <https://www.betterinternetforkids.eu/web/portal/practice/awareness/detail?articleId=2018677> accessed 26 July 2018

Montgomery KC and Chester J, 'Interactive Food and Beverage Marketing: Targeting Adolescents in the Digital Age' (2009) 45 Journal of Adolescent Health S18

—, 'Data Protection for Youth in the Digital Age: Developing a Rights-Based Global Framework' (2015) 1 European Data Protection Law Review 277

Moore ES and Rideout VJ, 'The Online Marketing of Food to Children: Is It Just Fun and Games?' (2007) 26 Journal of Public Policy & Marketing 202

Moore RS, Stammerjohan CA and Coulter RA, 'Banner Advertises-Website Context Congruity and Color Effects on Attention and Attitudes' (2005) 34 Journal of Advertising 71

Morin C, 'Neuromarketing: The New Science of Consumer Behavior' (2011) 48 Society 131.

Morrow V (2004) 15 Kings College Law Journal

Moschis GP and Churchill GA, 'Consumer Socialization: A Theoretical and Empirical Analysis' (1978) 15 Journal of Marketing Research 599

Nairn A and Fine C, 'Who's Messing with My Mind?: The Implications of Dual-Process Models for the Ethics of Advertising to Children' (2008) 27 International Journal of Advertising 447

Opree SJ and others, 'Children's Advertising Exposure, Advertised Product Desire, and Materialism: A Longitudinal Study' (2014) 41 Communication Research 717

Perse EM and Rubin RB, 'Attribution in Social and Parasocial Relationships' (1989) 16 Communication Research 59

Poullet Y, 'E-Youth before Its Judges – Legal Protection of Minors in Cyberspace' (2011) 27 Computer Law & Security Review 6

Raney AA and others, 'At the Movies, on the Web: An Investigation of the Effects of Entertaining and Interactive Web Content on Site and Brand Evaluations' (2003) 17 Journal of Interactive Marketing 38

Reed OLJ and Coalson JLJ, 'Eighteenth-Century Legal Doctrine Meets Twentieth-Century Marketing Techniques: F.T.C. Regulation of Emotionally Conditioning Advertising' (1976) 11 Georgia Law Review 733

Reijmersdal EA van and others, 'Disclosing the Persuasive Nature of Advergames: Moderation Effects of Mood on Brand Responses via Persuasion Knowledge' (2015) 34 International Journal of Advertising 70

Reynaert D, Bouverne-de-Bie M and Vandevelde S, 'A Review of Children's Rights Literature Since the Adoption of the United Nations Convention on the Rights of the Child' (2009) 16 Childhood 518

Rozendaal E and others, 'Reconsidering Advertising Literacy as a Defense Against Advertising Effects' (2011) 14 Media Psychology 333

—, 'Children's Responses to Advertising in Social Games' (2013) 42 Journal of Advertising 142

Rozendaal E, Buijzen M and Valkenburg P, 'Children's Understanding of Advertisers' Persuasive Tactics' 329

Schoefs R, 'Connected TV: Editorial Responsibility in a Converged Media Environment' (2014) 5 Droit des médias – Mediarecht 346

Sithigh DM, 'Multiplayer Games: Tax, Copyright, Consumers and the Video Game Industries' (2014) 5 European Journal of Law and Technology <http://ejlt.org/article/view/324> accessed 28 November 2017

Terlutter R and Capella ML, 'The Gamification of Advertising: Analysis and Research Directions of In-Game Advertising, Advergames, and Advertising in Social Network Games' (2013) 42 Journal of Advertising 95

Tobin J, 'Beyond the Supermarket Shelf: Using a Rights Based Approach to Address Children's Health Needs' (2006) 14 The International Journal of Children's Rights 275

Trusov M, Bucklin RE and Pauwels K, 'Effects of Word-of-Mouth versus Traditional Marketing: Findings from an Internet Social Networking Site' (2009) 73 Journal of marketing 90

Trzaskowski J, 'User-Generated Marketing – Legal Implications When Word-of-Mouth Goes Viral' (2011) 19 International Journal of Law and Information Technology 348

Tutaj K and van Reijmersdal EA, 'Effects of Online Advertising Format and Persuasion Knowledge on Audience Reactions' (2012) 18 Journal of Marketing Communications 5

Valcke P and Lievens E, 'Rethinking European Broadcasting Regulation: Unraveling Europe's Policy for the Digital Media Landscape: Critical Analysis of the Audiovisual Media Services Directive' (VUB Press 2009)

van der Hof S, 'I Agree, or Do I: A Rights-Based Analysis of the Law on Children's Consent in the Digital World' (2016) 34 Wis. Int'l LJ 409

van der Hof S and Lievens E, 'The Importance of Privacy by Design and Data Protection Impact Assessments in Strengthening Protection of Children's Personal Data under the GDPR' (2018) 23 Communications Law 33.

van Doorn J. and Hoekstra J.C., 'Customization of Online Advertising: The Role of Intrusiveness' (2013) 24 Marketing Letters 339

Van Eecke P, 'Online Service Providers and Liability: A Plea for a Balanced Approach' (2011101) 48 Common Market Law Review 1455

Verbruggen P, 'Gorillas in the Closet? Public and Private Actors in the Enforcement of Transnational Private Regulation' 7 Regulation & Governance 512

Verdoodt V, Clifford D and Lievens E, 'Toying with Children's Emotions, the New Game in Town? The Legality of Advergames in the EU' (2016) 32 Computer Law & Security Review 599

Verdoodt V and Lievens E, 'De AVG Bekeken Vanuit Een Kinderrechtenperspectief Pluspunten, Knelpunten & Vraagstukken' [2017] Computerrecht

Voorhoof D, 'European Court of Human Rights: Bohlen and Ernst August von Hannover v. Germany' (IRIS Merlin – The Audiovisual Law Information Wizard) <http://merlin.obs.coe.int/iris/2015/5/article1.en.html> accessed 30 August 2018.

Waiguny MKJ, Nelson MR and Terlutter R, 'The Relationship of Persuasion Knowledge, Identification of Commercial Intent and Persuasion Outcomes in Advergames – the Role of Media Context and Presence' (2014) 37 Journal of Consumer Policy 257

Ward J, 'CAP Guidance on Vlogging Advertising' [2016] Entertainment Law 49

Wauters E, Donoso V and Lievens E, 'Optimizing Transparency for Users in Social Networking Sites' (2014) 16 info 8

Weber F, 'The Law and Economics of Self-Regulation in Advertising' (2014) 3 Journal of European Consumer and Market Law 5

Wojdynski BW and Evans NJ, 'Going Native: Effects of Disclosure Position and Language on the Recognition and Evaluation of Online Native Advertising' (2016) 45 Journal of Advertising 157

Wolak J and others, 'Online "Predators" and Their Victims: Myths, Realities, and Implications for Prevention and Treatment.' (2008) 63 American Psychologist 111

Yan J and others, 'How Much Can Behavioral Targeting Help Online Advertising?', Proceedings of the 18th international conference on World wide web (ACM 2009) <http://dl.acm.org/citation.cfm?id=1526745> accessed 25 October 2017

Zarouali B and others, 'Adolescents' Advertising Competences and Institutional Privacy Protection Strategies on Social Networking Sites: Implications for Regulation'

—, 'Online Reclamewijsheid Bij Kinderen: Herkennen En Begrijpen van Reclamebanners En de Rol van Need for Cognition En Reclamewijsheidslessen' (2016) 44 Tijdschrift voor communicatiewetenschap.-Houten 24

—, 'The Impact of Online Peer Communication on Adolescents' Persuasion Knowledge and Attitudes toward Social Advertising', Paper presented at Etmaal van de Communicatiewetenschap 2017 (2017)

—, '"Do You like Cookies?" Adolescents' Skeptical Processing of Retargeted Facebook-Ads and the Moderating Role of Privacy Concern and a Textual Debriefing' (2017) 69 Computers in Human Behavior 157

Zuiderveen Borgesius FJ, 'Personal Data Processing for Behavioural Targeting: Which Legal Basis?' (2015) 5 International Data Privacy Law 163

—, 'Mensen Aanwijzen Maar Niet Bij Naam Noemen: Behavioural Targeting, Persoonsgegevens En de Nieuwe Privacyverordening' [2016] Tijdschrift voor Consumentenrecht en handelspraktijken <https://www.ivir.nl/publicaties/download/1786> accessed 17 October 2017

C. PHD THESES

De Pauw P, 'Children's Advertising Literacy: Empowering Children to Cope with Advertising – A Multi-Perspective Inquiry in Children's Abilities to Critically Process Contemporary Advertising' (Ghent University 2018)

Rozendaal E, Advertising Literacy and Children's Susceptibility to Advertising (2011) <https://dare.uva.nl/search?identifier=59a96c2a-1dd8-4fbc-8ac1-1c0cf4836420> accessed 8 February 2018

Van Alsenoy B, 'Regulating Data Protection: The Allocation of Responsibility and Risk among Actors Involved in Personal Data Processing' (KU Leuven 2016)

Zuiderveen Borgesius FJ, 'Improving Privacy Protection in the Area of Behavioural Targeting' (University of Amsterdam IViR 2015)

4. MISCELLANEOUS

A. INTERNET AND WORKING PAPERS

Al Abbas A, Chen W and Saberi M, 'The Impact of Neuromarketing Advertising on Children' <www.wasd.org.uk/wp-content/uploads/2017/05/AMANI-AL-ABBAS.pdf> accessed 13 August 2018.

Beales H, 'The Value of Behavioral Targeting' (2010) 1 Network Advertising Initiative <https://pdfs.semanticscholar.org/e2eb/6726f5a29d9c14dafaf056be9a3ade877b0a.pdf> accessed 24 October 2017.

Chiarella ML, 'The Regulation of Child Consumption in European Law: Rights, Market and New Perspectives' (Social Science Research Network 2009) SSRN

Scholarly Paper ID 1440251 <https://papers.ssrn.com/abstract=1440251> accessed 28 November 2017

Christl W, Kopp K and Riechert PU, 'How Companies Use Personal Data against People' (Cracked Lab – Institute for Critical Digital Culture 2017) <http://crackedlabs.org/dl/CrackedLabs_Christl_DataAgainstPeople.pdf> accessed 13 October 2017

Clifford D, 'Citizen-Consumers in a Personalised Galaxy: Emotion Influenced Decision-Making, a True Path to the Dark Side?' (2017)

Clifford D and Verdoodt V, 'Ad-Blocking-the Dark Side of Consumer Empowerment: A New Hope or Will the Empire Strike Back?' (2016)

Humphreys L and Santos C, 'Mapping Recitals to Normative Provisions in EU Legislation to Assist Legal Interpretation' <http://icr.uni.lu/leonvandertorre/papers/jurix2015.pdf> accessed 27 July 2018

Lodder A, 'European Union E-Commerce Directive – Article by Article Comments' (Social Science Research Network 2007) SSRN Scholarly Paper ID 1009945 <https://papers.ssrn.com/abstract=1009945> accessed 22 November 2017

Steiner T, 'Advertising in Online Games and EC Audiovisual Media Regulation' (Social Science Research Network 2008) SSRN Scholarly Paper ID 1101363 <https://papers.ssrn.com/abstract=1101363> accessed 22 November 2017

van der Sloot B, 'Where Is the Harm in a Privacy Violation? Calculating the Damages Afforded in Privacy Cases by the European Court of Human Rights' (2017) 4 <https://bartvandersloot.com/onewebmedia/Bart%20van%20der%20Sloot%20-%20PLSC.pdf> accessed 29 August 2018.

B. RESEARCH REPORTS

'Acumen Report: Youth Video Diet' (Defy Media) <http://defymedia.com/wp-content/uploads/2017/11/Acumen_DL_booklet_16_12_04.pdf> accessed 29 November 2017.

Angelopoulos C, Product Placement in European Audiovisual Productions (European Audiovisual Observatory 2010) <http://dare.uva.nl/search?metis.record.id=337442> accessed 25 July 2018.

Barnabé D and others, 'The Effect of Advertising and Marketing Practices on Child Obesity, A Study Requested by the European Parliament's Committee on the Environment, Public Health and Food Safety.' (2007).

BEUC, 'Data Collection, Targeting and Profiling of Consumers Online' (2010) BEUC discussion paper <www.beuc.eu/publications/2010-00101-01-e.pdf> accessed 26 October 2017.

Blázquez FJC and others, 'On-Demand Services and the Material Scope of the AVMSD' [2016] IRIS Plus, European Audiovisual Observatory 74.

Blázquez J and others, 'Commercial Communications in the AVMSD Revision, IRIS Plus' (European Audiovisual Observatory 2017) <www.obs.coe.int/documents/205595/8682894/IRIS+Plus+2017-2+Commercial+communications+in+the+AVMSD+revision/783f02df-ff10-447c-a144-43b70b19b218> accessed 13 October 2017.

Canetta E and others, 'EU Framework of Law for Children's Rights' (European Parliament) <www.europarl.europa.eu/RegData/etudes/note/join/2012/462445/IPOL-LIBE_NT(2012)462445_EN.pdf> accessed 12 July 2018

Capello M and Nikoltchev S (eds), New Forms of Commercial Communications in a Converged Audiovisual Sector (2014)

Cauberghe V and others, 'Reclamewijsheid Bij Kinderen En Jongeren: Onderzoeksrapport in Opdracht van Vlaams Ministerie van Cultuur, Jeugd, Sport En Media' (2012) <https://biblio.ugent.be/publication/4130480/file/4130494> accessed 25 October 2017

Chaudron S and others, Young Children (0–8) and Digital Technology: A Qualitative Exploratory Study across Seven Countries. (Publications Office 2015) <http://dx.publications.europa.eu/10.2788/00749> accessed 6 November 2017

—, 'Kaleidoscope on the Internet of Toys – Safety, Security, Privacy and Societal Insights' (European Commission) JRC Technical Report <http://publications.jrc.ec.europa.eu/repository/bitstream/JRC105061/jrc105061_final_online.pdf> accessed 6 February 2018

Children's Rights Alliance, 'Briefing Note on the Optional Protocol to the UN Convention on the Rights of the Child on a Communications Procedure' <www.childrensrights.ie/sites/default/files/information_sheets/files/BriefingNoteUNCRC3rdOptProtocol170914.pdf> accessed 12 July 2018

Closs W, Nikoltchev S and European Audiovisual Observatory (eds), The Regulation of On-Demand Audiovisual Services: Chaos or Coherence? (European Audiovisual Observatory : Council of Europe 2011)

Cole M, 'New Forms of Commercial Communications in a Converged Audiovisual Sector' [2014] Observatory/Observatoire/Informationsstellen-Shop <http://shop.obs.coe.int/en/iris-legal-publications/23-iris-special-new-forms-of-commercial-communications-in-a-converged-audiovisual-sector.html> accessed 16 April 2018

Committee on Consumer Policy, 'Industry Self-Regulation: Role and Use in Supporting Consumer Interest' (OECD 2015) www.oecd.org/officialdocuments/publicdisplaydocumentpdf/?cote=DSTI/CP(2014)4/FINAL&docLanguage=En

Daems K and De Pelsmacker P, 'Marketing Communication Techniques Aimed at Children and Teenagers. A Research Report within the Frame of the AdLit Project.' (2015) <www.AdLit.be/output> accessed 11 July 2018

Directorate of the Jurisconsult of the European Court of Human Rights, 'Guide on Article 6 of the European Convention on Human Rights – Right to a Fair Trial' <https://www.echr.coe.int/Documents/Guide_Art_6_ENG.pdf> accessed 17 May 2018

DLA Piper, 'European Telecommunications Network Operator's Association (ETNO) Study on the Revision of the EPrivacy Directive' (2016) <https://etno.eu/datas/publications/studies/DPTS_Study_DLA_04082016_ePrivacy_Final.pdf> accessed 16 April 2018

European Audiovisual Observatory, 'Co-Regulation of the Media in Europe' (2003) <https://www.ivir.nl/publicaties/download/IRIS-Special-Co-regulation-of-the-Media-in-Europe.pdf> accessed 31 July 2018

—, The Protection of Minors in the Case of New (Non-Linear) Media – European Legal Rules and Their National Transposition and Application (Susanne Nikoltchev ed, Council of Europe 2012)

European Union Agency for Fundamental Rights, 'Handbook on European Law Relating to the Rights of the Child' (2015) <http://fra.europa.eu/en/publication/2015/handbook-european-law-child-rights> accessed 12 July 2018

—, 'Mapping Minimum Age Requirements Concerning the Rights of the Child in the EU' (2017) <http://fra.europa.eu/en/publication/2017/mapping-minimum-age-requirements-concerning-rights-child-eu> accessed 4 January 2018

European Union Agency for Fundamental Rights and Council of Europe (eds), Handbook on European Data Protection Law (Re-ed, Publ Office of the Europ Union [u.a] 2014) <https://www.echr.coe.int/Documents/Handbook_data_protection_ENG.pdf> accessed 25 July 2018

Faculty of Law Antwerp, 'Access to Remedy in Belgium – The United Nations Guiding Principles on Business and Human Rights (UNGP) in Belgium, State-Based Judicial and Non-Judicial Mechanisms That Provide Access to a Remedy' (Federal Institute for Sustainable Development (FISD 2017) <https://www.sdgs.be/sites/default/files/publication/attachments/brochure_acces_to_remedy_in_belgium_2017.pdf> accessed 16 July 2018

Fenstad JE and Matsuura K, 'The Precautionary Principle, World Commission on the Ethics of Scientific Knowledge and Technology (Published by UNESCO)' 52

Helberger N, 'Form Matters: Informing Consumers Effectively – (Study Commissioned by BEUC)' <www.beuc.eu/publications/x2013_089_upa_form_matters_september_2013.pdf.> accessed 26 July 2018

Hans Bredow Institute for Media Research 'INDIREG – Indicators for Independence and Efficient Functioning of Audiovisual Media Services Regulatory Bodies for the Purpose of Enforcing the Rules in the AVMS Directive' (Hans Bredow Institute for Media Research 2011) <http://ec.europa.eu/archives/information_society/avpolicy/docs/library/studies/regulators/final_report.pdf> accessed 5 July 2018

Kabel J, 'Swings on the Horizontal – The Search for Consistency in European Advertising Law. Legal Observations of the European Audiovisual Observatory' (Council of Europe, European Audiovisual Observatory 1994)

Livingstone S, Carr J and Byrne J, 'One in Three: Internet Governance and Children's Rights' (Centre for International Governance Innovation and the Royal Institute of International Affairs 2015) 22 <https://www.cigionline.org/publications/one-three-internet-governance-and-childrens-rights> accessed 11 July 2018

Livingstone S, Haddon L and London school of economics and political science, EU Kids Online: Final Report. (London school of economics and political science 2009)

Lupiáñez-Villanueva F and others, 'Study on the Impact of Marketing through Social Media, Online Games and Mobile Applications on Children's Behaviour' (European Commission 2016) <http://ec.europa.eu/consumers/consumer_evidence/behavioural_research/docs/final_report_impact_marketing_children_final_version_approved_en.pdf> accessed 10 November 2017

Ólafsson K, Livingstone S and Haddon L, 'Children's Use of Online Technologies in Europe' 40

Ruxton S, 'Children's Rights in the European Union: What about Us? : Next Steps. Brussels: The European Children's Network' (2005) <https://www.crin.org/en/docs/Ruxton%20Report_WhatAboutUs.pdf> accessed 8 November 2017

Sartor DG, 'Providers Liability: From the ECommerce Directive to the Future' (European University Institute 2017)

Third A and others, Children's Rights in the Digital Age [Documento Elettronico]: A Download from Children around the World (Young and Well Cooperative Research Centre 2014)

Van Alsenoy B, 'Rights and Obligations of Actors in Social Networking Sites' <https://lirias.kuleuven.be/handle/123456789/453689> accessed 4 August 2017

—, 'From Social Media Service to Advertising Network – A Critical Analysis of Facebook's Revised Policies and Terms' <https://www.law.kuleuven.be/citip/en/news/item/facebooks-revised-policies-and-terms-v1-2.pdf>

Van Alsenoy B and Verdoodt V, 'Liability and Accountability of Actors in Social Networking Sites, Spion Project' (2014)

Van Boom WH and others, 'Handelspraktijken, Reclame En Zelfregulering: Pilotstudy Maatschappelijke Reguleringsinstrumenten' (Ten verzoeke van: Wetenschappelijk Ond erzoek – en Documentatiecentrum Ministerie van Justitie 2009) <www.professorvanboom.eu/pdf_files/2009_eindrapportage_Pilotstudy_zelfregulering.pdf> accessed 3 July 2018

Verbruggen P, 'Case Study Report – Transnational Private Regulation in the Advertising Industry. Conducted within the Framework of the Research Project Constitutional Foundations of Transnational Private Regulation' (2011) <www.hiil.org/data/sitemanagement/media/HiiL%20Case%20Study%20Advertising%20Executive%20Summary.pdf> accessed 12 July 2018

Van Wezenbeeck I and others, 'Minors' Advertising Literacy in Relation to New Advertising Formats – Identification and Assessment of the Risks' (2016) <www.adlit.be> accessed 16 November 2017

Verdoodt V, Lambrecht I and Lievens E, 'Mapping and Analysis of the Current Self- and Co-Regulatory Framework on Commercial Communication Aimed at Minors. A Report in the Framework of the AdLit SBO Project.' <www.adlit.be> accessed 20 November 2017

Verdoodt V, Lievens E and Hellemans L, 'Mapping and Analysis of the Current Legal Framework of Advertising Aimed at Minors.' (2015) <www.adlit.be/output>

Verdoodt V, Lievens E and Hellemans L, 'Mapping and Analysis of the Current Legal Framework on Commercial Communication Aimed at Minors. A Report in the Framework of the AdLit Research Project.' (2015) <www.adlit.be> accessed 20 November 2017

Zarouali B and others, 'Mediabezit En –Gebruik Bij Minderjarigen. Een Rapport in Het Kader van Het AdLit Onderzoeksproject' (2015) <www.adlit.be/output> accessed 11 July 2018

C. POLICY BRIEFS AND STATEMENTS

BEUC, 'Position Paper: Proposal for a Regulation on Privacy and Electronic Communications (e-Privacy)' <www.beuc.eu/publications/beuc-x-2017-059_proposal_for_a_regulation_on_privacy_and_electronic_communications_e-privacy.pdf> accessed 3 April 2018.

Conway L, 'The Role of the Advertising Standards Authority' <https://researchbriefings.parliament.uk/ResearchBriefing/Summary/SN06130> accessed 8 August 2018

Lievens E and Directorate-General for Internal Policies of the Union, Research for CULT Committee Solutions and Policy Dilemmas Regarding Minors' Protection Online: In-Depth Analysis. (2018)

Martuzzi M and Tickner J, The Precautionary Principle: Protecting Public Health, the Environment and the Future of Our Children (WHO Regional Office for Europe 2004) <www.euro.who.int/__data/assets/pdf_file/0003/91173/E83079.pdf> accessed 9 April 2018

Myrstad F, 'Connected toys violate European consumer law: Forbrukerrådet' (6 December 2016) <https://www.forbrukerradet.no/siste-nytt/connected-toys-violate-consumer-laws/> accessed 23 July 2018

Nairn A and Hang H, 'Advergames: It's Not Child's Play: A Review of Research' (Commissioned by the Family and Parenting Institute 2012) <www.agnesnairn.co.uk/policy_reports/advergames-its-not-childs-play.pdf> accessed 8 November 2017

Savirimuthu J, 'Unfair Commercial Practies, the Consumer Child and New Technologies: What Should We Regulate? Some Policy Provocations' (2014) <https://www.liverpool.ac.uk/media/livacuk/law/european-childrens-rights-unit/BriefingNote.pdf> accessed 13 November 2017

Senden LAJ and others, 'Mapping Self- and Co-Regulation Approaches in the EU Context' (Utrecht Centre for Shared Regulation and Enforcement in Europe 2015) <https://ec.europa.eu/digital-single-market/en/content/mapping-self-and-co-regulation-approaches-eu-context> accessed 7 August 2018

Sheahan F, 'Translating the Right to Non-Discrimination into Reality. Save the Children' (2005) <https://resourcecentre.savethechildren.net/sites/default/files/documents/2617.pdf> accessed 8 November 2017

Voorhees T, Spiegel DL and Cooper D, 'Neuromarketing: Legal and Policy Issues' <https://www.cov.com/files/upload/White_Paper_Neuromarketing_Legal_and_Policy_Issues.pdf> accessed 28 August 2018.

D. CONFERENCE PROCEEDINGS

Anteunis ML and van Noort G, 'Interactivity Effects in Social Media Marketing on Brand Engagement: An Investigation of Underlying Mechanisms, The 10th ICORIA Conference Berlin' (2011).

Cannie H and Voorhoof D, 'Audiovisuele media, reclame en minderjarigen: Veel regels, maar weinig toezicht, Etmaal van de Communicatiewetenschap' (2010) 8.

Covington P, Adams J and Sargin E, 'Deep Neural Networks for YouTube Recommendations' (ACM Conference Press 2016) <http://dl.acm.org/citation.cfm?doid=2959100.2959190> accessed 7 December 2017

Hudders L and others, 'Children's Advertising Literacy in a New Media Environment: An Introduction to the AdLit Research Project', *Etmaal van de Communicatiewetenschap, Proceedings* (2015) <http://hdl.handle.net/1854/LU-5811593> accessed 5 February 2018

Wilks L and others, 'Mapping Exercise Report on Self-Regulation. Prepared for the European Commission DG SANCO Institute for Social Marketing. The Open University & University of Stirling.' <https://ec.europa.eu/health/archive/ph_determinants/life_style/alcohol/forum/docs/regulation_en.pdf> accessed 12 July 2018

E. DOCUMENTS OR ONLINE INFORMATION BY ALTERNATIVE REGULATORY BODIES

Advertising Code Authority [Stichting Reclame Code], 'Yearly Report [Jaarverslag]' (2017) <https://www.reclamecode.nl/bijlagen/SRC_JV2017_internet.pdf> accessed 3 July 2018.

—, 'The Dutch Advertising Code and the Advertising Code Committee [De Nederlandse Reclame Code En de Reclame Code Commissie]' <https://www.reclamecode.nl/bijlagen/SRC_brochure_totaal_sep17.pdf> accessed 5 July 2018.

Advertising Standards Authority, 'Non-Broadcast Complaint Handling Procedures' <https://www.asa.org.uk/asset/171EB506-B4EF-4FEC-BDCEC62DC49E0BE2.1759E419-AD92-452B-865FC913C62CE312/> accessed 8 August 2018.

—, 'About the ASA and CAP' <www.asa.org.uk/about-asa-and-cap/about-regulation/about-the-asa-and-cap.html> accessed 7 June 2018.

—, 'Making a Complaint' <https://www.asa.org.uk/asset/8C4ECE0C-1EFA-43B9-885C0D18480E3F94/> accessed 8 August 2018.

—, 'Our History' <www.asa.org.uk/about-asa-and-cap/our-history.html> accessed 8 August 2018.

—, 'Our Proactive Work' <www.asa.org.uk/about-asa-and-cap/the-work-we-do/our-proactive-work.html> accessed 8 August 2018.

—, 'Video Blogs: Scenarios' <www.asa.org.uk/advice-online/video-blogs-scenarios.html> accessed 13 February 2018.

—, 'Working with Others' <www.asa.org.uk/about-asa-and-cap/the-work-we-do/working-with-others.html> accessed 7 August 2018.

Advertising Standards Authority and Committees of Advertising Practice, 'Annual Report 2017' (2017) <https://www.asa.org.uk/uploads/assets/uploaded/34872c48-106e-4f5f-a92983c95e92c84b.pdf> accessed 19 June 2018.

Dutch Advertising Code Authority, 'The Dutch Advertising Code – Information about the Working Procedures of the Advertising Code Committee and the Board of Appeal' <https://www.reclamecode.nl/bijlagen/20120701_NRC_Engels.pdf> accessed 29 June 2018

European Advertising Standards Alliance, Blue Book: Advertising Self-Regulation in Europe and Beyond (2010)

European Advertising Standards Alliance, 'Best Practice Recommendation on Online Behavioural Advertising' <www.easa-alliance.org/sites/default/files/EASA%20Best%20Practice%20Recommendation%20on%20Online%20Behavioural%20Advertising_0.pdf> accessed 12 April 2018

FEDMA, 'Code on E-Commerce & Interactive Marketing' <www.oecd.org/internet/ieconomy/2091875.pdf> accessed 26 July 2018

—, 'European Code of Practice for the Use of Personal Data in Direct Marketing' <https://ec.europa.eu/digital-single-market/en/content/european-code-practice-use-personal-data-direct-marketing> accessed 26 July 2018

—, 'European Code of Practice for the Use of Personal Data in Direct Marketing – Electronic Communications Annex (the On-Line Annex)' <http://ec.europa.eu/justice/data-protection/article-29/documentation/opinion-recommendation/files/2010/wp174_annex_en.pdf> accessed 14 November 2017

IAB Europe, 'EU Framework for Online Behavioural Advertising.' <www.iabeurope.eu/wp-content/uploads/2016/05/2013–11–11-IAB-Europe-OBA-Framework_.pdf> accessed 27 July 2018

International Chamber of Commerce, 'Interpretation of the Consolidated ICC Code' (2014) <www.codescentre.com/icc-code/general-provisions.aspx#gen1> accessed 31 July 2018

—, 'ICC Releases Statement on Age Considerations for Marketing and Advertising to Children and Teens – ICC – International Chamber of Commerce' (2016) <https://iccwbo.org/media-wall/news-speeches/icc-releases-statement-age-considerations-marketing-advertising-children-teens/> accessed 31 July 2018

—, 'ICC and the Code' <www.codescentre.com/about-us.aspx> accessed 31 July 2018

—, 'Consolidated Code of Advertising and Marketing Practice' <https://cdn.iccwbo.org/content/uploads/sites/3/2011/08/ICC-Consolidated-Code-of-Advertising-and-Marketing-2011-English.pdf> accessed 14 November 2017

—, 'Policy Statement on Freedom of Commercial Communication, 240/474 Rev'

—, 'Rules of the JEP [Reglement van de JEP]' <https://www.jep.be/sites/default/files/inline-media/reglement_jep_nl_-_februari_2017.pdf> accessed 8 June 2018

JEP, 'Yearly report 2016' <https://www.jep.be/sites/default/files/year_report/jaarverslag_2016_nl_-_hyperlinks.pdf> accessed 6 June 2018

Raad voor de Reclame, 'Reglementering van En Controle Op de Reclame – Repertorium Op 1 Januari 2013. 8th Edition.'

—, 'De Raad Voor de Reclame Wil de Europese Verankering van de JEP Versterken' (2016) <www.raadvoordereclame.be/nl/dossiers/115-de-raad-voor-de-reclame-wil-de-europese-verankering-van-de-jep-versterken> accessed 7 August 2018

Stichting Reclame Code, 'Stichting Reclame Code: Wie Zijn Wij?' <https://www.reclamecode.nl/adverteerder/default.asp?paginaID=1&hID=1> accessed 3 July 2018

F. NEWS ARTICLES

Advertising Standards Authority, Committees of Advertising, 'New Vlogging Advertising Guidance' <www.asa.org.uk/news/new-vlogging-advertising-guidance.html> accessed 15 February 2018.

Berg M, 'The Highest-Paid YouTube Stars 2016: PewDiePie Remains No. 1 With $15 Million' (Forbes) <https://www.forbes.com/sites/maddieberg/2016/12/05/the-highest-paid-youtube-stars-2016-pewdiepie-remains-no-1-with-15-million/> accessed 15 December 2017.

Costine J, 'Facebook Launches Watch Tab of Original Video Shows' (Techcrunch, 9 August 2017) <https://techcrunch.com/2017/08/09/facebook-watch/> accessed 15 December 2017

Flynn K, 'Musical.Ly Is Quietly Starting Another Big Advertising Push' <https://digiday.com/marketing/musical-ly-quietly-starting-another-big-advertising-push/> accessed 22 August 2018.

Jackson J, 'Children Spending Less Time in Front of the TV as They Turn to Online Media' The Guardian (6 August 2015) <www.theguardian.com/media/2015/aug/06/children-spending-less-time-in-front-of-tv-ofcom> accessed 7 December 2017

Meindersma C, 'Nieuwe Regels Voor YouTubers, de Social Code' (Marketingfacts, 21 November 2017) <https://www.marketingfacts.nl/berichten/nieuwe-regels-voor-youtubers-de-social-code> accessed 15 February 2018

Stokel-Walker C, 'Vloggers Unite: Youtubers Are Getting Organized after a Decade of Exploitation' Newsweek (8 October 2016) <www.newsweek.com/vloggers-youtube-organized-decade-exploitation-507592> accessed 11 December 2017

'Voorlopig toch geen strengere regels voor influencers' (De Standaard) <www.standaard.be/cnt/dmf20180515_03513682> accessed 2 August 2018

G. WEBSOURCES

Barkho G, 'Inside Instagram Pods: The Secret Trick to Increase Your Engagement' (Later Blog, 23 February 2017) <https://later.com/blog/instagram-pods/> accessed 18 January 2018.

Cadiot S, 'Status Update on the EU E-Privacy Regulation Proposal Discussions' (The WSGR Data Advisor, 1 September 2017) <https://www.wsgrdataadvisor.com/2017/09/eu-e-privacy-regulation/> accessed 3 April 2018.

Cavaliere FJ, 'People Can Make More Money on YouTube than Most Lawyers Earn – Is That Even Legal' (2016) <www.webwiselawyer.com>

Dheur J, 'Belgian CSA Conference – The Platform Is the Message' (2016) <www.csa.be/system/documents_files/2591/original/CI_20160310_The%20Platform%20is%20the%20Message_report.pdf?1458160565> accessed 11 December 2017

Ehle K, 'Digital Single Market Update: The European Commission's Proposal to Revise the Audiovisual Media Services Directive' (Lexology) <https://www.lexology.com/library/detail.aspx?g=dc9d66d9-f916-4f0b-b0cc-f3b6e2f45de4> accessed 15 December 2017

'EU Audiovisual and Media Policies – Historical Framework| Europa' <http://ec.europa.eu/archives/information_society/avpolicy/reg/history/index_en.htm> accessed 23 July 2018

'EU Audiovisual and Media Policies – History of TVwF| Europa' <http://ec.europa.eu/archives/information_society/avpolicy/reg/history/historytvwf/index_en.htm> accessed 23 July 2018

European Economic and Social Committee, 'The Database on Self- and Co-Regulation Initiatives: Federation of European Direct and Interactive Marketing (FEDMA)' (29 January 2007) <https://www.eesc.europa.eu/en/policies/policy-areas/enterprise/database-self-and-co-regulation-initiatives/48> accessed 25 July 2018

Federal Trade Commission, 'Complying with COPPA: Frequently Asked Questions – A Guide for Business and Parents and Small Entity Compliance Guide.' (Federal Trade

Commission, 20 March 2015) <https://www.ftc.gov/tips-advice/business-center/guidance/complying-coppa-frequently-asked-questions> accessed 26 July 2018

—, 'FTC Grants Approval for New COPPA Verifiable Parental Consent Method' (Federal Trade Commission, 19 November 2015) <https://www.ftc.gov/news-events/press-releases/2015/11/ftc-grants-approval-new-coppa-verifiable-parental-consent-method> accessed 26 July 2018

Fisk N, 'The Limits of Parental Consent in an Algorithmic World.' (LSE Media Policy Project Blog, 2016) <http://blogs.lse.ac.uk/mediapolicyproject/2016/11/28/the-limits-of-parental-consent-in- an-algorithmic-world/>

Global Privacy Enforcement Network, 'Children's Privacy Sweep' (2015) <http://194.242.234.211/documents/10160/0/GPEN+Privacy+Sweep+2015.pdf

Johnson N and Graham G, 'The Draft EPrivacy Regulation and Its Impact on Online Advertising and Direct Marketing' (Osborne Clarke LLP, 2017) <http://marketinglaw.osborneclarke.com/wp-content/uploads/sites/4/2017/04/DBL-January-2017–4–6.pdf>

Lievens E and Milkaite M, 'Better Internet for Kids – Age of Consent in the GDPR: Updated Mapping' (2017) <https://www.betterinternetforkids.eu/web/portal/practice/awareness/detail?articleId=2019355> accessed 26 July 2018

Livingstone S and Olafsson K, 'Children's Commercial Media Literacy: New Evidence Relevant to UK Policy Decisions Regarding the GDPR. LSE Media Policy Project Blog.' (Media Policy Project, 2017) <http://blogs.lse.ac.uk/mediapolicyproject/2017/01/26/childrens-commercial-media-literacy-new-evidence-relevant-to-uk-policy-decisions-regarding-the-gdpr/> accessed 17 July 2018

Medietilsynet, 'Advertisement, Sponsorship and Product Placement' (Medietilsynet) <www.medietilsynet.no/en/for-media-businesses/advertisement-sponsorhip-and-product-placement/> accessed 15 February 2018

Milkaite I, 'Sekmadienis Ltd. v. Lithuania: Can Religious Figures Be Featured in Commercial Advertising?' <https://strasbourgobservers.com/2018/03/13/sekmadienis-ltd-v-lithuania-can-religious-figures-be-featured-in-commercial-advertising/> accessed 30 August 2018.

'Schriftelijke Vraag Nr. 306 Door Katia Segers Aan Sven Gatz, Vlaams Minister van Cultuur, Media, Jeugd En Brussel: Jury Voor Ethische Praktijken – Klachtenbehandeling' <http://docs.vlaamsparlement.be/pfile?id=1287066> accessed 9 August 2018

Secretariat of the European Social Charter, 'Children's Rights under the European Social Charter' <https://rm.coe.int/1680474a4b> accessed 14 January 2018

Szajkowska A, 'The Impact of the Definition of the Precautionary Principle in EU Food Law' 24

Wharton University, 'A New Marketing Royalty: Why Digital Influencers Are on the Rise' (Knowledge@Wharton) <http://knowledge.wharton.upenn.edu/article/new-marketing-royalty-rise-digital-influencers/> accessed 20 November 2017

Woods L, 'Audiovisual Media Services Regulation and The "Newspaper Exception"'' <http://eulawanalysis.blogspot.com/2015/10/audiovisual-media-services-regulation.html> accessed 24 November 2017

YouTube Vloggers, 'Social Code: Richtlijnen Voor Reclame in Online Videos' (2017) <https://www.cvdm.nl/wp-content/uploads/2017/11/Social_Code_YouTube.pdf> accessed 15 February 2018

KU Leuven Centre for IT & IP Law

The KU Leuven Centre for IT & IP Law Series brings together the results of research activities of the Centre for IT & IP Law. The central research themes of the series concern the legal and ethical aspects of information technology, innovation and intellectual property.

Each book in the series focuses on the essential developments in the current legal framework, necessitated by the rapid evolution of technology in various fields, such as government, media, health care, informatics, digital economy, banking, transport and culture. The research is characterised by an interdisciplinary approach, constantly cross-fertilising legal, technical, economic, ethical and socio-cultural perspectives.

Books are published in English, Dutch and/or French.

Recently published in this series:

1. Rán Trygvadóttir, *European Libraries and the Internet: Copyright and Extended Collective Licences*, 2018.
2. Niels Vandezande, *Virtual Currencies*, 2018.
3. Aleksandra Kuczerawy, *Intermediary Liability and Freedom of Expression in the EU: From Concepts to Safeguards*, 2018.
4. Letizia Paoli, Jonas Visschers Cedric Verstraete, Elke van Hellemont, *The Impact of Cybercrime on Belgian Businesses*, 2019.
5. Niels Vandezande, *When An Original Is Not Original. The Originality Requirement in Belgian Law*, 2019.
6. Brendan Van Alsenoy, *Data Protection Law in the EU: Roles, Responsibilities and Liability*, 2019.
7. M-C. Janssens, *Handboek Merkenrecht*, 2019.
8. A. Vedder, J. Schroers, C. Ducuing and P. Valcke (eds.), *Security and Law. Legal and Ethical Aspects of Public Security, Cyber Security and Critical Infrastructure Security*, 2019.
9. KU Leuven Centre for IT & IP Law (ed.), *Rethinking IT and IP Law. Celebrating 30 Years CiTiP*, 2019.

www.ingramcontent.com/pod-product-compliance
Ingram Content Group UK Ltd.
Pitfield, Milton Keynes, MK11 3LW, UK
UKHW051041120926
8556IPUK00030B/491

9 781780 6886